Network Programming in C

Barry Nance

que®
CORPORATION
LEADING COMPUTER KNOWLEDGE

Network Programming in C

Library of Congress Catalog No.: 89-64226

ISBN: 0-88022-569-6

94 93 92 91 90   8 7 6 5 4 3 2

Interpretation of the printing code: the rightmost double-digit number is the year of the book's printing; the rightmost single-digit number, the number of the book's printing. For example, a printing code of 90-1 shows that the first printing of the book occurred in 1990.

DEDICATION ▼

To Susan, Scott, Chris, and Joel.
In many ways, this book was a family effort!

Publishing Manager

Allen L. Wyatt, Sr.

Technical Editor

Greg Guntle

Editorial Assistant

Ann K. Taylor

Index

Hilary Adams

Cover Design

Dan Armstrong

Book Design and Production

Bill Basham
Claudia Bell
Brad Chinn
Don Clemons
Sally Copenhaver
Tom Emrick
Dennis Hager
Tami Hughes
Bill Hurley
Charles Hutchinson
Jodi Jensen
Larry Lynch
Lori A. Lyons
Jennifer Matthews
Cindy L. Phipps
Joe Ramon
Dennis Sheehan
Louise Shinault
Bruce Steed
Mary Beth Wakefield
Nora Westlake

For information about our audio products, write us at:
Newbridge Book Clubs, 3000 Cindel Drive, Delran, NJ 08370

Composed in Garamond and OCRB
by Que Corporation

ABOUT THE AUTHOR ▼

Barry Nance

Barry Nance has written several articles for *BYTE* magazine. He is the Exchange Editor for the IBM Exchange on BIX (*BYTE*'s on-line information network). Barry is the author of the Lattice Communications Library. He has worked with various types of local area networks over the past four years. He programs in many languages and likes to share his software ideas with others.

Content Overview

TABLE OF CONTENTS ▼

II Network Programming Techniques

4 DOS-Level Programming

III   Reference

IV   Appendixes

TRADEMARK
ACKNOWLEDGMENTS

Que Corporation has made every reasonable attempt to supply trademark information about company names, products, and services mentioned in this book. Trademarks indicated below were derived from various sources. Que Corporation cannot attest to the accuracy of this information.

3Com is a registered trademark of 3Com Corporation.

3+ is a trademark of 3M Company.

Allen-Bradley and VistaLAN/PC are trademarks of Allen-Bradley Company, Inc.

Apple and AppleTalk are registered trademarks of Apple Computer, Inc.

LANTastic is a trademark of Artisoft, Inc.

AST is a trademark of AST Research, Inc.

UNIX is a trademark and AT&T is a registered trademark of AT&T Bell Laboratories.

Turbo C is a trademark of Borland International.

Corvus and Omninet are trademarks of Corvus Systems, Inc.

ARCnet and Datapoint are registered trademarks of Datapoint Corporation.

DEC is a registered trademark and VAX is a trademark of Digital Equipment Corporation; Ethernet is a registered trademark of Digital Equipment Corporation, Intel Corporation, and Xerox Corporation.

Intel is a registered trademark of Intel Corporation.

IBM AT, IBM PC, IBM XT, IBM Personal System/2, Micro Channel, NETBIOS, and PC DOS are trademarks of International Business Machines Corporation; IBM, IBM PC Network, OS/2, PS/2 are registered trademarks of International Business Machines Corporation.

Lattice is a trademark of Lattice, Inc.

1-2-3 is a registered trademark of Lotus Development Corporation.

Maxtor is a registered trademark of Maxtor Corporation.

Microsoft and Microsoft 3COM LAN Manager are registered trademarks and MS-DOS is a trademark of Microsoft Corporation.

Internetwork Packet Exchange (IPX), SFT, Transaction Tracking System, and TTS are trademarks of Novell, Inc.; Btrieve, NetWare, and Novell are registered trademarks of Novell, Inc.

Proteon and Proteon ProNET are registered trademarks of Proteon, Inc.

Rodime is a trademark of Rodime PLC.

Standard Microsystems is a trademark of Standard Microsystems Corporation.

Ungermann-Bass is a registered trademark of Ungermann-Bass, Inc.

Western Digital is a trademark of Western Digital Corporation.

Zenith is a registered trademark of Zenith Electronics Corp.

Introduction

The "Year of the LAN" never really happened; local area networks just sort of crept up on us and invaded our offices. The invasion shows no signs of slowing. LANs are here to stay.

What happens now that your personal computer is tied to your neighbor's computer with telephone wire, or with a thick cable that looks like it could easily carry 110 volts? Should you use the LAN just to share disk space or a printer? Does your company plan to develop applications that share files on the LAN—applications that a year or two ago would have been targeted for the big, expensive mainframe computer? What can you do with LANs that you cannot do with mainframes? Do you always have to use a file server, or can your users communicate PC-to-PC, as peers? What systems design, coding, and debugging skills do you need to take advantage of a LAN? These questions and more are answered in this book.

Forward-looking data processing departments now are developing significant (mission-critical) systems for LANs. Other systems, in other companies, soon will follow. These systems are cost-effective, bring the application closer to the user, take advantage of the PC's excellent capability of interacting with users, and distribute the work load across several computers.

1

LANs—a New Frontier

Local area networks are a new frontier in software technology. If you are accustomed to working with mainframe computers, you will like the way that a LAN gets you closer to your application's users through the screen and keyboard control afforded by personal computers. The file- and record-locking tools seem rudimentary, but you will grow used to them. After having worked with tools such as CICS, you will find the facilities for communicating information among users a breath of fresh air. On the other hand, if you have developed PC applications before, you have been in a single-user environment; you must adjust your thinking to account for the added dimension of having multiple concurrent users of your software. You will like the new facilities for user-to-user communications.

A medium-sized LAN represents, collectively, more raw computing horsepower than a mainframe. "Ah!" you say, "This fellow is mistaken. PCs will never stack up to a mainframe!" If that is your reaction, you are thinking of PCs in terms of individual users working at individual PCs, running individual off-the-shelf applications (word processors or spreadsheets, most likely). Until now, this sort of individual usage has been a classic way to treat PCs. But think of 50 personal computers on a LAN, being used by 40 people. Forty workstations are used as data-collection and inquiry vehicles, and 10 of the computers, unattended, run programs that perform the calculations, update the database, and work in close harmony with the software on the interactive workstations. These 10 "engines" are fast 80386 or 80486 computers with a total rating of about 60 MIPS. Each has a 300-megabyte hard disk (or perhaps I should refer to it as *DASD* in this context) with a 10-millisecond average access time. Each "engine" communicates with the other computers on the LAN at 16 megabits per second.

There. Without even sweating, I have defined an environment *much* more powerful than a mainframe. The icing on the cake is that you can incrementally add more horsepower by purchasing more personal computers; you do not have to write a check for $4 million every time you run out of gas.

Yes, I oversimplified things a bit. Later I will discuss issues that this thumbnail sketch avoided. But even at an introductory level, the unavoidable question arises: "Why aren't PCs being used all the time in a shared environment like the one just described?" The answer goes to the heart of this book.

The Purpose of This Book

Using networked PCs for more than sharing printers and spreadsheet files requires new systems-design techniques and new programming skills. These techniques and skills have been in short supply, so LANs have been used mostly to keep from wearing out the carpet ("sneakernet"—walking floppy disks around the office). This book gives you the techniques and skills you need to write LAN-aware applications.

After you read this book, you will be able to design and develop LAN-based systems that share files, that communicate directly from workstation to workstation, and that perform distributed processing.

Who Should Read This Book

This book is for you if you are interested in local area networks and are one of the following:

- ❏ A systems analyst and designer
- ❏ A programmer
- ❏ A LAN administrator or user who wants to use the free software presented in Chapter 8, "Network Applications," particularly the Remote Program Execution and Electronic Mail applications (this software is included on the diskette enclosed with this book)

What This Book Covers

Part I of this book lays the groundwork for the later discussions on design and programming. These chapters describe the characteristics of a LAN, the components of a LAN, and the differences among the LANs of various vendors. Part I also covers multiuser concepts, emphasizing the features and facilities that have been grafted onto the single-user PC DOS operating system to enable multiple users to coordinate with each other. Finally, Part I discusses the LAN environment itself—the things that happen "under the covers" to enable the LAN to appear as it does to users.

Part II delves deeply into the systems design and programming issues that you face when you develop for a LAN. These chapters first discuss file-level topics such as file sharing, record locking, access rights, journaling and rollback, and network printing. Part II then explains PC-to-PC communications in terms of conversations, dialogs, and protocols. I give simple, straightforward examples of NETBIOS and IPX/SPX calls. I also discuss the black art of debugging programs on a network.

Part II ends on a fun note, showing you how to write four complete, useful network applications. You can, of course, scavenge the code from these programs and use the code in your own network-aware applications, or, without changing a single line of code, you can use these programs "right out of the box." You get the following applications:

❑ *File and Record Collision-Tester*—If you do not have two users who can hit the Enter key at *exactly* the same time, this tool is for you. Use it to cause deliberate collisions between files and records so that you can see how your application reacts.

❑ *NETBIOS Microscope*—With this application, you can pick the NETBIOS functions you want to learn about and watch them happen step-by-step.

❑ *Remote Program Execution*—This application runs programs and DOS commands on a remote workstation. You queue up the programs and commands, cancel items that are in the queue, and see what is in the queue. The application works similar to the way that jobs are submitted on a mainframe—you even refer to the queued programs and commands by job number!

❑ *Electronic Mail*—This application will upset the people who sell commercial electronic mail products. The Electronic Mail program includes features that the commercial software lacks; furthermore, Electronic Mail is easy to use—and you can't beat the price.

Source code for these programs is listed in the appendixes. Chapter 8, "Network Applications," refers to the code to demonstrate specific techniques for programming on a LAN. The discussion of each application is divided into two parts—a programmer guide and a user guide. As a bonus, the disks enclosed with this book contain the source code and the executable files for these applications.

Part III, the technical reference for network programming, explains the following in detail:

❑ Network-related PC DOS function calls
❑ IBM PC LAN Program function calls
❑ Function call extensions added by Novell NetWare
❑ Network-related OS/2 Kernel API calls
❑ NETBIOS function calls
❑ Novell NetWare IPX and SPX function calls

What You Need, and What You Need to Know

To effectively use this book, you need access to a LAN (although the File and Record Collision Tester can be run on a stand-alone computer), and you need an IBM personal computer (such as a PC, XT, AT, or PS/2) or close compatible. You also should be aware that I used the Borland Turbo C compiler, version 2.0, to produce the applications discussed in Chapter 8, "Network Applications." Because I used the "inline assembler" facility of Turbo C, you need an assembler (such as Microsoft's MASM or Borland's TASM) if you want to compile and link the programs yourself.

Many of the code examples and fragments in Part II, however, consist of fairly standard C code. I provide specific examples of the differences between the Microsoft and IBM, Lattice, and Turbo C compilers.

You should already be somewhat familiar with the C language, although you do not have to be an expert to understand the examples in this book. I keep things simple, and avoid language-related issues as much as possible. One of the goals of this book is to make it easy for you to explore network programming.

You will find network programming challenging, fun, and an impressive addition to your resume. Turn the page and get started!

Part I

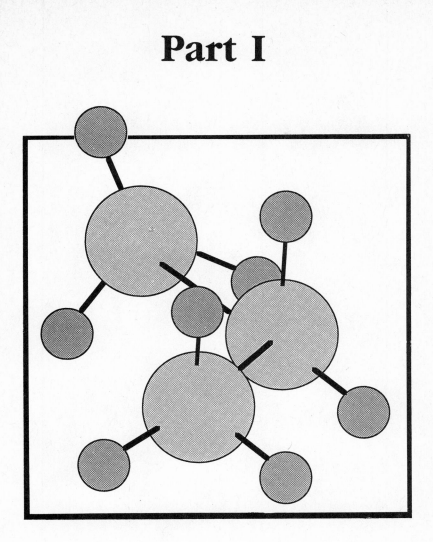

Local Area
Networks

1

The Basics of Networking

The best way to begin exploring local area networks is to start with the question "What is a LAN"? This chapter answers that question from a variety of viewpoints. A definition in terms of the essential ingredients and characteristics of a LAN is first. Next the discussion turns to an explanation of how a LAN works. The concepts of file sharing and file service redirection are introduced. This chapter then looks at the practical side of networking to see what different vendors offer. Ethernet, Token Ring, and the IEEE standards for networks are explained. After a look at cabling systems and other LAN hardware components, the discussion moves to network operating systems and network support software. Two of the more popular LAN software environments, Novell NetWare and the IBM PC LAN Program, are contrasted. The chapter ends with a brief explanation of other environments, such as TCP/IP.

This book deals with networks consisting of IBM microcomputers—PCs, XTs, ATs, PS/2s, or close compatibles. I refer to them simply as PCs throughout this book.

Characteristics

A local area network is a group of PCs that communicate with each other by message packets, with each packet containing sender and receiver address information for routing purposes. A LAN always has one or more file servers. Most of the processing occurs on the local PC, not on the file server. Furthermore, in a LAN environment, software mechanisms are provided so that a PC can share files, lock records, obtain its unique workstation name, and send messages to other computers.

Less formally, a LAN is a group of PCs connected to one another by cables. Each PC contains a network adapter card and network support software. Each PC has a unique address on the network and is known as a *node*, or *work-station*. The network support software in each workstation typically occurs in layers. The layer at the lowest level talks directly to the network adapter card; the layer at the highest level talks to your application program and provides a programmatic interface that your application can use to access the network. Each layer implements a well-defined method of communicating across the network (a *protocol*).

Now that you know what a LAN is, let's see how a LAN provides PC-to-PC communications and how it lets you access a file server's hard drive.

Message Packets (Frames)

At the lowest level, networked PCs communicate with one another and with the file server using message packets, often called frames. The foundation on which all LAN activity is based, these frames are sent and received by the network adapter and its support software. Chapter 3, "PC-to-PC Communications Concepts," discusses frames in detail. This section provides an overview of what frames are and how they work.

The network support software sends frames for many purposes, including the following:

❏ Open a communications session with another adapter.

❏ Send data (perhaps a record from a file) to a PC.

❏ Acknowledge the receipt of a data frame.

❏ Broadcast a message to all other adapters.

❏ Close a communications session.

PC-to-PC communications are easy to visualize in this way; you programmatically ask a protocol such as NETBIOS or IPX (both of which are described fully in Chapter 3, "PC-to-PC Communications Concepts") to send or receive a message, and the higher-level protocol works with the adapter support software to send and receive the appropriate data frames and acknowledgment frames. Different types of frames serve different purposes. For example, some of the frames used in implementations of NET-BIOS are Name Query frames, Session Request frames, data frames, and Close frames.

Figure 1.1 shows the layout of a typical frame. Different network implementations define frames in different ways, but the following data items are common to all implementations:

- ❏ The sender's network address
- ❏ The destination's network address
- ❏ An identification of the contents of the frame
- ❏ A data record or message
- ❏ A checksum or CRC for error-detection purposes

Fig. 1.1. *The basic layout of a frame.*

Sender ID	Dest ID	Frame type	Data/message	CRC

How are frames used in the context of sharing files on a file server? What happens when an application running on a workstation wants to open a file that resides on the file server? The answer lies in the *redirection of DOS function calls*.

Here is an ordinary program statement (in Turbo C) that opens a file; I am sure that you have coded something similar many times:

```
char filename[] = "DATABASE.FIL..;
int file_handle;

file_handle = open(filename, O_RDWR | O_DENYNONE);
```

The following statements are *exactly equivalent* to the preceding statements, but use the int86x() library function to explicitly invoke the DOS Open File service:

```
union REGS regs;
struct SREGS sregs;
char filename[] = "DATABASE.FIL..;
int file_handle;

regs.h.ah = 0x3D;
regs.h.al = 0x42;
regs.x.dx = FP_OFF( (void far *) filename);
sregs.ds = FP_SEG( (void far *) filename);
int86x(0x21, &regs, &regs, &sregs);
if (regs.x.cflag == 1)
   file_handle = -1;
else
   file_handle = regs.x.ax;
```

I show the longer, more complicated version to introduce the concept of DOS function calls. A DOS function call works as follows: the application loads certain CPU registers with certain values and executes an Interrupt 21 (hexadecimal). For example, to invoke Open File, the hex value 3D is placed in the AH CPU register, the DS:DX register pair is made to point to the name of the file to be opened, and the AL register is set to a value representing a combination of things—whether the file will be written to, and how the file should be shared.

On a stand-alone (non-LAN-attached) computer, Interrupt 21 is a primary entry point into DOS. On a LAN, however, Interrupt 21 is intercepted (filtered) by one of the higher levels of the LAN support software. This filtering allows the LAN software to shunt some of the function calls across the LAN to the file server, instead of letting DOS see them. The layer of the LAN support software that intercepts Interrupt 21 is referred to as the *shell* or sometimes *redirector*.

The shell/redirector software, which "sees" the Interrupt 21 requests first, detects that the file being opened is located on the file server. Thus the software knows to put the contents of the CPU registers into a message packet and send the packet along to the file server. The local copy of DOS running on the workstation does not process network requests. Instead, the file server gets the message, opens the file on behalf of the workstation, and sends back to the workstation a response saying, in essence, "Okay, the file was opened successfully." The shell/redirector software layer then passes this information back to the application in the appropriate CPU registers, just as though DOS had opened the file on the workstation's local hard disk. The net effect is that the shell/redirector software extends DOS functions (Open, Read, Write, Close, and other functions) across the network in a way that is transparent to an application. This redirection process is shown in figure 1.2.

Fig. 1.2. *Redirection of DOS functions.*

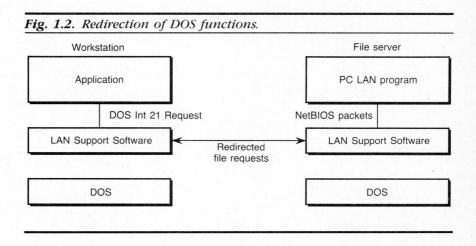

Note that the actual sending and receiving of frames are performed by the network support software and not by you. Your application causes network activity by doing I/O on files that are located on the file server, or by instructing a protocol such as NETBIOS or IPX to give a message record to another PC.

Types of Networks

LANs come in two basic flavors: collision-sensing and token-passing. Ethernet is an example of a collision-sensing network, and Token Ring is an example of a token-passing network.

In the collision-sensing environment, often referred to with the abbreviation CSMA/CD (Carrier Sense, Multiple Access, with Collision Detection), a network adapter card with a frame to send first listens to the network to see if it is quiet. If the adapter card hears another card sending a frame at that moment, it waits a microsecond or so and tries again. Even with this approach, collisions (two workstations attempting to transmit at exactly the same moment) can and do happen. CSMA/CD networks are designed to expect collisions and to handle them by retransmitting frames when necessary. These retransmissions are handled automatically by the adapter card and are transparent to the user. Although poor CSMA/CD network performance is often mistakenly blamed on the number of users simultaneously sending or receiving message traffic on the network, more than 90 percent of transmission problems on an Ethernet network are actually caused by faulty cables or malfunctioning adapter cards.

On an Ethernet network, data is broadcast throughout the network in all directions at the rate of 10 megabits per second. Each workstation receives every frame, but only those workstations meant to receive a frame (as specified in the frame's destination network address) respond with an acknowledgment. Figure 1.3 is a diagram of an Ethernet network.

Fig. 1.3. *An Ethernet network.*

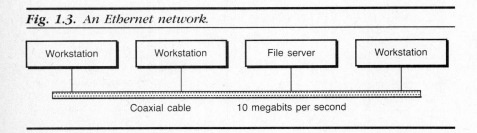

A token-passing network, on the other hand, can logically be viewed as a ring. This is true even though the network can be wired electrically as a star, because data (frames) move around the network from workstation to workstation (see fig. 1.4). Each network adapter card regenerates the signal from its "upstream" neighbor and passes the result along to the next workstation.

A token is a special type of frame. It contains no message data, but is circulated continuously around the ring during idle periods. When it wants to send a frame, the workstation waits for the token and, if the token is free (no other workstation is transmitting at the moment), the adapter card marks the frame "in use" and transmits the frame to the next downstream workstation. The frame is passed along from adapter to adapter until it eventually reaches its destination, which acknowledges its reception. On receiving an acknowledgment frame containing its own network address, the sending station relinquishes the network by recirculating a token. Unless an adapter card malfunctions and goes out of turn (without waiting for the token), collisions never occur on token-passing networks.

Fig. 1.4. *A Token Ring network.*

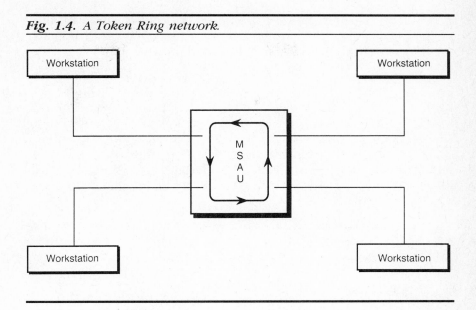

IBM offers Token Ring running at either 4 or 16 megabits per second. Several third-party companies make equipment compatible with IBM Token Ring, including the following:

3Com Corporation	DatAmerica
Gateway Communications	General Instrument
Harris Data Communications	Madge Networks
NCR	Proteon
Pure Data	Racore
RAD Data Communications	Siecor
Ungermann-Bass, Inc.	Western Digital

A few of these companies (such as Proteon and Siecor) make Token Ring hardware that operates at different rates or uses fiber optics.

Digital Equipment Corporation and 3Com Corporation are major suppliers of Ethernet hardware. Other companies that offer Ethernet equipment include the following:

AST Research, Inc.	Data General
Excelan	Gateway Communications
Micom-Interlan	Proteon
RAD Data Communications	Ungermann-Bass
Western Digital	Zenith Electronics Corporation

These lists are neither exhaustive nor endorsements. However, they should help you start your research into LAN hardware if you are planning to put together your own LAN.

The Institute of Electrical and Electronic Engineers (IEEE) defines a set of standards for the physical characteristics of both collision-sensing networks and token-passing networks: IEEE 802.3 (Ethernet) and IEEE 802.5 (Token Ring). Be aware, however, that there are minor differences between the frame definitions for "true Ethernet" and "true IEEE 802.3," and that IBM's 16-megabit-per-second Token Ring adapter card is considered an "802.5 Token Ring Extension." The definitions and layout of these low-level frames are given in Chapter 3, "PC-to-PC Communications Concepts."

Of course, some LANs do not conform to either IEEE 802.3 or IEEE 802.5. The most popular of these is ARCnet (Datapoint Corporation, Standard Microsystems Corporation, Thomas-Conrad); others include the following:

VistaLAN/PC (Allen-Bradley, Inc.)	LANTastic (Artisoft, Inc.)
STARLAN (AT&T)	Omninet (Corvus Systems, Inc.)
PC Network (IBM)	ProNET (Proteon)

In addition, an emerging physical standard called Fiber Distributed Data Interface (FDDI) uses fiber-optic cable. Subtly different from IEEE 802.5 standards, FDDI's token-passing scheme transmits data at 100 megabits per second.

Components of a LAN

Basic LAN hardware components consist of network adapter cards, cables, and either access units or repeaters. Depending on its type and complexity, your network may also include bridges, routers, concentrators, baluns, hubs, and transceivers. You don't need to understand these items to conceptualize a LAN for programming. One other component —the file server—is discussed later in this chapter.

Diskless Workstations

Imagine a fairly inexpensive PC consisting of just a keyboard, network adapter, and a monitor—no floppy drives, no hard disk. You turn the PC on and it immediately attaches itself to the network. Sounds like a great way to save money on LAN workstations, doesn't it?

Don't be fooled. It isn't. A diskless workstation relies completely on the file server's hard disk, which increases network message traffic. Furthermore, you cannot upgrade this single-purpose computer to run OS/2, and it cannot be used as a stand-alone computer.

Although diskless workstations do not save money in the long run, there is a reason for using them—security. If you have the sort of LAN environment in which it is important that users not be able to copy files to diskette and transport them, diskless workstations may give you just the security you need.

Network Adapter Cards

As mentioned before, network adapter cards can be either collision-sensing or token-passing. Both kinds of adapters contain sufficient on-board logic to know when it is okay to send a frame and to recognize when the frames they receive are intended for them. Along with the adapter support software, both types of cards perform seven major steps during the process of sending or receiving a frame. When data is being sent, the following steps are performed in the order shown; when data is being received, however, the steps are reversed:

1. *Data transfer.* Data is transferred from PC memory to the adapter card or from the adapter card to PC memory by DMA, shared memory, or programmed I/O.

2. *Buffering.* While being processed by the network adapter card, data is held in a buffer. The buffer gives the card access to an entire frame at once and lets the card manage the difference between the data rate of the network and the rate at which the PC can process data.

3. *Frame formation.* The network adapter has to break up the data (or, on reception, reassemble it) into manageable chunks. On an Ethernet network, these chunks are 4 kilobytes; at least one network uses 12 kilobytes. Most networks use a size between 1 and 4

kilobytes. A frame header is prefixed to the data packet; a frame trailer is suffixed to it. At this point a complete, ready-for-transmission frame has been created. (On reception, the header and trailer are removed at this stage.)

4. *Cable access.* In a CSMA/CD network such as Ethernet, the network adapter ensures that the line is quiet before sending its data. In a token-passing network, the adapter waits until it gets a token that it can grab and claim. (Cable access is irrelevant to message reception.)

5. *Parallel and serial conversion.* The bytes of data in the buffer are sent or received through the cables in serial fashion, with one bit following the next. The adapter card makes this conversion in the split second before transmission (or after reception).

6. *Encoding and decoding.* The electrical signals that represent the data being sent or received are formed. Most network adapters use *Manchester encoding*, a technique that has the advantage of incorporating timing information into the data by using *bit periods*. Instead of representing a 0 as the absence of electricity and a 1 as its presence, the 0s and 1s are represented by changes in polarity as they occur in relation to very short time periods.

7. *Sending and receiving impulses.* The electrically encoded impulses making up the data (frame) are amplified and sent through the wire. (On reception, the impulses are handed up to the decoding step.)

Of course, the execution of all these steps takes only a fraction of a second; while you were reading about these steps, thousands of frames would have been sent across the LAN.

Network adapter cards and the support software recognize and handle errors, which occur when electrical interference, collisions (in CSMA/CD networks), or malfunctioning equipment cause some portion of a frame to be corrupted. Errors are normally detected through the use of a cyclic redundancy checksum (CRC) data item in the frame. The CRC is checked by the receiver; if its own calculated CRC does not match the value of the frame's CRC, the receiver "NAKs the frame," which means that the receiver requests that the frame in error be retransmitted. If you suspect a malfunctioning adapter card or cable on your LAN, several vendors offer products that perform diagnostic and analytic functions on the different types of LANs.

The different types of network adapters vary not only in access method and protocol but also in the following:

- ❏ Transmission speed
- ❏ Amount of on-board memory for buffering frames
- ❏ Bus design (8-bit, 16-bit, or Micro Channel)
- ❏ Bus speed (some fail when run at high speed)
- ❏ Compatibility with various CPU chipsets
- ❏ DMA usage
- ❏ IRQ and I/O port addressing
- ❏ Intelligence (some adapters use an on-board CPU such as the 80186)
- ❏ Connector design

Cabling Systems

As you might imagine at this point, cabling systems for LANs vary widely in their appearance, characteristics, intended purpose, and cost. The three most popular ways to tie computers together on a LAN are

- ❏ The IBM Cabling System
- ❏ The AT&T Premises Distribution System
- ❏ The DEC cabling concept called DECconnect

The cabling systems discussed in this section can be categorized into three distinct cable types:

- ❏ Twisted pair (shielded and unshielded)
- ❏ Coaxial cable (thin and thick)
- ❏ Fiber-optic cable

Twisted pair is just what its name implies—insulated wires with a minimum number of twists per foot. Twisting the wires reduces electrical interference (attenuation). *Shielded* refers to the amount of insulation around the wire and therefore its immunity to data-corruption errors. You should already be familiar with unshielded twisted pair, because it is often used by the phone company. Shielded twisted pair, however, looks entirely different, somewhat resembling the wire used to carry "house current" (110 volts) throughout your home or apartment. But appearances are deceiving, because shielded twisted pair actually carries a relatively low voltage signal; the heavy insulation is for noise reduction, not safety.

Coaxial cable is fairly prevalent in our everyday lives; you often find it connected to the backs of television sets and audio equipment. "Thin" and "thick," of course, refer to the diameter of the coaxial cable. Standard Ethernet cable (thick Ethernet) is as thick as your thumb. The newer Thinnet cable is about the size of your little finger. The thick cable offers greater noise immunity and is more difficult to damage, and requires a vampire tap (a piercing connector) and a drop cable to connect to a LAN. Although it carries the signal over shorter distances than the thick cable, Thinnet uses a simple BNC connector, is lower in cost, and has become a standard in office coaxial cable.

Finally, fiber-optic cable, as its name suggests, uses light rather than electricity to carry information. Although it can send data over huge distances at high speeds, fiber-optic cable is expensive and difficult to install and maintain. Splicing the cable, installing connectors, and using the few available diagnostic tools for finding cable faults are skills that very few people have. Fiber-optic cable is simply designed, but unforgiving of bad connections. It consists of a hollow core fiber whose diameter is measured in microns, surrounded by a solid cladding, which in turn is covered by a protective sheath. The first fiber-optic cables were made of glass, but plastic fibers have also been developed. The light source for fiber-optic cable is a *light-emitting diode* (LED); information usually is encoded by varying the intensity of the light. A detector at the other end of the cable converts the received signal back into electrical impulses. There are two types of fiber, single mode and multimode. The more expensive single mode has a smaller diameter and can carry signals for a greater distance.

IBM Cabling System

The IBM Cabling System, oddly enough, is not manufactured or sold by IBM. Rather, the system consists of a published standard for building wiring systems that defines cabling system components and different cable types. When the IBM Cabling System was first introduced in 1984, IBM described it as the intended backbone for its Token Ring Network. The first such cables to be manufactured by third-party companies were tested by IBM itself, verified to IBM specifications, and actually given IBM part numbers. Now, however, cable manufacturers must rely on the independent testing laboratories ETL or UL, or industry-standard manufacturers such as AMP, to verify compliance with the specifications published by IBM.

The IBM specification defines workstation faceplates, adapters and connectors, access units, wiring closet termination methods, and the following cable types:

❏ Type 1—*data cable.* Used for data connections only, this copper-based cable is available in nonplenum, plenum, and outdoor varieties. It consists of two twisted pairs of 22-gauge solid conductors, shielded with both foil and braid, and covered with a polyvinyl-chloride (PVC) sheath. This cable type is used for connecting terminal devices located in work areas to distribution panels located in wiring closets, and for connecting between wiring closets. The plenum cable is installed in plenums, ducts, and spaces used for environmental air (in a fire, plenum cable emits less-toxic fumes than the nonplenum cable). The outdoor cable is protected in a corrugated metallic shield with a polyethylene sheath, and the core is filled with a jellylike compound to keep out moisture.

❏ Type 2—*data and telephone cable.* Used for both data and voice (telephone) applications, Type 2 is similar to Type 1, but has four additional twisted pairs (22-gauge). Type 2 cable also comes in plenum and nonplenum varieties.

❏ Type 3—*telephone twisted pair cable.* Consisting of four pairs of 24-gauge or 22-gauge wire in polyvinyl-chloride plastic, Type 3 cable is equivalent to the IBM Rolm specification and available in plenum. This cable is unshielded and not as immune to noise (when used for data) as Type 1 cable.

❏ Type 5—*fiber-optic cable.* This cable contains two 100/140-micron (100-micron core surrounded by 140-micron cladding layer) multimode optical fibers.

❏ Type 6—*patch panel cable.* This cable is used for connecting a workstation to a wall faceplate or making connections within a wiring closet. Type 6 is more flexible than Type 1 cable (which is why it is used as patch cable); it consists of two twisted pairs of 26-gauge stranded conductors.

❏ Type 8—*undercarpet cable.* An undercarpet cable useful for open office or workstation areas in which there are no permanent walls, Type 8 consists of two individually shielded pairs of 26-gauge solid conductors in a flat sheath.

❏ Type 9—*low-cost plenum cable.* An economy version of Type 1 plenum cable, Type 9 can transmit only about two-thirds the distance that Type 1 cable can. This cable consists of two twisted pairs of 26-gauge stranded conductors.

(Types 4 and 7 are not defined by IBM.)

AT&T Premises Distribution System

The AT&T Premises Distribution System is similar to the IBM Cabling System, but relies much more heavily on unshielded telephone twisted pair. It also integrates voice and data wiring. Connections are based on modular jacks and plugs, and on the cross-connect techniques originally designed for voice PBX to telephone-set wiring, which use multipair cable. PDS expands on the extensive base of this type of cable, which is already installed in many office buildings. Generally, the AT&T PDS parts cost is lower than the IBM system, but installation is more labor intensive.

DECconnect

The DECconnect cabling concept is based on the use of 50-ohm thin coaxial cable (Thinwire), which is commonly used in Ethernet networks. The DECconnect system has standardized much of the connecting hardware used in major DEC installations of VAX systems. DECconnect also defines a line of protocol converters, line drivers, and "satellite closet" rack and termination hardware. A DECconnect system consists of an Ethernet backbone (a central cable to which all other cables connect) wired throughout a building, with taps (connection points) provided at VAX computer sites and the satellite closets.

Access Units and Repeaters

In a token-passing network, the cables from the workstations (or from the wall faceplates) are centrally connected to a Multi-Station Access Unit (MSAU, or MAU). The MSAU keeps track of which workstations on the LAN are neighbors and which neighbor is upstream or downstream. It is an easy job; most MSAUs do not even need to be plugged into an electrical power outlet. The exception to this is an MSAU that provides for longer cable distances or the use of unshielded twisted pair (Type 3) cable in high-speed LANs. In these latter cases, the externally powered MSAU helps the signal along by regenerating it.

An MSAU has eight ports for connecting one to eight Token Ring devices. Each connection is made with a "genderless" Data Connector (as specified in the IBM Cabling System). The MSAU has two additional ports labeled RI (Ring-In) and RO (Ring-Out) that are used to link several MSAUs together (in a daisy chain) when you have more than eight workstations on the LAN.

It takes several seconds to "open the adapter connection" on a Token Ring LAN (something you may have noticed). During this time, the MSAU and your Token Ring adapter card perform a small diagnostic check, after which the MSAU establishes you as a new neighbor on the ring. After being established as an active workstation, your computer is linked on both sides to your neighbors (as defined by your position on the MSAU). In its turn, your Token Ring adapter card accepts the token, regenerates it, and gives it a swift kick to send it through the MSAU in the direction of your downstream neighbor.

In an Ethernet network, the number of connections (taps) and their intervening distances are limiting factors. Repeaters are used to regenerate the signal every 500 meters or so. If these repeaters were not used, "standing waves" (additive reflections) would distort the signal and cause errors. Because collision detection depends partly on timing, only five 500-meter segments and four repeaters can be placed in series before the propagation delay becomes longer than the maximum allowed time period for detecting a collision—otherwise, the workstations farthest from the sender could not detect any collisions. Computer systems designers, who generally hate limitations, made it possible to create Ethernet networks in star, branch, and tree designs that overcome these basic limitations. Thousands of workstations are possible on a complex Ethernet network.

In general, the limits on distances and numbers of workstations specified in both IEEE 802.3 Ethernet and IEEE 802.5 Token Ring are being overcome through the technologies of optical fiber, intelligent fast-acting repeaters, active bridges, routers, hubs, and gateways.

File Servers

You need a place to store the files that you want to share among the PCs. You can turn one of the PCs into a file server, or use a different kind of computer as the server. Either way, your file server must provide

❏ Fast access to the files
❏ Capacity to hold files and records for many users
❏ Security for the files
❏ Reliability

If you choose a computer other than a PC for a file server, you will also need to verify that the machine can be connected to the LAN and function as a file server.

On the other hand, if you use a PC as a file server, you should choose a PC that is faster and has larger, faster disks than its brothers and sisters. Why do you need the file server to be a faster computer if the software applications run on each of the individual PCs on the LAN and not on some central machine? Well, during busy periods, the server receives many requests for disk files and records; it takes a certain amount of CPU effort as well as disk rotation and access time to respond to each request. You want the requests to be serviced quickly so that each user gets the feeling that he or she is the only one using the file server at that moment.

File Server Hard Disks

The access speed and capacity of a server's hard disk are the most important criteria for a file server. The most common bottleneck in the average LAN is disk I/O time at the file server. And the most common complaint of LAN users is that the file server has run out of free disk space.

Disk access speed is determined by a number of factors, including the following:

❏ The recording method (MFM, RLL, ESDI, or SCSI)

❏ The type and on-board intelligence of the controller

❏ The type of hard disk (stepper band or voice coil)

❏ The interleave factor

❏ The location of the files on the disk (location affects how far the Read-Write head has to move to get to the file)

Disk access speed is measured by two variables, *data transfer rate* and *average seek time*. Data transfer rate expresses the number of bytes of data that the hard disk or controller can deliver to the computer in one second. Average seek time is the time taken by the disk to move the Read-Write head a small distance and then wait about a half-revolution of the disk platter for a given sector to appear under the head. The type of disk IBM installed as standard equipment in the IBM Personal Computer AT has a data transfer rate of about 180 kilobytes per second and an average seek time of 40 milliseconds. Third-party disks from companies such as Core, Maxtor, Micropolis, Priam, Rodime PLC, and Racet are faster, with average seek times in the 10- to 20-millisecond range. And of course IBM, not to be outdone, offers speedy drives in the current crop of high-end PS/2 machines.

Disk capacity tends to go hand in hand with speed; the larger drives are also the faster drives. The designers of 200- to 600-megabyte drives are obviously thinking "file server!" as they engineer their latest, technologically advanced products. Some of these huge beasts, however, cost as much as the computer you put them in. So how much space do you need on *your* file server? How many drives should you buy, and how many file servers will you need? A significant consideration is that you are limited in the number of drives that can be installed in a given file server machine (SCSI drives are less limited in this respect). A related consideration: it is generally better to have several medium-sized disks in multiple servers than one huge disk in one server, because you then have more Read-Write heads, more controllers, and more CPUs responding to user requests for files. This is only a general observation, of course; your situation may be different.

A rule of thumb (and another *very* general observation) is that you should allot 50 megabytes of disk-storage space for each user on the LAN. However, it is really impossible for me to guess what your own storage needs will be; you need to take a look at what you think the LAN will be used for and what type of applications your users will run. Another rule of thumb is that file server disks are much like closets and file cabinets—no matter how many you have, they tend to fill up pretty quickly. Let me offer these bits of advice:

- ❏ Encourage users to use their local hard drives for executable files and help files.
- ❏ Don't buy diskless workstations to try to save money.
- ❏ Don't let users store games on the file server.
- ❏ Set up a "retention period" scheme for the different kinds of files on the network. Houseclean regularly; do not wait for the server to run out of space.

Optical disks are another alternative for file servers. These durable and reliable disks use light to store data, or sometimes a combination of light and magnetism. With the proper software drivers, optical disks can be made to function just like any other file server drive. Until recently, two major drawbacks limited the popularity of optical disks; they tended to have slower access times than magnetic disks, and they could not erase files (Write Once, Read Many [WORM] drives). These drawbacks are being overcome by companies such as Maxtor and Racet, who now offer rewritable optical disks that are network-compatible.

File Server CPU, Memory, and Network Adapter

After capacity and access speed, the other considerations for the file server are CPU speed, amount of memory, network adapter speed, and dedicated versus nondedicated use.

Unless a LAN will have very few users and will never grow (that's hard to imagine!), a file server with an 80386 or 80486 CPU and plenty of memory is a wise investment. You can achieve significantly improved performance with a faster CPU and ample RAM, which make possible something called *caching*: with sufficient memory installed, a file server can "remember" those portions of the hard disk previously accessed and send these to the next user without having to actually access the hard disk for that subsequent user. Because it can avoid going to the hard disk, the file server can do its job quicker.

One of the characteristics of network adapter cards mentioned earlier in this chapter was buffer size. Some adapter cards have bigger buffers than others, and thus can hold more frames at one time. Such cards are ideal candidates for installation in a file server, which can be thought of as the Grand Central Station for message frames.

You can often set up a file server so that it can be used as a workstation at the same time it is acting as a file server. Such *nondedicated* file servers should be avoided—if a user runs an application at the server and the software crashes, the entire network crashes with it. This is not a pretty sight. Also, although not a common practice (especially in larger LANs), some networks are designed so that *every* workstation's hard drive is accessible to the other workstations on the network; conceptually, every workstation in such a network is a file server, and vice versa.

Network Support Software

We have covered a lot of ground so far. Take a moment to review what you would have if you had been building a LAN as we went along. You chose an access method—collision-sensing or token-passing—and installed the proper network adapter cards in several PCs. You also connected the PCs together with the appropriate cabling. If additional support hardware was needed, you obtained and installed it. And you designated one or more of the PCs as a file server and ensured that it is sufficient for your needs.

What can you do with the LAN you have assembled so far? Absolutely nothing.

You need to add network software to get the computers to talk to one another. And of course the software you use must be compatible with the hardware you acquired. (You can imagine the talk you would have with your boss if you bought Ethernet hardware and Token Ring LAN Support Software—not to mention the troubleshooting you would have to do to make it work!)

The network support software must

❑ Provide access to the network adapter card

❑ Enable PC-to-PC communications

❑ Emulate DOS so that the file server's disks are available to the applications run on the workstations

PC-to-PC Communications

Many vendors have created their own proprietary protocols for peer-level communications on LANs. Although most vendors of LAN products have endorsed the new standard published by the International Standards Organization (ISO), the *Open Systems Interconnection (OSI) Model*, it has not yet been fully implemented. The seven layers of the OSI Model are explained in Chapter 3, "PC-to-PC Communications Concepts," as are the internal formats and conventions used in some of the more popular vendor-created protocols.

Regardless of how each particular vendor's protocol is designed, certain basic functions and features are common:

❑ *Initiating communications.* Each protocol provides the means to identify a workstation by name, by number, or both. This identification scheme is made available to both the shell/redirector layer and to an application. Point-to-point communications are activated by one workstation identifying a destination workstation (often a file server) with which it wants to carry on a dialog. The originating workstation also designates the type of dialog: in a *datagram*, frames are addressed and sent to the destination without guarantee or verification of reception; in a *session*, a connection (or "pipe") is established that guarantees delivery of message data.

❑ *Sending and receiving data.* Each protocol provides the means for originating and destination workstations to send and receive message data. A protocol-specific limit on the length of a given message is imposed, and each participant in a session-type dialog is given the means to determine the status of the dialog (for example, a workstation may inadvertently power down in the midst of a dialog—perhaps someone kicked the power cord—and the other participants are notified that an error has occurred).

❑ *Terminating communications.* The protocol provides the means for the participants to gracefully end a dialog.

DOS Redirection and Emulation

As stated earlier, redirection of DOS function calls makes file-server access possible. An application running on a workstation goes through the motions of asking DOS for some part of a disk file, but the network software intercepts the request and sends it to the file server. The file server does the actual disk I/O to obtain that part of the disk file and returns the result to the workstation. The network software on the workstation hands the disk file contents to the application, and in doing so makes it look as though the local copy of DOS had been the one to obtain the file contents.

The network software performs several steps to send the request to the server and get back the response.

The first thing the network software needs to do is determine whether it should handle a DOS File Read request or pass it along to DOS. It does this by noting at File Open or File Create time whether a network drive letter is in effect for the Open or Create call. Because the network software maintains an internal table of which drives are network devices, it is fairly easy for the software to know whether an Open or a Create applies to a network drive. As the file is opened or created, the network software assigns a file handle (just as DOS would have done) or, if the old-style File Control Blocks (FCBs) are being used, it remembers the address of the FCB. When a File Read call occurs, the network software examines the file handle or FCB address to know whether the request should be shunted across the network to the file server or passed along for DOS to handle.

Let's assume that the network software detects that the File Read request is for a file on the file server. The software puts the contents of the appropriate CPU registers into a control block. The format and size of this control block vary among the different vendors' protocols, but its basic purpose, to request some file material from the file server, is the same for all protocols. The shell/redirector then passes this control block to the network support software, which puts the control block inside a frame and sends the result to the file server.

At the server, the frames are processed back into a File Read request by the network adapter card and its supporting software. If another user's request is currently being processed by the server (a common occurrence on a busy LAN), your File Read request is queued for scant-moments-later handling. In its turn, your request is processed by the File Service portion of the network software running on the server; the desired sectors of the file are found in the server's cache memory or, if not in memory, accessed directly from the server's hard disk.

During the I/O operation, the file server encounters one of three typical situations for a disk-read: the requested bytes are read, end-of-file is detected, or only some of the requested bytes are read (this happens if more bytes were requested than actually exist). The file server creates a control block containing an indication of which of these three situations was encountered, appends the file data (if any) to the control block, and then hands the result to the network support software for transmission back to the appropriate workstation.

After receiving the response from the file server, the workstation reverses the steps it took in sending the File Read request. The network adapter processes the frames containing the response, the frame headers and frame trailers are stripped off, and the shell/redirector emulates DOS by putting the file data into the application's buffer, setting the CPU registers to indicate the number of bytes actually read, and returning to the application at the next instruction after the DOS function call.

Vendor-Specific Protocols

Someday, perhaps, the OSI Model will be the only protocol the different LAN manufacturers use. Until that day, we are faced with a kaleidoscope of proprietary protocols from IBM (NETBIOS, APPC), Novell, Inc. (IPX/SPX), DEC, AT&T, Sun (NFS), Apple (Appletalk/AFP), and a smattering of other companies. Even the Department of Defense developed its own protocol, TCP/IP, to use over large networks; TCP/IP is also popular for tying together networks from diverse vendors.

Not only are the protocols from IBM and Novell two of the most popular, but they also represent fundamentally different approaches to managing communications on a LAN. Let's see what makes them different.

IBM sells four primary software products that implement IBM's LAN protocol. Three are DOS-based (PC LAN Support Program, PC LAN Program, and Advanced Program-to-Program Communications [APPC]), and the fourth (OS/2 LAN Server) is used under OS/2. Novell currently offers NetWare 286, NetWare 386, and Novell's own APPC product.

IBM PC LAN Support Program

A prerequisite product for DOS-based Token Ring LANs, the PC LAN Support Program implements the network adapter support software, as well as NETBIOS, in a set of device drivers (.SYS files) that are loaded when the system is booted. Typically, three driver files are used. Although the amount of memory used depends on how the drivers are configured, typical memory usage ranges from 40 to 50 kilobytes. The DXMA0MOD.SYS driver routes communications requests to the various subroutines in the layers of network support software. The file DXMC0MOD.SYS is the layer of adapter support software that talks directly to the IEEE 802.5 chipset on the Token Ring card. And the file DXMT0MOD.SYS is NETBIOS.

NETBIOS accepts communications requests from an application program or from the PC LAN Program. These requests fall into four categories:

❑ *Name support.* Each workstation on the network is identified by one or more names. NETBIOS maintains these names in a table; the first item in the table is automatically the unique, permanently assigned name of the network adapter. Optional user names (such as BARRY) can be added to the table to conveniently identify each user. These user-assigned names can uniquely identify a single workstation or, in a special case, they can refer to a group of workstations.

❑ *Session support.* A point-to-point connection between two names (workstations) on the network can be opened, managed, and closed under NETBIOS control. One workstation begins by "listening" for a call; the other workstation "calls" the first. The workstations are peers; both can send and receive message data concurrently during the session. At the end, both workstations "hang up" on each other.

❑ *Datagram support.* Message data can be sent to a name, a group of names, or to all names on the network. A point-to-point connection is not established and there is no guarantee that the message data will be received.

❑ *Adapter and session status.* Information about the local network adapter card, about other network adapter cards, and about any currently active sessions is available from NETBIOS.

IBM used to offer NETBIOS as a separate program product; it was implemented as a Terminate and Stay Resident (TSR) file named NETBEUI.COM. NETBEUI is now obsolete. If you have an older Token Ring network that uses NETBEUI, you should strongly consider replacing the low-level network support software on each workstation, including NETBEUI, with the later IBM PC LAN Support Program's device drivers.

IBM PC LAN Program

The PC LAN Program is a DOS shell/redirector that can be configured as a file server, as a simple workstation redirector, as a receiver, or as a messenger. The program requires that NETBIOS already be running on the workstation. The PC LAN Program creates and uses NETBIOS sessions to transfer file data and messages to and from the file server.

When configured as a file server, the PC LAN Program consumes the most memory; as a simple redirector, it consumes the least (taking about 46 kilobytes on a workstation). The other configurations, receiver and messenger, are in the middle. These in-between configurations allow users to send small notes back and forth, almost but not quite like an electronic mail system. Frankly, no one ever really sets up a workstation as a messenger or receiver. The note-passing facility is simply not worth the extra memory that these configurations take up. (Of course, a full-featured electronic mail product is included with this book. You can now safely forget about receivers and messengers.)

The PC LAN Program is flexible. Not only can you set it up to act as a file server or as a simple workstation redirector, you can install the program (network-wide) to provide *Base Services* or *Extended Services*. Base Services let users easily share resources, without user IDs and passwords. Extended Services implement the following concepts:

❏ The *System Administrator* is a user with special privileges on the network who can set up domains, define servers and Remote-IPL machines, and assign user IDs, passwords, and user access levels.

❏ A *domain* is a group of network resources (servers, server directories, and printers) and the mapping of users to these resources.

❏ The *user ID and password* mechanisms provide user identification and security.

❏ A *Fileset* is a named, shared disk resource (directory) that is part of a domain. Users are allowed Read-Only or Read-Write access to a fileset. A *Home Fileset* is particular to a user; when a user logs in, information in a user's Home Fileset is used to create that user's environment.

❏ A *Remote IPL machine* is a workstation whose network adapter card contains special program code. This code loads PC DOS and the network support software directly from a file server (the Program Server) at boot time.

❏ The *Application Selector* is a menu-driven, friendly-looking program launcher that lets each user have a unique list of applications to run. This list is initially set up by the System Administrator, but can be maintained by the user.

No matter whether Base Services or Extended Services are installed, the PC LAN Program manages the sharing of files between workstation and file server the same way. The PC LAN Program uses what IBM calls *Server Message Blocks* (SMBs) as a vehicle for shunting DOS function calls across the network. After a NETBIOS session is established between workstation and server, SMBs are sent to the file server to request remote DOS services and provide the response from the file server back to the work-station. A field in the SMB, *SMB_Function*, identifies the network request represented by a particular SMB. Each value of SMB_Function corresponds to a different DOS function call. Chapter 3, "PC-to-PC Communications Concepts," discusses SMBs, including the format of the SMB itself, in greater detail.

Advanced Program-to-Program Communications (APPC)

APPC is an IBM-designed programmatic interface that fundamentally changes the way PCs communicate with larger computers. This interface replaces the technique of talking to a host computer through a terminal emulator with a conversation- (peer-to-peer-) based technique. IBM designed APPC to be a programmer's view of the Systems Network Architecture (SNA) standard, *LU 6.2*. Before LU 6.2, PC and mainframe communications were accomplished by loading a terminal emulator program on the PC and forcing the emulator to handle each byte of data sent as though it were a keypress from the keyboard. Similarly, receiving data from the mainframe involved intercepting 3270 screen data before it reached the terminal emulator screen. Workable, but primitive.

APPC, on the other hand, assumes that two *computers* are talking to each other; both sides of the conversation are allowed to be "smart." APPC dispenses with 3270 keypress and screen-at-a-time transmissions, and instead provides that only the LU 6.2 verbs and raw data move through the communications link.

Because of its peer-to-peer technique, LU 6.2 (accessed through APPC) can be used as the basis for communications between workstations on a LAN as well as between a workstation and a mainframe (in fact, LU 6.2 can be used between any two computers on an SNA network). Application programs are unaware of which communications medium is being used, whether it is Token Ring, an SDLC mainframe link, or even a direct computer-to-computer link.

Two types of conversations are possible under LU 6.2, *basic* conversations and *mapped* conversations. With mapped conversations, the protocol converts the data into a standard *generalized data stream* for sending, and converts the data back into its original form upon reception. With basic conversations, the application must handle any necessary conversions. Programs that use basic conversations also are partly responsible for error recovery.

LU 6.2 implements a set of verbs. You can think of these as a programming language for developing the communications capabilities of an application. Each verb is a specifically formatted record with a particular purpose. The major verbs are shown in the following list:

❏ ALLOCATE initiates a conversation with a remote application. Parameters include the following:
LU_NAME, which gives the name of the Logical Unit that represents the remote program
TPN, which gives the name of the remote program
MODE_NAME, which specifies session properties for the conversation
SYNC_LEVEL, which specifies a synchronization level between the two conversants

❏ GET_ATTRIBUTES returns information about the conversation, such as mode name, partner LU name, and synchronization level.

❏ DEALLOCATE ends a conversation.

❏ CONFIRM asks the remote computer to confirm successful reception of data.

❏ CONFIRMED is the reply sent in response to a CONFIRM verb.

❏ SEND_DATA causes data to be sent.

❏ RECEIVE_AND_WAIT notifies a remote application that it is not okay to send data. The issuer of the RECEIVE_AND_WAIT then waits for a response.

You can see from this description of APPC and LU 6.2 that these are powerful tools. They also have some disadvantages, however. The PC implementation of APPC occupies a sizable chunk of memory (a resident program that offers a subset of APPC can be as small as 70 to 80 kilobytes; full APPC takes a little less than 200 kilobytes of resident code) and, under PC DOS, this is a big concern. Also, a significant programming investment is necessary to design and implement systems that use APPC.

OS/2 LAN Server

I can *almost* describe OS/2 Lan Server by asking you to imagine all of the aforementioned IBM products (LAN Support Program, PC LAN Program, and APPC) rolled into a single environment, with a dash of multitasking thrown in for spice. However, LAN Server (and its distant cousin, Microsoft Corporation's LAN Manager) is even more than that.

This is not the time or place to try to fully explain OS/2, so I am going to have to assume that you have already read some background material on IBM's newest PC-based operating system.

OS/2 is an excellent base for advanced, high-end PC networking. Its multitasking facilities make it a good candidate for distributed processing. OS/2 eliminates the memory-crunch problems so often faced on LANs, and is part of IBM's *System Application Architecture* (SAA) standards.

OS/2 Extended Edition is a prerequisite for OS/2 LAN Server, but only for the file server; you can have a mix of workstations on the network —some running DOS (with the PC LAN Program) and some running OS/2 EE. OS/2 EE comes with the optionally installable LAN Requester, which is IBM's shell/redirector software for OS/2. For the user, the network environment is similar to that of the PC LAN Program's Extended Services, including System Administrator, domains, and other concepts associated with Extended Services.

To a programmer, OS/2 LAN Server is altogether different from PC DOS and the PC LAN Program. In addition to the usual facilities for file sharing, printer sharing, and PC-to-PC communications through NETBIOS, OS/2 LAN Server offers built-in support for remote program execution and various kinds and levels of interprocess communications, including APPC (discussed earlier) and named pipes.

A pipe is a stream of data between two programs. One program opens the pipe and writes data into it; the other opens the pipe and reads the data from the first program. Does it sound easy, and simple to program? It is. A *named pipe* is a file whose name has a certain format:

```
\PIPE\path\name.ext
```

OS/2 provides a set of functions for opening, using, and closing named pipes. The application that wants to create the pipe (called the *server*, but do not confuse this with a file server) does so by calling DosMakeNmPipe. The server can then use DosConnectNmPipe to wait until another application (called the *client*) has opened the pipe with DosOpen. Both the server and the client can use a simple DosWrite to put data into the pipe or DosRead to get data from the pipe. DosPeekNmPipe can be used to inspect data in the pipe without removing the data. Finally, the server can close the pipe and destroy it with DosDisConnectNmPipe.

Named pipes can be treated as simple data streams or, if the programmer wants, as message pipes. In the latter case, each call to DosRead fetches one message at a time from the pipe.

Because named pipes do so much work yet require a programmer to code only a few simple program statements, named pipes are extremely popular on OS/2 LANs.

Novell NetWare 286

NetWare is the most popular network operating system used today; more than half of all LAN installations run a version of NetWare. People like it because it performs well, runs on several different kinds of hardware, and offers a useful, comprehensive set of security features. Novell NetWare also supplies a rich set of services and facilities to the programmer who develops a Novell-specific, LAN-aware application.

The NetWare Server and File System

A NetWare 286 file server, although it looks like a regular IBM AT or PS/2 from the outside, is really a minicomputer in disguise. The hard disk in the file server is formatted with a file system structure completely foreign to PC DOS. It is not possible, for example, to boot a NetWare 286 file server with a PC DOS diskette and then access the hard disk with DOS commands (especially CHKDSK!). A user at a workstation, however, is able to nonchalantly view the file server as just another DOS disk drive. The magic that allows this, of course, is the redirection of DOS function calls discussed earlier. Novell has simply carried the principle a bit further.

The proprietary format of a Novell file-server disk contains more information about files and subdirectories than is possible under PC DOS. Not only can a file have the DOS attributes Read-Only, Hidden, and Modified-Since-Last-Backup, but it also can be marked Shareable or Non-Shareable (a property that allows or disallows simultaneous access by more than one user). Each file is also tagged with its original creation date, the identification of the user who created the file (the file's owner), the date on which the file was last accessed, the date the file was last modified, and the date and time the file was last archived. Directories also have special properties (described in the "NetWare Security" section).

From this description of the file system used on NetWare 286 file server, you probably have guessed that the operating system software running on the server is not IBM PC DOS, and you are right. NetWare operates in protected mode (OS/2 does also, but NetWare did it first) and literally takes control of the entire computer. Because protected mode allows the 80286 CPU chip to address 16 megabytes of memory, NetWare uses whatever extra memory you install in the file server for caching (see the "File Servers" section earlier in this chapter).

NetWare also supports *Value Added Processes* (VAPs), separate program modules linked with NetWare that let the file server provide extra services. Novell's Btrieve file-access method is a good example of a VAP.

Instead of using DOS redirection to ask the file server for various portions of a file, an application running on a workstation sends Btrieve the key of the record that the workstation wants. Btrieve looks up the record right on the server and returns the appropriate record to the application.

NetWare Security

Novell NetWare implements four types of security to restrict or allow access to a file server, its directories, and its files:

❑ A user ID and password are required for file server access.

❑ *Trustee rights*, granted to a person or group of persons, can allow or disallow various levels of access to a directory and its subdirectories.

❑ Each directory has security restrictions that apply to that specific directory.

❑ A file can be marked Read-Only, to prevent inadvertent modification of the file.

Each directory has a *Maximum Rights Mask* that represents the highest level of privilege any of the directory's trustees can be granted. Each directory can have as many as five trustees, and each trustee can have the following eight rights expressed by the rights mask. A user can

❑ Read from open files

❑ Write to open files

❑ Open existing files

❑ Create new files

❑ Delete existing files

❑ Act parentally, by creating, renaming, or erasing subdirectories and setting trustee rights and directory rights in the directory and its subdirectories

❑ Search for files in the directory

❑ Modify file attributes

NetWare Fault Tolerance

Realizing that reliability is an important trait of a file server, the designers and programmers at Novell went to some lengths to protect the data stored on the server. Two versions of NetWare are available, Advanced NetWare 286 and SFT NetWare 286 (SFT stands for System Fault Tolerant). Both versions employ strategies and techniques that minimize and transparently handle the disk surface's failure to correctly record data; SFT NetWare goes a step further, providing *disk mirroring* and *disk duplexing*, which are software mechanisms for maintaining duplicate copies of disk data.

The NetWare operating system is also programmed to recognize signals from an uninterruptible power supply through UPS monitoring. The operating system knows when the UPS is supplying power, and the operating system notifies users of how much time they have left before the UPS batteries run down. If commercial power is not restored within the time period, NetWare closes any open files and shuts itself down gracefully.

Finally, SFT NetWare offers the NetWare Transaction Tracking System (TTS). An application programmed to use TTS can treat a series of database updates as a single, atomic operation—either all of the updates are made or none of them is made. A system failure in the midst of a multiple file update does not cause inconsistencies between the files.

A NetWare Workstation

Both of the software components running on each Novell NetWare workstation are TSR programs. *IPX* manages the PC-to-PC and PC-to-File Server communications by implementing Novell's IPX/SPX communications protocol. *NET3* (or NET2 or NET4, depending on the version of PC DOS you run at each workstation) is the shell/redirector that shunts DOS file requests to and from the file server by issuing commands to IPX. Together, these components make the file server's disks and printers look like DOS-managed peripherals. IPX takes about 19 kilobytes of memory; NET3 about 38 kilobytes.

You do not have to run NETBIOS on a NetWare workstation (unless of course you have applications that use NETBIOS' protocol), because the NetWare shell software uses IPX to communicate with the file server. Novell supplies a NETBIOS emulator that can be loaded on top of IPX and that converts NETBIOS commands into IPX commands for transmission across the network, if you want both protocols. The NetWare NETBIOS Emulator adds roughly 20 kilobytes of memory to the resident portion of NetWare.

As many as 100 workstations can be concurrently logged into each NetWare 286 file server.

Novell NetWare 386

NetWare 386 takes advantage of the 80386 CPU chip to extend the limits of NetWare. It supports as much as four gigabytes of memory for caching; as many as 250 users can be logged into a server; as much as 32 terabytes (32 trillion bytes) of disk storage can reside on a single server; each file can be as much as 4 gigabytes; and a file can span multiple physical drives. As many as 100,000 files can be open concurrently. NetWare 386 includes the features of SFT NetWare and adds enhanced security facilities. Also new is the concept of NetWare Loadable Modules (NLMs)—software modules that can be loaded into (or unloaded from) the file server even while the server is still running. Finally, to help programmers manipulate this new environment more easily, Novell offers The Developer's Workbench. This consists of a C compiler, linker, symbolic debugger, libraries of LAN-related code, and NetWare RPC. RPC stands for remote procedure code, a distributed processing concept in which different parts of an overall program and process are executed on separate computers.

Other Environments

Most LANs from other vendors look different externally from IBM and Novell LANs, but internally they work pretty much the same. Most, for example, are based on NETBIOS, just like the IBM PC LAN Program. And of course they strive to give users speedy PC-to-PC communications along with transparent PC DOS-like access to a file server. Some, such as 3+, from 3Com Corporation, offer easy-to-use system administration utilities and an enhanced NETBIOS that can route message packets across bridges (a bridge ties together two file servers or two LANs). Banyan offers Street-Talk, an easy-to-use naming convention for LAN resources.

TCP/IP, however, is a completely different animal. The Department of Defense designed TCP/IP (Transmission Control Protocol/Internet Protocol) for ARPANET, a geographically large network (not a LAN) that connects the various sites of the DoD Advanced Research Projects Agency. TCP/IP is a layer of protocols, not a LAN operating system. TCP is similar to NETBIOS in that it provides point-to-point, guaranteed-delivery communications between nodes; IP provides datagram communications between nodes on a network (like Novell's IPX). A set of fairly standard utilities for transferring files (FTP), executing simple remote programs (TELNET), and sending electronic mail (SMTP) is designed to work with TCP/IP. These utilities are not a PC DOS shell/redirector, of course; the remote computer is not a file server.

Because TCP/IP is a public, not proprietary, protocol, it has become extremely popular as the basis for interconnecting LANs from different vendors. However, this popularity is bound to wane—the federal government has already decreed that after August 1990 all major computer and network acquisitions must comply with the Government OSI Profile (GOSIP). By the late 1990s, OSI protocols will have replaced TCP/IP.

Summary

This chapter covered the basics of local area networking. You know that LANs are based on the exchange of message packets (frames) by the workstations on the network, and you have seen how a file server shares its resources through the redirection of DOS function calls. You have a basic familiarity with the different types of networks and their components. And you understand the different LAN environments presented by the popular IBM and Novell products.

If you built a LAN as we went along, it is certainly up and running now. The cabling is in place (you can put the ceiling panels back), the file server is humming nicely (you have put it in a safe location and surrounded it with signs telling users how to bring up the network and warning them to stay away from the server's power cord), and the PC workstations are happily sharing disk space, files, and printers across the network. The users might even be doing a bit of electronic mail.

2

Multiuser Concepts

C hapter 1, "The Basics of Networking," discussed the software products that create the LAN environment on a group of interconnected PCs. Let's explore that environment more closely.

This chapter explains the concepts on which multiuser network programming is based, and describes what the network support software does to enable multiple users to coexist peacefully on a LAN. Chapter 4, "DOS-Level Programming," contains a detailed discussion of network programming techniques.

This chapter shows how the various versions of PC DOS have provided LAN support, and discusses how DOS, the IBM PC LAN Program, and Novell NetWare transform a group of PCs into a multiuser setting for LAN-aware application programs. The role of the program SHARE.EXE is described, and the concepts of workstation identification, file sharing, and record locking are introduced. Printing to a shared network printer is also discussed. The chapter concludes with a brief look at how network security affects programs running on a LAN.

PC DOS and OS/2 by themselves are single-user operating systems. On a LAN, however, several users need to be able to run the same application on different workstations. The application coordinates the efforts of each user or workstation by understanding and manipulating the environment presented by the LAN. Network software adds an entirely new dimension to programming a PC.

The Multiuser PC DOS Environment

From a programming point of view, a multiuser operating system needs to provide three things:

1. It must offer some way to identify which user is which so that programs can know who they are talking to.

2. It must allow an application to share files and control whether a file can be shared among several users or accessed exclusively by the application.

3. For those files that are being shared, the system must allow an application to *lock records*—to momentarily gain exclusive access to all or a part of a file, update the file without fear of colliding with another application, and then release its temporary ownership.

In addition to these standard multiuser facilities, a LAN needs a fourth mechanism—a way to determine whether the PC is on a LAN.

The functions that Microsoft, IBM, and (in a completely separate way) Novell tacked onto PC DOS provide these capabilities and a little more. Microsoft and IBM, who obviously control what goes into PC DOS, placed these new and extended functions directly in PC DOS itself. Because Novell is not a partner in the maintenance and programming of the PC DOS operating system, Novell originally supported these capabilities with functions provided by the NetWare *shell* (called ANET2, ANET3, NET2, NET3, or NET4, depending on the version of DOS and on the version of NetWare). The NetWare shell supports these capabilities by intercepting the primary entry point into DOS (Interrupt 21 hex). Novell, in addition to offering its own proprietary set of multiuser functions, also recognizes and supports the Microsoft and IBM functions.

Both Novell NetWare and the IBM PC LAN Program can share an entire file server disk drive or, if you want, certain subdirectories on it. The Net-Ware command MAP is used to set up drive mappings that specify the relationship between the drive letters and directories that a workstation sees on the network and the actual drive and directory structure on the file server. Similarly, the commands NET SHARE (at the file server) and NET USE (at a workstation) are used with the IBM PC LAN Program to specify the drive and directory relationships. The way you use these commands determines which drive letters and directory structure are visible to your application. You may want to say a few words in the Installation section of your user documentation about how you expect these drive mappings to be set up. In any case, try to make your software as flexible as possible when you set up drive- and directory-naming conventions. Your program also can determine which drives are network drives, if for some reason it needs to know this. Chapter 4, "DOS-Level Programming," provides more detail and some source code examples of how to determine local versus network drives.

DOS Versions

Microsoft and IBM added LAN-related function calls to versions of PC DOS starting with 3.0. File-access control (exclusive and shared modes) and record locking are available to programs running under V3.0. Version 3.1 added the capabilities to obtain the identification of individual workstations, determine which disk drives are remote (that is, redirected or shared) and which are local, and find out the network name of a remote disk drive. Version 3.2 coincided with the release of IBM's Token Ring network adapter cards. Version 3.3 added a function allowing programs to commit file data to disk (a sort of *temporary close* action). And, DOS V4.0 makes the loading of the SHARE.EXE program mandatory rather than optional (the following section describes the SHARE program).

You probably will want to determine the DOS version early in your program. You then can decide whether to continue or warn the user to upgrade to a later version to run your application. In fact, if you detect either DOS V1.X or V2.X, you should *definitely* tell the user to upgrade.

DOS function call 30 (hex), Get Version, can be used to determine which version of PC DOS is running on a workstation and therefore which network-related programming services are available. This question is so frequently asked inside application programs that C compilers typically offer major and minor DOS-version information as a prefilled data item that application programs can access. Turbo C and Microsoft C both place DOS version in the global variable _osmajor (the minor part of the version is in _osminor). In Lattice C, version information is stored in the character array _DOS[]; _DOS[0] is the major portion and _DOS[1] the minor.

If you want to perform DOS function call 30 (hex) yourself, you can do it like this:

```
regs.h.ah = 0x30;
int86 (0x21, &regs, &regs);
dos_major = regs.h.al;
dos_minor = regs.h.ah;
```

A few years ago, V2.1 was the most popular PC DOS version. Its popularity lasted far beyond the release date of DOS V3.0. Because of the approach Novell took to create a LAN environment, based on a separate layer of software above DOS, users of PC DOS V2.1 who have the appropriate NetWare shell software were able to have access to a LAN without upgrading to a new operating system. This is one of the reasons Novell got an early toehold in the LAN marketplace. Today, of course, this is no longer a significant factor; most users have a later (LAN-compatible) version of DOS.

The LAN-related services provided by OS/2 are conceptually similar to the services provided by PC DOS. Support for file sharing and record locking has been a part of OS/2 from the beginning (version 1.0 of OS/2). Although OS/2 by itself is a single-user environment, it is also a multitasking environment. The same file-sharing and record-locking facilities you use on a LAN are used to control concurrently running OS/2 tasks that need to access and share the same files. If you have OS/2 and want to see an example of these facilities in action, go to the directory where your SWAPPER.DAT file resides (located in the \OS2\SYSTEM directory if you have version 1.1). Try to copy another file (doesn't matter which one) over SWAPPER.DAT with

```
COPY <anyfile> SWAPPER.DAT.
```

You will get a file-sharing error!

The SHARE.EXE Program

SHARE.EXE, which enables file sharing on a LAN, is distributed on the IBM PC DOS distribution diskettes. SHARE consists of a Terminate and Stay Resident (TSR) program that inserts hooks deep into DOS. So deep are these hooks that you cannot remove SHARE from memory without rebooting the computer.

If SHARE is not loaded, the special file-access modes that you specify when a file is opened (to acquire exclusive access to a file, for example) are ignored by DOS. In fact, you can corrupt a network disk quite thoroughly if SHARE is not in effect. This is one of the reasons that DOS V4.0 and subsequent versions load SHARE automatically so that users no longer can forget to run it. (SHARE is also automatically in effect under OS/2.)

You should put in the user documentation for your application (perhaps in the installation section) a few words that remind users to make sure that SHARE is run before they fire up your software. For those versions of DOS that don't load SHARE automatically, the best time to invoke the SHARE program is when the user types the sequence of commands for logging on to the network. Naturally, this sequence is often a .BAT file (and could likely even be the AUTOEXEC.BAT file). If you are a cautious programmer who wants to double-check whether users are following instructions, a technique for detecting the presence of SHARE is shown in Chapter 4, "DOS-Level Programming."

One interesting aspect of SHARE is that it enables file sharing even on a stand-alone, single-user PC. SHARE identifies the current owner of a file by the address at which the program is loaded, called the program's *Process ID* (PID). The PID consists of the segment address of the program's Program Segment Prefix. This segment address uniquely identifies different processes running on the same computer. Because you can have several TSR-type programs loaded underneath a running application program, DOS needs to keep separate track of the file I/O performed by each program—background and foreground. DOS does this by using the PID. If SHARE is loaded on a single-user computer, the same file sharing that occurs across the network can occur between two TSRs, or between a TSR and a foreground application. This aspect of SHARE allows the File/Record Collision Test software described in Chapter 8, "Network Applications," to work on a single-user computer.

Is This PC on a LAN?

When your program starts up, one of the first things it should do is determine whether it is running on a LAN. If your program is designed to run exclusively in a LAN environment and a user is trying to execute it on a stand-alone computer, you would naturally want to terminate processing and display to the user a message such as "Did you know that your computer isn't on the LAN right now?" On the other hand, your program may be sophisticated enough to run in both LAN and stand-alone environments; the program might do things one way on a LAN and a different way off the LAN.

If you scan the DOS Services section of Part IV ("Reference") of this book, or IBM's *PC DOS Technical Reference* manual, or any other DOS reference, you will see functions for opening files in shared mode, locking records, and other network-related operations. One thing you will *not* see, however, is a unique, standard mechanism for programmers to use to determine whether their programs are running on a LAN or just on a stand-alone PC. Different vendors have provided "Am I Installed?" schemes, and the programmer must code a series of tests and infer the presence or absence of the LAN by checking the results. Chapter 4, "DOS-Level Programming," shows how to make this inference.

Identifying the Workstation

Multiuser programming on a LAN is different from programming under "big computer" operating systems such as UNIX or MVS. On a mainframe or minicomputer, each user is running a copy of the application program on the same computer. On a LAN, each copy of the application runs on a different computer (the workstation). The LAN application may even be designed so that unattended computers acting as slaves (often called *engines*) perform some of the work.

Mainframes and minis identify the user with a Login Identifier/user ID/ account ID, which is then internally associated with the unique terminal address assigned to the terminal being used. On a LAN, each workstation can be given a *machine name* that identifies the workstation (not necessarily the user). To further complicate matters, on some LANs the same machine name can be assigned to more than one workstation, or machines names may not be assigned at all. Chapter 4, "DOS-Level Programming," describes ways to avoid these situations, because having unique machine names for all workstations can be helpful to your application.

Your program will need to distinguish the machine it is running on from the other workstations on the network. DOS function call 5E00 (hex), Get Machine Name, is used to determine whether a machine name exists and to obtain the name. Chapter 4, "DOS-Level Programming," presents techniques for obtaining and using machine name.

IBM PC LAN Program Workstation IDs

The IBM PC LAN Program uses machine names automatically; the Net Start command that loads and runs the PC LAN Program requires a machine name as part of the command line. The reason for this is that NETBIOS is a name-oriented PC-to-PC communications service, and PC LAN Program uses NETBIOS to shuttle file data back and forth to the file server. The machine names used by the PC LAN Program are always present and always unique.

If you use the NETBIOS Microscope program (see Chapter 8, "Network Applications") on a LAN running the PC LAN Program, you can examine (but please do not delete!) the NETBIOS names established by the PC LAN Program on each of the workstations.

Novell NetWare Workstation IDs

Novell NetWare, on the other hand, more closely resembles the minicomputer environment. Each of its users must log into the network with a user ID, but internally NetWare refers to each user (workstation) with a number that identifies the connection made to the file server (connection number). In fact, unless the System Administrator specifically prohibits it, the same user ID can be logged into the network from two or more workstations.

Although you can code your program to use NetWare-specific mechanisms for identifying workstations and users (by using either connection number or user ID), NetWare provides a facility for setting up machine names on a NetWare LAN. To establish a machine name under NetWare, you use the SYSCON utility to create a *login script* for each user, as shown in the following example:

```
machine name = "BARRY"
```

Login scripts are somewhat like .BAT files. They consist of a series of NetWare commands and, if you like, program invocations for one or more programs that you want to be run each time a user logs onto the network. The scripts are interpreted and executed as part of the processing done by the Login command.

Assuming that such NetWare login script entries are created, both user identifiers (connection number and machine name) are available to application programs. Be aware, of course, that your code will run only on NetWare networks if you use connection numbers. Also note that, under NetWare, the same machine name can be associated with more than one workstation. The best way to avoid non-unique machine names on a NetWare network is to have a System Administrator assign them carefully.

File Ownership and Locking

On a file server, every open file is owned by the workstation that opened it. The ownership can be possessive ("No one touches this file but me!") or communal ("If we cooperate, we can all own this file"). There are gradations in between these extremes. Applications specify how they want to share a file when it is opened.

What would happen if two workstations paid no attention to file-sharing concepts and tried to change the contents of the same file? If two workstations open the same file and attempt to update it at the same time, the results can be messy, to say the least! Here's an example of what can happen:

When a workstation reads a file or a portion of a file, the data is transferred from the file server into workstation memory. Writing the data transfers it back to the file server. Suppose that Workstation A reads the file and displays the data to the user. While User A is looking at the screen and keying in changes, Workstation B also reads the file into memory and displays the file's data to User B. User B, typing faster than User A, saves Workstation B's changes first. User A, after pondering a few minutes, then saves Workstation A's changes (by writing the data from workstation memory to the file server). The changes that User B made are now lost; they have been overwritten by those of the slower typist, User A.

An even more complicated situation arises when several *interrelated* files need to be updated. Because the contents of one file are supposed to have a certain correspondence to the contents of the other files, a helter-skelter series of updates from multiple workstations would be disastrous. Any relationships that existed before the updates would be quickly destroyed.

Deadlocks

Deadlock is a gruesome but well-chosen word for a situation you want very much to avoid. Suppose that Workstation A and Workstation B both are running different programs and both programs need to update the same two files on the file server. Both programs need to lock the two files so that the files can be updated with consistent data. At about the same moment, both programs reach the point in their execution at which they need to acquire the locks. The sequence of events goes like this:

❏ Program A locks file 1.

❏ Program A writes data to file 1 that absolutely also *must* be reflected in file 2.

❏ Program B locks file 2.

❏ Program B writes data to file 2 that also absolutely *must* be reflected in file 1.

❏ Program A tries to lock file 2—the request is denied.

❏ Program B tries to lock file 1—a Mexican standoff.

Another term for this situation is *deadly embrace*—a term just as gruesome as "deadlock," and perhaps a bit more descriptive. Untangling the participants in a deadlock usually involves rebooting both workstations, which leaves inconsistent data in the files that were open at the time. Chapter 4, "DOS-Level Programming," tells how to avoid deadlocks.

File Sharing under PC DOS

Beginning with V3.0, facilities were built into PC DOS that give programmers control over file sharing. These same facilities, although specified differently, are available also under OS/2. Novell NetWare supports the DOS function calls that involve file sharing and access, and also offers its own set of facilities (unique to NetWare), called *Synchronization Services*.

When an application opens a file, either by calling DOS directly or by performing an open() call, the application specifies three things to DOS: *access mode*, *sharing mode*, and *Inheritance*. How DOS handles the file also depends on whether the file has a Read-Only attribute.

Let me deal with Inheritance first, and then dismiss it, because it isn't directly related to LAN programming. You can set the Inheritance flag to File is Inheritable if you are spawning one or more child processes that need access to a file opened by the main program. Setting this flag allows the child process to use the same file handle issued to the main program by the open() call.

Access mode indicates to DOS whether you intend to write to the file. You should use this flag conservatively; if you only need to read from a file, open it with an access mode of Read-Only. This approach gives you a better chance of successfully opening the file, because DOS and the network software allow multiple readers of a file but reject a Read-Write open if others already have the file open in Read-Only mode. Similarly, if a workstation has opened a file for Read-Write access and other workstations subsequently attempt to open the file for Read-Only access, the subsequent attempts will fail.

Sharing mode lets you control how other workstations can open the file after it is opened successfully by your workstation. Sharing mode is expressed in terms of denying certain capabilities to the other workstations that attempt to open the file. The restrictions you can specify are DENY_NONE, DENY_READ, DENY_WRITE, and DENY_READ_WRITE. In addition, there is a special mode called compatibility mode.

DENY_READ_WRITE Mode (Exclusive Access)

When you open a file in DENY_READ_WRITE mode, you gain exclusive access to the file. While you have the file open, no other workstation can read from the file or write to it. The file belongs to you until it is closed. Your attempt to open the file will fail, however, if another workstation already has the file open in any other mode.

DENY_WRITE Mode

Opening a file in DENY_WRITE mode allows other workstations to open and read from the file, but not to write to it. The other workstations must open the file for Read-Only access in DENY_NONE mode, or their attempts to open the file will fail. Likewise, an attempt to open a file in DENY_WRITE mode will fail if any other workstation has the file open in a DENY_WRITE or DENY_READ_WRITE (exclusive) mode.

DENY_READ Mode

You can cause other workstations to fail to open a file for reading if you open it first in DENY_READ mode. Oddly enough, this mode allows multiple workstations to write to a file but not to read from it.

DENY_NONE Mode

DENY_NONE is the "communal ownership" mentioned earlier. It allows multiple workstations to open a file for Read-Write access, and defers control of concurrent reads and writes to the record-locking functions described later in this chapter.

Compatibility Mode

Compatibility mode confers exclusive control of a file. This mode is set automatically when a file is created (rather than opened) or when you use file control blocks (FCBs) rather than file handles. You should avoid this mode when you open a file, and you should also avoid using FCBs in LAN-aware software. FCBs are a holdover from DOS 1.X, continuing to be supported by PC DOS only so that users can run older programs. (That's where this mode got its name). For most compilers, compatibility mode is also in effect when you open a file with a call to fopen() rather than the more explicit open().

In certain cases, DOS changes compatibility mode to a different file-sharing mode during the process of opening the file. If a file has an attribute of Read-Only (as indicated by its directory entry), DOS replaces compatibility mode with DENY_WRITE. If other workstations attempt to open the file, access is allowed or denied based on the rules given under DENY_WRITE.

If a newly created file falls into the compatibility mode category, giving the creating workstation exclusive control of the file, how can you change the mode so that the new file can be shared with other workstations?

Unfortunately, there is no mechanism for changing sharing mode on the fly; you have to close the file and then open it with a suitable sharing mode.

File-Sharing Situations

Because these file-sharing modes use "negative logic" to control what happens when workstations try to open files, these modes can be pretty confusing. Figure 2.1 summarizes how access mode and sharing mode work together. The following examples should help explain the interactions.

Fig. 2.1. *Access mode and sharing mode.*

Workstation A (already open)		Sharing/Access modes Workstation B can use			
Sharing	Access	DENY_ALL	DENY_WRITE	DENY_READ	DENY_NONE
DENY_ALL	R/W	fail	fail	fail	fail
DENY_WRITE	R/W	fail	fail	fail	READ
DENY_READ	R/W	fail	fail	fail	WRITE
DENY_NONE	R/W	fail	fail	fail	R/W
DENY_ALL	READ	fail	fail	fail	fail
DENY_WRITE	READ	fail	READ	fail	READ
DENY_READ	READ	fail	WRITE	fail	WRITE
DENY_NONE	READ	fail	R/W	fail	R/W

Exclusive Access Example

Suppose that your application uses a B-Tree access method. Each file of data records is paired with a file of index entries that point into the various data records in the first file. Occasionally, a user (the System Administrator, perhaps) must run a utility program that rebuilds (reorganizes) the index file and physically deletes records from the data file that are marked as logically deleted. In this case, the utility program should open both the data and index files in DENY_READ_WRITE mode. If the open fails, the utility program detects the error and informs the user that another user is currently using the file. If the open succeeds, the utility program can go about its business, secure in the knowledge that no other user can open the file during the rebuilding process.

For another example, suppose that your application has a file which it opens, reads, and displays on-screen for a user to view and possibly update. After the user has keyed some changes, the application writes the data back to the file and closes it. The application needs to allow other workstations to read and view the data even while an update is under way. Should you open the file for exclusive (DENY_READ_WRITE) access, or perhaps DENY_WRITE access, and leave it open for the duration of the update? Probably not. A user may spend several minutes keying the update.

In this situation, the best approach is what I call the *library card* scheme. The application first puts a note in a separate file which indicates that the file is "charged out," and then proceeds with the open and read operations. After the update, the application removes the entry from the ChargedOut file. For any user, the application first checks the ChargedOut file against the type of operation the user has indicated. The application informs the user of what it finds in the ChargedOut file, if that information conflicts with the intended operation. If you record machine name (discussed earlier in this chapter) in the ChargedOut file, the application not only can inform users of the pending update but also can tell *who* has the file charged out. Chapter 4, "DOS-Level Programming," presents some pseudocode showing how to implement this scheme.

DENY_NONE Example

A multiuser environment commonly has two or three central files that all the workstations must be able to update concurrently, yet the contents of these files must remain consistent. Each time a user at a workstation starts up a copy of the application software, the common files are opened in DENY_NONE mode (with Read-Write access) so that all workstations can have the files open simultaneously. The control of concurrent access is then designed into the part of the program that performs the record-level updates. The concept of record locking is discussed later in this chapter.

Sharing Retry Count and Delay

DOS is smart enough to realize that many file-sharing conflicts are only momentary. It implements a *retry* mechanism that attempts to resolve sharing errors by delaying a certain length of time and then reexecuting the file-open request. If the conflict cannot be resolved after a certain number of retries, DOS gives up and signals that a sharing error has occurred.

There is a function call (IOCTL, hex 44; subfunction Set Sharing Retry Count/Delay, hex 0B) that your application can use to change the number of retries and the delay time between them. The delay itself consists of a simple "do nothing" loop. The default values used by DOS are *1 loop = 1 delay period* and *retries = 3*. If you expect your application to cause frequent but brief collisions, you can increase the retry count and the delay period. Chapter 4, "DOS-Level Programming," shows source-code techniques for setting these values.

Note that the DOS "do nothing" loop executes quicker on faster computers—DOS does not take into account the difference between a PC/XT and a PS/2 Model 70, for example. You have to consider the processing speed of the workstation computer as well as the estimated number of collisions and their duration as you fine-tune the Sharing Retry Count/Delay parameters. These parameters affect not only file locking but also the way that DOS processes record-locking conflicts (discussed later in this chapter).

NetWare Synchronization Services for Files

In addition to supporting the access mode and sharing mode concepts just discussed, Novell NetWare offers its own set of services that your program can use to control access to shared files. Novell calls these services *Synchronization Services*. They can be used to lock specific files individually, or together as a set. Chapter 4, "DOS-Level Programming," describes specific techniques for using these services.

Unlike the built-in PC DOS functions, the NetWare file-locking services let you treat a group of files as a related set. Novell suggests that you think of these services as four separate tasks which you insert into your code at strategic points:

❏ *Logging:* Your program first issues a LogFile request for each file that you are about to lock. This step informs the file server of what will come.

❏ *Locking:* Next, your program uses `LockFileSet` to lock all the files as a group. If the file server cannot successfully lock the entire set of files within a time period that you specify, an error is returned to your program.

❏ *Releasing:* After part or all of an update is complete, you can call `ReleaseFile` to release the lock on an individual file, or `ReleaseFileSet` to release all the locks associated with the group of files.

❏ *Clearing:* Finally, you undo the `LogFile` operation by using either `ClearFile` (one file at a time) or `ClearFileSet` (the entire group).

Novell designed these services to help programmers avoid deadlocks.

DOS Commands versus File Sharing

DOS itself is not immune to file-sharing problems—even something as simple as issuing a COPY command to DOS can cause problems on a network. It doesn't happen often, fortunately. But COMMAND.COM is not particularly LAN-aware. A nasty collision occurs when you tell DOS to copy a file that another workstation currently has open. It doesn't matter that the other workstation might only be reading from the file and that the COPY command just wants to share the file by also reading from it. To execute COPY, COMMAND.COM opens the input (source) file in compatibility mode, which, unless the file's directory entry is marked with the Read-Only attribute, asks for exclusive access to the file. What the COPY command *should* do is open the input file with a mode that denies other workstations the capability to write to the file.

Novell supplies NetWare users with a file-copy utility of its own, called NCOPY. Not only is NCOPY LAN-aware, but it also has a special feature for avoiding unnecessary message traffic across the LAN. If it detects that both the source and destination files reside on the same file server, NCOPY performs the file copy directly at the file server. NCOPY thus avoids transmitting the file out to a workstation, which in turn then would have to transmit the file back to the file server under the destination file name.

Record Locking

Because a file lock affects the entire file and extends from the time a file is opened until the time it is closed, file locking may be an awkward inconvenience to the users of your application. You can choose instead to implement locking at the record level. A record lock lasts only long enough to ensure that consistent data has been written to the files, and usually affects only a small portion of the file.

A record lock specifies a certain region of a file by giving the region's location in the file (its offset) and the region's size (its length). If the specified region cannot be successfully locked (if another workstation opened the file in other than DENY_NONE mode, or if another workstation locked the same region), an error is returned to your program. The locked region can encompass a portion of a data record, one data record, several physically adjacent data records, or the entire file. If each data record in a file is independent of all the others, simply locking the affected data record is appropriate. However, if there are relationships among the records in a file (perhaps one record contains a pointer to another, or the updating of the file implies that several records may need to be physically moved in the file), the correct approach is to lock the entire file as if it were a single large record.

Don't forget to unlock the record when you finish with it.

Deadlocks

The same sort of situation described earlier for file-level deadlocks can happen at the record level.

PC DOS Record Locks

DOS function call 5C (hex), Lock/Unlock File Access, is used to lock or unlock a range of bytes in a file. All workstations using the file should have opened it in DENY_NONE mode. If it cannot acquire the lock, DOS returns an error to your program. If another workstation tries to read from or write to a locked region, DOS generates a critical-error situation by invoking Interrupt 24 (hex), the Critical-Error Handler (which produces an Abort, Retry, Ignore, or Fail? message at that other workstation).

As the *PC DOS Technical Reference* manual mentions, a record lock is expected to last for only a brief duration. If your program needs to make sure that a portion of the file remains untouched while interacting with the user, you should consider implementing the library-card scheme discussed earlier.

It is incorrect for a program to discover that a region of the file is locked by attempting to write a record and finding that a critical error has occurred. You must first issue the lock request and, if it is successful, then proceed to write the record.

The DOS IOCTL function mentioned earlier for setting the duration of the delay loop and number of retries (Set Sharing Retry/Count) applies also to record locks. DOS uses the same retry mechanism for file locking and record locking.

NetWare Synchronization Services for Records

The record-locking services provided by Novell NetWare are conceptually similar to the NetWare file-locking services discussed earlier. The same four tasks of logging, locking, releasing, and clearing apply to record locking. Your application can choose to use either physical record locks or logical record locks.

NetWare's physical record locks work the same as PC DOS record locks. The protected region of the file is expressed in terms of a given number of bytes, starting at a given position in the file. To use the NetWare method of physical record locking, your program issues one or more calls to LogPhysicalRecord and then a call to LockPhysicalRecordSet. After the updates are complete, your program issues a ReleasePhysicalRecordSet and finally a ClearPhysicalRecordSet. If you choose to release or clear records one at a time, you can use ReleasePhysicalRecord and ClearPhysicalRecord.

NetWare also offers logical record locking—the capability to refer by symbolic name to a record that will be locked. Logical records are logged, locked, released, and cleared just as physical records are, but the lock applies only to the name of the record in a table residing in the file server and not to the actual file region itself. In other words, logical record locks provide a convenient coordination mechanism but no real security for file integrity. When a workstation requests a logical lock, the file server checks only the lock's name table to see whether another workstation previously issued a logical lock against that name. Therefore, if one program uses logical record locks, every program that accesses a file must use them. Both file locks and physical record locks override logical locks.

Printing across the LAN

You would think that sending print data to a shared network printer would be easy, painless, and not nearly as much trouble as trying to share files and records. Unfortunately, this isn't so.

Suppose that a user on the network runs 1-2-3 and needs to print a spreadsheet in condensed (small) print because the spreadsheet is several cells wide. The user sends control codes to the printer, prints the spreadsheet, and happily walks away from the network printer with a nicely formatted printout in hand. The next user to print a report (from your application!) mutters dark, nasty things about your software because the printout is scrunched on the left side of the page in small characters.

Here's another example: you have a series of programs that each print a section of a lengthy, complex report. You test the programs on a standalone, nonnetworked PC, and they seem to run perfectly. Each report section flows to the next one exactly as it should. Next, you run a test that sends the report to the network printer. To your bewilderment, stray page breaks occur throughout the report that destroy the report's appearance. It takes you an extra day or two to figure out that, because each of the programs in the series opens and closes the printer to print a given report section, the network software is inserting automatic page breaks each time the printer is closed.

Printer Control under the PC LAN Program

With the IBM PC LAN Program, a special form of the NET USE command is issued at a workstation to indicate that print data should be redirected across the network. A corresponding NET SHARE command must have been executed at the file server. The command can have optional arguments specifying how page breaks (form feeds) should occur at the printer:

- ❏ A form feed is automatically issued between printouts.
- ❏ The PC LAN Program detects whether the end of the print file contains a form feed; if not, a form feed is issued.
- ❏ The PC LAN Program does not send extra form feeds.

Additionally, you can create a file that the PC LAN Program uses to print job-separator pages between printouts. The PC LAN Program supports several printer-control options in the Job Separator file, and you can use them not only to specify what the separator page should look like but also to reset the printer to a default mode before each printout is produced. The default Job Separator file is PQ.SEP. You use the NET SEPARATOR command to specify the name of the Job Separator file and whether separator pages should be in effect.

You can use DOS function call 5E02 (hex), Set Printer Setup String, to programmatically designate a string of control characters to be sent to the printer each time the network printer is opened.

Printer Control under NetWare

With earlier versions of Novell NetWare, the workstation command that redirected print data was SPOOL; later versions use CAPTURE. CAPTURE offers more extensive control over the network printer. Using this command, you can control

❏ Whether automatic form feeds are added to the end of a file of print data

❏ Whether a separator page (Novell calls it a banner page) should be produced

❏ Whether tabs should be expanded into spaces and how many spaces to use

❏ The number of copies to be printed

❏ The type of form that must be mounted in the printer

❏ The variable text (user name or job name) that appears on the banner page

❏ The way NetWare detects the end of the print job (based on a time-out value or file close operation)

❏ The number of lines per page

❏ The width of each line

❏ Other miscellaneous items

Each of these parameters can be programmatically set by calling functions within Novell's Print Services.

Security Issues

As you design a LAN-aware application, you must consider security issues from two points of view.

First, you want to make sure that your application implements its own levels of security. Users should be instructed how to make backup copies of the files that your application uses; sensitive data should be protected in appropriate ways; and, as much as is possible, your application should be designed to guard users from even inadvertently damaging each other's work. Of course, you would have considered each of these points anyway. But you should revisit each aspect of your design that is related to either security or reliability, anticipating what could happen when multiple users run your software.

Second, the application must conform to the existing environment set up by the System Administrator. A shared network drive is not a local hard drive. Especially under Novell NetWare, situations are possible that would never occur on a single-user computer. For example, you recall that Chapter 1, "The Basics of Networking," discussed the rights associated with a directory on a NetWare server. If the System Administrator grants rights in your application's directory (or directories) only to certain users, your application may encounter I/O errors when it is run by an authorized person. Typically, the application will be incapable of finding its files in the directory. The files may actually exist (and be visible to users who have sufficient trustee rights), but unauthorized people can be restricted so that certain directories are "invisible." Your program will function differently when it is run by different users because of these rights.

Checking Return Codes and Handling Errors

Every programmer knows that it is important to check return codes after performing file I/O and to handle error situations correctly, but sometimes these tasks get short shrift. I am not accusing you personally, of course. It is just that I have often seen programs that (for example) display the message File Not Found when actually the file exists but is currently open at a different workstation. The program detected an error at file-open time, but neglected to find out exactly what error had occurred. Make sure in your own LAN-aware programs that you check return codes religiously, and that you offer your users good error-recovery options. You may even want to include retry options in your error-handling code so that your users have better control over their access to the LAN. Recognizing that error checking and processing would be a concern of many programmers, Microsoft and IBM added function call 59 (hex), Get Extended Error, to versions of DOS beginning with 3.0.

The DOS Critical-Error Handler, Interrupt 24 (hex), is particularly important to programmers on a LAN. On a single-user PC, the Abort, Retry, Ignore, or Fail? question usually pops up only for paper-out conditions at the printer or for true disk drive hardware problems such as Sector Not Found. On a network, however, the DOS Critical-Error Handler is also invoked for file-access collisions, which are caused when a workstation attempts to read from or write to a file that another workstation already has either locked or opened for exclusive access.

It is important to note that some errors are returned to the program by DOS and others are handled as critical errors—these are *sharing violations*. You should watch out for basically two situations that cause sharing violations:

1. *Files open in compatibility mode*—As was mentioned earlier, you should avoid opening a file in compatibility mode. Here's one reason why: if one workstation attempts to open a file in compatibility mode and another workstation has already opened the file in one of the other sharing modes, DOS generates an Interrupt 24 (hex) critical error. The error code from Interrupt 24 indicates Drive Not Ready, and a call to the Get Extended Error service (function call 59 hex) returns Sharing Violation.

2. *Reading and writing a locked region*—If a properly functioning program opens a file and locks a record in that file, and a rogue program then tries to read from or write into that region of the file (without testing first to see whether it is locked), DOS generates an Interrupt 24 (hex) with a General Failure error code.

Other situations, such as attempting to open for exclusive access a file that another workstation already opened, or attempting to lock a region of bytes in a file that another user already locked, return DOS error code 5, Access Denied, to your program.

Unless you specially intercept critical network errors, DOS uses the default Abort, Retry, Ignore, or Fail mechanism to give users a chance to decide how to handle the situation. This is not the friendliest message in the world, so you should consider incorporating your own Critical-Error Handler in the LAN-aware programs you develop. Under Novell NetWare, the wording of the message is different, but the effect is the same. Also under NetWare, you can perform a function call (SetNetWareErrorMode()) that tells NetWare to let your program handle critical errors rather than having NetWare handle them.

Summary

Some of the concepts presented in this chapter may be familiar to you already from your experiences with other multiuser environments, but now you understand how the concepts relate to the environment of networked PCs. The concepts discussed include identifying users, sharing files, locking records, printing, and handling the issues associated with security and error checking. This chapter also described the different environments presented by the IBM PC LAN Program and Novell NetWare, and introduced network-related services and functions offered by PC DOS that are common to both the PC LAN Program and NetWare.

3

PC-to-PC Communications Concepts

Chapter 1, "The Basics of Networking," briefly discussed frames, which form the basis for all activity on the LAN. This chapter describes frames in more detail and shows how they are used for both redirection of file-service functions as well as PC-to-PC communications. The chapter also explains the basics of the NETBIOS and IPX/SPX protocols.

Frames undergo several stages of processing during their lifetimes. On the outbound leg, before transmission, each processing stage adds information to the frame to help it along. For inbound (just-received) frames, each stage removes its layer of information and hands the frame to the next stage. The content, length, and usage of frames depend on which protocol the LAN is using. There are differences in the format of frames even between protocols as similar as Ethernet and the IEEE 802.3 protocol. Because vendors have implemented so many different protocols on LANs, you first must understand frames from a general perspective so that you can more easily focus on the individual protocols as this book explores them in depth.

After discussing frames in general, this chapter specifically examines how Ethernet frames, IEEE 802.3 frames, and Token Ring frames are formatted. In addition, you will be given a brief overview of frames on an FDDI fiber-optics network, and be introduced to the higher-level protocols IPX, SPX, and NETBIOS.

You may never need this chapter's information on how a low-level protocol's frames are formatted—you shouldn't have to go down to that level for application-level programming—but knowing what these frames look like and how they are used will help you understand what is happening "underneath" your program so that you can make better use of the LAN's facilities. You may even someday run across an odd-looking piece of data while using a debugger to pour through a memory dump and say to yourself, "Aha! That is the frame that contains the last message I sent."

General Features

Regardless of the protocol used, frames have certain common characteristics. The definition of a LAN in Chapter 1, "The Basics of Networking," said that a frame is a message packet that contains sender and receiver address information used in the routing of the message packet. As discussed in that chapter's description of network adapter cards and supporting software, each network adapter knows where to look in the frame for this routing information, so the adapter recognizes message packets intended for that adapter.

Frames are always layered (see fig. 3.1). When you give a message to a protocol such as NETBIOS, for example, and ask that the message be sent to another PC on the network, NETBIOS puts an "envelope" around your message packet and hands it to the next lower level, the network support software and network adapter card. Wrapping the NETBIOS envelope in an envelope of its own, this lower layer then sends the packet out across the network. After receiving the frame, the network support software on the receiver's computer removes the outer envelope and hands the result up to the next higher level, NETBIOS. The NETBIOS program running on the receiver's computer removes the NETBIOS envelope and gives the message, now an exact copy of the sender's message, to the receiver application.

The OSI Model

How many layers are there? Different vendors split the LAN communications functions in different ways, but they all compare themselves to the OSI Model (see fig. 3.2). This "soon-to-be" standard describes how communications between two computers *should* happen. During the early 1990s this theoretical standard will become a practical one as more and

Fig. 3.1. *Layering of frames.*

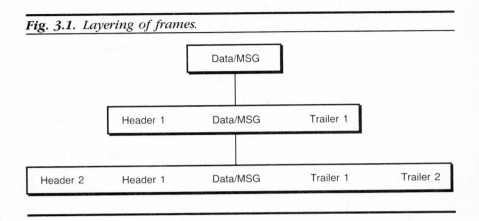

more vendors switch to it. The OSI Model declares seven layers and specifies that each layer is insulated from the others by a well-defined interface. The seven layers are

1. *Physical (lowest) Layer*—This part of the OSI Model specifies the physical and electrical characteristics of the connections that make up the network (twisted pair cables, fiber-optic cables, coaxial cables, connectors, repeaters, and so on). You can think of it as the hardware layer.

2. *Data Link*—At this stage of processing, the electrical impulses enter or leave the network cable. Bit patterns, encoding methods, and tokens are examples of elements known to this layer (and only to this layer). At this stage, errors are detected and corrected (by requesting retransmissions of corrupted packets). Because of its complexity, the data link layer is divided into a Medium Access Control (MAC) layer and a Logical Link Control (LLC) layer. The MAC layer manages network access (either token-passing or collision-sensing) and network control. The LLC layer, operating at a higher level than the MAC layer, sends and receives the user data messages themselves.

3. *Network Layer*—This processing step switches and routes the packets as necessary to get them to their destinations. It is the layer responsible for addressing and delivering message packets.

4. *Transport Layer*—When more than one packet is in process at any one time, this layer controls the sequencing of the message components and also regulates inbound traffic flow. If a duplicate packet arrives, this layer recognizes it as a duplicate and discards it.

5. *Session Layer*—The functions in this layer let applications running at two workstations coordinate their communications into a single session. A session is an exchange of messages (dialog) between two workstations. This layer supports the creation of the session, the management of the packets sent back and forth during the session, and the termination of the session.

6. *Presentation Layer*—When IBM, Apple, DEC, NEXT, and Burroughs computers all want to talk to each another, some translating and byte-reordering is needed. This layer converts data into (or from) a machine's native internal numeric format.

7. *Application (highest) Layer*—This is the layer seen by an application program, and therefore is also the interface to the OSI Model that the programmer sees. A message to be sent across the network enters the OSI Model at this point, travels downward toward the first layer (the Physical Layer), zips across to the other workstation, and then travels back up the layers until the message reaches the application on the other computer through its Application Layer.

Compare the way these layers function to the U.S. Postal Service:

❑ The Application Layer is a plain sheet of 8 1/2-by-11-inch paper, folded to fit in an envelope.

❑ The Presentation Layer is a #10 envelope (9 1/2 inches by 4 inches) with windows through which the addresses show.

❑ The Session Layer is the envelope with the names of the sender and recipient showing through the windows.

❑ The Transport Layer is the post office.

❑ The Network Layer is the mail carrier.

❑ The Data Link Layer is your mailbox.

❑ The Physical Layer is—of course—the mail truck.

Most vendors combine the functions expressed in the seven layers of the OSI Model into two or three layers of proprietary implementation.

Ethernet and IEEE 802.3 frames

Ethernet is a LAN standard based on the Experimental Ethernet network that Xerox designed and built in 1975 (before PCs!). Ethernet operates at ten megabits per second over 50-ohm coaxial cable. The current Ethernet version is 2.0, established in November 1982. The first edition of

Fig. 3.2. *The OSI Model.*

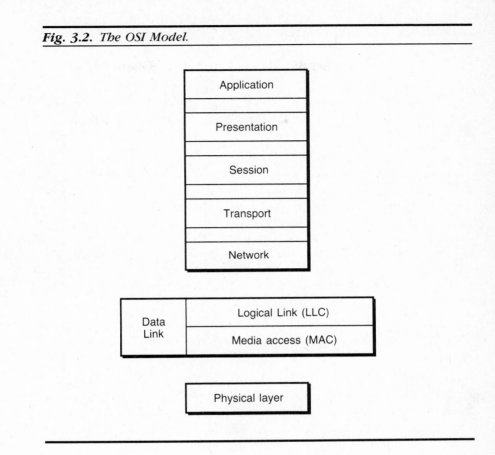

a similar LAN standard, IEEE 802.3, was published in 1985. The two standards differ subtly in network architecture and not so subtly in frame formats.

In terms of network architecture, IEEE 802.3 distinguishes between MAC and LLC layers. True Ethernet lumps these layers together into a single Data Link layer. Also, Ethernet defines an Ethernet Configuration Test Protocol (ECTP) that is absent from the IEEE 802.3 standard. However, the important differences between the two standards are in the types and lengths of the fields that make up a frame. These differences can cause the two protocols to be incompatible with one another.

Ethernet Frames

The fields in an Ethernet frame (see fig. 3.3) are defined as follows:

The 8-byte-long *preamble* field (the standard refers to a byte as an *octet*) is used for synchronization and framing. The preamble always contains the bit pattern 10101010...10101010 in the first seven bytes, with 10101011 in the last (eighth) byte.

The 6-byte *destination address* field contains the address of the workstation that will receive the frame. As the result of a naming scheme administered by Xerox, the first three bytes are a group address assigned by Xerox Corporation, and the last three are assigned locally. The first (leftmost) bit of the first byte has a special meaning. If the bit is 0, the destination address is a physical address unique throughout the entire Ethernet universe. If the leftmost bit is a 1, it represents a broadcast frame. In this case the remainder of the destination address can refer to a group of logically related workstations or to all workstations on the network (all 1s).

The *source address* address field, which is also six bytes long, identifies the workstation sending the frame. The leftmost bit of the first byte is always 0.

The *type* field contains two bytes of information that identify the type of the higher-level protocol that issued (or wants to receive) this frame. Xerox assigns the type field. Ethernet does not interpret the field. This field lets multiple high-level protocols (referred to as *Client Layers*) share the network without running into each other's messages.

The *data portion* of the frame, which can be from 46 to 1,500 bytes long, is the data message that the frame is intended to carry to the destination.

Finally, the frame contains four bytes of cyclic redundancy checksum (*CRC*) remainder, calculated by the CRC-32 polynomial. After receiving a frame, a workstation performs its own CRC-32 calculation on the frame, compares the calculated value to the CRC field in the frame, and thus determines whether the frame arrived intact or was somehow damaged in transit.

Disregarding the preamble, an entire Ethernet frame is between 64 and 1,518 bytes long, and the minimum size of a data message is 46 bytes.

Fig. 3.3. *An Ethernet frame.*

Preamble	Destination	Source	Type	Data	CRC
8	6	6	2	46-1500	4

Length of each field in bytes

IEEE 802.3 Frames

Figure 3.4 shows an IEEE 802.3 frame, which consists of the following fields:

The *preamble* field contains seven bytes of synchronization data. Each byte is the same bit pattern (10101010).

The *start frame delimiter* (SFD) consists of a single byte with the bit pattern 10101011. (These two IEEE 802.3 fields, the preamble and SFD, exactly match the single Ethernet preamble field.)

The *destination address* field, which can be either two or six bytes long, indicates which workstation is to receive the frame. The first bit of the destination address is the Individual/Group (I/G) bit; the bit is 0 if the address refers to a single workstation, or 1 if the address represents a group of workstations (a broadcast message). If the destination address is a 2-byte field, the remainder of the bits form a 15-bit workstation address. However, if the destination address is a 6-byte field, the bit following the I/G bit is a Universally/Locally (U/L) Administered bit; it is either a 0 for universally administered (global) addresses or a 1 for locally administered addresses. The remainder of the 6-byte field is a 46-bit workstation address. All addresses on a particular network must be either 2-byte or 6-byte addresses. The most popular type of IEEE 802.3 frame, 10BASE5, specifies 6-byte addresses.

In the 2- or 6-byte *source address* of the sending workstation, the I/G (first) bit is always 0.

The two *length* bytes express the length of the data portion of the frame.

The *data portion* can range from 0 to 1,500 bytes of data, but if the length of this field is less than 46 bytes, the next field (PAD) is used to fatten the frame to an acceptable (minimum) length.

The *PAD* field consists of enough bytes of filler to ensure that the frame has at least a certain overall length. This minimum length assures proper operation of the collision-detection mechanism. If the data portion is long enough, the PAD field does not appear in the frame (it becomes a zero length field).

The same as for Ethernet, the *CRC* field contains four bytes of remainder from the CRC-32 algorithm.

Fig. 3.4. *An IEEE 802.3 frame.*

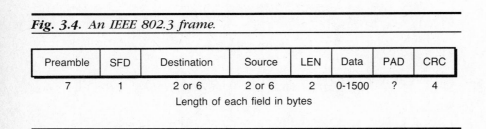

Preamble	SFD	Destination	Source	LEN	Data	PAD	CRC
7	1	2 or 6	2 or 6	2	0-1500	?	4

Length of each field in bytes

The size of a frame under both Ethernet and IEEE 802.3 (assuming Type 10BASE5), excluding the preamble and SFD, is the same—between 64 and 1,518 bytes. However, under IEEE 802.3, the application (or an upper-layer protocol) can send a data area that is less than 46 bytes long, because the MAC Layer will automatically pad it. Under Ethernet, too-small data areas are considered to be error situations.

Token Ring Frames

Let me briefly describe the magic that makes Token Rings work before I discuss actual frame formats. In 1985, Texas Instruments and IBM jointly developed the TMS380 Chipset (although, ironically, IBM does not use this chipset. IBM builds its own proprietary chipset that is *mostly* compatible with the TI/IBM set). The TMS380 chipset implements the IEEE 802.5 standards for the Physical Layer and the Data Link Layer of the OSI Model. The functions of both the MAC sublayer and the LLC sublayer of the Data Link Layer are supported. Originally released as a set of five chips, the TI product now can be produced as a single chip. In relation to the original five chips, the TMS380 functions are as follows:

❏ The *TMS38051* and *38052* chips handle the lowest level, the ring interface itself. They actually transmit and receive data (frames), monitor cable integrity, and provide clocking functions.

❏ The *TMS38020* chip is a protocol handler that controls and manages the 802.5 protocol functions.

❏ The *ROM* chip has program code burned into it. The permanently stored software performs diagnostic and management functions.

❏ The *TMS38010* chip, a 16-bit dedicated microprocessor, handles communications. It executes the code in the ROM chip and has a 2.75 kilobyte RAM buffer for temporary storage of transmitted and received data.

Be prepared for a bit of a letdown at this point, because I now have to tell you that a Token Ring is not a ring at all. Although most people think of a Token Ring as a single piece of cable that all the workstations tap into, in reality a Token Ring consists of individual point-to-point linkages. My workstation sends the token (or a frame) to your workstation, your workstation sends the token downstream to the next workstation, and so forth. Only the fact that one of your downstream neighbors happens also to be my *upstream* neighbor makes it a ring. From a communications standpoint, the messages go directly from one PC to another.

Not all workstations on the ring are peers, although the differences are invisible to the outside world. One of the workstations is designated the *active monitor*, which means that it assumes additional responsibilities for controlling the ring. The active monitor maintains timing control over the ring, issues new tokens (if necessary) to keep things going, and generates diagnostic frames under certain circumstances. The active monitor is chosen when the ring is initialized and can be any one of the workstations on the network. If the active monitor fails for some reason, there is a mechanism by which the other workstations (*standby monitors*) can negotiate which one becomes the new active monitor.

Tokens, Frames, and Abort Sequences

There are three different formats defined for IEEE 802.5 Token Ring message packets. Figure 3.5 shows the format of a token. In principle, a token is not a frame but simply a means by which each workstation can recognize when its turn to transmit has arrived. A token circulates the ring continuously until a workstation has a frame to send. The second format, seen in figure 3.6, is that of a true *data frame*. Data frames can contain messages that applications send to one another on the ring, and also sometimes contain internal messages used privately among the Token Ring network adapter cards for ring-management purposes. Figure 3.7 shows the format of the third type of message that can be transmitted on a

Token Ring, the *abort sequence*. It also is not considered a "frame." An abort sequence can occur anywhere in the bit stream and is used to interrupt or terminate the current transmission.

Fig. 3.5. *Token format.*

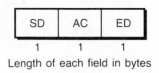

Length of each field in bytes

Fig. 3.6. *Token Ring data frame format.*

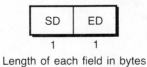

Length of each field in bytes

Fig. 3.7. *Abort sequence format.*

Length of each field in bytes

The Token

A token is three bytes long (24 bits) and contains the following three fields:

- ❏ Start delimiter
- ❏ Access control
- ❏ End delimiter

The start delimiter (SD) field appears at the beginning of the token (as well as at the beginning of every frame sent across the network). The field consists not of mere 0s and 1s, but of a unique series of electrical impulses that cannot be mistaken for anything other than a start delimiter field. Because there are four nondata symbols (each one bit long) and four (normal) 0 bits in the field, it totals one byte.

Next comes the access control (AC) field. This field is subdivided into four data items:

```
P P P   T   M   R R R
```

in which PPP are the priority bits, T is the token bit, M is the monitor bit, and RRR are the reservation bits.

Every token or frame is prioritized by setting the priority bits to a value from 0 to 7 (with 7 being the highest priority). A workstation can use the network (that is, change a token into a frame) only if that workstation receives a token with a priority less than or equal to its own priority. The workstation's network adapter sets the priority bits to indicate the priority of the current frame or token. See the description of reservation bits for details on how this works.

The token bit has a value of 0 for a token and 1 for a frame.

The monitor bit is set to 1 by the active monitor and set to 0 by any workstation transmitting a token or frame. If the active monitor sees a token or frame that contains a monitor bit of 1, the active monitor knows that this token or frame has been once around the ring without being processed by a workstation. Because a sending workstation is responsible for removing its own transmitted frames, and because high-priority workstations are responsible for grabbing a token they have previously laid claim to (see the next paragraph's discussion of reservation bits), the active monitor detects that something is wrong if a frame or a prioritized token circulates without being processed. The active monitor cancels the transmission and circulates a new token.

The reservation bits work hand in hand with the priority bits. A workstation can place its priority in the reservation bits (if its priority is higher than the current value of the reservation bits). That workstation then has dibs on the next use of the network. When transmitting a new token, a workstation sets the priority bits to the value that it found in the reservation field of the frame it just received. Unless preempted by an even higher-priority workstation, the workstation that originally set the reservation bits will be the next station to turn the token into a frame.

The final field of the token is the end delimiter (ED) field. Just as with the start delimiter field, this field contains a unique combination of 1s and special nondata symbols that cannot be mistaken for anything else. ED appears at the end of each token. Besides marking the end of the token, the field also contains two subfields: the intermediate frame bit and the error-detected bit. These subfields are discussed in the following section, because they pertain more to frames than to tokens.

The Data Frame

A frame consists of several groups of fields: the start frame sequence (SFS), the destination address (DA), the source address (SA), the data itself (INFO), the frame check sequence (FCS), and the end frame sequence (EFS). Together, these fields form a message record (envelope) that is used to carry either ring-management information (MAC data) or user data (LLC data). You already know about user data; these frames contain application-oriented data such as PC-to-PC messages or perhaps a portion of a disk file (from a file server) being shared by a workstation. MAC frames, on the other hand, are used internally by the network software. The IEEE 802.5 standard defines six MAC control frames. The frame control field (defined in the following list) indicates the type of the frame (MAC or LLC) and, if a MAC frame is specified, the field also identifies which one of the six MAC frame types is represented by this particular frame.

Briefly, the six MAC frames are the following:

- ❑ To ensure that its address is unique, a workstation sends a *duplicate address test* frame when it is first joins the ring.

- ❑ To let other workstations know that it is still alive, the active monitor circulates an *active monitor present* frame every so often.

- ❑ A *standby monitor present* frame is sent by any workstation other than the active monitor.

- ❑ A standby monitor sends *claim token* frames when it suspects that the active monitor may have died. The standby monitors then negotiate with one another to determine which one becomes the new active monitor.

- ❑ A workstation sends a *beacon* frame in the event of a major network problem, such as a broken cable or a workstation transmitting without waiting for the token. By detecting which station is sending the Beacon frame, diagnostic software can localize the problem.

❏ A *purge* frame is sent after a ring is initialized and a new active monitor establishes itself.

Each frame (MAC or LLC) begins with a *start frame sequence*, which contains the following three fields:

❏ The definition of *start delimiter* (*SD*) is the same for frames as for tokens.

❏ The *access control* (*AC*) field is also the same for frames as for tokens.

❏ *Frame control* (*FC*) is a 1-byte field containing two subfields, frame type and MAC control ID:

    F F   C C C C C C

The two frame type bits (FF) have a value of 00 for MAC frames and 01 for LLC frames. (Bits 11 and 10 are reserved.) The MAC control ID bits identify the type of ring management frame (see table 3.1).

Table 3.1. *MAC control ID bits.*

Bit Values (C C C C C C)	Ring management frame types
0 0 0 0 1 1	Claim Token
0 0 0 0 0 0	Duplicate Address Test
0 0 0 1 0 1	Active Monitor Present
0 0 0 1 1 0	Standby Monitor Present
0 0 0 0 1 0	Beacon
0 0 0 1 0 0	Purge

The destination address (DA), which follows the *start frame sequence* fields, can be either two or six bytes long. With 2-byte addresses, the first bit indicates whether the address is a group address or an individual address (just as in the collision-sensing IEEE 802.3 protocol). With 6-byte addresses, the first bit is also an I/G bit and the second bit (the U/L bit, which again is the same as in the IEEE 802.3 protocol) expresses whether the address is locally assigned or globally assigned. The remainder of the bits forms the address of the workstation to which the frame is addressed.

The *source address (SA)* is the same size and format as the destination address.

The data portion of the frame (*INFO*) can contain one of the MAC frames just described, or a user data message record intended for (or received from) a higher-level protocol such as IPX or NETBIOS. This field has no specified maximum length, although there are practical limits on its size based on the timing requirements of how long a workstation can control the ring.

The *frame check sequence (FCS)* field, which is used for error detection, is four bytes of remainder from the CRC-32 cyclic redundancy checksum algorithm.

The *end frame sequence (EFS)* consists of two fields: the end delimiter and the frame status.

I discussed the *end delimiter (ED)* field briefly as it relates to tokens, but in a frame it takes on additional meaning. Besides consisting of a unique pattern of electrical impulses, an ED also contains two 1-bit subfields. The intermediate frame bit is set to 1 if this frame is part of a multiple-frame transmission, or to 0 for the last (or only) frame. The error-detected bit starts as a 0 when a frame is originally sent; each workstation that passes the frame along checks for errors (verifying that the CRC in the frame check sequence field still corresponds to the contents of the frame, for example) and sets the error-detected bit to 1 if it finds anything wrong. The intervening workstations that see an already set error-detected bit will simply pass the frame along. The originating workstation notices that a problem occurred and retransmits the frame.

The 1-byte *frame status (FS)* field contains four reserved bits (R), and two subfields: the address-recognized bit (A) and the frame-copied bit (C):

```
A   C   R R   A   C   R R
```

Because the calculated CRC does not encompass this field, each of the 1-bit subfields is duplicated within frame status to ensure data integrity. When it originates a frame, a transmitting workstation sets the address-recognized bit to 0; to signal that it has recognized its destination address, the receiving workstation sets the bit to 1. The frame-copied bit also starts as 0 but is set to 1 by the receiving (destination) workstation when it copies the frame's contents into its own memory (in other words, when it actually receives the data). The data is copied (and the bit set) only if the frame is received without error. If its frame returns with both of these bits set, the originating (source) workstation knows that a successful reception occurred. However, if the address-recognized bit is not set by the time the frame gets back to the originating workstation, it means that the destination workstation is no longer on the network—it must have crashed.

Another situation happens when the destination address is recognized but the frame-copied bit is not set. This tells the originating workstation that the frame was damaged in transit (the error-detected bit in the end delimiter will also be set). There is one more possible combination of these bits: if both the address-recognized bit and the frame-copied bit are set, and the error-detected bit is also set, the originating workstation knows that the error happened *after* the frame was correctly received.

The Abort Sequence

An abort sequence, consisting of a start delimiter followed immediately by an end delimiter, signals that the current transmission of a frame or token is being canceled.

FDDI Frames

The fiber distributed data interface (FDDI) is a much newer protocol than Ethernet or Token Ring. The X3T9.5 Task Group of the American National Standards Institute (ANSI) designed FDDI to pass frames around a ring of optical fiber at a rate of 100 megabits per second. Purposely designed to be as much like the IEEE 802.5 Token Ring standard as possible, FDDI differs from Token Ring only where necessary to support faster speed and longer transmission distances.

If FDDI were to use the same bit-encoding scheme employed by Token Ring, every bit would require two optical signals: a pulse of light and then a pause of darkness. This means that FDDI would need to send 200 million signals per second to transmit at a rate of 100 megabits per second. Instead, the scheme used by FDDI, *4B/5B*, encodes four bits of data into five bits for transmission so that fewer signals are needed to send a byte of information. The 5-bit codes (*symbols*) were chosen carefully to ensure that network timing requirements are met. At a 100 megabit per second transmission rate, the 4B/5B scheme actually sends 125 million signals per second (125M baud). Also, because each carefully selected light pattern symbol represents four bits (a half-byte, or nibble), FDDI hardware can operate at the nibble and byte level rather than at the bit level, making the high data rate a little easier to achieve.

There are two major differences in the way the token is managed by FDDI and IEEE 802.5 Token Ring:

1. In Token Ring, a new token is circulated only after a sending workstation gets back the frame it sent. In FDDI, however, a new token is circulated immediately by the sending workstation after it finishes transmitting a frame.

2. FDDI doesn't use the priority and reservation subfields that Token Ring uses to allocate system resources. Rather, FDDI classifies attached workstations as asynchronous (those that are not rigid about the time periods that occur between network accesses) and synchronous (those that have very stringent requirements regarding the timing between transmissions). FDDI uses a complex algorithm to allocate network access to the two classes of devices.

Figure 3.8 shows an FDDI token. It consists of preamble, start delimiter, frame control, end delimiter, and frame status fields, which have the same definition for FDDI tokens as for FDDI frames.

Fig. 3.8. FDDI token.

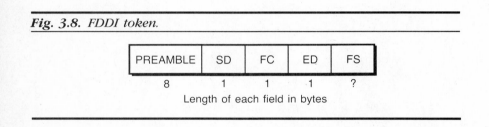

The layout of an FDDI frame, shown in figure 3.9, is similar to that of the IEEE 802.5 Token Ring frame just discussed. The FDDI frame, just like its slower Token Ring cousin, carries either MAC control data or user data. The fields in an FDDI frame are the following:

The *preamble* field is used for synchronization purposes. Although initially 64 bits (16 symbol-encoded nibbles), the preamble's length can be modified dynamically by subsequent workstations to satisfy their own clocking and synchronization requirements.

The pattern of the unique 2-symbol (1-byte) *start delimiter* (*SD*) field identifies the start of the frame.

The 2-symbol (1-byte) *frame control (FC)* field consists of the following subfields:

```
C   L   F F   T T T T
```

The C subfield designates frame class, which tells whether the frame is being used for synchronous or asynchronous service. The L bit is the frame address length and indicates whether 16-bit or 48-bit addresses are being used (both are possible on the same FDDI network). The F F bits are the frame format subfield, which expresses whether the frame is a

MAC frame carrying ring-management information or an LLC frame carrying user data. If this is a MAC frame, the T T T T bits specify the type of the MAC control frame contained in the information field.

The *destination address (DA)* field, which can be either 16 bits or 48 bits long, identifies the workstation to which the frame is being sent.

Either 16 or 48 bits long, the *source address (SA)* identifies the sending workstation.

The *information (INFO)* data portion of the frame contains either a MAC control record or user data. The length of this field can vary, but cannot cause the overall length of the frame to exceed 4,500 bytes.

The four bytes (eight symbols) of CRC data in the *frame check sequence (FCS)* are used for error checking.

In a frame, the *end delimiter (ED)* field is one nibble (one symbol) long. In a token, ED is one byte (two symbols) long. It always uniquely identifies the end of the frame or token.

Of arbitrary length, the *frame status (FS)* field contains the error-detected bit, the address-recognized bit, and the frame-copied bit. These subfields do the same job on an FDDI network as on a Token Ring network.

Fig. 3.9. *FDDI frame.*

PREAMBLE	SD	FC	DA	SA	INFO	FCS	ED	FS
8	1	1	DA/SA--2 or 6			4	1/2	

Length of each field in bytes

Higher-Level Protocols

Even I have to admit that some of the material we have just covered on low-level MAC and LLC frames is a bit dry. Fortunately, it is time to move on to the higher level protocols, where I discuss what goes into the data portion of each of the types of frames described so far. You will recall that frames are layered; the data portion of an LLC (user data) frame contains —you guessed it—a frame that has been constructed by a higher level protocol.

The protocols discussed next are IPX, SPX, and NETBIOS. Each of these is directly programmable by your software. The actual data messages that fly around the network come from either your software (when you do PC-to-PC communications) or from the shell/redirector software that shuttles DOS file-service requests to the file server and back.

Datagrams and Sessions

The two types of PC-to-PC or PC-to-server communications are *datagrams* and *sessions*. A datagram is a message never acknowledged by the receiver; if message delivery must be verified, the receiver must supply a return message. In other words, the sender and receiver must agree on a protocol of their own to safely use datagrams. Each datagram message stands on its own—if more than one datagram is outstanding, the order in which each is delivered is not guaranteed. In some cases, the maximum size of a datagram is much smaller than that of a session-related message. However, most networks can send and receive datagrams faster than session-related messages. In contrast to datagrams, a session is a logical connection between two workstations in which message reception *is* guaranteed. Datagrams can be sent at will. For messages to be sent during a session, however, more work must be done: the session must be established, data messages sent and received, and at the end of the dialog the session must be closed.

IPX—a Datagram Service

The underlying protocol in Novell NetWare, Internetwork Packet Exchange (IPX) is a close adaptation of a protocol developed by Xerox Corporation, the Xerox Network Standard (XNS). IPX supports only datagram messages (it is said to be "connectionless"). Corresponding to the Network Layer of the OSI Model, this protocol performs addressing, routing, and switching to deliver a message (packet) to its destination. IPX is speedier than the session-oriented SPX protocol (discussed later in this chapter). Datagram delivery is not guaranteed, but Novell indicates (or, alternatively, the word *says* could be used here) that IPX packets are correctly received about 95 percent of the time.

Incidentally, NetWare's shell/redirector software uses IPX (not SPX) to send and receive file service packets to and from the file server. Using IPX is safe and reliable because every such request from a workstation requires a response from the file server. Until the proper response is received, the shell/redirector never assumes that a file server has processed a file service packet (to write data to a file, for example).

If you use Novell NetWare, you already have IPX. Depending on the version of NetWare you have, you may already have SPX as well. All you need to begin developing programs that do PC-to-PC communications on a NetWare LAN is a good C compiler and the information in this book.

IPX Destination Address

The destination address in an IPX packet is an *internetwork address*, which consists of three components: *network number*, *node address*, and *socket*.

❑ Network numbers identify each segment of a multiserver network. System Administrators assign the numbers when the Novell NetWare file servers are initialized.

❑ Node address uniquely identifies each network adapter card.

❑ Socket represents the destination application itself, running on the target workstation. Your application opens and closes sockets in much the same way as it opens and closes files.

For IPX packets, the destination address can contain a group (broadcast) address; for SPX packets, the destination address must contain the address of a specific workstation on the network. If your application needs to communicate with a particular workstation, you can use services within IPX to find that workstation's destination address. Chapter 6, "IPX and SPX Programming," includes some examples showing how to obtain a destination address when all you know is the user ID under which the other workstation is logged on. You send IPX packets by specifying a destination address (network, node, and socket), but you receive them by specifying a socket.

IPX Program Services

You can manage PC-to-PC communications by using a set of services that IPX offers to your software. These services rely on the following three data structures that you construct and pass to IPX:

❑ The IPX Header, consisting of the first 30 bytes of the IPX Packet discussed later in this chapter

❑ The data record or message that you want to send or receive

❑ An Event Control Block (ECB) that is not actually transmitted but contains information about a particular IPX operation that you initiate

Chapter 6, "IPX and SPX Programming," covers IPX services in detail; at this point, let me just categorize them.

Initialization and Termination Functions

When two PCs on a network want to send message records back and forth using IPX, the application on both workstations first opens a socket using the IPXOpenSocket function. The socket number that is open on Workstation A must be known to the application running on Workstation B, and vice versa.

Both workstations need to know the destination address of the other workstation. Socket numbers are easily determined; you simply establish conventions for the sockets you use. However, your application does not automatically know the network number and node address—what you typically know is the other workstation's user ID.

To translate user ID into network number and node address, use the GetObjectConnectionNumbers and the GetInternetworkAddress IPX functions at the beginning of your program. Be aware, however, that Net-Ware lets a single user ID log on at several workstations simultaneously. The usual way to handle this situation is by using the first item from the list that is returned to you and ignoring any subsequent items in the list.

When finished sending and receiving message records, the two work-stations close the open sockets by calling IPXCloseSocket.

Sending and Receiving Packets

After you have opened a socket at Workstation A and determined the network number, node address, and socket number of Workstation B (presumably Workstation B has determined the same information regard-ing Workstation A), you are ready to send and receive message records. IPXSendPacket and IPXListenForPacket are used to do the sending and receiving. Each time you call IPXSendPacket, however, you must supply an additional data item, the *immediate address* field. If the message packet must cross a bridge (go through a linkage between two networks) to reach its destination, the immediate address field is the node address of the bridge. You call the function IPXGetLocalTarget to determine the value to be placed in the immediate address field. If the packet does not need to cross a bridge, `IPXGetLocalTarget` will return the node address of the destination workstation (which still goes into the immediate address field).

IPX does not wait for the packet to be sent or received before returning to your application program; the protocol only initiates the operation. The actual sending and receiving occur in the background. You can handle these operations in one of two ways: either the application can go into a loop that repeatedly checks to see whether the send or receive operation is completed, or the application can supply IPX with the address of a routine that IPX will execute when the operation finishes. Chapter 6, "IPX and SPX Programming," includes examples of these techniques, which are also discussed later in this chapter's description of SPX.

Miscellaneous Functions

Outstanding IPX operations (events) can be canceled with the `IPXCancelEvent` call. Your application can call `IPXScheduleEvent` to ask IPX to schedule a send or receive event to occur at a later moment. Especially while you are polling for the completion of a send or receive operation, you can call `IPXRelinquishControl` to give IPX control of the CPU; this gives IPX a chance to "breathe" while you wait for the operation to complete.

IPX Packet Format

Figure 3.10 shows the format of an IPX packet. This packet is the data record that is either placed inside an Ethernet frame or Token Ring frame for transmission, or extracted from the frame on reception. An SPX packet (discussed later in this chapter) contains an IPX packet header in its first 30 bytes. The fields within an IPX packet are the following:

Checksum—This 2-byte field is a holdover; Xerox defines it in the XNS protocol and so it appears here in the IPX packet. Because the lower-level protocol always performs error checking (as mentioned earlier in this chapter), you never need to set this field (IPX always sets it to 0xFFFF).

Length—The size of the complete packet, including both the IPX packet header and the data portion, is expressed by this 2-byte field. The smallest packet length is 30 bytes (just the IPX header itself) and the largest is 576 bytes (30 bytes of IPX header plus 546 bytes of data). IPX calculates the value of this field based on information you provide when you tell IPX to send a packet; you do not set this field directly.

Transport Control—An IPX packet can cross as many as 16 NetWare bridges. IPX sets this 1-byte field to 0 when the packet is originally transmitted, and then increments the field each time a bridge passes along the packet. If the count reaches 16, the packet is discarded; in normal situations, of course, this is not a concern. IPX sets and uses this field.

Packet Type—Xerox defines various types of packets for various purposes; an application that sends IPX packets should set this 1-byte field to a value of 4. This signifies that the packet is what the Xerox standard calls a Packet-Exchange Packet. Later, when this chapter discusses the SPX session-level protocol, you will see that SPX-oriented applications set this field to a value of 5.

Destination Network—This is a 4-byte field that, as mentioned previously, identifies the network on which the intended receiver workstation is located. Destination network is the first of three fields that you must specify to tell IPX/SPX where a packet should be delivered.

Destination Node—The second of the three fields in which you specify where IPX/SPX should deliver a packet, these six bytes identify the target workstation by its unique physical address. Chapter 6, "IPX and SPX Programming," includes examples showing how to obtain both destination network and destination node.

Destination Socket—This field contains a 2-byte socket number. Destination socket is the last of the three fields you specify to say where the packet should be delivered. The socket must have been opened by the application running on the destination workstation. Certain socket-number values are reserved by Novell and Xerox. You can ask Novell to assign a particular socket number to your application, or, if you want, you can use dynamic socket numbers, which are in the range 0x4000 to 0x8000. In any case, you must establish conventions regarding which socket numbers your IPX/SPX-based software will use.

Source Network—The network number of the originating workstation, this 4-byte field is set by IPX.

Source Node—The physical address of the network adapter card in the originating workstation, this 6-byte field is set by IPX.

Source Socket—The packet is sent through an open socket, which IPX sets in this field.

Data Portion—This field—the data record or message your application wants to send—can be from 0 to 546 bytes long. A zero-length data area might be appropriate, for example, if the presence of the packet itself is sufficient for a particular purpose, such as acknowledging reception of a previous packet.

Fig. 3.10. *IPX packet format.*

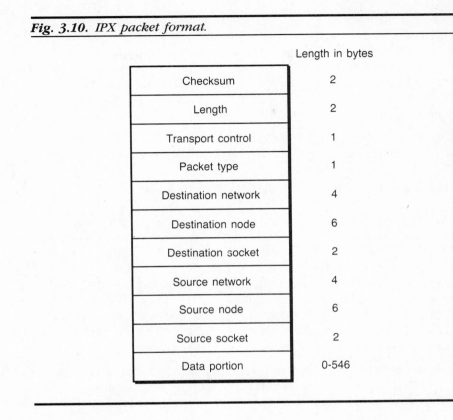

Length in bytes

Field	Length
Checksum	2
Length	2
Transport control	1
Packet type	1
Destination network	4
Destination node	6
Destination socket	2
Source network	4
Source node	6
Source socket	2
Data portion	0-546

All multiple-byte fields in an IPX packet are ordered so that the high-order byte is first (leftmost) and the low-order byte is last. This differs from the native format for multibyte fields in an IBM-type microcomputer.

SPX—Session-Level Communications

Sequenced Packet Exchange (SPX) is a session-level, connection-oriented protocol. Before SPX packets are sent or received, a connection must be established between the two sides that want to exchange information (SPX assigns a *connection ID* SPX at either end of the connection). After the connection is established, messages can be sent in either direction with the guarantee that they will be delivered. SPX also guarantees that packets will arrive in the correct order (if multiple packets are sent at once). Although IPX operates at the Transport Layer of the OSI Model, SPX operates at one layer above that, the Network Layer. SPX also has some of the characteristics of the Session Layer.

SPX uses IPX to actually send or receive message packets. If you have Novell NetWare, you know that IPX is available to your software. This is not necessarily true for SPX; early versions of NetWare did not support SPX. If you have version 2.0a of NetWare, you have SPX only if the version of the shell/redirector program (ANET3.COM) is 2.01-4. SPX is present in all later versions of NetWare (2.1 and higher). There is a function call, SPXInitialize, you can use to determine whether SPX is available.

Chapter 6, "IPX and SPX Programming," details the functions and services that SPX provides; for now, let's see how they are used.

Establishing and Terminating a Connection

The first thing both workstations do is initialize SPX with the SPXInitialize call; each workstation then opens one or more sockets by calling the IPXOpenSocket function. (If the call to SPXInitialize indicates that SPX is not installed, you should terminate your program with a message that tells the user to upgrade to a later version of NetWare to use your software). To establish a connection, Workstation A issues to SPX an SPXListenForConnection call that specifies an open socket. Workstation B must then issue a subsequent SPXEstablishConnection call that specifies Workstation A's destination address (network, node, and socket).

If it knows the listening workstation's user ID, the calling workstation (the one that issues the SPXEstablishConnection) can call the NetWare GetObjectConnectionNumbers and GetInternetworkAddress functions to determine the network or node that the workstation needs to use in the SPXEstablishConnection call. As was previously mentioned, the socket-number portion of the destination address is application-specific.

If the SPXEstablishConnection call is issued first, and if all the retry attempts performed by SPX are exhausted before the other workstation issues an SPXListenForConnection, the connection attempt fails.

Both workstations must issue a set of SPXListenForSequencedPacket calls to establish a connection. There are three reasons for this:

1. SPX uses some of the resulting packet buffers internally as it creates the connection.

2. A pool of packet buffers must be available to SPX so that the protocol can receive and queue incoming messages.

3. SPX sometimes "borrows" some packet buffers for its own internal use.

As it creates the connection, SPX assigns a connection ID at each work-station. Your application uses connection ID to refer to this particular connection when the application later wants to send or receive message packets.

To sever a connection, one of the workstations issues an SPXTerminateConnection call. This causes SPX to automatically send a packet containing a datastream type field of 0xFE to the other workstation (which your application must recognize and process). Both workstations should, of course, close all open sockets after the dialog is finished.

Does the listening application need to sit and do nothing while it waits for a call? No; if you give IPX or SPX the address of an *event service routine* (ESR) that it can execute when the call occurs, the listening application can continue doing other things. ESRs are most useful when your application is listening for another workstation to call, but they also can be used in other situations. An ESR can be associated with sending or receiving messages and can be used under both IPX and SPX. If you do not use an ESR, you can simply poll for the completion of the event by going into a loop that waits for IPX or SPX to set a completion code for that event.

Sending and Receiving Packets

Sending a message packet is fairly straightforward; you give SPX the address and length of the message data along with the connection ID assigned by SPX when the connection was created. Receiving a packet, however, is a little more complicated. Because multiple ListenForSequencedPacket calls are outstanding when the message is received (a set of them was issued as part of establishing the connection), you must devise a method for determining which call SPX used. Then you must issue another ListenForSequencedPacket call to return the packet buffer to SPX's pool. If you do not do this, SPX will starve and crash the machine.

You can attach an ESR to a send operation or a receive operation. The ESR will be awakened and executed when the send or receive operation finishes. Or, alternatively, you can simply poll for the completion of the event.

Miscellaneous Functions

For a quick, emergency exit, you can call SPXAbortConnection to uni-laterally end a connection. If you want status information about an existing connection, you can call `SPXGetConnectionStatus`. `SPXInitialize` returns information about SPX itself, including an indication of whether the protocol is installed.

SPX Packet Format

An SPX packet, as shown in figure 3.11, contains 30 bytes of IPX packet header followed by 12 bytes of SPX-specific header fields, for a total length of 42 bytes. The 30 bytes of IPX header have the same meaning for SPX as for IPX, except that the packet type field must be set to 5 to specify what Xerox and Novell call a Sequenced Packet Protocol Packet (an SPX packet). The fields in the SPX portion of the header are the following:

Some of the bits within the 1-byte *connection control* field are for your use and some for SPX's use. The byte is formatted like this:

S   A   !   E   X X X X

where the S bit is the system packet flag, A is the acknowledgement-required bit, ! is the attention bit, E is the end-of-message bit, and the remaining four bits are undefined. SPX uses the system packet flag and the acknowledgement-required flag internally. The attention flag and the end-of-message flag are available for your use. SPX passes them, untouched, along to the destination workstation.

Datastream type—You and SPX also share this 1-byte field. You can set this field to a value from 0 to 253 (0xFD) in each packet that you send, and thus use datastream type to identify the type of data contained in each packet (SPX does not touch values in this range). SPX uses values of 254 (0xFE) and 255 (0xFF) in the following way: when Workstation A tells SPX to terminate a connection, SPX sends to Workstation B a final message packet that contains a datastream type field of 254 (0xFE). On receiving this final packet, the application running on Workstation B knows that Workstation A has ended the dialog. For packets that it uses internally, SPX sets this field to a value of 255 (0xFF); your application never sees these packets.

Source connection ID—SPX sets this 2-byte field. It contains the SPX-assigned value of the connection ID that identifies this SPX session at the source workstation.

Destination connection ID—SPX also sets this 2-byte field. It contains the connection ID assigned at the destination. If multiple connections are associated with one socket, SPX uses this field to keep track of which message goes with what connection ID.

Sequence number—This 2-byte field is also set by SPX. SPX uses this field to identify and discard duplicate packets. (These can occur, for example, if SPX resends a packet after failing to get an acknowledgment back from the original transmission, but both packets eventually arrive at their destination.)

Acknowledge number—This field, also set by SPX, keeps track of the sequence number of the next packet SPX expects to receive for a particular connection ID.

Allocation number—This 2-byte-long field is also set internally by SPX. SPX uses this field to count the number of packets sent but not yet acknowledged by the other workstation.

The maximum size of the data portion of an SPX packet is 534 bytes, slightly less than that of IPX, to accommodate the SPX-specific fields.

NETBIOS

At this point, I end my discussion of Novell communications services and turn to NETBIOS, IBM's protocol for PC-to-PC transfer of messages and records. However, Novell does provide a NETBIOS emulator with NetWare (when the emulator is loaded, it sits on top of IPX/SPX). Because it uses a different frame format, Novell's NETBIOS software is incompatible with the IBM NETBIOS program product.

IBM NETBIOS on NetWare LANs

IBM NETBIOS services are provided by a device driver; under PC DOS, the driver file, DXMT0MOD.SYS, is part of the IBM PC LAN Support Program. I hate to muddy the waters even further at this point, but let me mention that it is possible to have an IBM Token Ring network on which Novell NetWare is running, and, if DXMT0MOD.SYS is loaded at each workstation, NETBIOS communications can take place just as described in this section. Does this mean that you should forget about IPX and SPX communications and concentrate on using NETBIOS? Not necessarily; NETBIOS (either in the form of the Novell emulator or the IBM device driver) takes up extra memory on a Novell NetWare workstation. A further complication is that a NetWare bridge will not pass IBM NETBIOS messages to a different physical Token ring. (Nothing is ever simple, is it?)

Fig. 3.11. *SPX packet format.*

	Length in bytes
Checksum	2
Length	2
Transport control	1
Packet type	1
Destination network	4
Destination node	6
Destination socket	2
Source network	4
Source node	6
Source socket	2
Connection control	1
Datastream type	1
Source connection ID	2
Destination connection ID	2
Sequence number	2
Acknowledge number	2
Allocation number	2
Data portion	0-534

NETBIOS, which stands for *Network Basic Input/Output System*, is the protocol that the IBM PC LAN Program uses to send file-service requests back and forth to the file server. The protocol's communications facilities are of course also available to the programs you write. NETBIOS corresponds to the Network Layer, Transport Layer, and Session Layer of the

OSI Model; the protocol operates at a higher level than either IPX or SPX. NETBIOS supports both datagram and session-oriented communications. IBM PC LAN Program file-service packets sent to and received from a file server are managed under session control rather than treated as individual datagrams; this is one of many differences between the IBM PC LAN Program and Novell NetWare.

Most of the NETBIOS commands come in both *wait* or *no-wait* flavors. When you use the wait version of a command, NETBIOS completes the operation before returning to your program. If you specify no-wait, you then have the option of polling (looping until an operation is complete) or giving NETBIOS the address of one of your routines that NETBIOS will invoke when the command is completed. This facility is similar to the IPX/SPX event service routine concept discussed earlier. Under NETBIOS, such a routine is called a *POST routine*. When the no-wait option is used, your program must inspect two different return codes to determine whether a command completed successfully: the first is the *immediate return code* (available as soon as NETBIOS returns to your application) and the other is the *final return code* (which holds a value of 0xFF until the operation finishes, at which time NETBIOS sets the appropriate value).

NETBIOS Names

NETBIOS is name-oriented; each workstation (and each file server, if the network is operating under the IBM PC LAN Program) is identified by one or more 16-byte names. A table of these names is kept inside NETBIOS. In addition to this table of names, a *permanent node name* is always present. The permanent node name is formed by taking the six bytes of network address from the network adapter card and prefixing them with 10 bytes of binary 0s. The permanent node name is always unique on the network.

Your program can inspect the names in the name table and, except for the permanent node name, can add or delete names at your application's convenience. A special *group name* can also be added to the table; unlike a regular name, a group name does not have to be unique on the network. Several workstations can use the same group name at the same time. The number of names and group names that the table can hold is configurable when the device driver is loaded, and usually defaults to 16 names. You use names (ones you have added, or the permanent node name) and group names as the destination address and source address when you establish a session. NETBIOS assigns a *name number* to each name you add. This name number is used to send datagrams.

Because names are always 16 bytes long, you must pad a short name (such as BARRY) with trailing spaces before adding it to the table. Also, don't add a name that starts with an asterisk (∗) or with a binary zero (0x00). One more caution: it is not a good idea to use names beginning with the three characters I, B, and M; such names are reserved.

The NETBIOS commands relating to name management are *Add Name*, *Add Group Name*, and *Delete Name*. The NETBIOS *Reset* command deletes all names from the name table (the permanent node name remains, of course). You should not use a Reset command when running under the IBM PC LAN Program; Reset will delete the names being used for DOS file redirection as well as the names you added.

To ensure that a name being added to the table is unique, NETBIOS first searches its local name table and then the entire network to check whether the name is already being used. To search the network, NETBIOS broadcasts a name claim frame. If a name claim response frame is received, NETBIOS knows that another workstation is already using the name. NETBIOS frames are discussed later in this chapter.

NETBIOS Datagrams

You will recall that a datagram is connectionless and not guaranteed to be delivered to the other workstation. NETBIOS support for datagrams allows them to be sent to an individual name, to a group name, or to all workstations on the network. NETBIOS datagrams can carry message records up to 512 bytes long.

The NETBIOS commands used for sending and receiving datagrams are *Send Datagram*, *Send Broadcast Datagram*, *Receive Datagram*, and *Receive Broadcast Datagram*.

NETBIOS Sessions

You can create a session between any two names on the network. Multiple sessions are possible between the two names, and you can even create a session between two names on the same workstation. While the session is active, you are assured that when you send and receive message records, each will be delivered at the proper destination in the proper sequence.

To create a session, one workstation issues a *Listen* command (with or without the wait option). The Listen command specifies whether it is listening for a call from a specific name or from any name. The other workstation then issues a *Call* command, specifying the name it is calling.

When each command completes on its respective workstation, NETBIOS returns a *local session number* (LSN) to each application. (The LSNs returned to each workstation are not necessarily the same.) Thereafter, each workstation uses the assigned LSN to refer to the open, active session.

Message records sent and received during a session can be up to 65,535 bytes long. The commands you use are *Send*, *Chain Send* (which can be used to send multiple messages back-to-back), and *Receive*.

At the end of the dialog, both workstations issue a *Hang Up* command to close the session.

Miscellaneous NETBIOS Services

You can use the *Session Status* command to obtain information about all active sessions for a specified name, or for all names in the local name table. The *Adapter Status* command is used when you want to find out, for example, the permanent node name of a particular workstation.

Network Control Blocks (NCBs)

To invoke a particular NETBIOS command, your application builds a *Network Control Block* (NCB) and then executes an Interrupt 5C (hex). Figure 3.12 shows the format of an NCB, and this section describes each of the fields:

You set the 1-byte *command* field to tell NETBIOS which command you want it to execute. If the high-order bit is set, the command is executed in no-wait mode.

The 1-byte *return code* field contains the immediate error code (set by NETBIOS when it begins executing the command).

After a Listen or Call command is executed, the 1-byte *local session number* field contains the LSN assigned to that session. For Send or Receive commands, you put the session's LSN in this field.

NETBIOS returns the 1-byte *name number* field after an Add Name or Add Group Name command. You use this number, not the name, when doing any datagram-related commands or the *Receive Any* command.

In this 4-byte (segment:offset) *data buffer address* field, you put a far pointer to the data buffer associated with a send or receive operation.

You set the 2-byte *data buffer length* field to indicate the length of the data buffer.

You set the 16-byte *call name* field to indicate the name of the other workstation with which you want to communicate.

You set the 16-byte *local name* field to indicate by which of the names in the local name table (or the permanent node name) you want your application to be known.

When you issue a Call or Listen command, you set the 1-byte *receive timeout* field to a value that indicates how many half-second intervals NETBIOS should use while waiting for a subsequent Receive command to be completed. A value of 0 indicates no time-out.

When you issue a Call or Listen command, you set the 1-byte *send timeout* field to a value that indicates how many half-second intervals NETBIOS should use when waiting for a subsequent Send command to be completed. A value of 0 indicates no time-out.

You put into the 4-byte *POST routine address* a far pointer (segment:offset) to a routine that NETBIOS invokes when the command is completed (this field is meaningful only when the no-wait option is in effect). If you set this field to 0 (NULL), you should poll the final return code to determine when the command is completed and whether it was completed successfully.

You set the 1-byte *adapter number* field to indicate which network adapter you want to use (0 for primary and 1 for alternate). (A workstation can contain as many as two Token Ring cards.)

The 1-byte *final return code* field contains 0xFF while a command is being processed; after the command is executed, the field is set to show whether the command was successful.

The 14-byte *Reserved* area in the NCB is not used by your program. NETBIOS reserves the 14 bytes shown in figure 3.12.

NETBIOS Frames

NETBIOS frames are created and managed exclusively by NETBIOS; you do not have to deal with them directly. To create its frames, NETBIOS uses the contents of the NCB that you build, plus what it knows about the sessions and names currently in effect. NETBIOS uses several types of frames; this section lists the more important types, along with a brief description of the purpose of each:

When you issue a Call command, NETBIOS broadcasts a *name query* frame to find out whether the destination workstation is on the network.

Fig. 3.12. *Network Control Block format.*

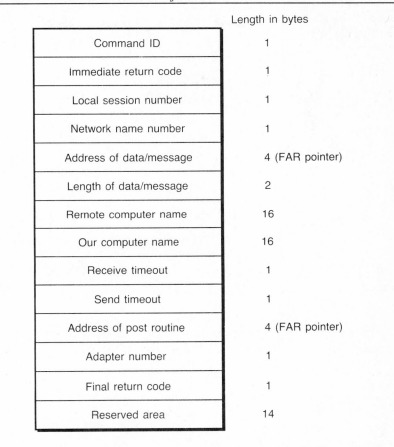

	Length in bytes
Command ID	1
Immediate return code	1
Local session number	1
Network name number	1
Address of data/message	4 (FAR pointer)
Length of data/message	2
Remote computer name	16
Our computer name	16
Receive timeout	1
Send timeout	1
Address of post routine	4 (FAR pointer)
Adapter number	1
Final return code	1
Reserved area	14

When you issue an Add Name command, NETBIOS sends an *add name query* frame around the network to ask if any other workstation is using the name.

When you issue an Add Group Name command, NETBIOS sends an *add group name query* frame to find out whether another workstation is already using the name as a unique name (several workstations can use the same group name, but it cannot already be established as a unique name).

A listening workstation returns a *name recognized* frame coded to indicate the outstanding listen in response to a name query frame. In essence, the frame announces "I exist, and I am listening."

If a workstation recognizes that one of its names is the same as the name in an *add name query* frame, that workstation returns an *add name response* frame to tell the workstation executing an Add Name command that the name is already in use.

A workstation doing a Call command sends a *session initialize* frame to establish the session.

A *session confirm* frame is returned to the calling workstation to indicate that the session is established.

A *data* frame is sent when you give NETBIOS a Send command to process.

Sent by a workstation that has just received a data frame, an *ACK* frame indicates successful reception.

NETBIOS sends the *session end* frame when you issue a Hang Up command.

A *datagram* frame is similar to a data frame, except that a datagram frame does not require that a session have been established.

NETBIOS transmits a *status query* frame when you give NETBIOS an Adapter Status command for a remote adapter.

Returned by the workstation that received a status query frame, the *status response* frame contains configuration and status information.

Server Message Blocks (SMBs)

As was previously mentioned, the IBM PC LAN Program intercepts network-related DOS function calls and shunts them across the network to the file server. The program uses a *Server Message Block* protocol to accomplish this redirection. The PC LAN Program running on a workstation opens NETBIOS sessions with the PC LAN Program running on the file server. The PC LAN Program then uses NETBIOS Send commands to send SMBs to the server to request that the server perform file operations on behalf of the workstation. There are four categories of SMBs: *session control*, *file access*, *print service*, and *messages*.

Session Control

After a NETBIOS session is established between a workstation and the server, the workstation sends a Verify Dialect SMB to the server. This message contains data indicating the capabilities of the PC LAN Program version running at the workstation. The server examines this message, then responds to the workstation with information about the server itself and the capabilities the server supports. This exchange is followed by one or more Start Connection SMBs, which create logical connections between the workstation and network resources at the file server. These logical connections are later terminated by the workstation when it sends End Connection SMBs to the server (or when the occurrence of an error aborts the NETBIOS session).

File Access

A workstation uses the SMBs in this category to gain remote access to the files on the server's hard disk. The functions included in this category allow the workstation to treat the server disk almost as though it were a local hard drive. The workstation can direct the file server to do the following:

- ❏ Create and remove directories
- ❏ Create, open, and close files
- ❏ Read from and write to files
- ❏ Rename and delete files
- ❏ Search for files
- ❏ Get or set file attributes
- ❏ Lock records

For remote files, these operations are intercepted at the workstation (the local copy of PC DOS never sees them) and turned into SMBs for the file server to execute.

Print Service

The SMBs in this category enable a workstation to queue files for printing by a server and to obtain print queue status information. The workstation can create a spool file, write data to the spool file, close the spool file, and ask that the server return a Print Queue Status SMB.

Messages

This category of SMBs supports simple message-passing through the following functions:

- ❏ Send Single Block Message
- ❏ Send Broadcast Message

❏ Send Start of Multiple Block Message

❏ Send Text of Multiple Block Message

❏ Send End of Multiple Block Message

❏ Forward User Name

❏ Cancel Forward

❏ Get Machine Name

The messenger and receiver configurations of the IBM PC LAN Program discussed in Chapter 1, "The Basics of Networking," use these functions.

Format of an SMB

Figure 3.13 shows the layout of a Server Message Block. It contains the following fields:

The *message type* field identifies the type of message that this SMB contains.

The *server type* field indicates the type of server component that this SMB addresses.

The *function ID* field identifies the type of network request that this SMB represents.

If an error occurs, the *return error class* code tells where the failure occurred (for example, during the execution of an Interrupt 21 [hex] function at the server).

The *critical error class* field gives information about critical errors that occur at the server.

The *return code* field indicates the command's completion status.

The *direction code* field indicates whether the SMB is a request to a server or a response to a workstation.

Reserved Area 1 bytes are reserved.

The *network path ID* field contains the computer name, path, and file name that identify a logical connection between a workstation and a particular file-server resource.

Process ID—This field identifies the program on the workstation which issued the DOS function call that resulted in this SMB.

Reserved Area 2 is another set of reserved bytes.

The *parameter count* field indicates the number of parameters that the parameters field represents.

The meaning of the *parameters* field varies with the function of the SMB.

The *buffer length* field gives the length of the SMB buffer area.

A variably formatted field containing function-specific data, the *SMB buffer* can include zero or more variable-length structures; the first byte of each structure identifies the type of the structure, and the next two bytes give the structure's length.

Fig. 3.13. *Server Message Block (SMB) format.*

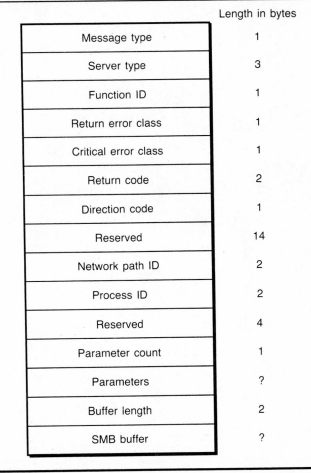

	Length in bytes
Message type	1
Server type	3
Function ID	1
Return error class	1
Critical error class	1
Return code	2
Direction code	1
Reserved	14
Network path ID	2
Process ID	2
Reserved	4
Parameter count	1
Parameters	?
Buffer length	2
SMB buffer	?

Summary

This chapter explored, literally from the bottom to the top, how PCs communicate on a LAN. You are familiar with the different layers of processing that messages and frames undergo as they are prepared for transmission. You now have a good grasp of the underlying differences between Ethernet, Token Ring, and FDDI. IPX, SPX, and NETBIOS are no longer vague, mysterious layers of software on the workstations you use; you now understand how these protocols operate. And, you have delved into the mechanisms the PC LAN Program uses to enable a file server to be shared across the network.

Part II

Network
Programming
Techniques

DOS-Level Programming

Programming for a multiuser LAN environment is mostly a matter of taking extra care to ensure that users do not bump into each other or destroy each other's files. This is easier said than done; it takes thorough planning and design.

So far, I have described what the LAN environment looks like. This chapter discusses how to design and program your applications so that they are LAN-aware. I raise several design issues you need to think about, such as how to choose a file and record-locking scheme and how to coordinate related file updates. This chapter also includes a series of tests for determining when your application is running on a LAN, and offers coding examples for identifying workstations, sharing files, locking records, printing to a shared printer, and handling file attributes on a network. Finally, this chapter closes with a discussion of the things you *cannot* do on a network, such as sorting directory entries on a file server.

The theme of this chapter is *how to develop programs that run well on many different kinds of networks*. Some of the more specialized features and facilities found on various LANs are touched on, but their full description is deferred to Part IV, "Reference." The aim is to work at the highest possible level that allows the job to get done.

Design Considerations

The extra care you take in designing your application will really pay off when people begin using it in a LAN environment. Users will not only be glad for the bugs they don't run into, but they will be impressed by the LAN-aware features you build into the environment. The following section describes several things to consider.

General Techniques

Whenever possible, avoid writing code that uses facilities specific to a particular LAN vendor. For example, you may find that Novell's Transaction Tracking System (TTS) exactly suits the design of your application. (TTS is a mechanism that Novell provides for grouping sets of database updates into atomic operations.) Be aware that, if you want your application to run on non-Novell LANs, you will have to provide your own substitute for TTS.

When is it impossible to avoid vendor-specific programming? To save you some time, let me mention the following situations in which vendor-specific coding is required.

❑ PC DOS does not provide a surefire, standard method of determining the presence of a LAN. Because you almost certainly need to be aware in your application whether it is running on a LAN, you will have to make several tests (some vendor-specific) and infer from the results whether a LAN is present. Later, this chapter describes some techniques for detecting the LAN.

❑ When a file is created on a NetWare LAN, the file is automatically given a file attribute of Nonshareable. To modify this NetWare-specific file attribute to make the file Shareable, you need to call a function within NetWare. The technique for doing this is described toward the end of the chapter, in the section called "Setting File Attributes."

❑ When the NetWare shell detects the termination of a program, the shell releases all locks, closes all files, and performs several general cleanup tasks. Normally, this behavior is exactly what you want. Under NetWare version 2.0a, however, the shell sometimes does not distinguish between a program that COM-MAND.COM executed and a program you executed from within your application. If your application expects files to remain open across the spawn() or exec() call, you must use a NetWare function call to temporarily disable NetWare's cleanup actions. You then should re-enable them before returning to DOS. This function, `SetEndOfJobStatus`, which turns the cleanup action off or on, is invoked as follows:

```
regs.h.ah = 0xBB;   /* SetEndOfJobStatus         */
regs.h.al = 0; /* 0 = disable; 1 = enable */
int86(0x21, &regs, &regs);
```

❑ Sometimes not enough memory is available to do things at the highest possible level. A good example of this is the choice you make to support NETBIOS or IPX/SPX for PC-to-PC communications (refer to Chapter 3, "PC-to-PC Communications Concepts"); you can run NETBIOS on a Novell NetWare network but the Novell NETBIOS Emulator takes up extra memory.

❑ Your application may absolutely *require* certain things to be true. For example, you may need PC DOS to be running on the file server, in which case you give up compatibility with Novell NetWare. On the other hand, you may find that your application cannot be designed and written without using NetWare's Print Services (see the "NetWare Print Services" section later in this chapter); in this case you give up compatibility with IBM PC LAN Program and OS/2 LAN Server. Of course, you compromise as much as possible in these situations, but (rarely, I hope) the application's requirements may not be at all flexible.

One of the most devastating things you can do on a network is to store user configuration data back inside the executable (.EXE) file itself. This scheme has two problems: first, you cannot store individual user configurations for every user on a LAN; second, you cannot mark the executable file Shareable, Read-Only. A better approach is to establish a configuration file for each user; in this file you can put machine name (discussed in Chapter 2, "Multiuser Concepts") to good use. If you tell users that they must set up a machine name for each workstation (or each user login account), and if you also give them guidelines for constructing the name (it must be unique, between one and eight characters long, consist of alphabetic or numeric characters, and otherwise conform to the requirements for a valid file name under DOS), you can use machine name as the basis for the name of each user's configuration file. An example of such a name is BARRY.CFG. Later, this chapter describes a method you can use to ensure that users have set up machine names.

A common programming technique that makes perfect sense in a single-user environment is to have the program read a control record into memory and hold it there while the program runs. In a multiuser environment, if the control record is modified while the application runs, soon each workstation has a different copy of the record and loses the capability to coordinate with the other workstations. Make sure that you recognize which files and records in your application can be updated by the general user population, and maintain these files and records on the file server, not in workstation memory.

Chapter 2, "Multiuser Concepts," discusses the importance of checking for I/O errors inside your software. On a LAN, you should offer users more options for handling these errors. For example, you may need to acquire a physical lock on a file and find that DOS returns `Access Denied` to your program. However you tune Sharing Retry Count/Delay, you still must prepare for the possibility that a locked region of a file may become inaccessible because of a network operating system bug, file server problem, or other difficulty. I suggest that you implement your own automatic retry logic, in addition to setting Sharing Retry Count/Delay. What if the lock cannot be acquired, however, even after a reasonable length of time? You should abort the current process as gracefully as possible—release any locks in effect, close any open files, and inform the user at the workstation that a significant error has occurred that will require the attention of a System Administrator. It may even be necessary to broadcast a message telling all users to log off so that the file server can be restarted.

Choosing a File- and Record-Locking Scheme

At the beginning of this chapter you read that it takes thorough planning and design to develop programs that live happily on a network. The key is knowing how each file is accessed and updated, including database files, help files, user-specific files, and temporary files. For each file or class of file, decide how you want to protect the contents from being damaged by users who are concurrently using the file. The following guidelines should help.

As the application retrieves records, displays retrieved records on the screen, and begins accepting keyboard input from the user, it is intuitively clear that physical record locking is an inadequate method of collision protection while the input data is being entered. Physical record locking is useful only when actual I/O is being performed on a file or group of related files. It is unfair to other users to physically lock records in a file during the relatively long time it takes to do keyboard entry, and there is no guarantee that users will actually fulfill their intentions of updating those records.

The best approach is to implement a user lock facility at the application level. This is the essence of the library-card scheme described in Chapter 2, "Multiuser Concepts." Such a facility uses a centralized control file on the file server, in which records representing user intentions and fulfillments are placed. This technique makes it possible for an application, running on several workstations simultaneously, to coordinate with itself.

The drawback to the library-card scheme is that all programs which access the charged-out files must be designed to check the control file before opening files. For a large, vertical market application (for example, an insurance claims handling system, a stock-market trading system, a shop floor control system, or an airline fleet maintenance system), the application should be the only software to touch the files and so the library-card scheme will work well. Horizontal market applications (such as word processors and business graphics presentation programs) have a tougher time enforcing this scheme. Users at other workstations can easily use other software—not developed by you—to access files.

Table 4.1 shows some possible fields of a control file.

Table 4.1. *An example of a control file's fields.*

Field	Purpose
User ID	Machine name of user doing an update
File ID	File the user intends to update
Key	Records affected by the update
Transaction	Code expressing the type of update
Date/Time	Date-and-time stamp
In Progress	Code giving the status of the update; 1 while in progress, 0 when finished

Of course, you may want to add other fields to this control file so that it supports your application exactly the way you want. You may want to tie this control file logically to a journal file, discussed later in this chapter.

When a user signals an intention to enter new or changed information, the application performs the following steps (note that the control file is opened in DENY_NONE [shared] mode):

1. Physically lock the control file.

2. Check whether it is okay for the user to proceed. (Is there an entry in the control file already which shows that another user has something in progress?)

3. If there is a conflict, unlock the control file and inform the user that the record (or file, or entity) is not presently available; perhaps a message should tell the user to try again later. (If the date/time stamp is old, this control file entry may be obsolete. Old entries will need housecleaning and should not cause conflicts.)

4. If there is no conflict, insert an entry in the control file for this user, unlock the file, and proceed with the update.

5. Read the necessary data files and display the data to the user. Accept the user's input.

6. When the user finishes, acquire a physical lock on the individual data records (or perhaps the entire file) that need to be updated, as prescribed by the guidelines following this list, and, after all the records are locked, do the I/O.

7. After the updates have taken place and the locks have been removed from the affected data records and files, remove the entry from the control file. You can delete the entry by marking it as unused (finished), or by copying the entry to a separate file for audit trail purposes and then marking the control file entry as unused.

8. If the user cancels the update, simply remove the entry from the control file.

If the data file being updated is a single common database that the application accesses record-by-record (each record is an independent entity, with no relationships among records), the locking that your application performs when it is time to write a record is rather simple. Because the file is open in DENY_NONE (shared) mode, all users have access to the file; various users may be updating different records within the file at the same time. To write a record, lock the appropriate region of the file (corresponding to the record about to be written), make sure that the lock is successful, actually write the record, and then unlock that region of the file.

You may have designed your application so that each entity it deals with is contained in a separate file. If the file is read into memory, updated, and immediately written back to disk without intervention or input from the user, it is appropriate for you to open the file in DENY_READ_WRITE (exclusive) mode for the duration of the quick update. On the other hand, if your application accepts input from the user between reading the entire file and writing it (a good example is the way a spreadsheet or word-processing program handles files), you can follow these steps to implement a secure, LAN-aware method of handling concurrent access:

1. Use the previously outlined library-card scheme to "own the file" while the user inputs data. When you put an entry in the control file, also record in the control file the file's last-modified-date, last-modified-time, and size.

2. Open the file for DENY_READ_WRITE (exclusive) access, read the file into memory, and close the file. Present the data to the user, and allow the user's changes.

3. Before updating the file, first check whether the file's current last-modified-date, last-modified-time, and size match the values you originally placed in the control file. If you detect a difference, inform the user that the file has changed since the user first loaded it and ask whether your software should proceed with the update.

4. If the file was not touched while the user keyed changes, or if the user signals approval to overlay the changed file with the more recent changes, open the file for DENY_READ_WRITE access, write the changes, and close the file. If your application uses the entries in the control file for audit purposes, you can mark this entry with a code that says "file was overlayed!" if the user authorized it.

Suppose that your application manages an index-type file, in which certain data records bear a relationship to one another or to the contents of records in another file. In this case, in addition to possibly employing the library-card scheme previously outlined, you can use the following mechanism:

1. Open the file for DENY_NONE (shared) access from each workstation, so that everyone can use the file.

2. To do an update, acquire a lock on the entire file (as though it were one big record) before writing records.

3. Write the records containing the related data and release the lock.

Help files and other files that are usually accessed on a Read-Only basis (but are periodically updated by a special maintenance program or upgrade/installation process) can benefit from the following design approach:

1. After initial installation or file creation, use DOS function call 43 (hex), Change File Mode, to mark the file Read-Only.

2. In everyday use, the Read-Only attribute protects the file from being modified (or inadvertently deleted), and also enables the file to be buffered locally at the workstation rather than remotely at the file server (local buffering helps performance).

3. When the file needs to be updated, the installation or special maintenance program can use that same DOS function call to give the file a Read-Write attribute and then proceed with the update.

4. During the update process, you can protect the file from multiuser access by opening the file with a DENY_READ_WRITE (exclusive) mode. After the update or installation is finished, the file should be marked Read-Only again.

Some programming environments provide their own locking schemes, over which you have little or no control. For example, if you find yourself coding *embedded SQL statements* in your C programs (or calling an SQL API directly), the programming manual may refer to *shared locks*, *exclusive locks*, and *isolation levels*. However, the underlying software that performs the actual I/O on the files probably uses one or more of the locking schemes described in this section to protect the data.

Coordinating Related File Updates

A special situation arises when a file contains data fields whose values have certain relationships to data fields in a second file. To handle such a situation, you need to do the following:

❑ Avoid deadlocks during the process of acquiring locks.

❑ Protect the data in both files while the update takes place.

❑ Prepare for the possibility that the machine may crash (perhaps from a power failure) after one file is updated but before the second update takes place.

By using a technique known as *journaling*, you can easily handle this potentially disastrous situation. The following are the steps you take in your application; note that step 1, which contains the exception-handling logic, is described last:

2. Acquire all locks on the related files before proceeding. This step avoids deadlock.

3. Read the records that the update will affect, and store their images in a separate file (the journal file). Mark the journal entry "update not yet applied."

4. Write the updated records to the files.

5. Mark the journal entry "update applied."

6. Release the locks.

7. If program execution reaches this point, the updates were fully applied and the journal file was marked accordingly. However, a power failure could have caused processing to halt after any one of the preceding steps, and you need to restore the related files to a consistent condition.

1. This step is described last so that you understand the context in which it executes. When your application starts up, it needs to inspect the journal file before letting users change any files in the system. If any of the items in the journal file are marked "update not yet applied," you can show these entries to the user, roll back the related files to a consistent state by copying the images from the journal file back to their respective file locations, and mark the journal file entry "rolled back."

Power failures are not the only culprits that can cause inconsistencies. If you are an especially conservative designer or programmer, or you are working on an especially sensitive application, you can take steps in your software at strategic points to check for inconsistencies in the data. If your defensive programming turns up an "impossible situation," you can fall back on a variation of the previously listed steps to make the related files consistent again. Naturally, this would be a good time to ask the user to notify you that something went wrong.

You may find other uses in your application for the audit trail provided by the journal file, incidentally.

Far Pointers

Far pointers are commonly used in network programming. IBM microcomputers have a segmented architecture in which the complete address of a structure or function is specified in segment:offset form. Because the network support software exists in a different segment from your application code, you must use far pointers to tell the network support software where your structures and functions are located. The current versions of the Borland Turbo C, Microsoft, and Lattice compilers support far pointers, but some differences exist in how the compilers' preprocessor macros and library routines handle far pointers. In particular, the process of separating a far pointer into its segment and offset components varies by compiler. The reverse process of creating a far pointer from a segment and an offset is also handled differently.

Throughout this book, I treat far pointers according to the descriptions of the following three macros. Each description is accompanied by a function prototype and a macro definition. If your compiler defines macros or functions that behave differently from the ones shown below, you can insert the given prototypes and macro definitions into your code.

MK_FP()—make a far pointer. This function (macro) takes two unsigned integer parameters, segment and offset. MK_FP() returns a far pointer that it creates from the segment and offset values. The Turbo C and Microsoft compilers conform to this definition, but the Lattice C compiler does not define MK_FP().

```
Function prototype:
void far *MK_FP()(unsigned int segment, unsigned int offset)
```

```
Macro definition
#define MK_FP(seg, ofs)    ((void far *)   \
  (((unsigned long) (seg) (( 16) | (unsigned) (ofs)))
```

FP_OFF()—obtain the offset portion of a far pointer. This function (macro) takes a far pointer as a parameter and returns the offset portion of the pointer. The Turbo C and Lattice compilers conform to this usage of FP_OFF(), but the Microsoft compiler defines this function differently.

```
Function prototype:
unsigned int FP_OFF(void far *pointer)
```

```
Macro definition:
#define FP_OFF(pointer)    ((unsigned) (pointer))
```

FP_SEG()—obtain the segment portion of a far pointer. This function (macro) takes a far pointer as a parameter and returns the segment portion of the pointer. The Turbo C and Lattice compilers conform to this usage of FP_OFF(), but the Microsoft compiler defines this function differently.

```
Function prototype:
unsigned int FP_SEG(void far *pointer)
```

```
Macro definition:
#define FP_SEG(void far *pointer)
    (unsigned long) (pointer) )) 16))
```

Detecting the LAN

Because there is no standard, PC DOS-supplied method for detecting the presence of a LAN, you must make a series of tests in your program and infer the LAN environment from the results. The following section describes the tests you can perform. After each of the tests is explained, some of them are combined into a custom *LAN-Presence Test* that you can use in your software.

SHARE Installed Test

The SHARE.EXE program hooks into DOS Interrupt 2F (hex), the *Multiplex Interrupt*. A strong caution about this interrupt: it was added to PC DOS beginning with version 3.0; if you invoke Interrupt 2F under earlier versions of DOS, your program likely will crash.

Each process that uses Interrupt 2F adheres to a general interface for recognizing and accepting function requests. A *multiplex number* identifying the particular interrupt handler is placed in the AH CPU register, and the specific function to be performed is indicated by setting the AL register. For SHARE.EXE, the multiplex number is 10 (hex) and the Get Installed State function code is 0. If SHARE is installed, it responds to this function code by setting the AL register to FF (hex). Any other value returned in the AL register indicates that SHARE is not installed, as shown in the following example:

```
if (_os_major < 3)
    {
    printf("Can't check for SHARE.\n");
    exit(1);
    }
else
    {
    regs.h.ah = 0x10;
    regs.h.al = 0;
    int86(0x2f, &regs, &regs);
    if (regs.h.al != 0xFF)
        {
        printf("SHARE.EXE is not loaded.\n");
        exit(1);
        }
    }
```

Network Drive Test

Another way to detect a LAN is with a DOS IOCTL call (Function 44 hex; Subfunction 9). The call tests whether a logical drive is local or remote. To use this function, put the number of the logical drive in the BL register (default drive is 0, drive A: is 1, drive C: is 3, and so on) and perform the call. After the call, if bit 12 of the DX register is a 1, the logical drive is remote. Perform this test for all possible nonremovable drives (C: through Z:) and look for at least one remote drive:

```
remote_drive_present = 0;

for (i=3; i<26; i++)
    {
    regs.h.ah = 0x44;
    regs.h.al = 9;
    regs.h.bl = (unsigned char_ i;
    int86(0x21, &regs, &regs);
    if ( (regs.x.dx & 0x1000) == 0x1000 )
        {
        remote_drive_present = 1;
        break;
        }
    }
```

There is one problem with the IOCTL method: it does not distinguish between a network drive and a CD-ROM drive. The software drivers that Microsoft developed to support CD-ROM machines use the same DOS internals that the network uses to identify remote drives. However, Microsoft CD-ROM Extension (MSCDEX) function calls can help us here. Interrupt 2F (hex) is the entry point for the MSCDEX functions. Function 15 (hex), Subfunction 0 returns the number of CD-ROM logical drives in the BX register. If BX is 0 after this call, you do not have to worry about CD-ROM drives. If BX is nonzero, however, things get complicated. The CX register contains the first CD-ROM drive (D: = 3, E: = 4, and so on) after this call, but there may be multiple CD-ROM drives. Function 15 (hex), Subfunction 0B (hex) checks whether a drive is a CD-ROM drive, and Subfunction 0D (hex) provides a list of all the CD-ROM drive letters. Unfortunately, only the newer MSCDEX version (2.0) supports the additional query subfunctions 0B and 0D, so they may not be available.

If your application detects a CD-ROM drive, you might take an approach that counts on the almost certain likelihood that the network drives, if any, are assigned drive letters that come after the CD-ROM drives because of the way DOS establishes drive letters. This means that you can look for network drives by starting with a drive letter one position beyond the count (in the BX register) of drives beginning with the first CD-ROM drive (the CX register).

The following code summarizes the situation with CD-ROM drives:

```
start_drive = 3;     /* tentatively start at C: */

regs.h.ah = 0x15;
regs.h.al = 0;
regs.x.bx = 0;
int86(0x2f, &regs, &regs);
if (regs.x.bx != 0)
     start_drive = regs.x.cx + regs.x.bx + 1;
                    /* CD-ROM found.  Start 1 beyond it. */


/*   Now do the 'network drives' test, starting beyond
     any CD-ROM drives that might exist.  */


remote_drive_present = 0;

for (i=start_drive; i<26; i++)
    {
    regs.h.ah = 0x44;
    regs.h.bl = (unsigned char) i;
    regs.h.al = 9;
    int86(0x21, &regs, &regs);
    if ( (regs.x.dx & 0x1000) == 0x1000 )
        {
        remote_drive_present = 1;
        break;
        }
    }
```

NETBIOS Installed Test

Many types of networks are based on NETBIOS. The test for its presence relies on getting an Invalid Command error code back after deliberately passing an incorrect command to the network support system. The following code shows how to make this test. The code uses the

Network Control Block (NCB) data structure, which is explained in Chapter 5, "PC-to-PC NETBIOS Programming."

```
NCB  test_ncb;
void interrupt  (*int_5C_vector)(void);


int_5C_vector = getvect(0x5C);
if (int_5C_vector == (void far *) NULL)
    {
    printf("ERROR. NetBios not loaded (Int5C not present).\n");
    exit(1);
    }

memset(&test_ncb, 0, sizeof(NCB));
test_ncb.NCB_COMMAND = 0x7F;
NetBios(&test_ncb);
if (test_ncb.NCB_RETCODE != 03)
    {
    printf("ERROR. NetBios not loaded (No response from Int5C).\n");
    exit(1);
    }

/* - - - - - - - - - - - - - - - - - - - - - - - - - */
/*
 *  Call NETBIOS, via Interrupt 5C.
 */

void    NetBios(NCB far *ncb_ptr)
        {
        ncb_ptr->NCB_CMD_CPLT = 0xFF;
        _ES    = FP_SEG(ncb_ptr);  /* Turbo C can directly */
        _BX    = FP_OFF(ncb_ptr);  /* access CPU registers.*/
        _AX    = 0x0100;
        geninterrupt(0x5c);
        }
```

Incidentally, the Lattice C 6.0 compiler library function for determining the presence of a LAN (isnet()) relies on a variation of the NETBIOS-is-loaded test. Some network operating systems, most notably the IBM PC LAN Program, put a layer of software over NETBIOS that consists partly of extra retry logic. The entry point for this layer is Interrupt 2A (hex), which the Lattice function isnet() uses to determine the presence of the LAN.

NetWare Installed Test

This test asks the NetWare shell for version information. Naturally, if the shell is not loaded, your cue is that no information is returned. The function code for this call is EA (hex) and the subfunction code is 1; these values go into the AH and AL registers, respectively. BX is set to 0 and the ES:DI register pair is loaded with a far pointer to a reply buffer (50 bytes of buffer area is enough). After the call, if the NetWare shell is loaded, the BX register contains major and minor version information. If the BX register remains 0 after the call, the shell is not loaded.

```
union REGS regs;      /* from <dos.h> with most compilers. */
struct SREGS sregs;
char reply_buffer[50];

regs.h.ah = 0xEA;
regs.h.al = 1;
regs.x.bx = 0;
sregs.es  = FP_SEG( (void far *) reply_buffer);
regs.x.di = FP_OFF( (void far *) reply_buffer);
int86x(0x21, &regs, &regs, &sregs);
if (regs.x.bx == 0)
    printf("Not a NetWare LAN.\n");
```

PC LAN Program Installed Test

The PC LAN Program (PCLP) also uses the Multiplex Interrupt. The program's multiplex number is B8 (hex). PCLP supports the same Get Installed State call as SHARE does. If the AL register remains 0 after the call to Interrupt 2F (hex), the PC LAN Program is not loaded.

```
if (_os_major < 3)
    {
    printf("Can't check for PCLP.\n");
    exit(1);
    }
else
    {
    regs.h.ah = 0xB8;
    regs.h.al = 0;
```

Listing continues

Listing *continued*

```
int86(0x2f, &regs, &regs);
if (regs.h.al == 0)
    {
    printf("PC LAN Program is not loaded.\n");
    exit(1);
    }
}
```

Custom LAN-Presence Test

There are pros and cons to using each of these tests as an indication of the presence of a LAN. The test for SHARE.EXE is not a good indicator of whether a workstation is on a LAN, because DOS version 4.0 loads SHARE automatically, even on stand-alone PCs. On the other hand, SHARE *must* be loaded to enable file sharing, so your application should test for the presence of SHARE before sharing files or locking records.

The test for network drives (with allowances for the possible existence of CD-ROM drives) is an excellent, highly accurate test for the presence of a network. In essence, this test says, "Yes, there is a file server." The only trouble with this test is that some vendors who implement low-cost networks may overlook this particular IOCTL call in the network support software they write, and so I will formulate a custom LAN-presence test as follows:

❑ SHARE must be loaded so that the application can share files and lock records.

❑ The test for network drives should find at least one drive letter to be remote; or, failing that, NETBIOS must be operational on the workstation.

Note that not all of the various tests mentioned are used. The other tests, such as the NetWare-present test, are handy for special situations—particularly if you need to perform a vendor-specific function and first want to verify the environment in which your program is running.

Identifying the Workstation

After you are satisfied that your application is running on a workstation and not just on a stand-alone PC, you next need to identify the workstation. Recall from Chapter 2, "Multiuser Concepts," that machine name is a common method of identification and is supported by PC DOS itself.

There are two drawbacks to using machine name:

1. If the workstation always boots up with one particular machine name, the name actually identifies the workstation and not the user. No matter who sits down at the workstation to use the network, the user has the same machine name as all the other users who happen to sit down at that same workstation.

2. On some LANs, more than one workstation can establish the same machine name, or a workstation may have no machine name at all.

The solution to both these problems is usually administrative. Each user who wants to use your application on the LAN should execute a program that identifies that user with a unique machine name. This program execution might consist (under the PC LAN Program) of rebooting the workstation and executing a new NET START command, or perhaps (under NetWare) simply telling each user how to properly use the Login and Logout commands so that he or she is correctly identified.

You can also take extra steps to ensure that each machine name is always unique by using the techniques described in Chapter 5, "PC-to-PC NETBIOS Programming," to route a simple message across the network. Any workstation that recognizes its machine name in the message can respond with a Present! message, thus alerting the new claimant to the presence of the name's current owner. You might use this technique if unique user or workstation identification is critical to your application. You also can set machine name yourself, from within your program, by using an undocumented DOS function call (documented later in this section).

Machine Name

The PC DOS Get Machine Name function call, hex 5E00, returns a 16-byte machine name. The name is padded on the right with spaces and is null-terminated in the 16th byte (in other words, the name is an ordinary C string). This function also returns NETBIOS name number, which is meaningful on NETBIOS-based LANs only. NETBIOS assigns this number when you do either of the NETBIOS functions Add Name or Add Group Name. The NETBIOS name number of the permanent

node name (refer to Chapter 3, "PC-to-PC Communications Concepts")
is always 1. If machine name is not defined, this function returns a 0 in
the CH register. The following is an example of the function:

```
char            machine_name[16];
unsigned char   netbios_name_number;

regs.x.dx = FP_OFF( (void far *) machine_name);
sregs.ds  = FP_SEG( (void far *) machine_name);
regs.x.ax = 0x5E00;
int86x(0x21, &regs, &regs, &sregs);
if (regs.h.ch == 0)
    {
    printf("ERROR.  Machine name not set.\n");
    exit(1);
    }


netbios_name_number = regs.h.cl;   /* not really useful */
                                   /* in this chapter.  */


/* If you want to use machine name as part of a */
/* filename, you should remove the spaces.      */

i = strlen(machine_name) - 1;
while (i > 0 && machine_name[i] == ' ')
    {
    machine_name[i] = '\0';
    i--;
    }
```

The following is an undocumented (not mentioned in the *PC DOS
Technical Reference*) variation of the Get Machine Name function call that
can be used to set machine name. You probably would not use this function on a NETBIOS-based LAN, because NETBIOS is already a name-
oriented environment. However, you might use this function in lieu of
NetWare's login script facility for setting machine name.

```
char machine_name[16];

/* At this point, set machine_name to a null-terminated, */
/* 15-byte string that is padded on the right with spaces.    */
/* The null terminator should appear in the 16th byte:    */
```

```
machine_name[15] = '\0';

regs.x.dx = FP_OFF( (void far *) machine_name);
sregs.ds  = FP_SEG( (void far *) machine_name);
regs.h.ch = 1;
regs.h.cl = netbios_name_number;
regs.x.ax = 0x5E01;
int86x(0x21, &regs, &regs, &sregs);
```

After glancing at this coding example, you probably wonder where you come up with a value for netbios_name_number. Because you should use this function only on a non-NETBIOS-based LAN, you have to fake it; put a value of 1 into the CL register, if you want.

NetWare User IDs

In addition to supporting machine name (set with a command in the login script), NetWare also has its own mechanism for identifying users. It is a two-step process: you first find out the workstation's *connection number* (assigned by the file server at login time) and you then use the result to get information about that connection number, including the user ID (which Novell calls the *object name*).

The first step is accomplished with a GetConnectionNumber function call. To perform the call, set the AH register to the function number DC (hex) and do an Interrupt 21 (hex). On return, the AL register contains the connection number (in the range of 1 to 100).

```
regs.h.ah = 0xDC;
int86(0x21, &regs, &regs);
connect_num = regs.h.al;
```

The second step consists of a GetConnectionInformation call. The addresses of two data areas are passed to this function. The first area is a four-byte request buffer:

```
struct
    {
    unsigned int    request_length;
    unsigned char   subfunction;
    unsigned char   buffer_connect_num;
    } request_buffer;
```

The other area is a 63-byte reply buffer:

```
struct
    {
    unsigned int    reply_length;
    unsigned long   object_id;
    unsigned int    object_type;
    char            object_name [48];
    char            login_time [7];
    } reply_buffer;
```

The call itself consists of setting the AH register to the function code (hex E3), the DS:SI register pair to the address of the request buffer, the ES:DI register pair to the address of the reply buffer, and doing an Interrupt 21 (hex):

```
request_buffer.request_length     = 2;
request_buffer.subfunction        = 0x16;
request_buffer.buffer_connect_num = connect_num;

reply_buffer.reply_length = 61;

regs.h.ah = 0xE3;
sregs.ds  = FP_SEG( (void far *) &request_buffer);
regs.x.si = FP_OFF( (void far *) &request_buffer);
sregs.es  = FP_SEG( (void far *) &reply_buffer);
regs.x.di = FP_OFF( (void far *) &reply_buffer);

int86x(0x21, &regs, &regs, &sregs);
```

Because it is null-terminated, the object name returned in the reply buffer can easily be treated as an ordinary string:

```
printf("The User ID is %s\n",
        reply_buffer.object_name);
```

Sharing Files

Earlier, this chapter discussed several strategies for sharing files, and Chapter 2, "Multiuser Concepts," explained the concepts behind sharing mode and access mode, which are specified when a file is opened. Let's look now at specific coding techniques that show how you indicate these modes from within your application.

The first thing to note is that the high-level call fopen() is not generally LAN-aware, and does not provide a means for indicating sharing mode
and access mode. For example, under Turbo C 2.0 and Microsoft C 5.1,
fopen() results in a *compatibility mode* open of a file—as discussed in
Chapter 2 ("Multiuser Concepts"), compatibility mode should be avoided
in LAN-aware programs. Lattice C 6.0 is a little more up-to-date in this
area; it uses a sharing mode of DENY_NONE for files opened with fopen()
. At any rate, avoid using fopen() in your LAN-aware applications; it just
does not give you enough control over the different file-sharing modes.
Use the open(), _open(), or sopen() calls instead, as outlined in the following sections. Under PC DOS, these functions wind up calling the same
DOS function call (3D hex, Open File) as fopen(), but they enable you to
specify the values for sharing mode and access mode.

Exclusive Access

The following code shows some examples of calls that open a file
named PRIVATE.FIL for exclusive access. After a particular workstation
opens the file in this mode, no other workstation can open the file. Also, if
another workstation already has the file open in any mode, the request for
exclusive access will fail. Note that the manifest constants are different
among the different compilers, but that all these calls do the same thing.

In Turbo C:

```
handle = _open("PRIVATE.FIL", O_RDWR | O_DENYALL);
if (handle == -1)
    {
    if (errno == ENOENT)
        printf("No such file.\n");
    else
    if (errno == EMFILE)
        printf("Too many open files.\n");
    else
    if (errno == EACCES)
        printf("File is READ-ONLY, or already open.\n");
    else
    if (errno == EINVACC)
        printf("Invalid access mode.\n");
    }

/* Note that I use UNIX-style error handling */
/* here, because it's fairly consistent       */
/* among different compilers.                  */
```

In Lattice C:

```
handle = open("PRIVATE.FIL", O_RDWR | O_SDRW);
if (handle == -1)
    /* same error handling as for Turbo C. */
```

In Microsoft C:

```
handle = sopen("PRIVATE.FIL", O_RDWR, SH_DENYRW);
if (handle == -1)
    /* same error handling as for Turbo C. */
```

One Writer; Many Readers

Occasionally, you will want to update a file in such a way that only one workstation writes to the file but others can read from it concurrently. The following examples show what the open() or sopen() call looks like for the workstation that wants to be the only one to write to the file. The error handling is omitted because it would be exactly as described earlier for establishing exclusive access.

In Turbo C:

```
handle = open("ONEWRITE.FIL", O_RDWR | O_DENYWRITE);
```

In Lattice C:

```
handle = open("ONEWRITE.FIL", O_RDWR | O_SDW);
```

In Microsoft C:

```
handle = sopen("ONEWRITE.FIL", O_RDWR, SH_DENYWR);
```

Of course, the other workstations want to open the file only for reading; their call would look like one of the following:

In Turbo C:

```
handle = open("ONEWRITE.FIL", O_RDONLY | O_DENYNONE);
```

In Lattice C:

```
handle = open("ONEWRITE.FIL", O_RDONLY | O_SDN);
```

And in Microsoft C:

```
handle = sopen("ONEWRITE.FIL", O_RDONLY, SH_DENYNO);
```

Shared Access

If you want record-level control over concurrent file access, you need to open the file in DENY_NONE mode. Here are some examples of how this is coded:

In Turbo C:

```
handle = open("SHARED.FIL", O_RDWR | O_DENYNONE);
```

In Lattice C:

```
handle = open("SHARED.FIL", O_RDWR | O_SDN);
```

In Microsoft C:

```
handle = sopen("SHARED.FIL", O_RDWR, SH_DENYNO);
```

Setting the Sharing Retry Count/Delay

You can fine-tune the way DOS retries network-related errors before DOS returns the errors to your program as failed function calls. The default is that DOS performs three retries, with one delay loop between attempts. You set both the retry count and the number of delay loops with the Set Sharing Retry Count/Delay IOCTL function call. The following example sets the delay period to two loops and tells DOS to retry six times before quitting:

```
regs.h.ah = 0x44;
regs.h.al = 0x0B;
regs.x.cx = 2;      /* number of delay loops into CX */
regs.x.dx = 6;      /* new retry count into DX        */
int86(0x21, &regs, &regs);
```

NetWare File Sharing

NetWare adds several individual function calls to PC DOS under the general category of *Synchronization Services*. If your software will be used only in a NetWare environment, these services might give you exactly the control you need.

As mentioned in Chapter 2, "Multiuser Concepts," the process of using Novell services consists of *logging* the files you are about to lock, *locking* that set of files, performing the updates, *releasing* the locks, and *clearing*

the list of logged files. The following shows what it would take to do these
steps in Turbo C for a pair of related files, FILE.ONE and FILE.TWO:

```c
void main(int argc, char *argv[])
    {
    char filename1[15] = "FILE.ONE";
    char filename2[15] = "FILE.TWO";
    char string[20];
    int  handle1;
    int  handle2;


/* Even though NetWare services are being used,        */
/* the file should still be opened in a sharing mode.  */


    handle1 = open(filename1, O_RDWR | O_DENYNONE);
    handle2 = open(filename2, O_RDWR | O_DENYNONE);

log_both_files:
    if (nw_log(filename1) != 0)
        abend("Couldn't log file 1.");
    if (nw_log(filename2) != 0)
        abend("Couldn't log file 2.");


issue_lock:
    if (nw_lock_set() != 0)
        {
        printf("1 or both already locked.  Retry? (Y/N) ");
        gets(string);
        if (string[0] == 'Y' || string[0] == 'y')
            goto issue_lock;
        abend("Couldn't lock.  Try later.");
        }

update_the_files:
    perform_update();   /* Your routine to write records. */

now_release_files:
    if (nw_release(filename1) != 0)
        abend("Couldn't release file 1.");
    if (nw_release(filename2) != 0)
        abend("Couldn't release file 2.");
```

```
clear_log_entries:
    nw_clear_files();

    close(handle1);
    close(handle2);
    printf("Update complete.\n");
    return;
    }


/*  -   -   -   - subroutines -   -   -   - */

int  nw_log(char *name)
    }
    struct REGPACK sregs;

/*
 * Function Call EB, Log File
 * AL = 0 to just log, 1 to log and lock.
 * DS:DX = pointer to drive, path, filename string.
 * BP = number of 1/18ths of a second to keep trying the
 *      lock before timing out.
 * Completion code returned in the AL register.
 */

    regs.r_ax = 0xEB00;
    regs.r_dx = FP_OFF( (void far *) name);
    regs.r_ds = FP_SEG( (void far *) name);
    regs.r_bp = 18;
    intr (0x21, &regs);
    return regs.r_ax;
    }


int  nw_lock_set(void)
    {
    struct REGPACK regs;

/*
 * Function Call C2, Lock Physical Record Set
 * AL = 0 to lock with exclusive locks;
 *      1 to lock with shareable, Read-Only locks.
 * BP = timeout limit, in 1/18ths of a second.
 * Completion code returned in AL.
 */
```

Listing continues

```c
        regs.r_ax = 0xC200;
        regs.r_bp = 18;
        intr(0x21, &regs);
        return regs.r_ax;
        }


int  nw_release(char *name)
        {
        struct REGPACK regs;

/*
 * Function Call EC, Release File
 * DS:DX = far pointer to filename.
 * Completion code in AL register.
*/

        regs.r_ax = 0xEC00;
        regs.r_dx = FP_OFF( (void far *) name);
        regs.r_ds = FP_SEG( (void far *) name);
        intr(0x21, &regs);
        return regs.r_ax;
        }


void nw_clear_files(void)
        {
        struct REGPACK regs;

/*
 * Function Call CF, Clear File Set
 * no parameters.
 * returns nothing.
*/
        regs.r_ax = 0xCF;
        intr(0x21, &regs);
        }

void abend(char *msg)
        {
        printf("%s\n", msg);
        exit(1);
        }
```

OS/2 File Sharing

In general, file sharing is accomplished under OS/2 in the same way as under DOS. Borland has not yet released an OS/2 C compiler, so the discussion in this section does not pertain to Turbo C. Of course, the Microsoft and Lattice compilers do produce code that runs under OS/2.

For both of these compilers, the code examples (open() and sopen()) listed previously are also applicable to the OS/2 environment. However, if you want even more control over the way a file is opened, you can call the DosOpen() kernel API function directly:

```
char           filename[80]; /* drive, path, name      */
unsigned       handle;       /* returned file handle    */
unsigned       action;       /* action that OS/2 took    */
unsigned long  filesize;     /* file's new size in bytes */
unsigned       file_attribute;/* used when creating file  */
unsigned       flag;         /* action to take           */
unsigned       open_mode;    /* Sharing Mode; Access Mode*/
unsigned long  reserved;
unsigned       return_code;  /* returns 0 if successful  */

strcpy(filename, "SHARED.OS2");
filesize       = 0l;
file_attribute = 0;
flag           = 0x0001;
open_mode      = 0x0042;
reserved       = 0l;

return_code = DosOpen     (filename,
                          &handle,
                          &action,
                          filesize,
                          file_attribute,
                          flag,
                          open_mode,
                          reserved);
```

This example does not create a new file, so the file_attribute and filesize items are set to 0. The flag value of 0x0001 signifies that if the file exists it should be opened, and that if the file does not exist, the call should fail (an error should be returned). The open_mode informs OS/2 that the file should be opened for Read-Write access in DENY_NONE mode. If the file is successfully opened, OS/2 returns a file handle in the handle field and sets the action field to 1 if the file exists, 2 if it was created, and 3 if the file was replaced. (It is much easier to call the open() and sopen() functions, so use them whenever possible.)

Setting File Attributes

Function call Change File Mode, hex 43, is used under PC DOS to set a file's attributes. To mark a file Read-Only, put the new file attribute value in the CX register, make DS:DX a far pointer to the name of the file, and do the call:

```
regs.h.ah = 0x43;
regs.h.al = 1;      /* 1=set mode; 0=return mode      */
regs.x.cx = 0x0001; /* set bit 1 to indicate Read-Only */
regs.x.dx = FP_OFF( (void far *) filename);
sregs.ds  = FP_SEG( (void far *) filename);
int86x(0x21, &regs, &regs, &sregs);
```

PC DOS does not know about or recognize the Shareable/Non-Shareable attribute; it is specific to NetWare. However, because NetWare intercepts Interrupt 21, Function 43, you can use this function call to control whether more than one workstation can access a file. NetWare turns the request into a Novell-specific function request and sends the result to the file server. Bit 8 of the attribute field, which is marked "reserved" in the *PC DOS Technical Reference*, is defined as the Shareable/Non-Shareable bit by Novell. In the preceding example, putting 0x8000 into the CX register would make a file Shareable; 0x8001 would make it Shareable/Read-Only.

Under OS/2, a file may be set to Read-Only with the DosSetFileMode() kernel API call:

```
ret_code = DosSetFileMode( (void far *) filename,
                          0x0001,
                          0l);
```

Locking Records

Before you look at the examples of the techniques used for locking individual records, two important rules should be mentioned:

1. You can have multiple locks in a file, but you should not overlap file regions.

2. Be careful to unlock all records that you lock.

To lock records the file must have been opened by your application for Read-Write access in Deny-None mode. You can then freely lock and unlock records within the file. If you need to lock the entire file as one large record, specifying a file region longer than the file itself is not an error, so you do not have to determine the current length of the file before locking records. The Sharing Retry Count/Delay parameters previously mentioned apply to record locking as well as to file sharing.

The following coding examples show how records are locked for the Turbo C, Lattice, and Microsoft compilers. Each compiler requires a slightly different syntax for the library calls, but all ultimately invoke DOS function call 5C (hex), Lock/Unlock File Range. In each example, the fifth (counting from 1) record in a file is locked, written, and unlocked. The record length is 100 bytes.

Invoking DOS Function 5C

If you do not mind coding your record-locking routines yourself (rather than using the library routines supplied with the compiler), you can create a fairly generic function that invokes DOS function 5C and that you can use with almost any compiler:

```c
int  lock_record    (int handle,
                     long file_position,
                     long record_length)
{
union REGS regs;
/* Function 5C */
/* AL = 0 to lock, 1 to unlock */
/* BX = file handle */
/* CX:DX = position in file */
/* SI:DI = byte count to lock/unlock */

regs.h.ah = 0x5C;

regs.h.al = 0;
regs.x.bx = handle;
regs.x.cx = (unsigned) file_position >> 16;
regs.x.dx = (unsigned) file_position & 0x0000ffff;
regs.x.si = (unsigned) record_length >> 16;
regs.x.di = (unsigned) record_length & 0x0000ffff;
int86(0x21, &regs, &regs);
return regs.x.ax;
}
```

The following code is an example of record locking that uses Turbo C library functions:

```
int  handle;
int  return_code;
int  my_retries;
long record_length;
long record_number;
long file_position;

handle = _open("SHARED.FIL", O_RDWR | O_DENYNONE);
if (handle == -1)
    /* Same error handling as mentioned earlier. */


/* Each record is 100 bytes in length. */
/* Lock the fifth record. */

my_retries     = 0;
record_length = 100l;
record_number = 5l;
file_position = record_length * (record_number - 1l);


do_the_lock:
return_code = lock(handle, file_position, record_length);
if (return_code != 0)
    {
    if (errno != EACCES)
        {
        close(handle);
        printf("Lock attempt failed; I/O error.\n");
        exit(1);
        }
    /* St this point you know someone else has */
    /* locked the record. */
    my_retries++;
    if (my_retries < 100)    /* app-specific number */
        goto do_the_lock;
    close(handle);
    printf("Lock failed after 100 retries.\n");
    exit(1);
    }

/* Lock succeeded; write the record(s). */
```

```
/* Notice that, if the write() fails, I make sure */
/* to unlock the file region before exiting. */

return_code = write(handle, &a_record, (int) record_length);
if (return_code == -1)
    {
    unlock(handle, file_position, record_length);
    close(handle);
    printf("Write attempt failed.\n");
    exit(1);
    }

unlock(handle, file_position, record_length);
close(handle);
printf("All done.  Update successful.\n");
exit(0);
```

Lattice C has two library functions for locking records, lockf() and rlock(). The lockf() function takes a parameter telling it whether to lock or unlock a file region; a separate function (runlk()) unlocks records that the rlock() call locked. The following code shows the rlock() and runlk() functions:

```
int   handle;
int   return_code;
int   my_retries;
long  record_length;
long  record_number;
long  file_position;

handle = open("SHARED.FIL", O_RDWR | O_SDN);
if (handle == -1)
    /* Same error handling as mentioned earlier. */

/* Each record is 100 bytes in length. */
/* Lock the fifth record. */

my_retries    = 0;
record_length = 100l;
record_number = 5l;
file_position = record_length * (record_number - 1l);

do_the_lock:
return_code = rlock(handle, file_position, record_length);
if (return_code != 0)
```

Listing continues

Listing continued

```
        {
        if (errno != EACCES)
            {
            close(handle);
            printf("Lock attempt failed; I/O error.\n");
            exit(1);
            }
        /* At this point you know someone else has */
        /* locked the record. */
        my_retries++;
        if (my_retries < 100)    /* app-specific number */
            goto do_the_lock;
        close(handle);
        printf("Lock failed after 100 retries.\n");
        exit(1);
        }

/* Lock succeeded; write the record(s).        */
/* Notice that, if the write() fails, I make sure */
/* to unlock the file region before exiting.     */

return_code = write(handle, &a_record, (int) record_length);
if (return_code == -1)
    {
    runlk(handle, file_position, record_length);
    close(handle);
    printf("Write attempt failed.\n");
    exit(1);
    }

runlk(handle, file_position, record_length);
close(handle);
printf("All done.  Update successful.\n");
exit(0);
```

The next example is in Microsoft C, which has a library function, locking(), that you use for both locking and unlocking file regions. This function assumes that your application has already used an lseek() call to position the file pointer to the correct location in the file before issuing either a lock or unlock operation.

```
int  handle;
int  return_code;
int  my_retries;
```

```
long record_length;
long record_number;
long file_position;

handle = _sopen("SHARED.FIL", O_RDWR, SH_DENYNO);
if (handle == -1)
    /* same error handling as mentioned earlier. */

/* each record is 100 bytes in length. */
/* lock the 5th record. */

my_retries   = 0;
record_length = 100l;
record_number = 5l;
file_position = record_length * (record_number - 1l);

do_the_lock:
lseek(handle, file_position, SEEK_SET);
return_code = locking(handle, LK_NBLCK, record_length);
if (return_code != 0)
    {
    if (errno != EACCES)
        {
        close(handle);
        printf("Lock attempt failed; I/O error.\n");
        exit(1);
        }
    /* at this point you know someone else has */
    /* locked the record. */
    my_retries++;
    if (my_retries < 100)    /* app-specific number */
        goto do_the_lock;
    close(handle);
    printf("Lock failed after 100 retries.\n");
    exit(1);
    }

/* lock succeeded; write the record(s)          */
/* Notice that, if the write() fails, I make sure */
/* to unlock the file region before exiting       */

return_code = write(handle, &a_record, (int) record_length);
if (return_code == -1)
```

Listing continues

Listing *continued*

```
    {
    lseek(handle, file_position, SEEK_SET);
    locking(handle, LK_UNLCK, record_length);
    close(handle);
    printf("Write attempt failed.\n");
    exit(1);
    }

  lseek(handle, file_position, SEEK_SET);
  locking(handle, LK_UNLCK, record_length);
  close(handle);
  printf("All done.  Update successful.\n");
  exit(0);
```

NetWare Record Locking

In addition to supporting DOS function call 5C, *Lock/Unlock File Range* (and therefore all the examples you have seen so far), Novell Net-Ware lets you access its own proprietary functions for locking and unlocking records. Like the NetWare-specific file-sharing functions discussed earlier, the record-level functions also fall into NetWare's Synchronization Services category. The approach is exactly the same: log the records you need to access, lock them as a single entity, perform any appropriate updates, release the locks, and clear the list of logged records. You can specify either physical record locks, which are similar to the PC DOS record locking discussed so far, or logical record locks, which consist of symbolic references to the actual records. In the latter case, the file server maintains a list of named records and denies or grants access to items in the list according to the logical locks that the application issued against a name. The use of logical locks requires that all programs accessing the files cooperate by using logical record locks exclusively; one uncooperative program can cause havoc by not adhering to the use of logical locks. For this reason, I suggest that you not use logical locks in your software. Stick with physical record locking.

OS/2 Record Locking

The Microsoft and Lattice compilers emit code for either OS/2 or DOS, so the preceding examples for these two compilers are equally applicable to OS/2. In a program running under OS/2, the locking() and rlock() library routines internally call the OS/2 kernel API for locking records

rather than PC DOS function call 5C. If you want, you can call the
DosFileLocks() kernel function directly. The data structures and general
calling interface look like this:

```
struct    FILE_REGION
    {
    unsigned long  file_offset;
    unsigned long  region_length;
    };

struct FILE_REGION lock_region;
struct FILE_REGION unlock_region;


return_code = DosFileLocks(handle,
                  (void far *) &unlock_region,
                  (void far *) &lock_region);
```

Calling DosFileLocks() is simple. You should pass a NULL pointer for a
parameter if you do not want its corresponding action to be taken.

```
/* to lock a record: */

lock_region.file_offset   = file_position;
lock_region.region_length = record_length;
return_code = DosFileLocks(handle,
                  (void far *) NULL,
                  (void far *) &lock_region);


/* later, to unlock that record: */

unlock_region.file_offset   = file_position;
unlock_region.region_length = record_length;
return_code = DosFileLocks(handle,
                  (void far *) &unlock_region,
                  (void far *) NULL);
```

Committing Changes to Disk

Under PC DOS, two methods exist for ensuring that the records you
have written (which are probably in DOS buffers) are actually flushed out
to the disk. In the first method, you use DOS function call 45 (hex),

Duplicate Handle, and then closes the resulting duplicate handle. A tad faster than closing the original handle and reopening it, this method also has the advantage of working with DOS version 2.1 and subsequent versions. In Turbo C, this method is coded as follows:

```
close ( dup(handle) );
```

The second method—using DOS function call 68 (hex), Commit File—is more explicit. Unfortunately, this function was not added to DOS until version 3.3. This method is coded as follows:

```
regs.h.ah = 0x68;
regs.x.bx = handle;
int86(0x21, &regs, &regs);
```

Under OS/2, the kernel API call `DosBufReset()` does the same job as the DOS Commit File function. Called with the handle of a single file, this API call flushes that file to disk. With a handle of -1, `DosBufReset()` causes the records for all open files to be flushed to disk. The following is an example of the call's use:

```
DosBufReset(handle);
```

Printing to a Shared Printer

As was noted in Chapter 2, "Multiuser Concepts," even something as simple as printing a report takes a little extra care on a network. After you have the print program tested and working on a stand-alone PC, you should run a few tests on the network to make sure that the report looks the way you expect. Your two main concerns are

1. The mode, font or typeface, pitch, and other printer characteristics used for your report

2. The possible insertion of stray page breaks into the report by the network operating system

To address these concerns, DOS, the PC LAN Program, and NetWare all offer services you can use to control printing (of course, the PC LAN Program and NetWare functions are available only if your program is running in that environment).

Whether or not you use these operating system services, you need to send a setup string of printer commands to the printer at the beginning of each printout you produce. If you want to be kind to the next printer user, at the end of the printout you can also send to the printer a setup string that resets the printer to a known, default state. Because every printer has a different set of commands, you definitely want to make your setup string processing file-driven. At some point in your application, ask the user to enter the setup strings and store them in a file; then you do not have to worry quite as much about supporting myriads of different printers.

Also, regardless of whether you use the operating system services this section describes, you should make sure that you open the printer (as a file) only once, at the top of the report. Although usually acceptable on a stand-alone PC, the technique of opening and closing the printer in the middle of a printout is definitely a bad idea on a shared, network printer. The spooler software could insert page breaks into the printout and, if the printer is being used heavily by many users, you could even find another user's printout interleaved with your own.

Setup Strings

DOS function call 5E02 (hex), Set Printer Setup, is used to insert a setup string in front of each and every printout sent to the printer from a workstation (until a subsequent 5E02 call or the workstation is rebooted). Unfortunately, the function does not send a reset setup string after the printout is produced, so you may find using this function less helpful than providing your own setup string processing. If you want to use this function, you first must use DOS function call 5F02 (hex), Get Redirection List Entry, to determine the Redirection List Index entry for the printer you want to use. Perform function call 5F02 repeatedly until you detect a redirected printer or until the list is exhausted (which returns an error code 18):

```
int  done, index;
char local_name[128];
char network_name[128];
union REGS regs;
struct SREGS sregs;

done  = 0;
index = 0;

while (!done)
    {
    regs.x.ax = 0x5F02;
    regs.x.bx = index;
    regs.x.si = FP_OFF( (void far *) local_name);
```

Listing continues

Listing *continued*

```
        sregs.ds  = FP_SEG( (void far *) local_name);
        regs.x.di = FP_OFF( (void far *) network_name);
        sregs.es  = FP_SEG( (void far *) network_name);
        int86x(0x21, &regs, &regs, &sregs);
        if (regs.x.cflag)
            break;
        if (regs.h.bl = 3) /* 3=printer; 4=file device */
            {
            if (strncmp(local_name, "LPT1", 4) == 0)
                done = 1;
            }
        else
            index++;
        }

/* at this point, if done == 1, the variable "index"     */
/* corresponds to the Redirection List Entry of the      */
/* printer whose device name is recorded in "local_name". */
```

Now that you have the Redirection List Entry index value for a redirected LPT1 printer, you can issue function call 5E02 to tell DOS to begin using a particular setup string. The string can be as much as 64 bytes long.

```
regs.x.ax = 0x5E02;
regs.x.bx = index;
regs.x.cx = strlen(setup_string);
regs.x.si = FP_OFF( (void far *) setup_string);
sregs.ds  = FP_SEG( (void far *) setup_string);
int86x(0x21, &regs, &regs, &sregs);
```

PC LAN Program Printer Control

The IBM PC LAN Program provides a service called *Network Print Stream Control* that you can use to specify how you want page breaks handled. This service is invoked by doing an Interrupt 2A (hex) after setting the AH CPU register to 6 and the AL register to a mode value, as follows:

01   Concatenation Mode—Use this value to tell PCLP to ignore its normal assumptions about when page breaks should occur. In this mode, PCLP inserts a page break (the form-feed character, hex 0C) into the redirected print stream only when COMMAND.COM regains control after a program ends or after an entire .BAT file of commands has been processed.

02 Truncation Mode (default)—In this mode, PCLP inserts a page break into the print stream in the following instances:

❏ Whenever a program ends

❏ When the files LPT1, LPT2, or LPT3 are closed

❏ When the program detects a transition to or from printing by Interrupt 17 (hex) and printing by DOS files

❏ When PCLP detects that a different program or process is using Interrupt 17 to print characters

03 Truncate Print Stream—Use this service to tell PCLP that a complete print stream was sent to the printer (when concatenation mode is in effect)

NetWare Print Services

As was mentioned in Chapter 2, "Multiuser Concepts," NetWare provides a rich set of programming services for controlling the network printers. As an example of how rich this set of services is, the following data structure is used at each NetWare workstation to manage nonlocal printing:

```
struct     PRINT_CONTROL_DATA
    {
    unsigned char status;
    unsigned char print_flags;
    unsigned char tab_size;
    unsigned char server_printer;
    unsigned char number_copies;
    unsigned char form_type;
    unsigned char reserved1;
    unsigned char banner_text[13];
    unsigned char reserved2;
    unsigned char local_lpt_device;
    unsigned int  flush_timeout_count;
    unsigned char flush_on_close;
    unsigned int  maximum_lines;
    unsigned int  maximum_chars;
    unsigned char form_name[13];
    unsigned char lpt_flag;
    unsigned char file_flag;
    unsigned char timeout_flag;
    char far       *setup_string_ptr;
```

Listing continues

```
char far      *reset_string_ptr;
unsigned char connect_id_queue_print_job;
unsigned char in_progress;
unsigned char print_queue_flag;
unsigned char print_job_valid;
unsigned long print_queue_id;
unsigned int  print_job_number;
};
```

Note that in this structure NetWare provides for both a setup string and a reset string. This enables NetWare to "bracket" a stream of print material with printer commands that put the printer into the proper mode for a report and then back into a default state after printing. The NetWare function call for obtaining the information in this structure, `GetSpecificCaptureFlags()`, is coded as follows:

```
struct PRINT_CONTROL_DATA print_data;

regs.h.ah = 0xB8;
regs.h.al = 2;
regs.x.cx = sizeof(struct PRINT_CONTROL_DATA);
regs.x.bx = FP_OFF( (void far *) &print_data);
sregs.es  = FP_SEG( (void far *) &print_data);

regs.h.dh = 0;      /* 0=LPT1, 1=LPT2, 2=LPT3 */

int86x(0x21, &regs, &regs, &sregs);
if (regs.h.al != 0)
    printf("Couldn't obtain print data.\n");
```

After you have performed this call, you can use the far pointers `setup_string_ptr` and `reset_string_ptr`, which are returned as part of the data structure, to access the respective control strings. The first two bytes (1 word) of each string contain the maximum length to which each string can be set. The actual setup and reset characters follow the length field.

The `print_flags` field within the structure contains bits that indicate how the end of the print job (EOJ) is detected (see fig. 4.1).

You can modify any of the first 42 bytes of the data structure (except for the *status* field) with the `SetSpecificCaptureFlags()` function call:

```
struct PRINT_CONTROL_DATA print_data;
```

Fig. 4.1. *Bits within* print_flags.

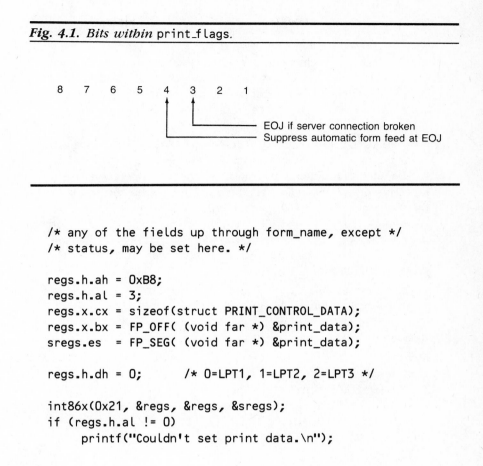

```
/* any of the fields up through form_name, except */
/* status, may be set here. */

regs.h.ah = 0xB8;
regs.h.al = 3;
regs.x.cx = sizeof(struct PRINT_CONTROL_DATA);
regs.x.bx = FP_OFF( (void far *) &print_data);
sregs.es  = FP_SEG( (void far *) &print_data);

regs.h.dh = 0;      /* 0=LPT1, 1=LPT2, 2=LPT3 */

int86x(0x21, &regs, &regs, &sregs);
if (regs.h.al != 0)
    printf("Couldn't set print data.\n");
```

Things You *Cannot* Do on a Network

So far, you have seen that redirecting DOS function calls from a workstation to the file server is a powerful concept. However, it just does not make sense to try to do the following things to the file server:

❏ *Do sector-level I/O*—You cannot do direct I/O to a shared disk at the sector level with Interrupts 25 and 26 (hex) or with the Interrupt 13 (hex) ROM BIOS service. There is no way to lock the sectors. Under NetWare, the layout of the server's disk (its *filesystem*) is completely different than the layout of a PC DOS-formatted disk. (CHKDSK, for example, does sector-level I/O.)

❏ *Treat directories as files*—Because you also cannot lock a directory on the server, you cannot do things such as read a directory into workstation memory to sort it and then write it back to the file server. The other users on the network would find the rug pulled from beneath their feet by the inconsistencies that would exist in the directory for the duration of the update. (Peter Norton's Directory Sort utility does not work on a LAN.)

❏ *Issue illegal FCB operations*—File control blocks (FBCs) are difficult for network software to handle; the usual approach taken by the shell/redirector is to translate each FCB operation into a corresponding file-handle operation and then send the result to the file server. Illegal FCB programming practices—such as constructing an already open FCB, saving an FCB in a disk file for later use, modifying the reserved areas inside an FCB, or closing an FCB and continuing to use it as though it were still open—are strictly forbidden on a network.

❏ *Turn interrupts off*—Leaving interrupts masked off for any but the briefest moment is always a bad idea on a PC, but in a network environment this practice is particularly deadly. The network software relies heavily on interrupts.

❏ *Remove SHARE from memory*—When you run SHARE.EXE, it does much more than just intercept an interrupt vector (as many TSRs do). SHARE actually modifies a set of user-exits inside PC DOS itself and becomes an integral part of DOS. Removing SHARE would take an effort analogous to doing brain surgery, and this is simply not worth while.

Summary

You have covered a lot of ground in this chapter. You now understand the design considerations involved in developing a LAN-aware application. You have seen how detecting the presence of a network is a matter of making some tests and inferring a LAN environment from the results. You know how to use machine name to distinguish between workstations. Sharing files and locking records are key operations on a LAN; you know how to write code that performs these operations properly. You can control file attributes as they relate to the LAN, and you know several techniques for managing a shared network printer. You also know the kinds of programming tactics that you cannot use on a network.

CHAPTER 5

PC-to-PC NETBIOS Programming

At this point, you might be thinking that the best (and easiest) way to share information among the workstations on the network is to write the data to a file on the file server and make the file available to the other workstations. Not always so! Using the file server has some disadvantages:

❑ It is relatively slow.

❑ It entails periodic housecleaning and maintenance of the files.

❑ It takes up disk space.

❑ It requires that users have the necessary rights and privileges to access the files.

There also are design questions: if you want to pass a message or data record to another workstation and get a reply, should you append the reply to the original file or should you write the reply to a separate file? How should the other workstation recognize that the message or record is intended for itself and not for another workstation? For many applications, direct PC-to-PC message passing is often a better technique than file sharing, and just as easy to design.

I want you to feel perfectly comfortable exploring the techniques outlined in this chapter. You may think that using NETBIOS or IPX/SPX can be dangerous—that you might crash the entire network unless you code things exactly right, according to some magic formula. However, when you have finished this chapter you will understand that peer-level communications on a LAN are simple and safe, and that it is actually difficult to bring down the entire network from within your program. The techniques and ideas presented in this chapter suggest several useful LAN applications and utilities—try your hand at them!

The most popular protocols for doing PC-to-PC communications on a LAN are NETBIOS, IPX, and SPX. This chapter offers some general design guidelines for developing applications that "talk directly to one another," and shows how to program NETBIOS applications. Chapter 6, "IPX and SPX Programming," covers the NetWare protocols IPX and SPX.

Designing the Dialog

Peer-level communications on a LAN can be used for simple applications, such as real-time chatting or electronic mail, and as the basis for sophisticated distributed processing systems that allocate a processing workload among several networked PCs. No matter how simple or complex your application is, you should consider the communications link as a dialog or conversation between two or more cooperative processes. Think of this dialog as a special kind of file. Receiving a message is equivalent to reading a record; sending a response is akin to writing a record. Your program defines the format and content of the messages just like records in a file.

Simple Dialogs

In a real-time chat facility, the record layout could not be simpler—the record needs to hold only a single keypress. When a key is pressed, the chat program echoes it to the screen and sends the keypress-record to the chat partner. Similarly, when the chat program receives a keypress-record from the chat partner, the chat program displays the incoming data on the screen. The toughest part of designing a chat program is managing two windows on the screen—incoming (remote) keypresses are displayed in the top window; outgoing (local) keypresses are echoed in the bottom window.

Electronic mail programs vary widely in their complexity, but the record layouts they use have much in common. Each typically contains header ("envelope") data, such as sender name, subject, and addressee. The remainder of the record is simply the text of the mail message.

Complex Dialogs

At the other end of the spectrum, distributed processing systems send and receive data records containing information that is highly application-specific. Each workstation in the system might have a particular task or subtask to do, in which case a workstation receives (reads) a data record, performs its processing, and sends the result along to the next work-station. In a different design, each workstation may run the same software and perform the same task; the next available (not already busy) work-station receives a set of input data to be processed. In a *really* complex design, the individual workstations might share (send and receive) various areas of memory along with the data records. You could consider this design as a form of parallel processing.

Design Considerations

The following guidelines will help you design a dialog between two or more workstations.

Each protocol limits the size of the data packet (data record) you can send or receive. For NETBIOS datagrams, the maximum length is usually 512 bytes. A NETBIOS session-related Send operation imposes a maximum data message length of 65,535 bytes, and a Chain Send operation doubles this by letting you send two data buffers with a single command. The maximum length of an IPX data packet (excluding the fixed, 30-byte IPX header) is 546 bytes. Because SPX uses a 42-byte packet header, the maximum length of an SPX data packet is 534 bytes.

There are a couple of ways to handle packet size limitations. One approach is to segment your data—break it into small chunks and perform a series of Send operations on the segments; on reception, reassemble the segments. Segmentation is a little harder to design and code, but it offers the advantage of insulating the main part of the program from the packet size limitation. Another approach is to deliberately and explicitly design the data records with the packet size limitation in mind. This approach is simpler to program initially, but it implies that, when you want to add new data fields to existing records, you must create new records to hold the fields.

You usually should not have to worry about your application increasing traffic on the network. You can consider the PC-to-PC communications link to be just another file that your software manages. The message traffic that occurs on the LAN is no more than the traffic that would result if the file were located on a file server (because the shell/redirector layer must send and receive a flurry of messages to accomplish the file redirection). However, avoid continuously polling another workstation. For example, suppose that you want to know when a key is pressed at a remote workstation. If you send a constant stream of packets to the remote computer, each one asking "Has a key been pressed yet?", you dramatically and unnecessarily increase message traffic. Design such a dialog so that you ask the remote computer only *once* about its keyboard activity (or modem activity, or whatever).

When you send a data packet on its outbound journey to a remote workstation, when can you count on the packet arriving at its destination? The answer can vary somewhat, of course, depending on the type and size of the network, as well as the current message traffic. On an Ethernet or Token Ring network, a 512-byte data packet usually takes only a millisecond or two to reach the application running on the remote workstation. However, even on a heavily loaded network, the sending and receiving of data packets takes less time than if the application were designed instead to access files on a file server.

Both NETBIOS and IPX/SPX are very good at supporting point-to-point message delivery. Designing one-to-many and many-to-many communications, however, can be a challenge. You can establish multiple NETBIOS sessions (or the equivalent, multiple SPX connections) between workstations, but each protocol limits the number of concurrent sessions (or connections). Even increasing these limits, by setting configuration parameters, may not give you the "elbow room" you want. It is usually a bad idea to go through the trouble of reestablishing a session (or connection) each time you have a data packet to send, because establishing a session requires significant overhead. If you need to send data packets from one workstation to several other workstations, or have several workstations share the same data packets among themselves, you might consider using the IPX or NETBIOS facilities for broadcasting data packets, or you might devise a table-driven, datagram-based scheme that builds the data packet and then sends it to multiple destinations by repeatedly copying a new destination into the packet and sending each copy.

Session or Datagram?

The preceding discussion brings us to the issue of when sessions are better than datagrams or vice versa. The most important difference between datagrams and the messages that are sent and received in a session is that datagrams sometimes get lost in transit and your program is not notified of the error. Messages sent within the framework of a session are guaranteed to be delivered (the protocol, transparent to your application, automatically detects and retransmits lost messages). If multiple packets are outstanding, session control also guarantees that they are delivered in the same sequence in which they were sent.

Sessions are a good environment for point-to-point dialogs in which two workstations pass back and forth several related data packets. Datagrams are a good design choice in applications whose dialogs consist of unrelated messages, only a few messages (brief dialogs), or a series of messages that do not always have to be a complete set. If you do not mind the extra design and coding work required to ensure that lost messages are properly retransmitted, datagrams can be particularly useful. Often all it takes to detect and retransmit lost messages is to add a sequence number field to your data packets, along with some logic to assign and check the sequence number values.

NETBIOS includes functions for doing both datagrams and session-related messages. Because NETBIOS datagrams do not cause return acknowledgments from the copy of NETBIOS running on the dialog partner PC, datagrams are speedier than their session-related counterparts. NETBIOS datagrams are limited in size, as was previously mentioned, but they are easy to program. The ease of programming is offset somewhat by the need to design some retry logic to detect and handle lost packets. Sessions require that you code a few extra program statements to establish and later dismantle the session itself, of course, but doing so requires fewer statements than handling the retransmission of lost packets.

NetWare's IPX protocol supports only datagrams; SPX is required to do connections (sessions). SPX is available in NetWare beginning with version 2.1. IPX is the speediest of the protocols discussed, and, for ease of programming, IPX is comparable to NETBIOS datagrams. However, SPX is much more difficult to program, as you will see in Chapter 6, "IPX and SPX Programming."

Polling versus Asynchronous Event Handling

As was mentioned in Chapter 3, "PC-to-PC Communications Concepts," your program can take either of two approaches while you wait for a NETBIOS or IPX/SPX event to complete. Messages are actually sent or received in the background; you can choose to go into a loop that simply waits for an event to finish, or you can specify that NETBIOS or IPX/SPX call one of your program's functions when the event completes. The techniques are a little different for NETBIOS and for IPX/SPX, of course. This chapter on NETBIOS and the next chapter on IPX/SPX programming techniques show you exactly how polling and asynchronous event handling are done. From a design standpoint, you should choose your approach based on what best suits your application. The only design constraint to keep in mind is that a program function called by NETBIOS or IPX/SPX should be coded to execute as quickly as possible and then return. Simply setting a flag that notifies the main program of event completion is often the best design.

Planning for Time-Outs and Errors

With any I/O that your program performs, good error handling is a must. In a NETBIOS or IPX/SPX environment, this means checking return codes to ensure that the PC-to-PC connection is still alive and healthy. If you design and test your application well, some of the possible return codes will never happen (such as "buffer too small," "invalid name," or "socket not open"). However, other return codes can crop up right in the middle of the communications link. Persistent "time-out" errors usually signify that the other workstation crashed or suffered a power failure. A return code indicating that a network hardware error occurred should be handled by telling the user about the error and gracefully terminating your program.

Programming NETBIOS

A useful way to begin looking at specific NETBIOS programming techniques is to see how similar NETBIOS programming is to disk file programming. In fact, you can treat peer-level communications as a special sort of file. Table 5.1 compares PC DOS file operations and equivalent NETBIOS functions.

Table 5.1. *File I/O compared to NETBIOS functions.*

File Operation	NETBIOS Equivalent
Open	Add Name, then Call (or Listen)
Read	Receive
Write	Send
Seek	<none>
Close	Hang Up, then Delete Name

Using NETBIOS datagrams (which lets you dispense with the session-oriented Call, Listen, and Hang Up NETBIOS commands), you send and receive data packets as shown in table 5.2.

Table 5.2. *A data packet sequence for NETBIOS datagrams.*

Workstation A	Workstation B
1. Add Name A	1. Add Name B
2. Send message to B	2. Receive a message
3. Receive a message	3. Send message to A
4. Delete Name A	4. Delete Name B

The NETBIOS commands Call, Listen, and Hang Up are your tools for managing sessions. Table 5.3 shows the sequence of events you would use for opening a session, exchanging messages, and closing the session.

Table 5.3. *A data packet sequence for NETBIOS sessions.*

Workstation A	Workstation B
1. Add Name A	1. Add Name B
2. Listen (wait for Call)	2. Call Workstation A
3. Send message to B	3. Receive a message
4. Receive a message	4. Send message to A
5. Hang Up on B	5. Hang Up on A
6. Delete Name A	6. Delete Name B

Invoking NETBIOS

To invoke any particular NETBIOS function, you set up a Network Control Block (NCB), put a far pointer to the NCB in the ES:BX register pair, and execute an Interrupt 5C (hex):

```
void NETBIOS (NCB far *ncb_ptr)
    {
    struct SREGS sregs;
    union  REGS regs;

    sregs.es  = FP_SEG(ncb_ptr);
    regs.x.bx = FP_OFF(ncb_ptr);
    int86x(0x5C, &regs, &regs, &sregs);
    }
```

Network Control Block

As the preceding description of how to invoke NETBIOS indicates, all you specify when you call Interrupt 5C is the address of a Network Control Block. The NCB is a self-contained vehicle that tells NETBIOS all it needs to know about each particular operation. The NCB itself does not get transmitted across the network. NETBIOS just uses the NCB as a set of directions specifying what you want done. You should declare a separate NCB for each operation; you will find this easier to manage than if you used one or two generic NCBs for multiple purposes. The following typedef'd struct shows the layout of the NCB:

```
typedef unsigned char byte;
typedef unsigned int  word;

/* Network Control Block (NCB)  */
typedef struct
    {
    byte NCB_COMMAND;
    byte NCB_RETCODE;
    byte NCB_LSN;
    byte NCB_NUM;
    void far *NCB_BUFFER_PTR;
    word NCB_LENGTH;
    byte NCB_CALLNAME[16];
    byte NCB_NAME[16];
    byte NCB_RTO;
    byte NCB_STO;
    void interrupt (*POST_FUNC)(void);
    byte NCB_LANA_NUM;
    byte NCB_CMD_CPLT;
    byte NCB_RESERVE[14];
    }
    NCB;
```

Each of these fields is described in Chapter 3, "PC-to-PC Communications Concepts," in the discussion on NETBIOS concepts. As a supplement to that chapter's discussion, table 5.4 briefly defines each field.

Table 5.4. *NCB fields.*

NCB_COMMAND	Command ID
NCB_RETCODE	Immediate return code
NCB_LSN	Local Session Number
NCB_NUM	Network name number
NCB_BUFFER_PTR	Far pointer to message packet
NCB_LENGTH	Length of message packet
NCB_CALLNAME	Name of the other computer
NCB_NAME	Our network name
NCB_RTO	Receive time-out, in 500-millisecond increments
NCB_STO	Send time-out, in 500-millisecond increments
POST_FUNC	Far (function) pointer to POST routine
NCB_LANA_NUM	Adapter number (0 or 1)
NCB_CMD_CPLT	Final return code

NETBIOS Commands

NETBIOS commands come in two flavors, *wait* and *no-wait*. When you use the wait option, control does not return to your program until the operation is completed. In contrast, the no-wait option tells NETBIOS to start the operation in the background and return immediately to your program. You can give NETBIOS a pointer to a function in your program (a POST routine), which NETBIOS calls when the event completes, or you can poll for the completion of the event by looping until the NCB_CMD_CPLT field changes from 0xFF to an actual return code (NETBIOS return codes are discussed next). You might want to include the following list of symbolically defined NETBIOS commands in your program:

```
#define RESET              0x32
#define CANCEL             0x35
#define STATUS             0xb3
#define STATUS_WAIT        0x33
#define UNLINK             0x70
#define ADD_NAME           0xb0
#define ADD_NAME_WAIT      0x30
#define ADD_GROUP_NAME     0xb6
#define ADD_GROUP_NAME_WAIT 0x36
#define DELETE_NAME        0xb1
#define DELETE_NAME_WAIT   0x31
#define CALL               0x90
```

List continues

List continued

```
#define CALL_WAIT                      0x10
#define LISTEN                         0x91
#define LISTEN_WAIT                    0x11
#define HANG_UP                        0x92
#define HANG_UP_WAIT                   0x12
#define SEND                           0x94
#define SEND_WAIT                      0x14
#define SEND_NO_ACK                    0xf1
#define SEND_NO_ACK_WAIT               0x71
#define CHAIN_SEND                     0x97
#define CHAIN_SEND_WAIT                0x17
#define CHAIN_SEND_NO_ACK              0xf2
#define CHAIN_SEND_NO_ACK_WAIT         0x72
#define RECEIVE                        0x95
#define RECEIVE_WAIT                   0x15
#define RECEIVE_ANY                    0x96
#define RECEIVE_ANY_WAIT               0x16
#define SESSION_STATUS                 0xb4
#define SESSION_STATUS_WAIT            0x34
#define SEND_DATAGRAM                  0xa0
#define SEND_DATAGRAM_WAIT             0x20
#define SEND_BCST_DATAGRAM             0xa2
#define SEND_BCST_DATAGRAM_WAIT        0x22
#define RECEIVE_DATAGRAM               0xa1
#define RECEIVE_DATAGRAM_WAIT          0x21
#define RECEIVE_BCST_DATAGRAM          0xa3
#define RECEIVE_BCST_DATAGRAM_WAIT     0x23
```

NETBIOS Return Codes

NETBIOS passes back to your program both an immediate return code (NCB_RETCODE) and a final return code (NCB_CMD_CPLT). If you use the wait option for a command, or if you use a command that does not have a no-wait option, you should look at the NCB_RETCODE field to find out whether the command succeeded. If you use the no-wait option, however, NETBIOS sets the NCB_CMD_CPLT field to a value of 0xFF while the operation is under way. Only on completion does NETBIOS put an actual, final return code in NCB_CMD_CPLT. Appendix L, "NETBIOS Error Codes," lists the specific error codes.

POST Routines

If you do not want to associate a POST routine with a particular NCB, set the POST_FUNC pointer to NULL. If you are executing a no-wait command, your program should then loop on NCB_CMD_CPLT until it changes from 0xFF to a real return code.

For a no-wait command, you can code a function that NETBIOS will call when the operation is completed. Place the address of the routine in POST_FUNC, as a pointer to a function:

```
void interrupt   answer_the_call()
    {
    ...
    }

listen_ncb.POST_FUNC = answer_the_call;
```

As the appearance of the `interrupt` keyword in the declaration of `answer_the_call()` indicates, the POST routine must behave as though it were an interrupt service routine. The following conditions are true at the time of the call:

❑ Interrupts are masked (turned off).

❑ The register pair ES:BX contains a far pointer to the NCB associated with the completed event.

❑ The NCB_CMD_CPLT field contains the final return code.

❑ The AL CPU register also contains the final return code.

❑ The other registers, including the data segment (DS) register, have no particular value.

❑ Performing DOS function calls (disk file operations, for example) from within the POST routine may not be safe.

You should code the POST routine to execute as quickly as possible. An IRET machine instruction must be used to exit the routine after its completion. The compiler automatically generates the IRET as one of the side effects of using the `interrupt` keyword. A simple POST routine, coded in Turbo C (note the direct reference to CPU registers, as well as the `interrupt` keyword), looks like this:

```
/*  Turbo C POST routine */

unsigned es_reg, bx_reg;
unsigned msg_received_flag;
NCB far *posted_ncb_ptr;
```

Listing continues

Listing continued

```
void interrupt post(void)
    {
    es_reg  = _ES;
    bx_reg  = _BX;
    posted_ncb_ptr = MK_FP(es_reg, bx_reg);
    msg_received_flag = TRUE;
    }
```

The following is the same routine coded according to the conventions of the Microsoft C compiler:

```
/*  Microsoft C POST routine */

unsigned msg_received_flag;
NCB far *posted_ncb_ptr;

void interrupt cdecl far post
                    (unsigned es,
                     unsigned ds,
                     unsigned di,
                     unsigned si,
                     unsigned bp,
                     unsigned sp,
                     unsigned bx,
                     unsigned dx,
                     unsigned cx,
                     unsigned ax,
                     unsigned ip,
                     unsigned cs,
                     unsigned flags)
    {
    posted_ncb_ptr = MK_FP(es, bx);
    msg_received_flag = TRUE;
    }
```

If you are using a C compiler that does not offer the `interrupt` keyword, the following assembler implementation of a POST routine lets you handle the completion of an NCB event (scavenge the code at will for your own purposes):

```
;  Assembler function whose address (far pointer) you
;  can put in the POST_FUNC field in a NETBIOS NCB.
```

```
;   The prototype of the assembler function should appear
;   as follows somewhere near the top of your program.

;        extern void far post_func(void);

;   And you should declare the following two global
;   data items in your C program:

;        NCB far *posted_ncb_ptr;
;        char    msg_received_flag = 0;

;   When this POST routine is invoked, it puts the
;   address of the NCB associated with the POST in
;   the 'posted_ncb_ptr' pointer, and it sets
;   'msg_received_flag' to 1.

;   If you want, you can modify this assembler routine
;   to call one of your C routines, once the registers
;   have been set up correctly.

;   You can change the following line to match the
;   memory model you're using:

      .model small

      public _post_func
         extrn   _posted_ncb_ptr : dword
         extrn   _msg_received_flag : byte

      .code
_post_func      proc far
         push    ds
         push    ax

         mov     ax, @DATA
         mov     ds, ax

;   Let the C program know which NCB has completed.

         mov     word ptr _posted_ncb_ptr+2, es
         mov     word ptr _posted_ncb_ptr, bx

;   Set a flag to indicate the completion of an operation.
```

Listing continues

Listing *continued*

```
        mov     _msg_received_flag, 1


;  If you have a C function declared like this:
;
;       void post_handler(void)
;           {
;           ... do something brief here ...
;           }
;
;  you could call it here:
;
;       extrn   _post_handler : near
;       call    _post_handler

        pop     ax
        pop     ds
    iret
_post_func      endp
        end
```

NETBIOS Installed Test

Chapter 4, "DOS-Level Programming," introduced the following useful component of the LAN-presence test, the "NETBIOS installed" test, which is rewritten here in Turbo C:

```
NCB  test_ncb;
void interrupt  (*int_5C_vector)(void);

int_5C_vector = getvect(0x5C);
if (int_5C_vector == (void far *) NULL)
    {
    printf("ERROR. NetBios not loaded (Int5C not present).\n");
    exit(1);
    }

memset(&test_ncb, 0, sizeof(NCB));
test_ncb.NCB_COMMAND = 0x7F;
```

```
NetBios(&test_ncb);
if (test_ncb.NCB_RETCODE != 03)
    {
    printf("ERROR. NetBios not loaded (No response from Int5C).\n");
    exit(1);
    }


/* - - - - - - - - - - - - - - - - - - - - - - - - - */
/*
 *  Call NETBIOS, via Interrupt 5C.
 */

void    NetBios(NCB far *ncb_ptr)
        {
        ncb_ptr->NCB_CMD_CPLT = 0xFF;
        _ES     = FP_SEG(ncb_ptr);  /* Turbo C can directly */
        _BX     = FP_OFF(ncb_ptr);  /* access CPU registers.*/
        _AX     = 0x0100;
        geninterrupt(0x5c);
        }
```

NETBIOS Names and Workstation IDs

The fields in an NCB that relate to NETBIOS names are NCB_NAME, NCB_CALLNAME, NCB_LSN, and NCB_NUM. NCB_NAME represents the name you are inserting into the local name table (for an Add Name call) or the name by which you want to be known (for a Listen or Call command). NCB_CALLNAME, on the other hand, expresses the name of the other (remote) workstation. Except for when you are performing an Add Name or Add Group Name command, NCB_NAME should already be in the local name table. The name you add with an Add Name command must be unique on the network. Group names, on the other hand, do not have to be unique, but must not already be on the network as a regular name. For example, you can add the group name TEAM_ONE to the local name tables of several different workstations as long as TEAM_ONE has not been added to any local name table with an Add Name command.

Chapter 3, "PC-to-PC Communications Concepts," mentioned that a permanent node name "pre-identifies" each workstation. This workstation ID is constructed by obtaining the 6-byte identification number that is "burned into" the network adapter, and prefixing the number with 10 bytes of binary 0s. The name thus formed is always unique on the network and always available to you in your software. You cannot add or delete the name, but you can use it to establish sessions with other work-stations. The Adapter Status command (described later in this section) returns the network adapter's 6-byte ID number. Be careful how you handle the permanent node name; it is not a normal, null-terminated C string.

The Local Session Number returned from a successful Listen or Call command, NCB_LSN, represents an established session. In subsequent calls to Send, Receive, and Hang Up, you use NCB_LSN to refer to this session.

NCB_NUM is the NETBIOS name number returned by an Add Name or Add Group Name command. Use the value in NCB_NUM when you send datagrams to other workstations.

One more note about NETBIOS names: for the Adapter Status command, you can specify an asterisk (∗) in the first byte of NCB_CALLNAME to indicate that you are interested in the local adapter. For the Session Status command, you can put an asterisk in the first byte of NCB_NAME to tell NETBIOS that you want session status information for all names. Finally, for the Chain Send command, the first two bytes of NCB_CALLNAME specify the length of the second buffer (to be appended or concatenated to the first) and the next four bytes of NCB_CALLNAME specify a far pointer to the second buffer.

Adding Names

Each name you add to the local name table should be checked to ensure that the name is both a normal C string you can easily manipulate in your program and a proper name entry for the table. The name should be 15 bytes long with a null byte after the last string character, as shown in the following example:

```
char netbios_name[16];

struct SREGS sregs;
union  REGS  regs;

NCB    add_name_ncb;

strcpy(netbios_name, "BARRY");
while (strlen(netbios_name) < 15)
     strcat(netbios_name, " ");
```

To add this name to the local name table as a unique name, follow these steps:

```
memset(&add_name_ncb, 0, sizeof(NCB));
add_name_ncb.NCB_COMMAND = ADD_NAME;
strcpy(add_name_ncb.NCB_NAME, netbios_name);

sregs.es  = FP_SEG( (void far *) &add_name_ncb);
regs.x.bx = FP_OFF( (void far *) &add_name_ncb);
int86x(0x5C, &regs, &regs, &sregs);

while (add_name_ncb.NCB_CMD_CPLT == 0xFF)
    ;

if (add_name_ncb.NCB_CMD_CPLT != 0)
    {
    printf("Error.  Could not add name %s\n",
            netbios_name);
    exit(1);
    }
```

To add a group name to the local name table, follow the preceding example and use ADD_GROUP_NAME instead of ADD_NAME.

NETBIOS Datagrams

If the preceding Add Name operation was completed successfully, NETBIOS assigns a name number and returns it in add_name_ncb.NCB_NUM. You use this name number to identify the local workstation when you issue datagram commands. The destination of a datagram is specified simply as a name (or a group name) in the NCB_CALLNAME field.

Datagrams can be sent point-to-point (Send Datagram; Receive Datagram) or broadcast throughout the network (Send Broadcast Datagram; Receive Broadcast Datagram). The following example sends a point-to-point datagram:

```
NCB send_ncb;
char destination[16];
char sql_message[] =
  "SELECT AIRCRAFT_ID, AGE WHERE AGE > 20";

strcpy(destination, "DATABASE_ENGINE");
memset(&send_ncb, 0, sizeof(NCB));
send_ncb.NCB_COMMAND    = SEND_DATAGRAM;
```

Listing continues

```
send_ncb.NCB_NUM        = add_name_ncb.NCB_NUM;
send_ncb.NCB_BUFFER_PTR = (void far *) sql_message;
send_ncb.NCB_LENGTH     = strlen(sql_message);
strcpy(send_ncb.NCB_CALLNAME, destination);
sregs.es  = FP_SEG( (void far *) &send_ncb);
regs.x.bx = FP_OFF( (void far *) &send_ncb);
int86x(0x5C, &regs, &regs, &sregs);

while (send_ncb.NCB_CMD_CPLT == 0xFF)
    ;

if (send_ncb.NCB_CMD_CPLT != 0)
    {
    printf("Error.  Could not send message\n");
    exit(1);
    }
```

Next you want to receive the reply message from "DATA-
BASE_ENGINE" (which, in this example, retrieved some information from
a relational database based on the query you specified). The Send Datagram command performed by the other workstation is exactly like the
preceding example, except that the destination is "BARRY" and the message itself contains the reply. To do the receive operation, you give NET-
BIOS an NCB that contains the name number assigned to the name
"BARRY" along with information about where to put the reply:

```
NCB recv_ncb;
struct
    {
    int  aircraft_count; /* number of entries (0-50) */
    int  aircraft_id[50];
    int  age[50];
    } sql_response;

memset(&recv_ncb, 0, sizeof(NCB));
recv_ncb.NCB_COMMAND    = RECEIVE_DATAGRAM;
recv_ncb.NCB_NUM        = add_name_ncb.NCB_NUM;
recv_ncb.NCB_BUFFER_PTR = (void far *) &sql_response;
recv_ncb.NCB_LENGTH     = sizeof(sql_response);

sregs.es  = FP_SEG( (void far *) &recv_ncb);
regs.x.bx = FP_OFF( (void far *) &recv_ncb);
int86x(0x5C, &regs, &regs, &sregs);
```

```
while (recv_ncb.NCB_CMD_CPLT == OxFF)
    ;
        /* Might want to put a timeout loop here, */
        /* in case there's no response at all.   */

if (recv_ncb.NCB_CMD_CPLT != 0)
    {
    printf("Error.  Could not receive reply.\n");
    exit(1);
    }
```

After you receive the reply "DATABASE_ENGINE" sent to "BARRY", no further communication is necessary. For example, you do not need to tell NETBIOS that you are finished talking to "DATABASE_ENGINE". (Also, for what it is worth, the preceding example assumes that you do not have more than 50 aging aircraft in your fleet!)

NETBIOS Sessions

Establishing a Session

If the dialog you designed is going to be longer than the preceding example, you might consider establishing a session between the two workstations. You create a session by having one workstation issue a Listen command and subsequently causing another workstation to issue a Call command. The Listen NCB that you construct and give to NETBIOS can specify "listen for a call from anyone" or, if your design dictates, "listen for a call from a specific name." In the first case, you put an asterisk (*) in the first byte of the NCB_CALLNAME field. When listening for a call from a specific name, that name goes into the NCB_CALLNAME field. The names (caller and who-can-call) must match on all 16 bytes; this is where the previously mentioned convention for padding the name with spaces comes in handy.

After the Listen command finishes on the first workstation, NETBIOS returns a Local Session Number (LSN) that you use in the Send and Receive NCBs to refer to that session. On the other workstation, NETBIOS also returns an LSN after the Call command finishes. Additionally, if you are listening for a call from anyone, the caller's name is returned in the NCB_CALLNAME field. At either workstation (listener or caller), you can begin sending and receiving messages just as soon as the Listen (or Call) command finishes.

When you fill out the Listen NCB, you specify NCB_CALLNAME as the name to listen for ($*$ = anyone) and NCB_NAME as the name in the local name table by which you want to be known. You also specify the time-out intervals that NETBIOS uses for the Send and Receive commands issued in this session. NCB_RTO is the Receive Time Out and NCB_STO is the Send Time Out. Both are expressed in 500-millisecond (1/2 second) intervals. If you use a value of 0 in either field, NETBIOS will not signal a time-out for that command.

The Listen command itself does not time out (use the wait option carefully!). A Call command will time out after a few retries; this indicates that the remote workstation has not issued a Listen command. The occurrence of a time-out during a Send operation aborts the session, but the occurrence of a time-out for a Receive operation merely invalidates that particular NCB, so you can reissue the Receive command if that suits your design.

You can code the Listen function like this:

```
/* - - - - - - - - - - - - - - - - - - - - - - - - - */
/*
 *     Build the 'listen' NCB and send it out
 *     across the network.  Set the POST address to
 *     point to a 'background' routine to handle a caller.
 */
void    net_listen_post(char *caller, char *us,
                        void interrupt (*post_function)(),
                        unsigned char rto, unsigned char sto)
        {
        memset(&listen_ncb, 0, sizeof(NCB));
        listen_ncb.NCB_COMMAND = LISTEN;
        strcpy(listen_ncb.NCB_NAME,     us);
        strcpy(listen_ncb.NCB_CALLNAME, caller);
        listen_ncb.POST_FUNC = post_function;
        listen_ncb.NCB_RTO = rto;
        listen_ncb.NCB_STO = sto;
        sregs.es  = FP_SEG( (void far *) &listen_ncb);
        regs.x.bx = FP_OFF( (void far *) &listen_ncb);
        int86x(0x5C, &regs, &regs, &sregs);
        }
```

Then, to invoke this `net_listen_post()` function, you can code the following:

```
net_listen-
_post("*", "DATABASE_ENGINE", handle_call, 20, 20);
```

In this function call, `handle_call()` is a POST routine (discussed earlier), `..DATABASE_ENGINE..` is the name that was added to the local name table to identify that workstation, `*` says "listen for a call from anyone," and the `rto` and `sto` values of 20 tell NETBIOS to wait as long as 10 seconds for each Send or Receive operation before timing out.

Similarly, the calling workstation ("BARRY") constructs and issues an NCB as follows:

```
/* - - - - - - - - - - - - - - - - - - - - - - - - - */
/*
 *  "Call" another workstation.
 */
void    net_call(char *who, char *us,
                unsigned char rto, unsigned char sto)
        {
        memset(&call_ncb, 0, sizeof(NCB));
        call_ncb.NCB_COMMAND = CALL;
        memcpy(call_ncb.NCB_NAME,     us,  16);
        strcpy(call_ncb.NCB_CALLNAME, who);
        call_ncb.NCB_RTO = rto;
        call_ncb.NCB_STO = sto;
        sregs.es  = FP_SEG( (void far *) &call_ncb);
        regs.x.bx = FP_OFF( (void far *) &call_ncb);
        int86x(0x5C, &regs, &regs, &sregs);
        }
```

The call to this function, elsewhere in the program, is coded as follows:

```
net_call("DATABASE_ENGINE", "BARRY           ", 20, 20);

while (call_ncb.NCB_CMD_CPLT == 0xFF)
     ;

if (call_ncb.NCB_CMD_CPLT == 0)
     local_session_number = call_ncb.NCB_LSN;
else
     abort("Call was unsuccessful.");
```

Sending and Receiving Session Messages

While a session is under way, you can issue Send and Receive commands (NCBs) to transfer information back and forth. In fact, you have a choice of NETBIOS commands—Send, Chain Send, or Send No ACK—for sending data. The Send command can be used for data packets as long as

65,535 bytes, and the Chain Send command concatenates two Send buffers, which you specify, into a message that can be as long as 131,070 bytes. The Send No ACK command is coded just like a Send command, but functions much like a datagram; no (internal) acknowledgement is sent between NETBIOS on the two workstations. This section discusses the basic Send and Receive commands. Refer to the next part of this book, "Reference," for descriptions of the Chain Send and Send No ACK commands.

To construct an NCB that causes data to be sent to the other session partner, you fill in the NCB_LSN field to identify the session, and you fill in the NCB_BUFFER_PTR and NCB_LENGTH fields to describe the data message you want sent. The following is an example of a function that performs a NETBIOS Send:

```
/* - - - - - - - - - - - - - - - - - - - - - - - - - */
/*
 *      Build the 'send' NCB and send it out
 *      across the network.
 *
 */
void     net_send(unsigned char lsn,
                  void far *packet_ptr, int packet_len)
         {
         memset(&send_ncb, 0, sizeof(NCB));
         send_ncb.NCB_COMMAND = SEND;
         send_ncb.NCB_LSN = lsn;
         send_ncb.NCB_LENGTH = packet_len;
         send_ncb.NCB_BUFFER_PTR = packet_ptr;
         sregs.es  = FP_SEG( (void far *) &send_ncb);
         regs.x.bx = FP_OFF( (void far *) &send_ncb);
         int86x(0x5C, &regs, &regs, &sregs);
         }
```

You might call the net_send() function with the following parameter values:

```
net_send(local_session_number,
         &aircraft_age_rcd, sizeof(struct AGE_RECORD));
while (send_ncb.NCB_CMD_CPLT == 0xFF)
     ;
```

The Receive command also uses the LSN to refer to the session. The following example shows how you can specify a POST routine when the Receive is issued:

```
/* - - - - - - - - - - - - - - - - - - - - - - - - */
/*
 *     Build the 'receive' NCB and send it out
 *     across the network.  When the operation completes,
 *     let NETBIOS call the POST routine to handle it.
 */
void    net_receive_post(unsigned char lsn,
                             void interrupt (*post_function)(),
                             void *packet_ptr, int packet_len)
        {
        memset(&receive_ncb, 0, sizeof(NCB));
        receive_ncb.NCB_COMMAND = RECEIVE;
        receive_ncb.NCB_LSN = lsn;
        receive_ncb.NCB_LENGTH = packet_len;
        receive_ncb.NCB_BUFFER_PTR = packet_ptr;
        receive_ncb.POST_FUNC = post_function;
        sregs.es  = FP_SEG( (void far *) &receive_ncb);
        regs.x.bx = FP_OFF( (void far *) &receive_ncb);
        int86x(0x5C, &regs, &regs, &sregs);
        }
```

At the point in your program at which you want to let NETBIOS know that you are ready to receive some data, you invoke net_receive_post() as follows:

```
net_receive_post(local_session_number,
     post_handler, &input_buff, sizeof(input_buff));
```

Terminating the Session

When the exchange of data messages is complete, both session partners issue a Hang Up command to end the session. Before issuing a Hang Up command, your program should make sure that any pending operations are canceled with the Cancel command. To cancel an outstanding NCB, you put the address of the NCB into another NCB's NCB_BUFFER_PTR field as a far pointer and issue the Cancel:

```
/* - - - - - - - - - - - - - - - - - - - - - - - - */
/*
 *     Build the 'cancel' NCB and send it out
 *     across the network.
 *
 */
void    net_cancel(NCB *np)
```

Listing continues

```
        {
        memset(&cancel_ncb, 0, sizeof(NCB));
        cancel_ncb.NCB_COMMAND = CANCEL;
        cancel_ncb.NCB_BUFFER_PTR = np;
        sregs.es  = FP_SEG( (void far *) &cancel_ncb);
        regs.x.bx = FP_OFF( (void far *) &cancel_ncb);
        int86x(0x5C, &regs, &regs, &sregs);
        }
```

The following is a specific example of how to use net_cancel() to cancel
a pending Listen command:

```
net_cancel(&listen_ncb);
while (cancel_ncb.NCB_CMD_CPLT == 0xFF)
    ;
```

To hang up on a session, all you need to specify is the LSN. The Hang
Up command that both session partners should execute looks like this:

```
/* - - - - - - - - - - - - - - - - - - - - - - - - - */
/*
 *      Build and issue a 'hang up' NCB
 *
 */
void    net_hangup(unsigned char lsn)
        {
        memset(&hangup_ncb, 0, sizeof(NCB));
        hangup_ncb.NCB_COMMAND = HANG_UP;
        hangup_ncb.NCB_LSN = lsn;
        sregs.es  = FP_SEG( (void far *) &hangup_ncb);
        regs.x.bx = FP_OFF( (void far *) &hangup_ncb);
        int86x(0x5C, &regs, &regs, &sregs);
        }
```

Deleting Names

When you are done sending and receiving datagrams, or after you have
closed a session by canceling any outstanding commands and performing
a Hang Up, you should delete any names you added to the local name
table. Not only does deleting names keep things neat and tidy, it also prevents users from encountering the error Duplicate Name if they run your
software again without rebooting the workstation (because the name

remains in the local name table). The following is an example of Delete Name:

```
/* - - - - - - - - - - - - - - - - - - - - - - - - */
/*
 *     Build the 'delete_name' NCB and issue it
 *
 */
void    net_delete_name(char *name)
        {
        memset(&delete_name_ncb, 0, sizeof(NCB));
        delete_name_ncb.NCB_COMMAND = DELETE_NAME;
        strcpy(delete_name_ncb.NCB_NAME, name);
        sregs.es  = FP_SEG((void far *) &delete_name_ncb);
        regs.x.bx = FP_OFF((void far *) &delete_name_ncb);
        int86x(0x5C, &regs, &regs, &sregs);
        }
```

Make sure that the NCB_NAME and NCB_CALLNAME fields are properly set up (using all 16 bytes) so that an exact match for the name you are trying to delete is found in the local name table.

Determining Session Status

The Session Status command returns information about all of the sessions for a particular name in the local name table, or for all names in the local name table. Session Status information is not available for remote sessions. You can use this command to find out

❏ The name number assigned to the name

❏ The number of sessions associated with the name

❏ The number of Receive Datagram and Receive Broadcast Datagram commands that are outstanding

❏ The number of Receive Any commands that are outstanding
The remainder of the data is a series of entries, one per session. The "number of sessions associated with this name" field tells you how many entries are filled. The remaining fields are

❏ The session's LSN

❏ The current state of the session (see table 5.5)

❏ The local session partner's name

❏ The remote session partner's name

❏ The number of Receive commands outstanding

❏ The number of Send and Chain Send commands outstanding

Table 5.5. *Session Status codes.*

State	Meaning
1	Listen pending
2	Call pending
3	Session established
4	Hang Up pending
5	Hang Up complete
6	Session ended abnormally

When you want to issue a Session Status command, set up an NCB whose NCB_BUFFER_PTR points to the following STATUS_INFO structure, and put sizeof(STATUS_INFO) in the NCB_LENGTH field. Specify the name you are interested in by placing it in the NCB_NAME field, or put an asterisk in the first byte of NCB_NAME to obtain session status for all local name table items. The following STATUS_INFO structure allows as many as 40 sessions, but you can adjust the number of sessions as necessary for your application.

```
typedef struct {
        unsigned char   name_num;
        unsigned char   session_count;
        unsigned char   datagram_count;
        unsigned char   recv_any_count;
        struct {
            unsigned char   lsn;
            unsigned char   state;
            char            local_name[16];
            char            remote_name[16];
            unsigned char   recv_count;
            unsigned char   send_count;
            } session_data[40];
        }
        STATUS_INFO;

STATUS_INFO     session_status_info;
```

Determining Adapter Status

The Adapter Status command, unlike the Session Status command, can be used to obtain information about a remote copy of NETBIOS as well as about the local copy in the requesting workstation. The following three categories of information are returned in a structure pointed to by NCB_BUFFER_PTR:

❏ The six bytes of network adapter ID, which represent the unique address of that particular network adapter card

❏ A set of statistics showing traffic and error counts

❏ A copy of the name table from the remote (or local) workstation, including status information about each name

One thing to watch out for is that the implementations of NETBIOS from different manufacturers can define the information differently, especially in the traffic- and error-count category. The following Adapter Status layout shows the information returned by the IBM NETBIOS device driver, DXMT0MOD.SYS. I have given suggestive names to the fields, but a few of them need further explanation:

The `release_level` field identifies the major version number of the NETBIOS software:

0x00 = version 1.X, 0x02 = version 2.X, and 0x03 = version 3.X

The definition of the `type_of_adapter` field depends on the NETBIOS version. For NETBIOS 1.X, it is always 0xFF. For later versions, this field contains 0xFE if the adapter is a PC Network interface card and 0xFF if it is a Token Ring card.

The `old_or_new_parameters` field contains two subfields: the second nibble (half byte) indicates the minor version of NETBIOS, and the first nibble indicates whether NETBIOS was started with old or new parameters. For NETBIOS version 1.X, the first nibble is always 0. For later versions, the nibble contains 1 if NETBIOS was started with old parameters and 2 if started with new parameters.

The `exhausted_resource_count` field contains the number of times data was lost because NETBIOS ran out of buffers. All the count fields roll over from 0xFF..FF to 0 except for `exhausted_resource_count`.

The last two bytes of each name table entry express the name number assigned to the name (`tbl_name_number`) and the status of the name (`tbl_name_status`). The `tbl_name_status` byte is encoded as follows:

```
G    x x x x    S S S
```

where G, the first bit, is a 1 if the name is a group name and 0 for a unique name. The xxxx bits are reserved for NETBIOS to use and are not necessarily 0. The S S S bits indicate the status of the name. Table 5.6 lists the status values.

Table 5.6. *NETBIOS SSS bits.*

SSS Bits	Meaning
000	Name registration in progress
100	Registered name
101	Deregistered name (a Delete Name was issued, but the name still has active sessions)
110	Detected duplicate name
111	Duplicate name, deregistration pending

The following is the layout of the Adapter Status buffer area:

```
typedef struct {
        unsigned char    card_id[6];
        unsigned char    release_level;
        unsigned char    reserved1;
        unsigned char    type_of_adapter;
        unsigned char    old_or_new_parameters;
        unsigned int     reporting_period_minutes;
        unsigned int     frame_reject_recvd_count;
        unsigned int     frame_reject_sent_count;
        unsigned int     recvd_data_frame_errors;
        unsigned int     unsuccessful_transmissions;
        unsigned long    good_transmissions;
        unsigned long    good_receptions;
        unsigned int     retransmissions;
        unsigned int     exhausted_resource_count;
        unsigned int     t1_timer_expired_count;
        unsigned int     ti_timer_expired_count;
        char             reserved2[4];
        unsigned int     available_ncbs;
        unsigned int     max_ncbs_configured;
        unsigned int     max_ncbs_possible;
        unsigned int     buffer_or_station_busy_count;
        unsigned int     max_datagram_size;
        unsigned int     pending_sessions;
```

```
      unsigned int    max_sessions_configured;
      unsigned int    max_sessions_possible;
      unsigned int    max_frame_size;
      int             name_count;
      struct {
          char            tbl_name[16];
          unsigned char   tbl_name_number;
          unsigned char   tbl_name_status;
          } name_table[20];
      }
      ADAPTER_DATA;

ADAPTER_DATA    adapter_data;
```

The NCB that you construct for an Adapter Status command must have the NCB_CALLNAME, NCB_BUFFER_PTR, and NCB_LENGTH fields set, as shown in this example:

```
/* - - - - - - - - - - - - - - - - - - - - - - - - */
/* Build and issue an 'adapter status' command
 * for the workstation named "DATABASE_ENGINE"
 */
    memset(&status_ncb, 0, sizeof(NCB));

    status_ncb.NCB_COMMAND = STATUS;
    strcpy(status_ncb.NCB_CALLNAME, "DATABASE_ENGINE");
    status_ncb.NCB_LENGTH = sizeof(ADAPTER_DATA);
    status_ncb.NCB_BUFFER_PTR = (void far *) &adapter_data;

    sregs.es  = FP_SEG((void far *) &status_ncb);
    regs.x.bx = FP_OFF((void far *) &status_ncb);
    int86x(0x5C, &regs, &regs, &sregs);
```

Resetting the Adapter

NETBIOS processes the Reset Adapter command by

❏ Deleting all names from the local name table (the permanent node name is not deleted, of course)

❏ Aborting all active sessions

❏ Discarding any outstanding NCBs

If you put a nonzero value in the NCB_LSN field, that value is used as the new maximum number of sessions. A value of 0 tells NETBIOS to use the default (usually 6). If you put a nonzero value in the NCB_NUM field, NETBIOS uses that value as the new maximum number of NCBs that can be outstanding at any one time. A value of 0 tells NETBIOS to use the default, which is usually 12.

You should avoid using the Reset Adapter command in such NETBIOS-based environments as the IBM PC LAN Program. Reset deletes not only the names and sessions belonging to your application but also the PCLP names and sessions. This effectively disables PCLP and kicks you off the network.

The layout for a Reset Adapter command is as follows:

```
/* the Reset Adapter command */

    memset(&reset_ncb, 0, sizeof(NCB));

    reset_ncb.NCB_COMMAND = RESET;
    reset_ncb.NCB_LSN = max_sessions;
    reset_ncb.NCB_NUM = max_ncbs;

    sregs.es  = FP_SEG((void far *) &reset_ncb);
    regs.x.bx = FP_OFF((void far *) &reset_ncb);
    int86x(0x5C, &regs, &regs, &sregs);
```

Summary

This chapter explained how to program NETBIOS applications. You know how a Network Control Block is constructed and what it is used for. You are now familiar with the NETBIOS commands for adding and deleting names, sending and receiving datagrams, creating sessions, and sending and receiving data messages within a session. You have also picked up a useful set of design guidelines for PC-to-PC communications.

Next, we turn to the programming techniques you use on NetWare LANs to do IPX and SPX peer-level communications.

IPX and SPX Programming

In addition to NETBIOS, Novell NetWare offers the IPX and SPX protocols for PC-to-PC communications. Why would you code your program to use IPX or SPX if NETBIOS is available on Novell networks as well as on IBM networks? You will probably want to use IPX or SPX rather than NETBIOS for two reasons: speed and memory. Novell's NETBIOS software layer translates your NETBIOS function calls into IPX functions; you can "avoid the middleman" by coding your program to call IPX directly. IPX is faster than NETBIOS, and, if NETBIOS is not loaded, you have between 20K and 25K more memory for your application.

Programming IPX

IPX is a datagram service available on NetWare LANs. The previous chapter on NETBIOS showed how NETBIOS commands relate to disk file I/O options; table 6.1 compares IPX functions and equivalent PC DOS operations.

Table 6.1. *File I/O compared to IPX functions.*

File Operation	IPX Equivalent
Open	Open Socket
Read	Listen for Packet
Write	Send Packet
Seek	<none>
Close	Close Socket

Table 6.2 lists the sequence of events you would use to send and receive IPX packets.

Table 6.2. *Data packet sequence for IPX.*

Workstation A	Workstation B
1. Open Socket	1. Open Socket
2. Get network address of B	2. Get network address of A
3. Send packet to B	3. Receive data packet
4. Receive data packet	4. Send packet to A
5. Close Socket	5. Close Socket

IPX is a datagram-based protocol. When you choose to use IPX to send and receive data packets, make sure that you design a scheme for verifying that the packets are delivered to the destination and received in the correct sequence. If you want to use a protocol that handles these details for you, use the SPX protocol discussed in the next section.

IPX Installed Test

The test for the presence of IPX uses Interrupt 2F (hex), *Multiplex Interrupt*. Put 0x7A, the multiplex number, in the AH register and put 0 in the AL register, then do the Interrupt 2F. If IPX is installed, the Interrupt 2F call returns 0xFF in the AL register. As a side effect, the entry point for IPX (and SPX) is returned in the ES:DI register pair as a far pointer to a function. The following ipx_installed() function shows the technique. The function returns −1 if IPX is not installed, 1 if it is. The function also sets up a far function pointer, *ipx_spx, that you can use to call IPX:

```
void far    (*ipx_spx)(void);

int     ipx_installed(void)
        {
        union REGS      regs;
        struct SREGS    sregs;

        regs.x.ax = 0x7a00;
        int86x(0x2f, &regs, &regs, &sregs);
        if (regs.h.al != 0xff)
            return -1;

        ipx_spx = MK_FP(sregs.es, regs.x.di);
        return 1;
        }
```

Invoking IPX

There are two ways to call IPX, and there are pros and cons to both methods. To use the first method, you set up the CPU registers as specified for a particular IPX function. You then call IPX using the ipx_spx function pointer obtained during the installed test. This first method is easy to do in Turbo C, as long as you are careful about directly accessing CPU registers.

The following examples of IPX calls show how to invoke IPX. For now, study the part of the code that calls IPX; the functions being performed and the actual contents of the CPU registers are not important now.

```
/* example IPX call in Turbo C */

void    ipx_listen_for_packet(struct ECB *ecb_ptr)
        {
        _ES = FP_SEG( (void far *) ecb_ptr);
        _SI = FP_OFF( (void far *) ecb_ptr);
        _BX = 0x0004;
        ipx_spx();       /* from the installed test */
        }
```

The second method uses Interrupt 7A (hex) to call IPX. This interrupt is a secondary entry point into IPX. Lattice and Microsoft C compiler users can use this second method:

```
/* example call to IPX (Int 7A) in Microsoft C */
void    close_socket(unsigned socket)
        {
        union REGS regs;

        regs.x.bx = 0x0001;
        regs.x.dx = socket;
        int86(0x7A, &regs, &regs);
        }
```

Interrupt 7A has one major drawback—it is also used by the IBM 3270 Emulator product, and by a few other software products. Unless you can be absolutely certain that your application will not be used concurrently with another product that uses Interrupt 7A, you should avoid using the Interrupt 7A entry point into IPX.

Lattice C and Microsoft C users can benefit from the following call_ipx() function. This short, assembler "helper" routine takes a single parameter—a pointer to a structure containing register values to be passed to IPX. call_ipx() puts the indicated values in the CPU register, calls IPX, and returns the values of the AX and DX registers in the same structure.

Before you look at the assembler code, study this typical calling sequence:

```
/* first, the layout of the structure containing */
/* the registers                                  */

struct IPX_REGS {
        unsigned   ax_reg;
        unsigned   bx_reg;
        unsigned   dx_reg;
        unsigned   si_reg;
        unsigned   di_reg;
        unsigned   es_reg;
        };

/* next, the prototype for the function */

extern void far call_ipx(struct IPX_REGS far *ipx_regs);


/* now use 'call_ipx' to receive a packet */

void    ipx_listen_for_packet(struct ECB far *ecb_ptr)
        {
        struct  IPX_REGS ipx_regs;
```

```
                ipx_regs.bx_reg = 0x04;
                ipx_regs.si_reg = FP_OFF(ecb_ptr);
                ipx_regs.es_reg = FP_SEG(ecb_ptr);
                call_ipx (&ipx_regs);
                }
```

The assembler routine itself follows:

```
; - - - - - - - - - - - - - - - - - - - - - - - - - - -
;        call_ipx()
;
;  Assembler function to set up the CPU registers
;  and call IPX:
;
;        1. Get IPX entry point, if not already set.
;        2. Load up the registers (AX, BX, DS, SI, DI, ES).
;        3. Call IPX via the IPX entry point (far call).
;        4. Return the AX and DX registers.
;
;  Code these statements early in your program:
;
;     struct IPX_REGS {
;         unsigned  ax_reg;
;         unsigned  bx_reg;
;         unsigned  dx_reg;
;         unsigned  si_reg;
;         unsigned  di_reg;
;         unsigned  es_reg;
;         };
;
;     extern void far call_ipx(struct IPX_REGS far *ipx_regs);
;
;
; - - - - - - - - - - - - - - - - - - - - - - - - - - -


;  Change the following line to match the memory model
;  you're using:

        .model small

        public _call_ipx

;  Symbolically map the stack area
```

Listing continues

Listing continued

```
parms   struc
sav_bp  dw      ?
ret_ip  dw      ?
ret_cs  dw      ?
reg_ofs dw      ?
reg_seg dw      ?
parms   ends


; Map the C structure in which the registers are passed

ipx_regs struc
ax_reg  dw      ?
bx_reg  dw      ?
dx_reg  dw      ?
si_reg  dw      ?
di_reg  dw      ?
es_reg  dw      ?
ipx_regs ends

        .data
ipx_epa dd      0


     .code
_call_ipx proc    far
        push    bp
        mov     bp, sp

;  See if IPX Entry Point has been established yet

        cmp     word ptr ipx_epa, 0
        jne     set_up_regs

; Call Interrupt 2F to get entry point of IPX

        mov     ax, 7A00h
        int     2Fh
        cmp     al, 0FFh

; Just exit if IPX is not present (shouldn't be true!)

        jne     call_ipx_exit
```

```
;  Set up far pointer to IPX

        mov     word ptr ipx_epa+2, es
        mov     word ptr ipx_epa, di

set_up_regs:
        push    ds
        mov     ds, [bp].reg_seg
        mov     bx, [bp].reg_ofs

        mov     es, ds:[bx].es_reg
        mov     di, ds:[bx].di_reg
        mov     si, ds:[bx].si_reg
        mov     dx, ds:[bx].dx_reg
        mov     ax, ds:[bx].ax_reg
        mov     bx, ds:[bx].bx_reg

        pop     ds
        call    far ptr ipx_epa

;  Now hand back AX and DX

        push    ds
        mov     ds, [bp].reg_seg
        mov     bx, [bp].reg_ofs

        mov     ds:[bx].ax_reg, ax
        mov     ds:[bx].dx_reg, dx
        pop     ds

call_ipx_exit:
        pop     bp
    ret

_call_ipx endp
    end
```

Event Control Block

An Event Control Block (ECB), like the NETBIOS Network Control Block, is not transmitted across the network. Instead, the ECB merely serves as a set of directions to IPX and as an IPX storage area for the current operation. You should set up a separate ECB for each IPX operation you plan to do in your application. Chapter 3, "PC-to-PC Communications Concepts," describes the fields in the ECB. The following code shows the layout of an ECB:

```
struct ECB
    {
    void far        *link_address;
    void far        (*event_service_routine)(void);
    unsigned char   in_use;
    unsigned char   completion_code;
    unsigned int    socket_number;
    unsigned char   ipx_workspace [4];
    unsigned char   driver_workspace  [12];
    unsigned char   immediate_address [ 6];
    unsigned int    packet_count;
    struct {
        void far    *address;
        unsigned int length;
        } packet [2];
    };
```

The event_service_routine (ESR) field, which this chapter discusses shortly, is a pointer to a function. The in_use flag is nonzero while IPX is processing a particular event in the background. You can poll for the completion of an event by looping until in_use becomes 0. When an event is completed, completion_code holds the return code from IPX for that event. You use socket_number to identify a socket you have opened and through which you are sending packets. For a Send Packet operation, you set the immediate_address field to the network address of a bridge the packet must cross. The last items in the ECB, packet_count and the packet[].address and packet[].length fields, describe the data areas that IPX gathers into a single data packet or that IPX uses to break apart a received packet as the protocol hands the data back to your software.

IPX Packet Header

The first 30 bytes of each IPX data packet that travels across the network contain an IPX packet header. IPX sets and manages some of the fields. The fields you are responsible for are packet_type (set it to a value of 4) and the destination address fields dest_network_number, dest_network_node, and dest_network_socket. Destination address is discussed shortly.

```
struct IPXHEADER
    {
    unsigned int      checksum;
    unsigned int      length;
    unsigned char     transport_control;
    unsigned char     packet_type;
    unsigned char     dest_network_number [4];
    unsigned char     dest_network_node   [6];
    unsigned int      dest_network_socket;
    unsigned char     source_network_number [4];
    unsigned char     source_network_node   [6];
    unsigned int      source_network_socket;
    };
```

IPX Commands

When you call IPX, you put a value in the BX register that identifies the function you want IPX to do. If an ECB is to be passed to IPX, you place a far pointer to the ECB in the ES:SI register pair. The following code lists the IPX functions, which the "Reference" section describes in more detail:

```
#define ipx_open_socket              0x00
#define ipx_close_socket             0x01
#define ipx_get_local_target         0x02
#define ipx_send_packet              0x03
#define ipx_listen_for_packet        0x04
#define ipx_schedule_ipx_event       0x05
#define ipx_cancel_event             0x06
#define ipx_get_interval_marker      0x08
#define ipx_get_internetwork_address 0x09
#define ipx_relinquish_control       0x0A
#define ipx_disconnect_from_target   0x0B
```

Event Service Routines

An Event Service Routine (ESR) for IPX works much the same way as does a POST routine for NETBIOS. When the event finishes, IPX calls the ESR that you coded. If you specify a NULL pointer in the event_service_routine function pointer in the ECB, IPX does not invoke an ESR at the completion of the event. When you take this no-ESR approach, it is important that you give IPX a chance to "breathe" while you poll for the completion of the operation. The following example is a function that invokes the relinquish_control service in IPX:

```
/* example of ipx_relinquish_control in Turbo C */

void    ipx_relinquish_control(void)
        {
        _BX = 0x000A;
        ipx_spx();
        }
```

This code shows how to poll for the completion of an IPX operation. It uses the function example just coded.

```
/* assume that a no-ESR IPX operation is started here */

while (receive_ecb.in_use)          /* poll */
        ipx_relinquish_control();
```

On the other hand, when you do specify an ESR in the associated ECB, your function is called with the following conditions true:

❑ Interrupts are disabled (masked off).

❑ The routine has been invoked with a far call.

❑ A far pointer to the ECB is in the ES:SI register pair.

❑ The CPU registers have been saved.

❑ The DS register does not necessarily point to your program's data area.

❑ The ECB's in_use flag has been reset to 0.

❑ Doing DOS function calls (disk file I/O, for instance) may not be safe.

An ESR is another case in which Turbo C is convenient, because Turbo C lets you directly access CPU registers inside the ESR. You can set the DS register to point to your program's data area, and you can make a far pointer to the just-completed ECB from the ES:SI register pair, as shown in this routine:

```
/* an Event Service Routine in Turbo C */

struct  ECB far *completed_ecb_ptr;
int     event_completed_flag;
```

```
void    far receive_esr(void)
        {
        _AX = _ES;
        _DS = _AX;

        completed_ecb_ptr = MK_FP(_ES, _SI);
        event_completed_flag = TRUE;
        }
```

If you use Microsoft C or Lattice C, you will want to call the following assembler function as the first statement in your ESR. The function sets up the DS register (by copying the ES register) and returns the ES:SI register pair in the parameter list:

```
; - - - - - - - - - - - - - - - - - - - - - - - - - - - - - -
;       esr_set()
;
;  Assembler function that sets DS equal to ES and returns
;  ES and SI.
;
;  extern void far esr_set(unsigned far *es_reg,
;                          unsigned far *si_reg);
;
; - - - - - - - - - - - - - - - - - - - - - - - - - - - - - -
;
;  A typical calling sequence:
;
;unsigned es_reg, si_reg;
;struct   ECB far *completed_ecb_ptr;
;
;void far receive_esr(void)
;       {
;       esr_set(&es_reg, &si_reg);
;       completed_ecb_ptr = MK_FP(es_reg, si_reg);
;       }
;
; - - - - - - - - - - - - - - - - - - - - - - - - - - - - - -

;  Change the following line to match the memory model
;  you're using:

        .model small

        public _esr_set
```

Listing continues

Listing continued

```
;  Symbolically map the stack area

parms    struc
sav_bp   dw      ?
ret_ip   dw      ?
ret_cs   dw      ?
es_ofs   dw      ?
es_seg   dw      ?
si_ofs   dw      ?
si_seg   dw      ?
parms    ends


        .code
_esr_set proc     far
        push    bp
        mov     bp, sp

        mov     ds, [bp].es_seg
        mov     bx, [bp].es_ofs
        mov     ds:[bx], es
        mov     ds, [bp].si_seg
        mov     bx, [bp].si_ofs
        mov     ds:[bx], si

        push    es
        pop     ds

        pop     bp
        ret

_esr_set endp
     end
```

Sockets

One of the first things you want to do in a program that uses IPX is open a socket (or perhaps more than one socket). You send a data packet through a socket to its destination; you receive a data packet through a socket. Chapter 3, "PC-to-PC Communications Concepts," mentioned some guidelines and cautions for assigning socket numbers. You must avoid using the same socket numbers that NetWare is using. You also need to assign them in such a way that your application can easily determine the destination socket number when it wants to send a data packet.

Another consideration is that NetWare defines the two bytes of socket number "backward"; NetWare expects to see the most significant byte first (leftmost), which is contrary to the way the PC's CPU chip usually stores numbers. Some creative programmers have contrived to sidestep this issue altogether by using socket numbers such as 0x4545 or 0x6767. The two bytes of such a number have the same value, so it does not matter which comes first.

A socket can be short-lived or long-lived. You can close either kind of socket with a call to `ipx_close_socket`. A short-lived socket will also be closed automatically when a program terminates. If you write Terminate and Stay Resident programs, you should use long-lived sockets.

To open a socket, put the socket number in the DX register and set AL according to the longevity you want the socket to have. Set AL to 0 for a short-lived socket; set AL to 0xFF for a long-lived socket. The function code for `open_socket` is 0, which goes into the BX register. This code makes use of Turbo C's direct access to CPU registers:

```
/* opening a socket in Turbo C */

int     open_socket(unsigned int socket)
        {
        _DX = socket;
        _BX = 0x0000;
        _AL = 0x00;         /* short-lived */
        ipx_spx();
        _AH = 0;
        return _AX;
        }
```

The translation between the IPX calling conventions for both Turbo C (just shown for `open_socket`) and the `call_ipx()` ASM function (listed earlier for Microsoft C programmers) should be readily apparent. Both have conventions that are simply different ways of loading up the registers. For example, compare the following call to the assembler `call_ipx()` function with the preceding Turbo C function for opening a socket:

```
/* open_socket, using the call_ipx ASM function */

void    open_socket(unsigned int socket)
        {
        struct  IPX_REGS ipx_regs;
```

Listing continues

Listing *continued*

```
        ipx_regs.dx_reg = socket;
        ipx_regs.bx_reg = 0;
        ipx_regs.ax_reg = 0;
        call_ipx (&ipx_regs);
        }
```

To close a socket, put its number in the DX register and call IPX with a function code of 1 in BX. If a Send or Receive IPX operation is outstanding when you close the socket, IPX cancels that operation. A function that closes a socket:

```
void    close_socket(unsigned int socket)
        {
        _BX = 0x0001;
        _DX = socket;
        ipx_spx();
        }
```

Destination Address

Chapter 3, "PC-to-PC Communications Concepts," listed three things you must know to send a data packet to another workstation. The destination of a packet is made up of *network number*, *node address*, and *socket number*. Socket number is easy; you assign values yourself, as was previously mentioned. However, network number and node address take a little more work. Recall from Chapter 3 that network number identifies each segment of a multiserver NetWare LAN, and node address identifies a particular workstation. Suppose, however, that all you know is the user ID logged on at the remote workstation; how do you turn user ID into a network number and node address?

Each user or workstation is assigned a connection number at login time. To make the user ID a useful destination address, you first ask NetWare to give you the connection number for a particular user ID. You then ask NetWare for the network number and node address associated with that connection number. As a simple example to start with, the following NetWare function call obtains the connection number of the *local* user or workstation. You can code

```
my_connect_num = get_local_connection_num();
```

to invoke the following function:

```
/* get connection number for local workstation */
```

```
unsigned char get_local_connection_num(void)
        {
        _AH = 0xDC;
        geninterrupt(0x21);
        return _AL;
        }
```

Except through careful system administration, there is no way to guarantee that a user will not be logged on at multiple workstations on a NetWare LAN. For point-to-point message sending, you can usually disregard any logins but the first. Given a particular user ID, the following function returns the first connection number for that user ID; you can call the function as follows:

```
unsigned    dest_connect_num;

dest_connect_num = get_1st_connection_num ("BARRY");
if (dest_connect_num == 0)
    printf("Not logged on.\n");
```

The following code is the get_1st_connection_num() function itself. It uses the NetWare function *GetObjectConnectionNumbers*, which returns an array of from 0 to 100 connection numbers for the given user ID. Incidentally, Novell classifies *GetObjectConnectionNumbers* as a Connection Service, not as an IPX function.

```
unsigned int    get_1st_connection_num (char *who)
        {
        union REGS      regs;
        struct SREGS    sregs;

        struct {
                unsigned int    len;
                unsigned char   buffer_type;
                unsigned int    object_type;
                unsigned char   name_len;
                unsigned char   name [47];
                } request_buffer;

        struct {
                unsigned int    len;
                unsigned char   number_connections;
                unsigned char   connection_num [100];
                } reply_buffer;
```

Listing continues

Listing *continued*

```
        regs.h.ah = 0xe3;

        request_buffer.len = 51;
        request_buffer.buffer_type = 0x15;
        request_buffer.object_type = 0x0100;
        request_buffer.name_len    = (unsigned char) strlen(who);
        strcpy(request_buffer.name, who);

        reply_buffer.len = 101;

        regs.x.si = FP_OFF( (void far *) &request_buffer);
        sregs.ds  = FP_SEG( (void far *) &request_buffer);
        regs.x.di = FP_OFF( (void far *) &reply_buffer);
        sregs.es  = FP_SEG( (void far *) &reply_buffer);

        int86x(0x21, &regs, &regs, &sregs);

        if (regs.h.al != 0) return 0;
        if (reply_buffer.number_connections == 0) return 0;

        regs.h.ah = 0;
        regs.h.al = reply_buffer.connection_num[0];
        return regs.x.ax;
        }
```

Now that you have obtained the connection number of the user ID you want to send packets to, the final step is the translation of connection number into network number and node address. The following function is a call to the NetWare function *GetInternetAddress*, which Novell also classifies as a Connection Service. The call returns a connection's network number and node address, as well as the socket number through which the connection communicates with the file server. You are interested in the first two items, of course, but the returned socket number is one you should avoid using!

```
int     get_internet_address(unsigned char connection_number,
                            unsigned char *network_number,
                            unsigned char *physical_node)
        {
        union REGS      regs;
        struct SREGS    sregs;
```

```
                    struct  {
                            unsigned int     len;
                            unsigned char    buffer_type;
                            unsigned char    connection_number;
                            } request_buffer;

                    struct  {
                            unsigned int     len;
                            unsigned char    network_number [4];
                            unsigned char    physical_node  [6];
                            unsigned int     server_socket;
                            } reply_buffer;

             regs.h.ah = 0xe3;
             request_buffer.len = 2;
             request_buffer.buffer_type = 0x13;
             request_buffer.connection_number = connection_number;

             reply_buffer.len = 12;

             regs.x.si = FP_OFF( (void far *) &request_buffer);
             sregs.ds  = FP_SEG( (void far *) &request_buffer);
             regs.x.di = FP_OFF( (void far *) &reply_buffer);
             sregs.es  = FP_SEG( (void far *) &reply_buffer);
             int86x(0x21, &regs, &regs, &sregs);

             memcpy(network_number, reply_buffer.network_number, 4);
             memcpy(physical_node,  reply_buffer.physical_node,  6);
             regs.h.ah = 0;
             return regs.x.ax;
             }
```

Before I leave the topic of destination addresses, user IDs, and connection numbers, I want to show you an example of how to obtain the user ID for a given connection number. This function is sort of the reverse of the preceding procedure for turning a user ID into a connection number/destination. Suppose, for instance, that you need to find out the user ID logged in at the current (local) workstation. You first call get_local_connection_num() (shown earlier) to get the connection number of this workstation. Then you call the following get_user_id() function:

```
unsigned char   my_connect_num;
unsigned char   my_user_id[48];

my_connect_num = get_local_connection_num();
get_user_id(my_connect_num, my_user_id);
```

The get_user_id() function uses the NetWare *GetConnectionInformation*
function (classified as a Connection Service):

```
/* get user ID for a given connection number */

void    get_user_id(unsigned char connection_number,
                unsigned char *user_id)
        {
        union REGS      regs;
        struct SREGS    sregs;

        struct {
                unsigned int    len;
                unsigned char   buffer_type;
                unsigned char   connection_number;
                } request_buffer;

        struct {
                unsigned int    len;
                unsigned char   object_id[4];
                unsigned char   object_type[2];
                char            object_name[48];
                char            login_time[7];
                } reply_buffer;

        regs.h.ah = 0xe3;
        request_buffer.len = 2;
        request_buffer.buffer_type = 0x16;
        request_buffer.connection_number = connection_number;

        reply_buffer.len = 61;

        regs.x.si = FP_OFF( (void far *) &request_buffer);
        sregs.ds  = FP_SEG( (void far *) &request_buffer);
        regs.x.di = FP_OFF( (void far *) &reply_buffer);
        sregs.es  = FP_SEG( (void far *) &reply_buffer);
        int86x(0x21, &regs, &regs, &sregs);
        strncpy(user_id, reply_buffer.object_name, 48);
        }
```

Receiving IPX Messages

You just did a lot of work to find out the destination address of the remote workstation. You cannot relax yet, though. It is time now to actually receive a data packet from the remote workstation, and then send one back. After you fill in the ECB for a Receive operation, you do the Receive by putting 4 in BX, making ES:SI a far pointer to the ECB, and invoking IPX:

```
void    ipx_listen_for_packet(struct ECB *ecb_ptr)
        {
        _ES = FP_SEG( (void far *) ecb_ptr);
        _SI = FP_OFF( (void far *) ecb_ptr);
        _BX = 0x0004;
        ipx_spx();
        }
```

To receive a data packet, you fill in an ECB and pass it to IPX. As you fill in the ECB, you tell IPX which socket number you are "listening on" (and which you previously opened). You also tell IPX where to put the received data. The incoming packet consists of an IPX header followed by the data message, so you need to have two areas set aside to receive the packet. In the following code, packet_count gets set to 2, to tell IPX that there are two data areas. The *address* and *length* fields of packet[0] express the IPX header, and the *address* and *length* fields of packet[1] describe the application's message buffer. After the ECB is set up, you then call IPX. When the event is completed, the ECB's completion_code indicates whether the event succeeded.

```
struct ECB receive_ecb;
struct IPXHEADER receive_header;
char    message[81];

memset(&receive_ecb, 0, sizeof(struct ECB));
memset(&receive_header, 0, sizeof(struct IPXHEADER));

receive_ecb.socket_number = 0x4545;
receive_ecb.packet_count  = 2;
receive_ecb.packet[0].address = &receive_header;
receive_ecb.packet[0].length  = sizeof(struct IPXHEADER);
receive_ecb.packet[1].address = message;
receive_ecb.packet[1].length  = strlen(message);

ipx_listen_for_packet(&receive_ecb);
```

Listing continues

Listing continued

```
while (receive_ecb.in_use)
    ipx_relinquish_control();

if (receive_ecb.completion_code == 0)
    printf("Message received: %s\n", message);
else
    printf("Error occurred while receiving message\n");
```

Sending IPX Messages

When you receive an IPX data packet, you need to specify only the data areas into which the incoming packet goes and the socket number on which you are listening. Outbound, however, you need to give IPX more information:

❏ The data areas to be sent, including an IPX header

❏ The socket number through which you are sending messages

❏ The "immediate address" of a bridge that will route the message

❏ A packet type (always 4 for IPX)

❏ A destination address, consisting of network number, node address, and socket

After you build the ECB and the IPX header for an IPX Send operation, you use the following function to invoke IPX:

```
void    ipx_send_packet(struct ECB *ecb_ptr)
        {
        _ES = FP_SEG( (void far *) ecb_ptr);
        _SI = FP_OFF( (void far *) ecb_ptr);
        _BX = 0x0003;
        ipx_spx();
        }
```

The immediate_address field of the ECB must contain the 6-byte node address of the bridge that will route the message. IPX provides a get_local_target function that returns the address of the bridge. If no bridge is involved in sending the message, get_local_target returns the node address of the destination workstation. In either case, the result goes into immediate_address. The following function shows how to use IPX get_local_target:

```
int get_local_target(unsigned char *dest_network,
                      unsigned char *dest_node,
                      unsigned int   dest_socket,
                      unsigned char *bridge_address)
```

```
{
unsigned int    temp_ax;

struct {
        unsigned char    network_number [4];
        unsigned char    physical_node [6];
        unsigned int     socket;
        } request_buffer;

struct {
        unsigned char    local_target [6];
        } reply_buffer;

memcpy(request_buffer.network_number, dest_network, 4);
memcpy(request_buffer.physical_node, dest_node, 6);
request_buffer.socket = dest_socket;

_ES = FP_SEG( (void far *) &request_buffer);
_SI = FP_OFF( (void far *) &request_buffer);
_DI = FP_OFF( (void far *) &reply_buffer);
_BX = 0x0002;
ipx_spx();
_AH = 0;
temp_ax = _AX;
memcpy(bridge_address, reply_buffer.local_target, 6);
return temp_ax;
}
```

The following send() function shows how to send an IPX message. The function's parameters are the destination (dest_network, dest_node, and dest_socket) and the data message to be sent (packet_ptr and packet_len). send() puts the socket number (the local one, not the destination socket) into the ECB. After calling the preceding get_local_target() routine to set the immediate_address field, the function then puts the address and length of two buffer areas—an IPX header and the data message—into the ECB.

The IPX header is the first 30 bytes of the packet that IPX transmits. The send() function inserts the destination address into the IPX header, sets the packet_type to 4, and calls IPX to send the message on its way.

```
struct ECB send_ecb;
struct IPXHEADER send_header;
```

Listing continues

Listing continued

```
void    send(char  *dest_network,
             char  *dest_node,
             int   dest_socket,
             void  *packet_ptr,
             int   packet_len)
{
int i;

memset(&send_ecb, 0, sizeof(struct ECB));
send_ecb.socket_number = our_socket;

i = get_local_target(dest_network,
                     dest_node,
                     dest_socket,
                     send_ecb.immediate_address);
if (i != 0) return;

send_ecb.packet_count = 2;
send_ecb.packet[0].address = &send_header;
send_ecb.packet[0].length  = sizeof(struct IPXHEADER);
send_ecb.packet[1].address = packet_ptr;
send_ecb.packet[1].length  = packet_len;

send_header.packet_type = 4;

memcpy(send_header.dest_network_number,
            dest_network, 4);
memcpy(send_header.dest_network_node,
            dest_node,    6);
send_header.dest_network_socket = dest_socket;

ipx_send_packet(&send_ecb);
}
```

Programming SPX

Do not skip to this section without first reading the previous section on IPX programming. SPX uses IPX functions (SPX is a higher layer), and many of the IPX concepts and techniques just mentioned also apply to SPX. SPX creates connections (sessions) between workstations, monitors the exchange of application messages for the duration of the connection, and dismantles the connection when your application finishes. This section covers some of the trickier steps to establishing an SPX connection between two workstations. After you establish a connection, sending and receiving messages under SPX is similar to the operations you perform under NETBIOS or IPX.

SPX Installed Test

If your application is running on a NetWare LAN, you know that IPX is present. Not so with SPX. Novell added SPX to its LAN operating system software beginning with the 2.01–4 version of NetWare. The following function uses the SPX Initialize service to determine if SPX is present; the function returns 1 if SPX is available, and 0 if not. You should always call this function once, early in your program, to enable SPX to initialize itself.

```
int     spx_installed(void)
        {
        _BX = 0x0010;
        _AL = 0x00;
        ipx_spx();
        if (_AL == 0)
            return 0;

        return 1;
        }
```

Note that SPX uses the same entry point as IPX.

ECBs, ESRs, and Sockets

The ECB format provided previously in the discussion of IPX applies to SPX as well. There are only a couple of differences in the way an ECB is used under SPX:

1. Your program does not have to set the `immediate_address` field before an SPX Send operation; SPX fills in the field automatically.

2. The first two bytes of the `ipx_workspace` field contain the assigned connection ID after a successful *SPXListenForConnection* call.

For SPX, the following is a better definition of an ECB:

```
struct ECB
    {
    void far        *link_address;
```

Listing continues

Listing continued

```
    void far          (*event_service_routine)(void);
    unsigned char     in_use;
    unsigned char     completion_code;
    unsigned int      socket_number;
    unsigned int      connection_id;
    unsigned char     reserved [2];
    unsigned char     driver_workspace  [12];
    unsigned char     immediate_address [ 6];
    unsigned int      packet_count;
    struct {
        void far      *address;
        unsigned int length;
        } packet [2];
};
```

ESRs work the same for SPX as for IPX. The same environment exists when SPX invokes one of your program functions, and you code the ESR the same way. Also, socket numbers have the same characteristics for SPX as for IPX. You must open a socket before doing SPX functions, and you must specify a socket number as part of the destination address when you establish an SPX connection.

SPX Header

The first 30 bytes of an SPX header are actually an IPX header. The remaining 12 bytes are unique to SPX. You treat the SPX header a little differently from how you treat the IPX header. You do not have to set the packet_type field; SPX automatically gives the field a value of 5 to identify an SPX packet. You need to set the destination address fields (dest_network_number, dest_network_node, and dest_network_socket) only before you issue an *SPXEstablishConnection* call. After the connection is created, you use an assigned connection ID to refer to the connection. The datastream_type field becomes important when the connection is terminated. One workstation issues the termination request, and the other receives a data packet whose datastream_type field was set to 0xFE by SPX.

```
    struct SPXHEADER
        {
        unsigned int      checksum;
        unsigned int      length;
        unsigned char     transport_control;
        unsigned char     packet_type;
        unsigned char     dest_network_number [4];
```

```
unsigned char    dest_network_node    [6];
unsigned int     dest_network_socket;
unsigned char    source_network_number [4];
unsigned char    source_network_node   [6];
unsigned int     source_network_socket;
unsigned char    connection_control;
unsigned char    datastream_type;
unsigned int     source_connection_id;
unsigned int     dest_connection_id;
unsigned int     sequence_number;
unsigned int     acknowledge_number;
unsigned int     allocation_number;
};
```

SPX Commands

Just as with IPX functions, you specify an SPX command by setting the BX register to a certain value before calling SPX. The SPX functions are symbolically defined as:

```
#define spx_initialize                  0x10
#define spx_establish_connection        0x11
#define spx_listen_for_connection       0x12
#define spx_terminate_connection        0x13
#define spx_abort_connection            0x14
#define spx_get_connection_status       0x15
#define spx_send_sequenced_packet       0x16
#define spx_listen_for_sequenced_packet 0x17
```

Establishing a Connection

SPX assigns a connection ID to each connection that you establish, much the same way NETBIOS assigns Local Session Numbers when you create NETBIOS sessions. In subsequent Send and Receive operations, you use the connection ID to refer to the established connection.

The way that you use SPX to create a connection is similar to the way that you use NETBIOS to create a session. Under NETBIOS, one workstation issues a Listen command, and the other issues a Call command. Under SPX, the first workstation issues a *ListenForConnection* command, and the other workstation issues a subsequent *EstablishConnection*. There are some extra steps you must take under SPX, however.

Under SPX, you must do at least a few (preferably five) calls to *SPXListenForSequencedPacket* before the call to either *ListenForConnection* or *EstablishConnection*. This gives SPX a pool of ECBs and packet buffers to use. SPX uses some of these ECBs and buffers internally, and this usage is transparent to your program. Some are used to receive incoming message packets after the connection is created. Later, when this chapter discusses receiving and sending SPX messages, you will learn how to handle these multiple outstanding events.

When you issue the set of *ListenForSequencedPacket* (receive) calls, fill in the following ECB fields for each call:

event_service_routine	An ESR to handle incoming messages
socket	One your application has opened
packet_count	Set to 2
packet[0].address	Pointer to an SPX header
packet[0].length	Length of an SPX header (42 bytes)
packet[1].address	Pointer to an incoming message buffer
packet[1].length	Length of the incoming message buffer

The ECB fields to fill in before calling *ListenForConnection* are the event_service_routine function pointer, socket, and the packet_count and packet address and length fields. packet_count should be set to 1, packet[0].address should point to an SPX header, and packet[0].length should be set to 42 bytes (the length of an SPX header).

Some of this will become clearer as you study the following code examples. The first example shows how to issue the five receive (*ListenForSequencedPacket*) operations. The example declares an array of five ECBs and an array of five SPX headers so that you can conveniently use a program loop to issue the five commands.

```
for (i=0; i<5; i++)
    {
    memset(&ecb_list[i], 0, sizeof(struct ECB));
    memset(&spxheader_list[i], 0, sizeof(struct SPXHEADER));

    ecb_list[i].event_service_routine = receive_esr;
    ecb_list[i].socket_number    = socket;
    ecb_list[i].packet_count     = 2;
    ecb_list[i].packet[0].address = (void far *) &spxheader_list[i];
    ecb_list[i].packet[0].length  = sizeof(struct SPXHEADER);
    ecb_list[i].packet[1].address = (void far *) packet_buffer;
    ecb_list[i].packet[1].length  = sizeof(packet_buffer);
```

```
        /* now issue a ListenForSequencedPacket */
        _ES = FP_SEG( (void far *) ecb_list[i]);
        _SI = FP_OFF( (void far *) ecb_list[i]);
        _BX = 0x0017;
        ipx_spx();
        }
```

Next, the following code actually does the *ListenForConnection* call:

```
memset(&listen_ecb, 0, sizeof(struct ECB));
memset(&listen_header, 0, sizeof(struct SPXHEADER));

listen_ecb.event_service_routine = listen_esr;
listen_ecb.socket_number         = socket;
listen_ecb.packet_count          = 1;
listen_ecb.packet[0].address     = (void far *) &listen_header;
listen_ecb.packet[0].length      = sizeof(struct SPXHEADER);


/* do the listen_for_connection call */

_ES = FP_SEG( (void far *) &listen_ecb);
_SI = FP_OFF( (void far *) &listen_ecb);
_BX = 0x0012;
_AH = 0xFF;
_AL = 0;
ipx_spx();
```

Now one workstation has gone through the preceding steps and is waiting for another workstation to establish the connection. Before issuing its *EstablishConnection* call, the other workstation also must do a series of *ListenForSequencedPacket* calls:

```
for (i=0; i<5; i++)
    {
    memset(&ecb_list[i], 0, sizeof(struct ECB));
    memset(&spxheader_list[i], 0, sizeof(struct SPXHEADER));

    ecb_list[i].event_service_routine = receive_esr;
    ecb_list[i].socket_number     = our_socket;
    ecb_list[i].packet_count      = 2;
    ecb_list[i].packet[0].address = (void far *) &spxheader_list[i];
    ecb_list[i].packet[0].length  = sizeof(struct SPXHEADER);
    ecb_list[i].packet[1].address = (void far *) packet_buffer;
    ecb_list[i].packet[1].length  = sizeof(packet_buffer);
```

Listing continues

Listing *continued*

```
        /* now issue a Listen For Sequenced Packet */
        _ES = FP_SEG( (void far *) ecb_list[i]);
        _SI = FP_OFF( (void far *) ecb_list[i]);
        _BX = 0x0017;
        ipx_spx();
        }
```

Like IPX, SPX uses destination addresses (network, node, and socket) to identify the target workstation. If you know the user ID but not the destination address, you use the same NetWare Connection Services functions defined earlier (for IPX) to obtain a destination address. Notice that you let get_internet_address() put the network number and node address directly into the SPX header:

```
    connection_number = get_1st_connection_num(dest_user_id);
    if (connection_number == 0)
        return 1;                /* not logged on */

    memset(&call_header, 0, sizeof(struct SPXHEADER));

    get_internet_address(connection_number,
            call_header.dest_network_number,
            call_header.dest_network_node)
    call_header.dest_network_socket= dest_socket;
```

You are finally ready to establish the connection:

```
    memset(&call_ecb, 0, sizeof(struct ECB));

    call_ecb.event_service_routine = call_esr;
    call_ecb.socket_number         = our_socket;
    call_ecb.packet_count          = 1;
    call_ecb.packet[0].address     = (void far *) &call_header;
    call_ecb.packet[0].length      = sizeof(struct SPXHEADER);

    /* do the Establish Connection call */
    _ES = FP_SEG( (void far *) &call_ecb);
    _SI = FP_OFF( (void far *) &call_ecb);
    _BX = 0x0011;
    _AH = 0xFF;
    _AL = 0;
    ipx_spx();
```

After the *EstablishConnection* event is completed, the assigned connection ID is found in the DX register and also in the call_header SPX header (as call_header.source_connection_id). On the other workstation, after the *ListenForConnection* event is completed, the assigned connection ID for that connection partner is found inside the listen_ecb ECB (listen_ecb.connection_id).

For both the *ListenForConnection* and *EstablishConnection* calls, you specify a retry count and a watchdog flag. See the Reference section for a discussion of these fields.

Sending and Receiving Messages

To send a data message to a connection partner, you give SPX a connection ID, an SPX header, and an ECB. Fill in the ECB with the ESR function pointer (optional), packet count, and the address and length of both the SPX header and the data message you want to send.

```
void    send(unsigned connect_id, void *packet, int packet_length)
        {
        memset(&send_ecb, 0, sizeof(struct ECB));
        memset(&send_header, 0, sizeof(struct SPXHEADER));

        send_ecb.event_service_routine = send_esr;
        send_ecb.packet_count          = 2;
        send_ecb.packet[0].address     = (void far *) &send_header;
        send_ecb.packet[0].length      = sizeof(struct SPXHEADER);
        send_ecb.packet[1].address     = (void far *) packet;
        send_ecb.packet[1].length      = packet_length;

        /* issue send_packet */
        _ES = FP_SEG( (void far *) &send_ecb);
        _SI = FP_OFF( (void far *) &send_ecb);
        _DX = connection_id;
        _BX = 0x0016;
        ipx_spx();
        }
```

Receiving an SPX data message is a little more complicated. SPX chooses one of the ECBs from the pool of five you issued earlier and uses the chosen ECB to signal that an incoming message has been received. Typically, you code a receive_esr() ESR that hands the data message to the main part of the program and then returns that ECB to the pool. To return the ECB to the pool, you issue another *ListenForSequencedPacket* call, using the same steps that put the ECB into the pool in the first place.

Terminating a Connection

When one connection partner issues an *SPXTerminateConnection* call, SPX processes the request by automatically sending a packet to the other workstation. This packet consists of an SPX header only, with its datastream_type set to 0xFE. The other connection partner, after receiving this packet, should recognize that the connection no longer exists. Both partners should close any open sockets before going back to DOS.

The following code shows how to issue an SPX Terminate Connection (function 0x0013). Note that the termination activity occurs in the background and you must wait for the function to finish. You can poll the in_use flag or set up an ESR to be invoked when the termination actually occurs.

```
struct ECB term_ecb;
struct SPXHEADER term_header;
unsigned int connection_id;


memset(&term_ecb, 0, sizeof(struct ECB));

term_ecb.packet_count       = 1;
term_ecb.packet[0].address = (void far *) &term_header;
term_ecb.packet[0].length  = sizeof(struct SPXHEADER);

_ES = FP_SEG( (void far *) &term_ecb);
_SI = FP_OFF( (void far *) &term_ecb);
_DX = connection_id;
_BX = 0x0013;
ipx_spx();

while (term_ecb.in_use)
    ;
```

Summary

In Chapter 5, "PC-to-PC NETBIOS Programming," and this chapter, "IPX and SPX Programming," you have acquired a solid, comprehensive set of communications tools. This chapter addressed the IPX and SPX protocols present on NetWare LANs. You understand Event Control Blocks,

IPX headers, and SPX headers. You can send and receive IPX datagrams, and you can create, use, and dismantle SPX connections. You might try writing a small "chat" facility using the techniques and code fragments from these two chapters. It will be good practice and a lot of fun!

CHAPTER 7

Testing and Debugging Your Program

Testing your software is a matter of running it and verifying that it does what it is supposed to do. Having a test plan helps; most of my test plans are just checklists that guide me through the testing. Debugging, on the other hand, is a lot less scientific! Most people think that finding and fixing bugs is a black art.

The information in this chapter is not intended to teach you how to test or debug your programs. Indeed, you should be able to apply most of the techniques you have learned from your other programming adventures. Instead, this chapter describes network-related items that you can add to your test-plan checklists. These items are categorized according to whether they pertain to DOS-level program functions, such as file sharing and record locking, or to NETBIOS, IPX, and SPX PC-to-PC communications functions. Next, the chapter discusses debugging network-related program errors. For each of the techniques covered in the previous chapters, this chapter describes some of the things that can go wrong and ways to find and fix the errors.

Do not think of testing as a measure of your coding skills; that would be unrealistic, unfair, and counterproductive. Instead, approach the testing phase as a chance to learn new things about how the computer functions. Especially when you are getting into an unfamiliar area of software technology (networks, for instance), you need to realize that programming can be a trial-and-error proposition.

207

When I try to do something new and it does not work the first time, I ask the following questions:

- ❏ Did I omit a statement?
- ❏ Do I have statements out of order?
- ❏ Did I misunderstand the concepts?
- ❏ Is there something else I should know that the reference manual is not telling me?

In each case, I check whether my code looks like it should do what I want. A careful rereading of the code often points out a minor discrepancy between what I thought I said to do and what I actually coded. Sometimes, however, the code looks perfectly fine and still does not work. Then I start experimenting to find out what I need to do differently. If I think major surgery is required, I first make a copy of the existing source file (it could have bugs, but it is a starting point to which I can always return). If I think that I can try a different approach by making only a few small changes, I make the existing code a comment (by surrounding it with /*...*/) and put some new code next to the old. If the new code works okay, I sigh in relief and quickly delete the old (commented out) code. If the new code does not work, I then go back through the same process. This time around, I have two routines I can use as a base for further experimentation. I pick the routine that worked best, make a few changes, and try again.

DOS-Level Testing

You may develop software for in-house use in your company, or you might be an analyst or programmer whose efforts become products that are sold to other companies. In the first case, you can run tests on whatever sort of LAN you have at work and not worry about making your code widely compatible. However, if your software will be used on different types of LANs, you must test your code on as many LANs as possible.

The following example shows why this testing is necessary (as a analyst and programmer, I have run into a few odd situations).

The Record Locking function call in DOS (hex 5C) says `Locking beyond end-of-file is not an error`. I took this to mean that I could lock an entire file by using 0xFFFFFFFFl as the `Length of Region` to be locked. I knew from the description of the 5C function call that 0xFFFF would go into the SI register and 0xFFFF into the DI register, and this seemed to be exactly what I wanted to do. I put the code into the application, tested it under both the IBM PC LAN Program and Novell NetWare, and the application worked just fine.

Later, a client said that he wanted to use an IBM RT, running AIX (IBM's flavor of UNIX) as a file server on a Token Ring LAN. IBM's AIX Access for DOS Users (AADU) would redirect the DOS file.

"Fine," I said, "but let's try it out first." With a borrowed RT computer, I tested the software. I discovered that AADU rejected the Record Locking function call because I used a Region Length of 0xFFFFFFFFl bytes! Changing the code to a value that AADU would accept only took a moment (I used 0x0FFFFFFFl, because AADU obviously was treating the value as a signed quantity). I was glad that I tested the software before it was sent to the client.

Incidentally, I also found that AADU does not support machine name; I had to put a small workaround in the code to make up for it.

LAN Detection

The custom LAN-presence test described in Chapter 4, "DOS-Level Programming," is designed to work on any LAN. The test even worked under AADU! Testing should be simple—run your software on a stand-alone PC and your program should tell you right away that "the network is not active" (or whatever). If clients say that they cannot run your LAN software product, you can confidently tell them to recheck their LAN configuration and setup. If that does not fix things, a client's "XYZ-Net LAN Operating System" is not quite as full-featured a LAN environment as the system's manufacturer claims.

Workstation IDs

If you use machine name or NetWare user IDs in your application, you should test to make sure that you are obtaining the string correctly and that you are handling it properly in your program. Fortunately, both fields are normal, null-terminated C strings. Remember that machine name is 16 bytes long (including the terminator) and that a user ID can be as much as 48 bytes long. I usually ignore long NetWare user IDs in my software. I initially acquire user ID into a 50-byte string and drop a null terminator (\0) into the 16th byte. Thereafter I treat user ID just as I would machine name.

If your program dies completely when you obtain the workstation identifier (either name or user ID), compare the code with the examples provided in this book. Probably something is wrong with the way the registers are set up for the function call.

If your program fails to match the workstation identifier (or a substring of it) with some other string, check the case of both strings. You may have to use strupr() or strlwr() to get them to match.

In the previously mentioned situation with AADU, in which I found that AADU does not support setting and obtaining machine name, I solved the problem with a small (400-byte) TSR called NAME and a couple of programs called GETNAME and SETNAME. NAME provides support for getting and setting machine name. I had each user, at each workstation, put NAME and SETNAME into the AUTOEXEC.BAT file as follows:

```
NAME
SETNAME 001_STATION      <different for each workstation>
```

In case you need them, all three of these programs are included on the diskette that comes with this book.

File Sharing

Whether you open a file on the file server for shared (DENY_NONE) or exclusive (DENY_ALL) access, the test you need to perform is to open the same file concurrently from two different workstations and see how your software reacts. If you get an Abort, Retry, or Ignore? message from DOS (or if your Interrupt 24, Critical Error Handler is invoked) at the second workstation, recheck the way that you are opening the file. If you omit parameters in the open() call, or if you inadvertently used fopen() rather than open(), the second workstation could be opening the file in compatibility mode.

Do not forget to test your "Is SHARE loaded?" routine. You will want to run your program on a just-booted workstation, without SHARE having been run, and look for your program to terminate with a message indicating that SHARE has not been run.

The NETWORK.C program can be useful in your file-sharing tests (see Chapter 8, "Network Applications"). Appendix A, "Source Listing for File and Record Collision Tester," lists the program's source code, and the disk includes the program's source and executable code.

Record Locking

For record locks, you need to test essentially the same as you do for file sharing: cause a controlled, concurrent collision between two work-stations. This test is not easy—a well-designed record lock lasts for only a brief moment. If you test by having two users at two workstations run your software and try to hit the Enter key (to cause a record update) at exactly the same time, you will quickly become frustrated; causing a collision this way is virtually impossible.

One possible approach is to temporarily change the copy of your program on the first workstation. Insert a `wait for keypress` function call (such as `getch()` after acquiring the record locks. This approach lets you deliberately hold the lock longer. While the lock is present, the user at Workstation B can attempt an update. You can then watch to see how your program behaves.

The NETWORK.C program (Chapter 8, "Network Applications") can also be useful in your record-locking tests.

What can go wrong inside your record-locking routines? If the machine crashes at the point that you issue the lock request, check your function call carefully. If you call function 5Ch directly, check how the CPU registers get set.

If DOS returns an error in response to your lock request, check the error code value. If it indicates that the region is already locked (and you know it should not be), you may be encountering the residue of a lock that was issued (without an unlock) during an earlier test. In this case, you may be able to use NETWORK.C to unlock the file region so that you can proceed with your testing. Another possibility is that the flow of your program took you through the lock request twice, without an intervening unlock. If DOS indicates some other error (perhaps invalid handle, or invalid function), carefully check your parameters in the call to the lock function.

DOS Function Call Tracking

If you have trouble figuring out what is wrong with a file open or lock/unlock request, you can run your program under a debugger and watch how the program reacts. In particular, you can set a breakpoint on the Interrupt 21 (hex) DOS entry point. The address of this entry point is found in the interrupt vector table, in segment:offset form (four bytes, low-order byte first), at 0x0000:0x0084. Of course, if you set an unconditional breakpoint at the Interrupt 21 entry point, you will see *every* DOS function call as it happens! This can get tedious, to say the least. If your debugger supports conditional breakpoints, tell it to stop at the breakpoint when the AH register has a value of 0x5C (for record locks) or 0x3D (for file opens). When the debugger stops, inspect its display of the CPU registers to see whether they seem to be set correctly.

The File Server as a Debugging Tool

You can ask the NetWare file server to tell you about files and records that are currently locked. From a separate workstation, run the FCONSOLE utility to view a display of file activity. Make sure that you give yourself SUPERVISOR rights before using FCONSOLE, as well as rights to use the remote console facilities in FCONSOLE.

Sometimes you can use the file server itself as a debugging tool. Under NetWare, for example, you can use the MONITOR command to view file activity. Before you begin a test, use the NetWare utility USERLIST at your workstation to find out your connection number. Then, while a test is under way, go to the file server and issue MONITOR <connection number>.

At the NetWare file server, you will see each file operation happen; NetWare shows you a list of file names and a mnemonic for the most recent file activity. If your program issues a flurry of file operations, the display of activity whizzes by and you will not be able to read it. For the displays you can read, however, be aware that the mnemonic for the file operation is NetWare-related, not DOS-related. For example, you will see Clr Phys Rec after an unlock has occurred. See the Synchronization Services part of the Reference section for an explanation of these mnemonics.

The IBM PC LAN Program has a similar facility, although it does not present the information in real-time. You can issue a NET FILE command at the file server to check which files are open. For each open file, the PC LAN Program displays the machine name of the workstation that opened the file as well as the number of locks in effect for that file. NET FILE can also be used to close an open file (of course, you want to do this only if the application running at the workstation has crashed). If you want a continuous display of open files, create a .BAT file, on the server, that contains these statements:

```
ECHO OFF
:AGAIN
NET FILE
GOTO AGAIN
```

Although the file still is not quite real-time, it does free you from having to type the command over and over again. Press Ctrl-C to stop the display.

NETBIOS Debugging

The first time you test a program that passes messages from workstation to workstation is exciting. You tell yourself that the program will not work the first time, but you are hopeful nevertheless. You start the programs, and—the two workstations refuse to talk to one another. It is a bit of a letdown. After you reboot the computers, you start wondering what went wrong.

This section ("NETBIOS Debugging") and the next ("IPX and SPX Debugging") offer some things you can look for that might be the culprit.

Adding and Deleting Names

One of the first things you need to verify is that your program has added or deleted NETBIOS names correctly. If you have two workstations that seem to have gone out to lunch, do not reboot them quite yet. Go to a third workstation and run the NETTEST.C program (source code in Appendix B, "Source Listing for NETBIOS Microscope"; executable on the diskette). Pick the Adapter Status menu option and specify that you want information about one of the test machines. If the computers are "alive" but unable to talk to one another, the display from the Adapter Status command tells you the contents of the local name table from one of the test machines. You then know whether your program at least performed a correct Add Name operation. Of course, you should check the return code from the Add Name operation and take appropriate action in your program if the call fails.

If the name is not present in the local name table from the test machine, or if the command times out, you can start looking for the problem in the part of the program that constructs the name and adds it to the local name table. If that code looks okay, you can try backtracking from there to check whether the problem occurred earlier in the execution of the program.

If the Adapter Status command times out, the Add Name operation may have been executed properly but your program subsequently damaged NETBIOS or crashed the workstation entirely. If you cannot find the problem in or prior to the code that does the Add Name, you can make what I call a "temporary assumption"—assume that the name was added correctly, and try looking for the problem later in the program.

Are there clues you can look for to tell you whether the workstation has crashed completely? Yes. The following technique sounds strange, but I assure you that it is well founded: Press the Caps Lock, Scroll Lock, or

Num Lock key; if the green LEDs on the keyboard respond normally by toggling off and on, the computer is in a loop. The loop may well be in your program. If the LEDs do not respond, the computer has crashed. (You will have to use the Red Switch to reboot the computer.) Of course, the loop (or the crash) may not be related to your calls to NETBIOS, but this technique can be informative.

Passing NETBIOS Datagrams

If you design your program to pass datagram messages "silently," without some outward sign (such as a screen message) that you can use to monitor what is going on, you should include in the program some temporary code that indicates when the program is transmitting or receiving messages. It can also be advantageous to test on two workstations that are physically adjacent so that you can watch both at the same time.

Suppose that you determine that Workstation A is sending a datagram, but Workstation B is not receiving the message. The first place to check is the code that does the Send Datagram. Does the code properly fill in the NCB_NUM field? Does the NCB_CALLNAME field contain the exact 16-byte name of the destination workstation? Is the NCB_LENGTH field non-zero? Are you getting a good return code from the Send Datagram call?

The next place to check is the Receive Datagram call. Is the NCB_NUM field properly filled? Do NCB_BUFFER_PTR and NCB_LENGTH correctly express the address and length of the input buffer? Is the Receive Datagram call returning an error code? And, more generally, is the Receive Datagram call actually outstanding when the Send Datagram is issued?

Another possible source of error is that the two workstations could be on separate LANs, and the Bridge machine is not transferring NETBIOS messages from one LAN to the other. This error can happen, for example, if you have two separate Token Ring LANs, running Novell NetWare, that are bridged internally at the NetWare file server. If you are using the IBM NETBIOS device driver DXMT0MOD.SYS, NetWare will not transfer the IBM NETBIOS frames from one LAN to the other. In this instance, you can use the Novell NETBIOS emulator rather than DXMT0MOD.SYS.

Establishing Sessions

Again, to find out whether a session is being established correctly, you should put in your program some temporary code which gives you some sign that the Call (or Listen) command has completed. As an alternative, you can use a debugger to trace through the code to find out exactly how the NETBIOS calls take place. In either case, make sure that you check return codes!

If you issued the Call and Listen commands on the two workstations but it appears that the session is not being established, you should first check the NCB_CALLNAME field in both NCBs. For the Call command, make sure that the NCB_CALLNAME field contains the name of the listening workstation. For the Listen command, make sure that the first byte of NCB_CALLNAME is an asterisk (*) if you are listening for a call from anyone, or that NCB_CALLNAME is the exact name of the caller.

If you have a complicated design that generates multiple sessions, your program could exceed the number of available sessions. In this case, check the installation and configuration documentation for the NETBIOS software. You may be able to configure it for a greater number of available sessions.

After a session is created successfully, make sure that you save the value of NCB_LSN. You will need this value in subsequent references to the session.

Sending and Receiving Session Messages

After you get the session under way, you should be able to easily verify whether the program is sending and receiving messages correctly—your program is working! If you encounter problems, however, the cause is probably either that the NCB_LSN (Local Session Number) is not set properly or that the NCB_BUFFER_PTR and NCB_LENGTH fields do not properly describe the input or output buffers. For the Receive operation, make sure that you set NCB_LENGTH to the size of the input buffer. Neglecting to set NCB_LENGTH is a common error; if the field is 0 when the Receive is issued, you cannot receive any data.

The Send and Receive operations time out according to the NCB_STO and NCB_RTO values given when the Call and Listen commands are issued. If your program seems to work only intermittently, you should check whether these fields are set correctly. A Send operation that times out causes the session itself to be aborted.

Do not forget that both workstations should do a Hang Up command to dismantle the session. Unless you want to deliberately leave the names you have added in the local name table, make sure that you do a Delete Name after the Hang Up operation is completed.

IPX and SPX Debugging

Many of the pitfalls of NETBIOS programming have counterparts in IPX and SPX. One difference you will notice is that there are more things to keep track of with IPX and SPX. This makes debugging a little tougher, because there are more statements in your program that can go wrong. As you test and debug a program that uses IPX or SPX, watch out for the following potential problems.

Opening Sockets

When you open one socket or more in preparation for sending and receiving data messages, always check the return code from the *OpenSocket* call to make sure that the socket was opened successfully. If you write a TSR that uses IPX or SPX, make sure that you set the Longevity Flag appropriately when you open a socket. NetWare closes any open sockets when the TSR operation (DOS function call hex 31) occurs, unless the sockets are marked as "long-lived." Trying to use a closed socket causes a strange reaction. When I encountered this bug, the program in error continued to run on some workstations, but on other workstations the program would crash after putting stray garbage on the screen.

Also remember that NetWare expects the socket value with the high byte first, in contrast to the way the CPU normally represents integer-type items. Finally, if you use both IPX and SPX in the same application, assign different sockets to the operations you do under each protocol.

Determining Destination Addresses

Chapter 6, "IPX and SPX Programming," introduced some programming techniques for determining the destination address (network number and node address) which assume that you already know the destination user ID. You also could obtain the destination address through another approach; for example, you could maintain in your program a table of target workstations. In either case, the FCONSOLE utility (which was mentioned previously) is useful when you must verify a workstation's destination address. If you need to insert some temporary code in your program to display the value of network number and node address, you can use the following technique:

```
for (i=0; i<4; i++)
    printf("%2.2X ", network_number[i]);

for (i=0; i<6; i++)
    printf("%2.2X ", node_address[i]);
```

The preceding statements show the network number and node address in hexadecimal notation, the same notation that FCONSOLE displays. The fields can contain null bytes; a common error is to use `strcpy()` to move these fields around. Use `memcpy()` or an equivalent.

In addition, if you are using connection number to obtain the destination address, invoking the USERLIST utility from a separate workstation helps verify whether you have the correct connection number.

Sending and Receiving IPX Messages

If you seem to be using the correct destination address for an IPX *SendPacket* call and yet the message is not being received, the problem could be that the IPX *ListenForPacket* call (the receive operation) is not issued before the data packet is sent. Make sure that IPX always has an outstanding ECB for receiving messages.

On the incoming side (a Receive operation), you should also check the contents of the ECB to make sure that the socket is correct and that you have properly expressed the length and address of the input buffers for both the IPX Header and the data packet.

On the outbound side (Send), check the value of `packet_type` (it should be 4). Make sure that the `immediate_address` field is filled in with the result of a call to *GetLocalTarget*. The length and address of the output buffers (IPX Header and data packet) should be properly set in the ECB.

Establishing an SPX Connection

If you are having trouble getting an SPX connection established, first check whether the listening workstation issued its *ListenForConnection* call before the other workstation did an *EstablishConnection* call. Especially for the first test (no matter what retry logic you programmed), make sure that you start up the software on the listening workstation before firing up your software on the calling workstation.

As was mentioned in Chapter 6, "SPX and IPX Programming," several *ListenForSequencedPacket* calls absolutely *must* be issued before you attempt to establish a connection. Compare your code to the examples I have given to make sure that the ECBs and input buffers are available to SPX. If a supply of these ECBs and buffers is not available for SPX to use as it creates the connection, SPX starves and crashes the workstation. As your program is executed, check to make sure that completed ECBs (which you have used to receive incoming messages) are returned to the SPX pool of available ECBs.

Sending and Receiving SPX Messages

If you traced through your program and verified that the SPX connection was successfully established, and yet the data packets do not seem to be getting to their destination, check first whether you are properly using the connection ID to refer to the connection. You even may want to code an *SPXGetConnectionStatus* call and display the result, just to make the whole process more visible during testing. If it appears that you are using the connection ID correctly, check the way you are describing the input and output buffers. Make sure that you are providing for both the SPX Header and your data packet with the `packet_count`, `packet[].address`, and `packet[].length` fields of the ECBs.

Before processing each received message, be sure to inspect the `datastream_type` field of the SPX Header. A value of 0xFE indicates that the other workstation issued an *SPXTerminateConnection* call. When the dialog between the two machines is finished, do not forget to cancel any outstanding events and close any open sockets.

Summary

I wish that I could anticipate and help you with every bug you might encounter in your programs. Although I cannot do that, this chapter provides the basics of how to find and fix each bug. Outlining many of the things that can go wrong with sharing files, locking records, and obtaining workstation IDs, this chapter discussed the kinds of problems you are likely to run into with NETBIOS, IPX, and SPX when you add names, use destination addresses, establish sessions (and connections), send and receive messages, and terminate the dialog.

CHAPTER 8

Network Applications

Sometimes code fragments alone are not enough to explain how to use a new programming facility. If you are like me, you want to see a complete example that shows how to put the pieces together. With this thought in mind, I wrote four working programs, described in this chapter, that use the techniques discussed in previous chapters. Each of the four source code files is listed in an appendix at the end of this book, and the source and executable files are contained on the enclosed floppy disk.

I used the Borland Turbo C compiler, version 2.0, to compile the programs. Some of the programs contain "inline" assembler code, so you also need an assembler (such as Microsoft's MASM, or Borland's TASM) to compile and link the files yourself.

Each program is discussed in two parts. The first part is a user guide that explains how to use the program. The second part is a programmer guide that shows how the program works and that highlights the network-related features of the program.

I will have to gloss over some aspects to these programs. Details about PC interrupt vectors, Terminate and Stay Resident (TSR) techniques, or the way that I manipulate the screen are beyond the scope of this book. For some detail on these non-network-related topics, I recommend the *MS-DOS Encyclopedia* (by Ray Duncan), and *Turbo C Programming* and *DOS Programmer's Reference,* 2nd Edition, (both published by Que Corporation). You also can use the Turbo Debugger, if you have it in your

219

arsenal, to trace through the code. Even without these aids, however, you should learn much just by studying the program listings.

File and Record Collision Tester

The Collision Tester is a TSR tool that you use to cause deliberate file-sharing situations and record-locking collisions. Pressing Alt-RightShift pops up a window. In that window, you open the same files that your application will open, or you lock the same records that your application will lock. Then return to your application to watch how your software reacts when it encounters the already open file or already locked record. You can run your application and the Collision Tester on the same workstation. You even do not have to be connected to a network to use the Collision Tester.

User Guide

Installing the Collision Tester is easy; just copy the NETWORK.EXE executable file to any one of the directories expressed by the PATH you have set on your computer. If you already have a .COM, .BAT, or .EXE file named NETWORK on your computer, you will want to rename NETWORK.EXE during the installation. Renaming the file will not affect its operation.

To load the Collision Tester before testing your application's file sharing and record locking, type **NETWORK** at the DOS prompt. The program asks for a drive letter that will be your network drive (which is important only if you are running the test program on a stand-alone, non-LAN-attached computer). The Collision Tester then becomes a resident program and displays a message reminding you to press Alt-RightShift to pop it up. While the Collision Tester is resident, it forces DOS to return a machine name of **"01TEST   "** to your application. The test program also forces DOS to return a Yes response to your application if your program issues DOS function call *Is Drive Remote?* (0x4409) for the drive letter you specified.

When you press Alt-RightShift, the program displays the menu shown in figure 8.1.

Fig. 8.1. *Main Menu of the Collision Tester.*

```
┌─[ LAN EMULATOR ]──────────────────────┐
│                                       │
│  E)xit to application                 │
│  R)emove Emulator from RAM            │
│  O)pen a file                         │
│  C)lose a file                        │
│  L)ock a record                       │
│  U)nlock a record                     │
│  S)how current files/locks            │
│                                       │
│                                       │
└─(Select option by first letter)───────┘
```

To select a menu option, type its first letter. For example, to choose Open a File, press the **O** key.

To unload the Collision Tester from memory when you are finished testing your application, pop up the program and pick the menu option Remove Emulator from RAM. If another program is loaded on top of NETWORK.EXE when you choose this option, the Collision Tester waits until the other program is removed from memory before unloading itself.

You should unlock any locked records and close any open files before removing the Collision Tester from memory (when you are finished testing).

The Collision Tester works only in text mode. You should not use it to test applications that put the computer into graphics mode.

Opening and Closing Files

Before you use the Collision Tester to check how your application handles file-sharing collisions, first put together a test plan. The plan should at least call out each of the files that you open and give some information about how you open the file and how you expect the file to be shared. You need this plan to determine what collisions you want to cause and how to specify them to the Collision Tester. This same information is useful in your record-locking tests.

To open a file in the Collision Tester, pop up the program by pressing Alt-RightShift, and pick the Open a File option. Figure 8.2 shows a partially filled-in example of the screen you see when you choose this option.

Fig. 8.2. Opening a file.

```
┌─[ OPEN A FILE ]─────────────────

    Filename: c:network.c
 Inheritance: N
    Sharing:
     Access:
  Record Len:

1=Compatibility Mode; 2=Deny R/W;
3=Deny Write; 4=Deny Read; 5=None
```

You are prompted for a file name (specify a drive letter and path, if necessary). If you press the Esc key in response to the file-name prompt, the program returns to the Main Menu.

You are asked whether the file is Inheritable (answer by pressing Y or N). At the Sharing prompt, specify the sharing mode that the Collision Tester should use by typing 1 for Compatibility Mode, 2 for Deny Read/Write, 3 for Deny Write, 4 for Deny Read, or 5 for Deny None. The next prompt asks for access mode; respond by typing 1 for Read access, 2 for Write access, or 3 for Read/Write access. Finally, at the Record Length prompt, type a number that expresses the length of each of the logical records in the file. When you press the Enter key, an Open File request is issued to DOS. If the request is successful, you see the message File successfully opened. If the request fails, you see Failed. DOS error XX, where XX represents the error code that DOS returns. In either case, press a key to return to the Main Menu. Unless you want to lock a record at this time, you now can pick Exit to application. As your program executes, the files that you opened remain open just as though another workstation were operating on the file.

Locking and Unlocking Records

Before locking a record in the Collision Tester window, you must first open the file as outlined in the previous section. You should use a sharing mode of Deny None and an access mode of Read-Write.

Pick the menu option Lock a record. You see a numbered list of open files; choose the file you want by its number. The next screen asks for the Record Number that you want the Collision Tester to lock. Note in figure 8.3 that Record Numbers start at 1, not 0.

Fig. 8.3. Locking a record.

```
┌─[ LOCK A RECORD ]─────────────────────┐
│                                       │
│  1. c:network.c                       │
│  2.                                   │
│  3.                                   │
│  4.                                   │
│  5.                                   │
│                                       │
│ Which record number? 2                │
│ (numbers start at 1)                  │
│                                       │
│                                       │
└───────────────────────────────────────┘
```

If the DOS function call 5C request (*Lock Record*) succeeds, you see Record X locked X is the Record Number you specified). If the call fails, you see Failed. DOS error XX, where XX represents the error code that DOS returns. In either case, press a key to return to the Main Menu.

Programmer Guide

Appendix A, "Source Listing for File/Record Collision Tester," lists the source code for the Collision Tester. If you put a bookmark or finger on Appendix A, you can trace through the code as the text describes the program. The start of the program, main(), appears at the end of the program listing.

The main() function initializes the program, says hello, sets certain interrupt vectors to point to certain functions in the program, and then issues a TSR function call. Initialization consists of the following series of actions:

❏ Determining whether color or monochrone attributes should be used.

❏ Detecting whether the program is loaded already.

❏ Checking the DOS version.

❏ Making sure that SHARE has been run.

❏ Obtaining pointers to variables inside DOS.

❏ Allocating a private stack for later use.

❏ Asking for a drive letter that will be considered as a network drive.

The interrupt vectors that this program uses are (in hex) the following:

08   *BIOS Timer Tick*—Invoked 18.2 times a second by the computer hardware, the int08() function first calls the previous Interrupt 8 handler. The program then calls the do_popup() function if (1) the hotkey flag is on, (2) the DOS variables and other flags indicate that it is safe to pop up, and (3) the program is not already popped up.

09   *BIOS Keyboard*—The computer hardware invokes this vector when a key is pressed or released. The interrupt is used here to detect when the hotkey combination has been pressed (int09() sets the hotkey flag).

10   *BIOS Video Functions*—A program wanting to perform screen-related events invokes this interrupt. While Interrupt 10 is active, a flag (in_int10) is set that is used to prevent the program from popping up inside Interrupt 10.

13   *BIOS Disk Functions*—DOS or a program that wants to do direct disk I/O invokes this interrupt, which is also flagged to prevent the program from popping up while active.

16   *BIOS Read Keyboard Functions*—DOS or a program that wants to read a character from the keyboard invokes this interrupt (Interrupt 9, defined previously, places keypresses in a buffer; Interrupt 16 gets a keypress from the buffer and returns that keypress to the caller). Interrupt 16 is flagged (in_int16) and, if it must wait for a keypress to appear in the buffer, this interrupt is also used as an opportunity to pop up. This interrupt works similarly to the way that Interrupt 8 works, which was described previously.

21   *DOS Function Call Entry Point*—All function calls can flow directly into DOS except for *Is Drive Remote?* and *Get Machine Name*. The Predetermined Network Environment section explains the interception of these functions.

24   *DOS Critical Error Handler*—DOS invokes Interrupt 24 to signal such errors as Sector Not Found or Sharing Violation. The Interrupt 24 handler inside DOS displays the Abort, Retry, Ignore? message. By intercepting Interrupt 24, the program avoids this message.

28   *DOS Idle*—When DOS is idle, it periodically invokes this interrupt. This mostly happens at the DOS prompt, when COMMAND.COM waits for you to enter a command or program name to execute. The Collision Tester uses Interrupt 28 as an opportunity to pop up. This interrupt works similarly to the way that Interrupt 8 works, which was described previously.

1B   Keyboard Ctrl-Break

1C   Auxiliary Timer Tick

23   DOS Ctrl-Break

    During the pop-up, these interrupts are disabled. Each is essentially turned into a `No Operation` for the duration of the pop-up.

Predetermined Network Environment

As was mentioned in Chapter 2, "Multiuser Concepts," the SHARE.EXE program can be used to enable file sharing on a stand-alone machine as well as on a network workstation. The Collision Tester exploits this capability to allow you to test file sharing and record locking, obtain the machine name, and determine network drives on a stand-alone machine. In other words, you do not have to be on a network to use the Collision Tester.

Inside the `int21()` function, function 0x4409 is intercepted so the Collision Tester can respond positively to the *Is Drive Remote?* call. Function 5E00 is intercepted so the Collision Tester can return machine name `"01TEST      "` to a request from your program. These "pretend network conditions" remain in effect until your program is finished running.

Files and Records

When you pop up the Collision Tester and tell it to open a file, the program prompts you for the file name, the Inheritance Flag, the sharing mode, the access mode, and the record length. The program uses the first few items to issue DOS function call 3D, *Open File*. To construct the Open mode byte required by the DOS Open File function, the Collision Tester uses your responses to set the fields `file_inherit`, `file_sharing`, and `file_access` to values that the test program simply ORs into the AL register for the call to function 3D. If the open succeeds, the file name, file handle, and other data are inserted into a table. The record length you specify is used later if you tell the program to lock a record in the file. If the open fails, the DOS error code is displayed.

When you tell the Collision Tester to lock a record, the test program asks you Which file? and Which record number?. The program uses your responses to issue a function call 5C request to DOS (*Lock/Unlock File Region*). The program calculates the starting file position of the file region as follows:

```
Record Length × (Record Number - 1)
```

NETBIOS Microscope

The NETBIOS Microscope (NETTEST.EXE) is a simple test bed you can use to explore NETBIOS PC-to-PC communications. From a menu, you pick the NETBIOS command that you want to execute. NETTEST issues the command and shows you the result. Using NETTEST, you can do the following:

- ❑ Add and delete names to and from the local name table.
- ❑ Create and destroy sessions.
- ❑ Send and receive messages.
- ❑ Obtain session status and adapter status information.

If you have a willing partner (or two physically adjacent workstations you can operate), you can establish NETTEST sessions across the network. You can even establish sessions between two names within a single workstation.

User Guide

To install NETTEST, copy the executable file NETTEST.EXE into one of the directories expressed by the PATH that you set up on your computer. To run the program, type **NETTEST** at a DOS prompt. NETTEST checks to make sure that NETBIOS is active and displays the menu shown in figure 8.4.

To pick a NETTEST menu item, type its number and press Enter. When you choose the Exit option, NETTEST does *not* perform any cleanup activity. Sessions that you created and names that you added remain intact when you exit. Use the Session Status and Adapter Status menu items to reveal the status of current sessions and names if you are in doubt about

Fig. 8.4. *Main Menu of NETBIOS Microscope.*

```
NET-TEST Menu:

0...exit
1...reset adapter
2...adapter status
3...add name
4...add group name
5...delete name
6...call
7...listen
8...send
9...receive
10...receive any
11...hang up
12...session status

Choice?
```

them. Unless you are deliberately doing something unusual, you should close sessions with the Hang Up command and clean up the local name table with the Delete Name command before exiting NETTEST.

When you select a NETBIOS command from the menu, NETTEST may ask you for additional information (such as the name you want to add for an Add Name operation). NETTEST then issues the command in its no-wait form to NETBIOS and redisplays the Main Menu. While you look at the menu (and possibly issue another command), NETBIOS executes the command in the background. At the completion of the command, a window pops up to show the results. The only command that is executed immediately is Reset Adapter.

If a command fails to execute, NETTEST displays an error message in the pop up window.

Session Status and Adapter Status

NETTEST displays the result of a Session Status command in the format shown in figure 8.5.

For an Adapter Status command, NETTEST displays the returned information in a series of screens, shown in figures 8.6 through 8.10.

Fig. 8.5. Session Status results.

```
NET-┌[NetTest POST results]─────────────────────────────────────┐
  0..│Command: SESSION STATUS                                    │
  1..│Immed: success.  Final: success.                           │
  2..│Names: 255   sessions: 3                                    │
  3..│lsn = 3  (Active session)  recvcount = 0  sendcount = 0     │
  4..│localname = 'CHRIS        '  remotename = 'SCOTT         '  │
  5..│lsn = 2  (Active session)  recvcount = 0  sendcount = 0     │
  6..│localname = 'SCOTT        '  remotename = 'CHRIS         '  │
  7..│lsn = 1  (Active session)  recvcount = 0  sendcount = 0     │
  8..│localname = 'BARRY        '  remotename = 'SERVER1       '  │
  9..│                                                           │
 10..│                                                           │
 11..│                                                           │
 12..│                                                           │
     │                                                           │
     │            (Press a key)                                  │
     └───────────────────────────────────────────────────────────┘
```

Fig. 8.6. First part of Adapter Status data.

```
NET-┌[NetTest POST results]─────────────────────────────────────┐
  0..│Command: ADAPTER STATUS                                    │
  1..│Immed: success.  Final: success.                           │
  2..│Card ID (hex): A8 B3 00 5A 00 10                           │
  3..│                                                           │
  4..│   Release level: 02                                       │
  5..│                                                           │
  6..│    Adapter type: FF                                       │
  7..│                                                           │
  8..│   Old/new parms: 13                                       │
  9..│                                                           │
 10..│                                                           │
 11..│                                                           │
 12..│                                                           │
     │                                                           │
     │            (Press a key)                                  │
     └───────────────────────────────────────────────────────────┘
```

Fig. 8.7. *Second part of Adapter Status data.*

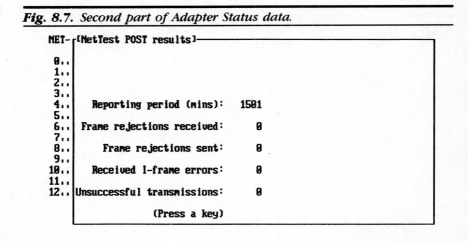

```
NET-┌[NetTest POST results]─────────────────────────────────┐
 0..│                                                        │
 1..│                                                        │
 2..│                                                        │
 3..│                                                        │
 4..│     Reporting period (mins):   1501                    │
 5..│                                                        │
 6..│ Frame rejections received:        0                    │
 7..│                                                        │
 8..│    Frame rejections sent:         0                    │
 9..│                                                        │
10..│  Received I-frame errors:         0                    │
11..│                                                        │
12..│Unsuccessful transmissions:        0                    │
    │                                                        │
    │              (Press a key)                             │
    └────────────────────────────────────────────────────────┘
```

Fig. 8.8. *Third part of Adapter Status data.*

```
NET-┌[NetTest POST results]─────────────────────────────────┐
 0..│                                                        │
 1..│                                                        │
 2..│                                                        │
 3..│                                                        │
 4..│Good transmissions:        1596                         │
 5..│                                                        │
 6..│   Good receptions:          74                         │
 7..│                                                        │
 8..│                                                        │
 9..│                                                        │
10..│                                                        │
11..│                                                        │
12..│                                                        │
    │                                                        │
    │              (Press a key)                             │
    └────────────────────────────────────────────────────────┘
```

Fig. 8.9. Fourth part of Adapter Status data.

```
NET-┌[NetTest POST results]────────────────────────────────┐
 0..│                                                      │
 1..│                                                      │
 2..│                                                      │
 3..│                                                      │
 4..│          Retransmissions:       0                    │
 5..│       Exhausted resources:      0                    │
 6..│           Available NCB's:      8                    │
 7..│      Max configured NCB's:      8                    │
 8..│       Max possible NCB's:     255                    │
 9..│         Pending sessions:       1                    │
10..│ Max configured sessions:        6                    │
11..│    Max possible sessions:     254                    │
12..│          Max frame size:     1028                    │
    │                                                      │
    │              (Press a key)                           │
    └──────────────────────────────────────────────────────┘
```

Fig. 8.10. Last part of Adapter Status data.

```
NET-┌[NetTest POST results]────────────────────────────────┐
 0..│MIDI            (#2)  Registered        Unique name    │
 1..│MIDI            (#3)  Registered        Unique name    │
 2..│MIDI            (#4)  Registered        Unique name    │
 3..│                                                       │
 4..│                                                       │
 5..│                                                       │
 6..│                                                       │
 7..│                                                       │
 8..│                                                       │
 9..│                                                       │
10..│                                                       │
11..│                                                       │
12..│                                                       │
    │                                                       │
    │              (Press a key)                            │
    └───────────────────────────────────────────────────────┘
```

NETTEST Sessions

To create a session between two NETBIOS names (on the same workstation or on different workstations), first add the names to the local name tables. Choose the Add Name menu option for each name and watch for a successful completion of each command. For example, you could add the name SCOTT and then add the name CHRIS.

Next, issue a Listen command for one of the names. Specify one of the names as the listener (CHRIS) and specify the other name as the one being listened for (SCOTT). Alternatively, you can specify that CHRIS "listen for a call from anyone" by using an asterisk (*) in place of a specific name. You now have a Listen command outstanding.

Establish the session by having SCOTT call CHRIS. Choose the Call menu option and designate SCOTT as the caller (the local name) and CHRIS as the name to be called (the remote name).

If all goes according to plan, when both the Listen and Call commands finish you will see a display of screens similar to those shown in figures 8.11 and 8.12. Make a note of the Local Session Number (LSN) assigned to each partner in the session. You will need each LSN to send and receive messages.

Fig. 8.11. *POST result of a Listen command.*

```
NET-┌[NetTest POST results]──────────────────────────────┐
    │Command: LISTEN                                      │
  0..│Immed: success.  Final: success.                    │
  1..│                                                    │
  2..│                                                    │
  3..│Session established with 'SCOTT        ',  LSN = 3. │
  4..│                                                    │
  5..│                                                    │
  6..│                                                    │
  7..│                                                    │
  8..│                                                    │
  9..│                                                    │
 10..│                                                    │
 11..│                                                    │
 12..│                                                    │
    │                                                    │
    │          (Press a key)                             │
    └────────────────────────────────────────────────────┘
```

Sending and Receiving Messages

Now that you have established a session, you can use the Send and Receive menu options to transfer text messages between the two workstations (or between the two names on the same workstation). Have one session partner issue a Receive (you will be prompted for the LSN you made a note of earlier). Then have the other session partner issue a Send. When you pick the Send menu option, you will be prompted for both the LSN (use the one assigned to the sending session partner!) and the text of a message. When the Receive command is completed, NETTEST displays a

Fig. 8.12. POST result of a Call command.

```
NET-┌[NetTest POST results]──────────────────────────────┐
    │Command: CALL                                        │
 0..│Immed: success.  Final: success.                     │
 1..│                                                     │
 2..│                                                     │
 3..│Session established.  LSN = 2.                       │
 4..│                                                     │
 5..│                                                     │
 6..│                                                     │
 7..│                                                     │
 8..│                                                     │
 9..│                                                     │
10..│                                                     │
11..│                                                     │
12..│                                                     │
    │                                                     │
    │               (Press a key)                         │
    └─────────────────────────────────────────────────────┘
```

screen similar to that shown in figure 8.13. You will also be notified when the Send command completes.

Fig. 8.13. Received message.

```
NET-┌[NetTest POST results]──────────────────────────────┐
    │Command: RECEIVE                                     │
 0..│Immed: success.  Final: success.                     │
 1..│                                                     │
 2..│                                                     │
 3..│Message says:                                        │
 4..│This is a simple text message.                       │
 5..│                                                     │
 6..│                                                     │
 7..│                                                     │
 8..│                                                     │
 9..│                                                     │
10..│                                                     │
11..│                                                     │
12..│                                                     │
    │                                                     │
    │               (Press a key)                         │
    └─────────────────────────────────────────────────────┘
```

Programmer Guide

Appendix B, "Source Listing for NETBIOS Microscope," contains the code listing for this program (each of the programs described in this chapter is listed in one of the appendixes). You can trace the code with a bookmark or finger as the text describes the program.

The user guide implied how the program functions. When you pick a menu option, the program issues the appropriate NETBIOS command in its no-wait form. A POST routine is used to signal the end of each command. As many as 10 Network Control Blocks can be outstanding at any one time; a wraparound (circular) buffer maintains these NCBs; after the 10th item is POSTed, the next item goes into the first slot. Each item consists of the segment and offset portions of the completed NCB's address.

While waiting for a menu selection to be typed at the keyboard, the program also awaits a signal from the POST routine indicating that a command has completed. Touching a key sends the program into the code that processes each menu selection. The completion of a NETBIOS command, as signaled by the POST routine, sends the program into the `report_result()` function, where the results from a completed command are displayed. The Reset command, however, does not cause the POST routine to occur.

For any command but Reset, the program constructs a Network Control Block, issues it to NETBIOS, and lets NETBIOS process the command in the background. For the Reset command, the program waits for the command to finish before continuing. Some of the commands require information (a name, a Local Session Number, or a text message) to fill in the NCB. These items are requested as necessary. Defaults are used for some of the parameters in the NCB. In particular, the Receive time-out and Send time-out values given in the Call and Listen commands are hard-coded. You may want to change these and recompile the program if the defaults do not suit your needs.

The function `post()` is used as a POST routine. The completion of any command (except Reset) causes NETBIOS to call `post()`. The function inserts the address of the completed NCB into a table of far pointers (segments and offsets), and returns to NETBIOS.

The `report_result()` function interprets the NCB_COMMAND field as well as the NCB_RET_CODE and NCB_CMD_CPLT fields in the completed NCB. For each different command, this function then displays the data returned by NETBIOS. For the Adapter Status command, this data consists of a series of screens showing the information in the `adapter_status` structure. For an Add Name or Add Group Name operation, the assigned name number is shown. The Call and Listen commands cause the assigned Local Session Number to be displayed. The contents of the text message are displayed when a Receive command is completed. A Session Status command results in a display of information about each of the sessions for a name in the local name table.

Remote Program Execution

With the Remote Program Execution (RPE) facility, you designate one of the workstations on the LAN as an unattended slave machine on which you run batch (noninteractive) programs. The programs (and DOS commands) executed on the slave machine are submitted remotely through NETBIOS. One component of the RPE facility, RPE.EXE, runs on the slave machine and executes the submitted "jobs." You use the other component, REMOTE.EXE, to submit the jobs that RPE executes.

What sort of programs are good candidates for RPE to run as jobs? Compilers and linkers are obviously good examples, as are unattended tape backups. A good candidate program has the following attributes:

- ❏ Takes more than a few seconds to run
- ❏ Does not require keyboard interaction
- ❏ Terminates after running a finite length of time

RPE maintains a queue of as many as 50 jobs that are awaiting execution. Not only can you use REMOTE to submit jobs to RPE, you can issue Status, Cancel, and Quit commands to find out what is in the queue, cancel a job in the queue, or terminate RPE when the queue is empty. Output from the command or program that ordinarily would go to the screen is automatically redirected into a file you can inspect when the job is completed. RPE also maintains a log of all job activity.

User Guide

To install the RPE.EXE component, copy the executable file into one of the directories expressed by the PATH statement on the slave machine. To start up the facility on the slave machine, type **RPE** at a DOS prompt. The program prompts you for a network (file server) drive letter and path where RPE should write its log file. If you answer, for example, H:\JOBS, the full name of the log file will be H:\JOBS\RPE.LOG. The redirected output of each program will be written to this same directory. When RPE is running, you can submit jobs remotely from one of the other workstations on the network.

The drive letter must represent a file server disk; otherwise, nobody on the network will be able to view either the log file or the redirected output files.

Install the REMOTE.EXE component by copying the executable file into one of the PATH directories on each workstation.

Submitting a Job Using REMOTE

To submit a job to RPE, type the word **REMOTE**, followed by a space, followed by the exact DOS command or program name that you want executed on the RPE slave computer, as shown in the following examples:

```
remote chdir \compile
```

or

```
remote tcc bigprog
```

If RPE is not running, you will see the following:

```
Couldn't connect: no answer.
REMOTE ended (unsuccessfully).
```

If RPE is already running a job, REMOTE informs you that your job will go into the queue and asks whether this is okay. If the queue is full (50 jobs are awaiting execution), you will see the following message:

```
The queue is full at this time.  Try later.
```

Otherwise, REMOTE and RPE exchange a few data messages and you next should see the following:

```
Job # XXXX in queue on machine NNNNN
```

where *XXXX* represents the assigned job number and *NNNNN* represents the machine name of the slave computer.

RPE writes an entry in the log file RPE.LOG when each job starts and when it finishes. Elapsed time is shown for each job, and each entry in the log file carries a date-and-time stamp. When initiating the job, RPE uses the angle bracket (<) notation on the DOS command line. This notation redirects the STDOUT screen output to a file named *jXXXX.out*, where *XXXX* is the assigned job number.

When the job is completed, you can inspect the contents of the *jXXXX.out* file to see how the execution went.

Using Status, Cancel, and Quit Commands

You can find out what is in the queue by invoking REMOTE as follows:

```
remote status
```

After REMOTE and RPE exchange a few messages, you next see a display similar to the following example:

```
There are 3 jobs in MAINFRAME's queue.

JOB       COMMAND
--------  ----------------------------------------
J0030     tcc bigfile     EXECUTING
J0031     tcc applic      PENDING
J0032     lc -L othprog   PENDING
```

You can cancel a job anytime before it begins executing. Use this syntax to cancel, for example, job number 31:

```
remote cancel j31
```

You can also tell RPE to stop. Type

remote quit

and RPE terminates as soon as the queue is empty.

Programmer Guide

Appendix C, "Source Listing for RPE.C," and Appendix D, "Source Listing for REMOTE.C," list the source code for these programs. If you are using a bookmark or finger to hold your place in the appendixes, note that the text discusses the RPE program first.

RPE (Program Launcher)

First, RPE creates a far pointer to the transient portion of COMMAND.COM, located in upper memory. I will soon explain how this far pointer is used. Next, the job queue is initialized. RPE checks to make sure that the following conditions are true:

❏ The DOS version is 3.0 or later.
❏ SHARE.EXE is loaded.
❏ The machine name has been set.
❏ NETBIOS is active.

After asking NETBIOS to add its name (RPE) to the local name table, RPE then asks which network drive letter and path to use for the log file. RPE attempts to create a new file with the name RPE.LOG. If the file exists already, the call fails and RPE then attempts to open the existing file for Read/Write access, using a sharing mode of Deny None. The file is opened in Append mode, so the existing contents of the file are not disturbed. If the file cannot be opened, RPE instructs NETBIOS to delete the name RPE from its name table before RPE displays an error message and terminates.

If RPE does not encounter any problems, it displays RPE Started and issues a NETBIOS Listen command. This command specifies:

❑ Listen for a call to RPE.

❑ The call can be from anyone.

❑ The POST routine is called background_listen().

❑ A time-out value of 10 seconds for the Send and Receive commands issued in the upcoming session.

RPE then goes into a loop, waiting for a user to stop it manually at the slave machine's keyboard, or for a NETBIOS error to happen. Inside the loop, if RPE finds that the background processing established a session and placed an item in the queue, the program calls execute_program() to satisfy the job submission request.

A Call from another workstation triggers background (asynchronous) processing in RPE. A session is established (RPE saves the assigned Local Session Number), and RPE begins the dialog by sending a message to the Caller. The message contains the machine name of the slave computer and an indicator of whether the queue is empty. RPE then receives from the Caller a message containing either a command line to be executed, or a Status, Cancel, or Quit signal. If the message contains a command line, RPE puts the job in the queue, assigns a job number, sends this job number back to the Caller in a NETBIOS message, and closes the session by doing a Hang Up. If the message contains a Status, Cancel, or Quit signal, RPE sends the Caller the requested information (if appropriate) and closes the session. Unless RPE receives a Quit signal, the program reissues a Listen command to restart the process.

RPE executes a job by using the system() library function to invoke a secondary copy of COMMAND.COM and instructing COMMAND.COM to run the program represented by the job. Before executing the program, RPE sets to zero the far pointer to the top of COMMAND.COM. (This step prevents an obscure bug in some versions of DOS, by forcing COMMAND.COM to reload its upper-memory command processor.) An entry is written to the log file, the DOS command line is constructed, and the job is run. Elapsed time is measured and written to the log file when the job is completed.

REMOTE (Job Submission)

When you tell REMOTE to submit a job, the program begins processing by checking the DOS version and making sure that NETBIOS is active. REMOTE obtains the permanent node name from NETBIOS by performing an Adapter Status command and prefixing 10 binary 0s to the first six bytes of data returned by Adapter Status.

REMOTE then makes an exact copy of its command line and builds a data message to send to RPE. REMOTE issues a Call command to NETBIOS, specifying the following:

❑ A remote name of RPE

❑ A local name equal to the permanent node name

❑ Time-out values of 10 seconds each for Send and Receive commands issued in the upcoming session

Because RPE always starts the conversation by sending its machine name in a data message, the first thing REMOTE does after the session is established is issue a Receive command. The data message also contains an indication of whether RPE's queue is empty. If the queue is not empty, REMOTE asks whether the submitted job can go into the queue.

REMOTE then sends its command line to the RPE machine. This command line might contain a DOS command, a program to be executed, the word cancel, the word status, or the word quit. REMOTE receives a reply from RPE and closes the session with a Hang Up command.

The reply from RPE is an assigned job number, the contents of the awaiting-execution queue (status), or confirmation of a cancel or quit request. REMOTE displays the information contained in the reply and terminates.

Dialog Design

The dialog between RPE and REMOTE is outlined as follows:

```
                    SESSION DIALOG DESIGN


      RPE (listener)                REMOTE (caller)
   ----------------------------    --------------------------------
1. Send:
   - machine name
   - idle/busy status

                                1. Receive:
                                   - machine name
                                   - status

                                2. Send:
                                   - command line
                                   if command line = 'quit',
                                   hang up

2. Receive:
   - command line

   if command line = 'quit',
    hang up and don't take
    further job requests

3. if command line = 'status', Send:
   - count of pending items
   - 0 to 50 pending items
   (then hang up)

                                3. Receive:
                                   - queue status
                                   (then hang up)

4. If command line = 'cancel', Send:
   - job-not-found, or confirmation
   (then hang up)
```

```
                              4. Receive:
                                 - cancellation response
                                 (then hang up)

     5. Send:
        - job number packet
          (then hang up)

                              5. Receive:
                                 - job number packet
                                 (then hang up)
```

Electronic Mail

The E-Mail application lets you send memos to other users on your LAN. By using the "carbon copy" feature, you can attach a binary or text file (such as a spreadsheet, a long letter, a report, or a .EXE) to each memo, and then you can send your memo to a list of people. E-Mail does not require any disk space or special rights on the file server; the memos are sent directly from user to user through NETBIOS.

User Guide

Two programs make up the E-Mail application. The first is the Postman. This small TSR, which has no user interface, simply receives and delivers mail. Postman places incoming mail in a specified directory, and periodically checks whether your out basket has any mail messages that need to be delivered.

The second program, Mail, is a somewhat larger TSR that contains the user interface for sending and receiving mail, including a simple text editor. You can pop up the Mail program to send a memo or to read your incoming mail. To send mail, you use the text editor to compose a memo and, when you finish, you specify a file attachment (if any) and a CC list (if any). The Postman then is triggered so that it can deliver your message. The text editor supports memos as much as one screen long. You use the Alt-RightShift keyboard combination to pop up the Mail program. The Mail program is text-based. When you are running a program that has put your workstation into graphics mode and you try to pop up the Mail program, Mail beeps to let you know that it currently cannot use the screen.

To read a mail message, you scroll through your in basket and pick the item you want to read. After you read the item, you then can reply to the message, delete it, print it, or save it as a regular file.

Mail is delivered only if the recipients are running the Postman program at their workstations. If your Postman and the recipient's Postman cannot make a connection when you put the item in your out basket, your Postman tries again every ten minutes thereafter. Presumably, the recipient will run his or her Postman program at some time during the day!

In addition to the NETBIOS version of these programs, the disk accompanying this book contains an IPX and SPX version of both Postman and Mail in the disk directory named NETWARE. If you use Novell NetWare on your LAN, you can choose to load the Novell NETBIOS emulator (NETBIOS.EXE) and run the NETBIOS version of these programs, or you can choose to use the IPX and SPX version of Postman and Mail found in the NETWARE disk directory.

When you run the Postman, the program notes the current drive and directory. All incoming mail and attached files are placed in the current directory. The Postman also sets its "alarm clock" to wake up every ten minutes, at which time the program checks your out basket for undelivered mail. Before exiting to DOS as a TSR, the Postman displays a message reminding you to run the Mail program if you want to view your in basket or out basket. While the Postman is loaded, it is always ready to receive mail.

The Mail program is also a TSR. Although larger than the Postman program (Mail is 48 kilobytes, Postman is 24 kilobytes), Mail is easily unloaded from memory to give you room to run other applications. Unless you are *really* cramped for memory space, you should consider leaving Postman running for as long as you are on the network.

Installing the Mail Program and Popping Up

If you have a hard drive on your workstation, you should make a directory named MAIL on your C: drive and copy the POSTMAN.EXE and MAIL.EXE programs to that directory. If you do not have a hard drive, you can make a directory on the file server and copy the programs to the directory, but make sure that all users have their own directory for receiving mail. The Postman program will get confused if two users try to share the same file server directory for E-Mail! The mail messages are not encrypted in any way, so for privacy I strongly recommend that you use the local hard disk installation method.

After you log on to the network, you run the Postman program and then the Mail program. You should first make your MAIL directory your current directory so that the Postman knows where to put your incoming mail. If you construct a .BAT file to load the Postman and Mail programs, it should look like this:

```
C:
CD \MAIL
POSTMAN
MAIL
```

After the Postman is loaded, you can change drives and directories without affecting where the files containing your mail messages are placed.

When you pop up the Mail program by pressing Alt-RightShift, the program displays a screen similar to that shown in figure 8.14.

Fig. 8.14. *Main screen of the Mail program.*

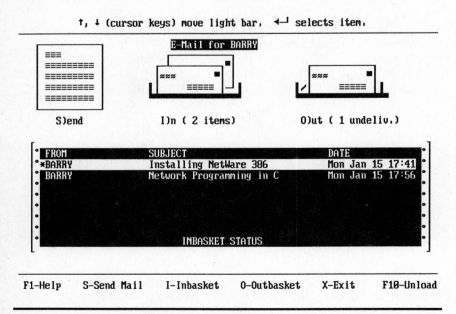

The bottom line of the screen shows the keys you press to tell the Mail program what to do:

❑ The F1 key to get help.

❑ The S key to send a memo.

❑ The I key to view your in basket.

❑ The O key to view your out basket (that is, any undelivered mail).

❑ The X key to exit E-Mail.

❑ The F10 key to unload the Mail program from memory.

Sending and receiving mail are described later. For now, note that the I and O keys toggle the display between the in basket and the out basket. The X key returns you to the foreground application (or to the DOS prompt). Not only can you use the F10 key to remove MAIL.EXE from memory, but also, if you need the extra memory, you can press Alt-F10 to cause both MAIL.EXE and POSTMAN.EXE to be removed from memory. Remember, however, that you cannot receive mail from other users if Postman is not running. After running your memory-intensive application, you should go back to the C:\MAIL directory and reload the Postman.

For each item in your in basket, Mail shows the sender's name, the subject of the memo, and the date and time the memo was sent. For out-basket items, Mail shows the recipient's name, the subject, and the date and time the memo was placed in the out basket.

Sending Mail

Press the S key to send mail. You can practice sending mail by sending a message to yourself. From a DOS prompt, follow these steps to send the mail message:

1. Pop up the Mail program with Alt-RightShift. Note your workstation name; it is displayed as *XXXXXX* in the E-Mail for *XXXXXX* message on the screen.

2. Press the *S* key.

3. Respond to the TO: prompt by typing the name by which your workstation is known on the network. Press Enter.

4. For SUBJECT:, type **Practice Test** and press Enter.

5. You are now in the text editor. Type a couple of lines (remember that the editor does not have word wrap; press Enter before you get to the end of a line). You can type anything at all. No one but you will see the message.

6. Press F2 when you are finished composing the message to yourself.

7. Press Enter when you are prompted for an attachment file name.

8. To receive two copies of the message, respond to the CC: prompt by typing your workstation name again, and press Enter.

The next thing you see is the main screen for the Mail program. Very soon afterward, you should hear a beep and see the message You have mail at the bottom of your screen. The message goes away by itself. You then should see your mail message appear in the in basket on the screen. The beep and the momentary message repeat themselves when the CC message is also received and placed in your in basket.

Do not read your mail yet. Press X to return to DOS, and select a file in another directory (not C:\MAIL) that you would not mind having two copies of. Note the drive, directory, and file name. Then pop up the Mail program again and follow the preceding steps to send another message to yourself. This time, when you see the Attach File: prompt, specify the drive, directory, and file name of the file you just found. After the test, pop back to DOS and look in the C:\MAIL directory to see what the Postman delivered.

Reading and Disposing of Mail

If you have several items in your in basket (which holds as many as 50 memos), use the up-arrow or down-arrow cursor keys to select one item to read. Press Enter when the item you want is highlighted. The text of the selected mail message appears; a sample of such a screen is shown in figure 8.15.

You can press the Esc key to leave the item in your in basket; you can press D to delete the item; or you can press P to print the message (make sure that your printer is ready). You also can press S to save the message as a regular text file, in which case Mail prompts for a file name. Finally, you can press R to reply to the mail message. Selecting this last option causes the Mail program to automatically switch the TO: and FROM: fields and put you in the text editor, where you can compose your reply.

In the display of your in basket, an asterisk (*) before the sender's name identifies items that you have already read.

If an item sits in your out-basket for a long time, you may have misspelled the name of the recipient. To correct the name, press O to switch to the out-basket display and select the item by highlighting it with the up-arrow or down-arrow cursor keys. Press Enter. You next see options

Fig. 8.15. *A mail message screen.*

```
TO: BARRY            FROM: BARRY              DATE: Mon Jan 15 17:56
SUBJECT: Network Programming in C

    This is the Electronic Mail application that accompanies the
"Network Programming in C" book from Que Publishing.  It allows
short memos to be quickly routed across the LAN to the addressee.
Binary or text files may be attached to the E-Mail memos.  And you
can send "carbon copies" to multiple addressees.

    The text editor is simple but adequate.  You can insert and
delete lines, cursor to anywhere on the memo, and erase-to-end-of-
line.  It does not, however, support word wrap.  It also only allows
a single screen's worth of text to be edited (this constitutes one
memo).




ESC - Exit    D - Delete Mail    S - Save as file    P - Print    R - Reply
```

for changing or deleting the message. If you press C, to pick the Change option, you can retype the recipient's workstation name. The Postman then can successfully deliver the mail message.

Using the Text Editor

You can use the text editor to compose mail messages as much as one screen long. To send a longer memo, use a more powerful text editor or word processor to write the memo and attach the memo to a mail message.

The first two lines of the text editor screen are significant. The prompts TO: and SUBJECT: should not be modified. The Mail program looks for these phrases to identify the recipient and the subject of the mail message. The remainder of each line after the words TO: and SUBJECT:, however, is modifiable. The name you specify in the TO: area is used as the destination of the mail message and should contain the workstation name associated with the user who should receive the message. The phrase you specify after the word SUBJECT: will identify the message in the recipient's in-basket display. If you inadvertently put in your out-basket an item that contains an invalid workstation name, you can use the procedure described earlier to correct the name.

As with any text editor, certain keys cause certain things to happen. Figure 8.16 shows the layout of the text editor screen. Pressing the following keys results in the following actions:

❏ Esc quits the text editor without sending the message.

❏ F2 schedules the message for delivery to the recipient.

❏ F4 erases the text from the cursor to the end of the line.

❏ F5 inserts a blank line between two existing lines.

❏ F10 deletes the line that the cursor is on.

❏ The up-arrow, down-arrow, left-arrow, and right-arrow keys move the cursor around the editor screen.

❏ The Tab key moves the cursor four spaces to the right.

❏ The Home key moves the cursor to the beginning of the line.

❏ The End key moves the cursor to the end of the line.

❏ The Del key deletes the character that the cursor is on.

❏ The Backspace key moves the cursor to the left, just as the left-arrow cursor key; Backspace does not delete characters that the cursor is on.

❏ The Ins key toggles Insert mode.

Word wrap is not supported; make sure that you press Enter at the end of each line, before you reach the right side of the screen.

```
TO: <addressee>
SUBJECT: <subject phrase>

<body of message>

ESC-Quit  F2-Save  F4-Erase EOL  F5-Insert Line  F10-
Delete Line
```

Programmer Guide

The source code for the Postman program is listed in Appendix E, "Source Listing for the Postman Program." The Mail program is listed in Appendix F, "Source Listing for the Electronic Mail Program." The NetWare-specific (IPX and SPX version) program code is not listed in this book, but appears in the NETWARE directory on the accompanying disk.

The Postman program occupies about 24 kilobytes of memory when it is resident. The Mail program, on the other hand, occupies about 48 kilobytes. Both programs originally were a single program, but I split the functions into two programs after I realized that some users might want to unload the Mail program to have enough memory to run large applications. Leaving the smaller Postman program in memory just to receive incoming mail is a good compromise.

Quite a bit of effort went into the TSR and interprocess communication techniques used by these two programs. I could write an entire book just on these techniques! However, because this book focuses on network programming techniques, the following program descriptions concentrate on the programs' PC-to-PC communications.

The Postman Program

Although smaller than the Mail program, Postman is easily the more complex of the two programs. At its outset, Postman performs the same sort of TSR initialization described earlier in the Collision Tester discussion. Postman also does a getcwd() call to find out the current working directory. Before making itself resident, Postman gets machine name, prefixes the name with a ! character, and uses the result to do an Add Name operation. Postman uses the ! character to avoid conflicts with the IBM PC LAN Program, which is already using machine name in its sessions with the file server. The program then issues a Receive Datagram call to NETBIOS and terminates to DOS with a TSR function call.

The mail messages (and optional attached files) that one Postman sends to another Postman are sent as a series of datagrams. Each datagram packet is formatted as follows:

```
typedef struct
    {
    char type;
    int  sequence;
    int  data_length;
    char data [500];
    }
    MAIL_PACKET;
```

The type field identifies the type of packet:

```
01 - Acknowledgment (returned by recipient)

10 - Mail Header    (first one in each set)
20 - Mail Data      (carries mail message text)
```

Listing continues

Listing continued

```
30 - Mail EOF        (signals the end of the mail message)
50 - File Header     (first packet for an attached file)
60 - File Data       (carries parts of the attached file)
70 - File EOF        (signals the end of the attachment)
99 - Trailer         (last packet of each set)
```

The *sequence* field is used to ensure that datagrams arrive in the proper order and that none is missed. The data_length field tells how long the data area is. The *data* field contains a portion of the mail message or attached file.

The function POST_routine() handles each datagram that the Postman receives. This function merely sets two flags, mail_flag (which triggers Postman to do background processing) and incoming_msg (which tells the background code that a datagram was received and needs to be processed).

Several events trigger Postman to do background processing:

❏ The reception of a datagram, as was previously mentioned. (incoming_msg).

❏ The expiration of a 10-minute time period, which causes Postman to look for out-basket items that it can attempt to deliver. The Mail program can alter this time-out value to cause mail to be sent without waiting the full 10 minutes. (outbasket_alarm).

❏ The expiration of a 60-second time-out. Postman sets up this counter for incoming mail. Because a mail message (and optional attached file) are transmitted as several datagrams, this counter tells the Postman that 60 seconds have passed since the program last received the previous packet in a series of incoming packets. (incoming_alarm).

❏ The expiration of a 5-second time-out. When Postman sends an initial datagram to a mail recipient, the program waits five seconds for an acknowledgment. If no acknowledgment is received, the sending Postman assumes that the recipient's Postman is not running and goes on to the next item in the out-basket. (no_answer_alarm).

When one of these events happens, Postman uses the next timer tick (Interrupt 8), the next keyboard idle time (Interrupt 16), or the next DOS idle time (Interrupt 28) to wake itself up. Background processing begins in the process_mail() function, which saves the current machine context, switches to a private stack, and calls the `post_office()` function. After `post_office()` is completed, `process_mail()` restores the machine context and returns, through the interrupt handler, to the foreground process.

The `post_office()` function is the clearinghouse for all background activity. If Postman is sending a mail message to another workstation, and an Acknowledgment datagram packet is received from that workstation, `send_next_packet()` is called to send the next packet in the series.

If another workstation is sending mail (Postman is in the recipient mode rather than the sender mode), and if the datagram packet checks out okay (it is the expected type, and the sequence number is valid), `post_office()` sends an Acknowledgment packet to the other workstation.

If `post_office()` is receiving mail and sees that 60 seconds have passed without receiving the next datagram packet, the function cancels the reception of incoming mail and assumes that the sender workstation will try again later.

If an exploratory Mail Header was sent to another workstation to check whether that workstation is ready to receive mail, and if five seconds elapse without an Acknowledgment of that Mail Header, `post_office()` assumes that the other workstation currently is not logged on or not running the Postman program. The function leaves the item in the out basket and goes on to the next item.

If `post_office()` detects that it is time to check the out basket to see whether another item can be delivered (10 minutes have elapsed since the last attempt), the function invokes the `send_mail()` function to process whatever items are in the out basket.

If an incoming datagram packet has been processed, `post_office()` issues another Receive‑Datagram call to NETBIOS.

The Mail Program

The Mail program creates out basket files named *XXXXXX*.`OUT`, where *XXXXXX* is an ASCII representation for the number returned by the `time()` library function. Similarly, the Postman creates in-basket files named *XXXXXX*.`IN`. When you pop up the Mail program, it looks in Postman's startup directory (usually C:\MAIL) for `*.IN` files and `*.OUT` files. The information from the header portion of each of these files is placed in a table (which can have a maximum of 50 items). The contents of the tables are shown on the screen as in-basket or out-basket items.

Again, I hate to gloss over such things so quickly. The aspects of the Mail program dealing with becoming a TSR and popping up on a hotkey are much like those described earlier for the Collision Tester. There are two important things to look for in the code, however.

The first is the way that Mail does an Interrupt 16 call early in the program, with AH set to PO. If the AH register is returned as po (notice the lower case), Mail knows that Postman is active. From this call, Mail obtains pointers to certain variables inside Postman. One of these pointers is to the outbasket_alarm field. When you send a mail message, the Mail program sets Postman's outbasket_alarm field to 0 and thus causes Postman to wake up and send the mail. Otherwise, you would have to wait for a 10-minute period to elapse before the mail message got delivered. Another pointer that Mail obtains is that of a de_install flag inside Postman. When you press Alt-F10 to tell both the Mail program and the Postman program to remove themselves from memory, Mail uses its pointer to Postman's de_install flag to tell Postman to unload itself.

The other thing to look for is sort of subtle. When the Mail program knows that the keyboard is idle and that DOS is safe to use, the program does a dummy Interrupt 28 call from within the program's own Interrupt 16 handler. This extra DOS Idle Interrupt is important because it gives the Postman program a chance to "breathe"—Postman can take the opportunity to do some background processing even though the Mail program is popped up and active.

When you tell the Mail program that you want to send a memo, the program puts you in the text editor. When you finish composing the message, Mail asks you for the file name of an attachment file and the list of names to which carbon copies should be sent. This information goes into the header of the mail message. The CC list causes the Mail program to create copies of the mail message file, one copy for each recipient. The copies are identified with an alphabetic suffix in the file name (*XXXXXX*A.OUT, *XXXXXX*B.OUT, and so on).

When you use the Mail program to read a mail message, the program loads the text of the mail message into the text editor work area and displays the memo on the screen.

The only network-related action that the Mail program performs is to obtain machine name, which the program uses in the FROM: field of each mail message.

E-Mail Functional Design

The following is the functional specification used for the Postman and Mail programs. Notes regarding NetWare (IPX) calls appear in parentheses and refer to the source code listings on the disk rather than to the listings in the appendixes.

A. Main routine

```
1. Make sure that we are not already loaded
2. Make sure that NETBIOS (or IPX) is loaded
3. Do Add_Name (or IPX_Open_Socket)
4. Install interrupt handlers
5. Issue Receive_Datagram (or IPX_Listen_For_Packet)
6. Terminate and Stay Resident
```

B. De-install routine (de_install flag ON)

```
1. Do nothing until we're last in memory
2. Restore interrupt vectors
3. Cancel Receive_Datagram (or IPX_Listen_For_Packet)
4. Delete_Name (or IPX_Close_Socket)
5. Deallocate memory
6. Exit
```

C. Incoming Mail routine, triggered by POST (or ESR) or timer tick

```
1. If processing incoming mail:
     a. If expected packet not received (60 sec. timeout)
          1. close files
          2. delete files
          3. reset sequence number, etc.
          4. exit
     b. If not a packet-type that we logically expect
          1. close files
          2. delete files
          3. reset sequence number, etc.
          4. reissue receive/listen
          5. exit
     c. If duplicate packet
          1. just resend acknowledgment
          2. reissue receive/listen
          3. exit
```

```
        d. If missing packet
            1. close files
            2. delete files
            3. reset sequence number, etc.
            4. reissue receive/listen
            5. exit
        e. Packet okay; process it
            1. Mail-Header packet
                a. Determine local mail message file name
                b. Create file
            2. Mail-Message-Data packet
                - Write to mail message file
            3. Mail-Message-EOF packet
                - Close mail message file
            4. Attached-File-Header packet
                - Create new file
            5. Attached-File-Data packet
                - Write to file
            6. Attached-File-EOF packet
                - Close file
            7. Mail-Trailer packet
                a. Put item in in basket
                b. Set Expected-Sequence-Number to zero
        f. Ask for next packet
            1. Return an acknowledgment
            2. Increment sequence number (0 if Trailer)
            3. Reissue Receive_Datagram (or IPX_Listen_For_Packet)
            4. Exit


    2. If receiving acknowledgment for mail we sent:
        a. Prepare to send the next packet, if any (see the following)
```

Deliver an out-basket item

```
    1. Occurs every 10 minutes, or when new item in out basket
    2. Send Mail-Header for an out basket item
    3. If no acknowledgment within 5 seconds
        - go on to next item
    4. After checking last item, go back to sleep
    5. If acknowledgment received, proceed:
    6. Send packets
        a. Mail-Message-Data (as many as needed)
        b. Mail-Message-EOF
```

    c. If no attached file, send Mail-Trailer and exit
    d. Attached-File-Header
    e. Attached-File-Data (as many as needed)
    f. Attached-File-EOF
    g. Mail-Trailer
7. For each packet sent, expect an acknowledgment
    a. If ACK not returned in 5 seconds, resend the packet
    b. If 10 error-
s in a row, cancel (leave item in out basket)

Exit pop-up routine

1. Pop up on hotkey flag
2. Wait until DOS is safe to use
3. Switch contexts (just beep if machine in graphics mode)
4. Save application screen
5. Determine status of in basket
6. Determine status of out basket (undelivered mail)
7. Put up our screen, including menu icons
8. Get menu choice and perform subroutine to handle it
    a. Send Mail
    b. Read Mail
    c. Change out basket item
    d. Remove From Memory (sets de_install flag)
    e. Quit
9. If menu option isn't 'Remove', or 'Quit'
    - go back to step 5
10. Restore application screen
11. Restore context
12. Exit from popup routine

Send Mail subroutine

1. Clear the editor area
2. Ask "TO: "
3. Ask "SUBJECT: "
4. Invoke simple text editor
5. After edit session, ask:
    a. Attach file?
    b. Carbon copies?
6. If "attach file", ask for file name and verify that it exists
7. Put mail in out basket
8. Trigger mail-delivery routine
9. Exit

Read Mail routine

```
1. Read mail message into Editor area
2. Show it on screen
3. When done, show submenu:
     a. Leave
     b. Delete
     c. Print
     d. Save as regular file
     e. Reply
4. Mark message as read
5. Exit
```

Change out-basket item

```
1. Suspend mail delivery
2. Allow out basket mail to be withdrawn or changed
3. Trigger mail-delivery routine
4. Exit
```

Summary

This chapter presented four complete applications for you to study and use. Each application is described from both a user perspective and a programmer perspective. The Collision Tester is a tool for seeing how your program reacts when it encounters already open files and already locked records. The NETBIOS Microscope is a menu-driven interface to NETBIOS that lets you easily explore PC-to-PC communications. The Remote Program Execution facility runs batch-type jobs and lets you treat one of the workstations on the LAN almost as a mainframe computer. The E-Mail programs implement LAN-based interoffice mail with an attached-file feature.

As gently and nicely as I possibly can, let me mention something to you at this point. Buying this book gives you the equivalent of a single-user license of the software. If you use any of the software on your LAN, or a modified derivative of the software, you should (for both moral and legal reasons) arrange to purchase a copy of this book for each user. Thank you for your support!

This ends the narrative section of this book. When you turn the page, you will be in the Reference section. As its name suggests, the Reference section is intended to be a source of detailed programming information you can use as you design and code your LAN-aware applications.

Part III

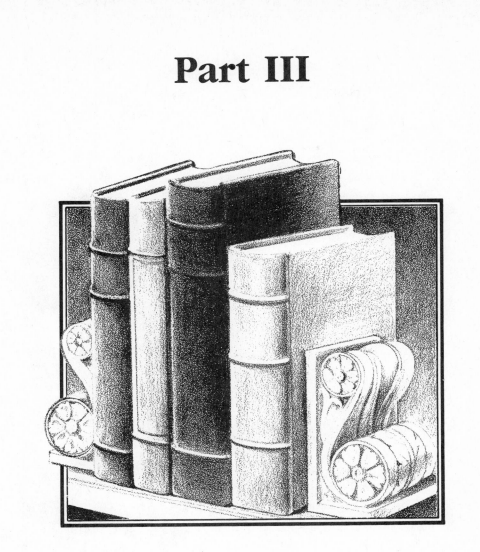

Reference

DOS Services for
Network Programming

This section describes the DOS function calls related to network programming. The descriptions presume that SHARE.EXE is loaded.

Create a File   0x3C

Description: If the file does not exist, this function creates it. If the file exists, the existing contents are discarded by giving the file a length of 0 bytes. DOS then opens the file and returns a file handle. If specified in the CX register, a Read-Only file attribute takes effect only if the file did not previously exist. The Read-Only attribute also takes effect only after the file is closed; you may, of course, write to the file you have just created. The file position is set to the first byte of the file.

Input Registers: AH   0x3C
                              CX   File attributes
                              DS:DX   Far pointer to file name string

Output Registers: Carry flag clear if successful
        AX   File handle

                     Carry flag set if error
        AX   Error code
                  0x03   Path not found
                  0x04   No handles left
                  0x05   Access denied

Network Considerations: If the file already exists and is marked Read-Only, an error is returned. If the file already exists and is currently opened by another workstation, the Critical-Error Handler, Interrupt 24 (hex), signals a Sharing Violation. The file is opened with an access mode of Read-Write and a sharing mode of compatibility mode. Under NetWare, the file is given the default attribute of NON-SHAREABLE. Also under NetWare, the user must have sufficient rights in the directory.

Invoked by C Library Functions: `creat()`, `open()`, `sopen()`, and `fopen()`

Open a File   0x3D

Description: If the file exists on the file server, and if there is no conflict among (1) how the file is already open by another workstation, (2) the file's current attribute, and (3) the intentions you express in the Open mode field, the file is opened and a file handle is returned. The file position is set to the first byte of the file.

Input Registers: AH   0x3D
                   DS:DX   Far pointer to file name string
                   AL   Open mode:

76543210	
.....000	Access mode: Read
.....001	Access mode: Write
.....010	Access mode: Read-Write
....0...	Reserved, always 0
.000....	Sharing mode: Compatibility
.001....	Sharing mode: Read-Write denied (exclusive)

.010....	Sharing mode: Write denied
.011....	Sharing mode: Read denied
.100....	Sharing mode: None denied (shared)
0.......	Inheritable
1.......	Not inheritable

Output Registers: Carry flag clear if successful

      AX   File handle

Carry flag set if error

      AX   Error code

             0x02   File not found

             0x03   Path not found

             0x04   No handles left

             0x05   Access denied

Network Considerations: If you try to open in compatibility mode a file that another workstation already opened in any other mode, Interrupt 24 (hex), the Critical-Error Handler, signals a sharing violation. Under NetWare, if you open a file marked Read-Only with an access mode of Read-Write, an entry in the SHELL.CFG file controls whether an error is returned to your program when you try to open the file or when you ever try to write to it. (This entry is the READ ONLY COMPATIBILITY = ON statement.)

Invoked by C Library Functions: fopen(), open(), sopen()

IOCTL—Is Drive Remote?   0x4409

Description: This function returns an indication of whether a logical drive is local or remote.

Input Registers:

	AH	0x44
	AL	9
	BL	Drive number (0 = default, 1 = A:, 3 = C:, and so on)

Output Registers:

	DX	Bit 12 (bit mask 0x1000) = 1 if drive is remote, 0 if local

Network Considerations: CD-ROM drives also return an indication that drives are remote (see Chapter 4, "DOS-Level Programming").

C Library Function: The following is_drive_remote() function takes the single parameter drive_num and returns 1 if the drive is remote, 0 if it is local:

```
#include <dos.h>

int  is_drive_remote(int drive_num)
    {
    union REGS regs;

    regs.x.ax = 0x4409;
    regs.h.bl = (unsigned char) drive_num;
    int86(0x21, &regs, &regs);
    if ((regs.x.dx & 0x1000) == 0x1000)
        return 1;
    return 0;
    }
```

IOCTL—Is Handle Remote?   0x440A

Description: This function returns an indication of whether a file handle is for a local or remote file.

Input Registers:	AH	0x44
	AL	0x0A
	BX	File handle
Output Registers:	DX	Bit 15 (bit mask 0x8000) = 1 if handle is remote, 0 if local

Network Considerations: Files on CD-ROM drives also return an indication that the handle is remote.

C Library Function: The following is_handle_remote() function takes the single parameter file_handle and returns 1 if the handle is remote, 0 if it is local:

```
#include <dos.h>

int  is_handle_remote(int file_handle)
    {
    union REGS regs;

    regs.x.ax = 0x440A;
    regs.x.bx = file_handle;
    int86(0x21, &regs, &regs);
    if ((regs.x.dx & 0x8000) == 0x8000)
        return 1;
    return 0;
    }
```

Set Sharing Retry Count/Delay   0x440B

Description: This function sets the number of retries that DOS performs, as well as the delay between tries, when a file-sharing or record-locking conflict occurs. If the conflict persists after the specified number of retries, an error is returned to your program (or a sharing violation is handled as a critical error—see Chapter 2, "Multiuser Concepts"). Each delay loop consists of a simple "do nothing" sequence:

```
XOR  CX, CX     ; zero the CX register
back:
LOOP back       ; cycle 64K times
```

The default values that DOS uses are 1 loop = 1 delay period and retries = 3. The loop is sensitive to the speed of the CPU on which it executes, so faster workstations will have shorter delay periods.

Input Registers:	AH	0x44
	AL	0x0B
	CX	Number of CPU loops (equals 1 delay period)
	DX	Number of retries
Output Registers:	None	

Network Considerations: See the Description.

C Library Function: The following set_retries() function takes two parameters. The first is retry_count and the second is delay_loops. Nothing is returned.

```
#include <dos.h>

void set_retries(unsigned retry_count, unsigned delay_loops)
    {
    union REGS regs;

    regs.x.ax = 0x440B;
    regs.x.cx = delay_loops;
    regs.x.dx = retry_count;
    int86(0x21, &regs, &regs);
    }
```

Create Unique File   0x5A

Description: This function is exactly like 3C, Create a File, except that the file name is generated by DOS rather than you, and the name is guaranteed to be unique in the target directory. The same caveats (as mentioned for Create a File) regarding permissions and compatibility mode apply. You indicate the directory in which the unique file should be created. This function is useful for creating temporary files that need to be specific to each workstation.

Input Registers:	AH	0x5A
	CX	File attributes
	DS:DX	Far pointer to directory name string. The final character of the string must be a backslash (for example, H:\\MYAPP\\); the string area must be long enough to hold the directory name plus the generated file name.

Output Registers:	Carry flag clear if successful	
	AX	File handle
	DS:DX	Far pointer to directory name string, to which the unique file name has been appended

Carry flag set if error
AX	Error code
	0x03 Path not found
	0x04 No handles left

Network Considerations: See function 3C.

Invoked by C Library Functions: `creattemp()`, `tmpfile()`, `tmpnam()`, `tempnam()`

Create New File 0x5B

Description: This function is exactly like 3C, Create a File, except that 5B fails if the file already exists. The same caveats regarding permissions and compatibility mode apply as for function 3C.

Input Registers:
AH	0x5B
CX	File attributes
DS:DX	Far pointer to file name string

Output Registers:
Carry flag clear if successful
| AX | File handle |

Carry flag set if error
AX	Error code
	0x03 Path not found
	0x04 No handles left
	0x05 Access denied

Network Considerations: See function 3C.

Invoked by C Library Functions: `dcreatx()`, `creatnew()`

Lock/Unlock File Region 0x5C

Description: This function locks or unlocks a given number of bytes in a file, starting at a certain file position. Other workstations are denied access to the file region from the time it is locked until the time it is unlocked. Several regions can be locked, but they cannot overlap. Each locked region must be unlocked individually; a single call cannot unlock physically adjacent locked areas. If another workstation attempts to read from or write to the locked region, Interrupt 24 (hex), the Critical-Error Handler, signals a sharing violation. If another workstation attempts to lock all or any part of an already locked region, `Access Denied` is returned to the program running on that workstation. Each locked region must be unlocked before your program terminates. Locking beyond the end-of-file is not an error.

Input Registers:	AH	0x5C
	AL	0 to lock, 1 to unlock
	BX	File handle
	CX:DX	File position (start of region)
	SI:DI	Length of region

Output Registers:	Carry flag set if error	
	AX	Error code
		0x05 Access denied

Network Considerations: Some network operating systems clear dangling locks for you when your program terminates, but you should not rely on this behavior.

Invoked by C Library Functions: `lock()`, `lockf()`, `locking()`, `rlock()`, and `runlk()`

Get Machine Name   0x5E00

Description: This function obtains the workstation's machine name and NETBIOS name number, if available. The name, a 15-character string with a null byte in the 16th character, is padded on the right with spaces.

| **Input Registers:** | AX | 0x5E00 |
| | DS:DX | Far pointer to machine name string |

Output Registers:	Carry flag clear if successful	
	CH	0 if name and number not present
	CL	NETBIOS name number
	DS:DX	Far pointer to filled-in machine name

> Carry flag set if error
>
> | AX | Error code |
> |----|------------|
> | | 0x01 Invalid function (if network is not active) |

Network Considerations: Machine name may not be set in all cases. Duplicated machine names are possible.

Invoked by C Library Function: pcngmn(), or you can use the following library routine:

```c
#include <dos.h>

/* pass back machine name and name number, if available, */
/* in the name/number fields */
/* return 0 if not available, else return 1 */

int  get_machine_name(char *name, int *number)
    {
    union REGS regs;
    struct SREGS sregs;

    regs.x.ax = 0x5E00;
    regs.x.dx = FP_OFF( (void far *) name);
    sregs.ds  = FP_SEG( (void far *) name);
    int86x(0x21, &regs, &regs, &sregs);
    if (regs.h.ch == 0)
        return 0;
    number = (int) regs.h.cl;
    return 1;
    }
```

Set Machine Name 0x5E01

Description: This undocumented function call sets machine name and name number for later retrieval by the Get Machine Name function. You must prepare the name carefully before calling this function. Pad the name on the right with spaces, and make the string 15 characters long by putting a null byte in the 16th position.

Input Registers:

AX	0x5E01
CL	Name number
DS:DX	Far pointer to machine name string

Output Registers: Carry flag set if error

AX	Error code	
	0x01	Invalid function (if the network is not active)

Network Considerations: If NETBIOS is loaded, you should not need this function; it is useful only on non-NETBIOS LANs.

C Library Function: The following set_machine_name() routine sets machine name and name number:

```c
#include <dos.h>

void set_machine_name(char *name, int number)
    {
    union REGS regs;
    struct SREGS sregs;

    regs.x.ax = 0x5E01;
    regs.x.dx = FP_OFF( (void far *) name);
    sregs.ds  = FP_SEG( (void far *) name);
    regs.h.cl = (unsigned char) number;
    int86x(0x21, &regs, &regs, &sregs);
    }
```

Set Printer Setup   0x5E02

Description: This function call designates a printer setup string of up to 64 bytes. These bytes are sent to the network printer each time the printer is opened as a file. With this function, each user of a shared printer can set the printer into a particular mode (character pitch, font, page orientation, and so on) for generating printouts from that user's workstation. Before you invoke this function, you must know the shared printer's Redirection List Index; it is usually obtained by calling Get Redirection List Entry (see function 0x5F02).

Input Registers:

AX	0x5E02	
BX	Redirection List Index for specified printer	
CX	Setup String length (0 to 64)	
DS:SI	Far pointer to Setup String	

Output Registers: Carry flag set if error

    AX   Error code

             0x01   Invalid function (if the network is not active)

Network Considerations: If one workstation uses this function, all workstations should use it. Otherwise, the network printer will be left as set by the most recent user of this function.

Invoked by C Library Function: pcnspi(), or the following:

```
#include <dos.h>

void set_printer_setup(int index, char *setup, int len)
    {
    union REGS regs;
    struct SREGS sregs;

    regs.x.ax = 0x5E02;
    regs.x.bx = index;
    regs.x.cx = len;
    regs.x.si = FP_OFF( (void far *) setup);
    sregs.ds  = FP_SEG( (void far *) setup);
    int86x(0x21, &regs, &regs, &sregs);
    }
```

Get Printer Setup   0x5E03

Description: This function obtains any Setup String specified in the latest Set Print Setup call.

Input Registers: AX   0x5E03

                BX   Redirection List Index

                ES:DI   Far pointer to Setup String buffer (maximum 64 bytes)

Output Registers: Carry flag clear if successful

    CX   Length of returned Setup String

    ES:DI   Far pointer to Setup String (now filled in)

                Carry flag set if error

    AX   Error code

             0x01   Invalid function (if the network is not active)

Network Considerations: See function 5E02, Set Printer Setup.

Invoked by C Library Function: pcngpi(), or the following:

```
#include <dos.h>

void get_printer_setup(int index, char *setup, int *len_ptr)
    {
    union REGS regs;
    struct SREGS sregs;

    regs.x.ax = 0x5E03;
    regs.x.bx = index;
    regs.x.di = FP_OFF( (void far *) setup);
    sregs.es  = FP_SEG( (void far *) setup);
    int86x(0x21, &regs, &regs, &sregs);
    *len_ptr = regs.x.cx;
    }
```

Get Redirection List Entry   0x5F02

Description: This function returns information about a particular redirected disk or printer device, for a given Redirection List Index value. A call establishes each entry to the Redirect Device function (0x5F03), which is normally issued only by network operating-system software. You must perform a series of calls (one for each Redirection List Index value) to obtain all redirections. When the list is exhausted, error code 12 (hex) is returned. The information returned for each call consists of the following:

❑ The local device name string (for example, H:\)
❑ The network device name string (for example, \\SERVER\C:)
❑ The device status flag
❑ The device type
❑ A user-defined parameter

Input Registers:

AX	0x5F02	
BX	Redirection List Index	
DS:SI	Far pointer to 128-byte local device name	
ES:DI	Far pointer to 128-byte network device name	

Output Registers: Carry flag clear if successful

BH	Device status	
	76543210	
	0	Device is valid
	1	Device is invalid
	xxxxxxx.	Reserved
BL	Device type (3 = printer, 4 = file)	
CX	Stored user-defined parameter	
DX	Undefined (register not preserved)	
DS:SI	Far pointer to filled-in local name	
ES:DI	Far pointer to filled-in network name	
BP	Undefined (register not preserved)	

Carry flag set if error

AX	Error code	
	0x01	Invalid function (if the network is not active)
	0x12	No more entries

Network Considerations: Under the PC LAN Program, the user-defined 2-byte parameter should not be used.

Invoked by C Library Function: pcngdr(), or the following:

```
/* For a Redirection Index value, get local_name, */
/* network_name, et al.  Return 0 if successful,  */
/* else return DOS error code.                     */

#include <dos.h>

int  get_redirection_entry(int index,
                    char *local_name,
                    char *network_name,
                    int  *device_status,
                    int  *device_type,
                    int  *stored_parm)
```

```
{
union REGS regs;
struct SREGS sregs;

regs.x.ax = 0x5F02;
regs.x.bx = index;
regs.x.si = FP_OFF( (void far *) local_name);
sregs.ds  = FP_SEG( (void far *) local_name);
regs.x.di = FP_OFF( (void far *) network_name);
sregs.es  = FP_SEG( (void far *) network_name);
int86x(0x21, &regs, &regs, &sregs);
if (regs.x.cflag)
     return regs.x.ax;
*device_type   = (int) regs.h.bl;
*device_status = (int) regs.h.bh;
*stored_parm   = (int) regs.x.cx;
return 0;
}
```

Redirect Device   0x5F03

Description: This function sets up the relationship between a network device and its local workstation name, for both disk drives and printers. This function should rarely be used by application programs; use existing redirections where possible.

Input Registers:	AX	0x5F03
	BL	Device type (3 = printer, 4 = file)
	CX	Parameter value (retrievable with Get Redirection List Entry)
	DS:SI	Far pointer to local name string
	ES:DI	Far pointer to network name string

Output Registers:	Carry flag set if error		
	AX	Error code	
		0x01	Invalid function (if the network is not active)

Network Considerations: For compatibility with the PC LAN Program, the parameter value should always be 0. If you use this function to redirect a device, it will not show up in the display produced when you issue a NET USE command.

Invoked by C Library Function: pcnsdr(), or the following library code:

```
#include <dos.h>

int   redirect_device(int type,
                      char *local_name,
                      char *network_name)
      {
      union REGS regs;
      struct SREGS sregs;

      regs.x.ax = 0x5F03;
      regs.h.bl = (unsigned char) type;
      regs.x.cx = 0;
      regs.x.si = FP_OFF( (void far *) local_name);
      sregs.ds  = FP_SEG( (void far *) local_name);
      regs.x.di = FP_OFF( (void far *) network_name);
      sregs.es  = FP_SEG( (void far *) network_name);
      int86x(0x21, &regs, &regs, &sregs);
      if (regs.x.cflag)
          return regs.x.ax;
      return 0;
      }
```

Cancel Redirection 0x5F04

Description: This function terminates a logical local-name-to-network-name relationship established with the Redirect Device function call. You can cancel redirections only in the same program or process that created the redirection.

Input Registers:	AX	0x5F04
	DS:SI	Far pointer to redirected local name string

Output Registers:	Carry flag set if error		
	AX	Error code	
		0x01	Invalid function (if the network is not active)

Network Considerations: After a redirection is terminated, the logical drive or device name (for example, F:, or LPT1) reverts to whatever meaning it had before the redirection. For a disk drive, this usually means that DOS goes back to treating the drive as an "Invalid Drive Specification"; for a printer, printouts appear on the local printer if a local printer exists.

Invoked by C Library Function: pcnrdr(), or the following library code:

```
#include <dos.h>

int  cancel_redirection(char *local_name)
     {
     union REGS regs;
     struct SREGS sregs;

     regs.x.ax = 0x5F04;
     regs.x.si = FP_OFF( (void far *) local_name);
     sregs.ds  = FP_SEG( (void far *) local_name);
     int86x(0x21, &regs, &regs, &sregs);
     if (regs.x.cflag)
         return regs.x.ax;
     return 0;
     }
```

Commit File   0x68

Description: This function causes file data in DOS buffers to be written to disk.

Input Registers: AH   0x68
                          BX   File handle

Output Registers: Carry flag set if error
                               AX   Error code
                                         0x06   Invalid handle

Network Considerations: None.

C Library Function:

```
int  flush(int handle)
     {
     union REGS regs;

     regs.h.ah = 0x68;
     regs.x.bx = handle;
     int86(0x21, &regs, &regs);
     if (regs.x.cflag)
          return regs.x.ax;
     return 0;
     }
```

PC LAN Program Services

This section describes the programming services available under the IBM PC LAN Program. Interrupts 2A (hex) and 2F (hex) are used to call these functions, rather than the regular DOS interrupt, 21 (hex). See the cautions in Chapter 4, "DOS-Level Programming," regarding the use of Interrupt 2F with DOS versions earlier than 3.0.

Interface Installation Check — Int 2A, service 0

Description: This service returns an indication of whether the Int 2A interface is installed.

Input Registers:	AH	0
Output Registers:	AH	Status (0 = not installed, 1 = installed)

C Library Function Code: isnet(), or use the following:

```
#include <dos.h>

int int_2A_installed(void)
    {
    union REGS regs;

    regs.h.ah = 0;
    int86(0x2A, &regs, &regs);
    if (regs.h.ah == 0)
        return 0;
    return 1;
    }
```

Check Direct I/O   Int 2A, service 3

Description: This service returns an indication of whether Interrupts 25 (hex), 26 (hex), or 13 (hex) can do direct disk I/O (at the sector level) for a particular disk device.

Input Registers:	AH	3
	AL	0
	DS:SI	Far pointer to disk device name string (an example of such a string is F:)

Output Registers: Carry flag clear if direct I/O allowed
Carry flag set if direct I/O not allowed

C Library Function Code:
```
#include <dos.h>

int direct_io_allowed(char *device_name)
    {
    union REGS regs;
    struct SREGS sregs;

    regs.x.ax = 0x0300;
    regs.x.si = FP_OFF( (void far *) device_name);
    sregs.ds  = FP_SEG( (void far *) device_name);
    int86x(0x2A, &regs, &regs, &sregs);
    if (regs.x.cflag)
        return 0;
    return 1;
    }
```

Execute NETBIOS   Int 2A, service 4

Description: This small, extra layer of software provides a second interface to NETBIOS in addition to that offered by the usual Interrupt 5C (hex) NETBIOS entry point. If the value in AL is 0 when the function is called, this service will perform automatic retries for the following NETBIOS error codes:

- ❏ 0x09 No Resource Available
- ❏ 0x12 Session Open Rejected
- ❏ 0x21 Interface Busy

Input Registers:	AH	4	
	AL	0	Enable error retries
		1	Disable error retries
	ES:BX	Far pointer to a Network Control Block (see Chapter 5, "PC-to-PC NETBIOS Programming," for NCB definition)	

Output Registers:	AH	0	Successful completion
		1	Error
	AL	NETBIOS error code if AH = 1	

C Library Function Code:

```
#include <dos.h>

int  call_netbios_with_retry(void *ncb_ptr)
     {
     union REGS regs;
     struct SREGS sregs;

     regs.x.ax = 0x0400;   /* use 0x0401 to disable retries */
     regs.x.bx = FP_OFF( (void far *) ncb_ptr);
     sregs.es  = FP_SEG( (void far *) ncb_ptr);
     int86x(0x2A, &regs, &regs, &sregs);
     if (regs.h.ah == 0)
          return 0;
     regs.h.ah = 0;
     return regs.x.ax;
     }
```

Get Network Resource Information

Int 2A, service 5

Description: This service asks the PC LAN Program how many network resources remain for your use after PCLP establishes its sessions with the file server. The network resources counted are the following (refer to Chapter 5, "PC-to-PC NETBIOS Programming," for an explanation):

- ❏ Names
- ❏ Commands
- ❏ Sessions

Input Registers:

	AH	5
	AL	0

Output Registers:

	AX	Reserved
	BX	Number of network names available
	CX	Number of network commands available
	DX	Number of network sessions available

C Library Function Code:

```c
#include <dos.h>

void get_net_info(int *names, int *commands, int *sessions)
    {
    union REGS regs;

    regs.x.ax = 0x0500;
    int86(0x2A, &regs, &regs);
    *names    = regs.x.bx;
    *commands = regs.x.cx;
    *sessions = regs.x.dx;
    }
```

Network Print Stream Control   Int 2A, service 6

Description: This service sets the mode that the PC LAN Program uses to determine when one printout ends and another begins. The service also indicates the end of a printout. In truncation mode (the default), the end of a print stream is indicated by any one of the following:

- ❏ The end of the program
- ❏ Opening and closing of file names LPT1, LPT2, or LPT3
- ❏ Switching from printing through DOS to printing through Interrupt 17 (hex), or vice versa
- ❏ Printing through Interrupt 17 (hex) from different programs (processes)

In concatenation mode, the preceding conditions are ignored; the only delimiter or transition recognized in this mode is when COMMAND.COM issues a new DOS prompt after executing one complete program or a complete .BAT file.

Input Registers: AH   6
                        AL   1   Set concatenation mode
                              2   Set truncation mode
                              3   Signal end-of-print-stream
                                   (truncate it)

Output Registers: Carry flag set if error
                         AX   DOS error code

C Library Function Code:

```
#include <dos.h>

int  print_stream_control(int flag)
     {
     union REGS regs;

     regs.h.ah = 6;
     regs.h.al = (unsigned char) flag;
     int86(0x2A, &regs, &regs);
     if (regs.x.cflag)
          return regs.x.ax;
     return 0;
     }
```

PC LAN Program Installation Check

Int 2F, service 0xB8

Description: This service returns an indication of whether the PC LAN Program is installed; if it is installed, the service returns configuration information. This information tells you whether PCLP is running on this workstation as a redirector, receiver, messenger, or as a server (see Chapter 1, "The Basics of Networking"). These configurations can be cumulative; a server configuration includes lower-level components. Check for configuration information in the following order:

❏ Server

❏ Messenger

❏ Receiver

❏ Redirector

If you check first for redirector, you may never find out that the PC is also a server because a server includes the redirector function.

Input Registers:	AH	0xB8 (multiplex number for the PC LAN Program)
	AL	0
Output Registers:	AL	Status (0 = PC LAN Program not installed, nonzero = PCLP installed)
	BX	Bit flags for configuration information:

76543210	Configuration
1.......	Receiver
.1......	Server
....1...	Redirector
.....1..	Messenger

C Library Function Code:

```
/* pclp_installed() returns:                */
/*    0 - if PCLP is not installed          */
/*    1 - if configuration is Redirector    */
/*    2 - if configuration is Receiver      */
```

```
/*   3 - if configuration is Messenger    */
/*   4 - if configuration is Server       */
/*   -1 if error occurs                    */

#include <dos.h>

int  pclp_installed(void)
    {
    union REGS regs;

    regs.x.ax = 0xB800;
    int86(0x2F, &regs, &regs)
    if (regs.h.al == 0)
        return 0;
    if ( (regs.x.bx & 0x0040) == 0x0040)
        return 4;
    if ( (regs.x.bx & 0x0004) == 0x0004)
        return 3;
    if ( (regs.x.bx & 0x0080) == 0x0080)
        return 2;
    if ( (regs.x.bx & 0x0008) == 0x0008)
        return 1;
    return -1;
    }
```

PC LAN Program Version Information   Int 2F, service 0xB8

Description: This service returns the major and minor version of the PC LAN Program, if it is installed. Do not use this service to determine the installed state of the PC LAN Program; use the PC LAN Program Installation Check function call.

Input Registers:	AH	0xB8	(multiplex number for the PC LAN Program)
	AL	9	
Output Registers:	AH	Minor version number	
	AL	Major version number	

C Library Function Code:

```c
#include <dos.h>

void get_pclp_version(int *major, int *minor)
    {
    union REGS regs;

    regs.x.ax = 0xB809;
    int86(0x2F, &regs, &regs);
    *major = (int) regs.h.al;
    *minor = (int) regs.h.ah;
    }
```

Novell's Extended DOS Services

Several categories of services are available to an application running on a NetWare workstation. This section describes each of the function calls in these frequently used categories:

- ❏ Bindery Services
- ❏ Connection Services
- ❏ Print Services
- ❏ Synchronization Services
- ❏ Transaction Tracking Services
- ❏ Workstation Services

NetWare's IPX and SPX services for PC-to-PC communications are described separately in their own section.

A few other categories of programmer services offered by NetWare are not covered in this section. You probably won't need these services to develop your application programs. These other categories are the following:

- ❏ Accounting Services
- ❏ AppleTalk Services

❏ Diagnostic Services

❏ Directory Services

❏ File Server Services

❏ Server-Based Message Services

❏ Queue Services

❏ Service Advertising Services

❏ Value Added Process (VAP) Services

If you want to use any of the services in these categories, Novell offers technical reference products—*NetWare System Calls for DOS* and *NetWare C Interface for DOS*—that explain the categories in depth. The latter includes software libraries on diskette.

Numeric Formats and Buffer Lengths

NetWare defines the format of multibyte numeric items a little differently from the native representation internal to the PC. Instead of expecting the least significant byte first, NetWare looks for the most significant byte first. This means that you will have to swap the bytes of int and long items as you prepare to call functions in this section.

The following typedefs denote these high-byte-first items:

```
typedef struct NW_INT
    {
    unsigned char high_byte;
    unsigned char low_byte;
    } nw_int;

typedef struct NW_LONG
    {
    unsigned char highest_byte;
    unsigned char higher_byte;
    unsigned char lower_byte;
    unsigned char lowest_byte;
    } nw_long;
```

For each of the functions in this section, the buffer_length field in each of the request_buffer and reply_buffer data structures does not include itself as part of the length. Make sure that you set the `buffer_length` field in both the `request_buffer` and `reply_buffer` before calling a function.

Bindery Services

Not only can you use the information in this category in your applications, but the information also helps explain what goes on within NetWare itself. Although they function somewhat more abstractly than other NetWare services, *Bindery Services* reveal the interesting architecture of Novell's LAN operating system.

Two hidden files, NET$BIND.SYS and NET$BVAL.SYS, exist in the SYS:SYSTEM directory of each NetWare file server. These files contain information about the users and other entities that can use the file server. The information is hierarchical, in three levels:

1. Each entity (or *object*)

2. Each object's *property* or *properties*

3. Each property's *value* or *values*

NetWare uses the bindery internally to maintain the list of user IDs, passwords, groups, security equivalences, and the like. If you adhere to the conventions discussed in this section, you can also use Bindery Services in your NetWare-specific applications.

Objects

The following information is maintained about each object:

❑ Object ID number
❑ Object name
❑ Object type
❑ Object flag
❑ Object security
❑ Properties flag

Object ID is a 4-byte number NetWare assigns to each object. The high-order byte is stored first (in contrast to the CPU's native representation for numeric items, which is low-byte first).

Object name is a 48-byte field containing a null-terminated string of printable characters; for a user, this is the user ID.

Each entity is classified according to its *Object type*:

Entity	Object Type
Unknown	0x0000
User	0x0001
User group	0x0002
Print queue	0x0003
File server	0x0004
Job server	0x0005
Gateway	0x0006
Print server	0x0007
Archive queue	0x0008
Archive server	0x0009
Job queue	0x000A
Administration	0x000B
Remote bridge	0x0026
Reserved	Up to 0x8000
Wild card object type	0xFFFF (−1)

Object flag defines an object as being either static (0x00) or dynamic (0x01); static objects are explicitly created and deleted, but dynamic objects exist only until the file server is rebooted (or until the object is deleted).

The *Object security* field expresses which users are granted access for the following:

❏ Viewing the information in the bindery for an object

❏ Modifying the information

Security permission levels for both types of access are encoded in four bits (1 nibble) each:

Access Level	Object Security
Anyone	0 0 0 0
Logged in	0 0 0 1
Object itself	0 0 1 0
Supervisor	0 0 1 1
NetWare only	0 1 0 0

The *Properties flag* indicates whether the object has any properties associated with it (0 = no properties; 0xFF = at least one property).

Properties of an Object

The following information is maintained for each property of an object:

❏ Property name
❏ Property flags
❏ Property security
❏ Property values flag

Property flags indicates two things: whether the property is static or dynamic, and whether the property is an item or a set, as defined by the two low-order bits of the field:

Bit position	Meaning
76543210	
.......0	Static
.......1	Dynamic
......0.	Item
......1.	Set
xxxxxx..	Reserved

An item property has a value maintained inside the bindery but not recognized by Bindery Services. User name is an example of an item property. A set property, on the other hand, is defined by Bindery Services as a list of object ID numbers. An example of a set property is the list of users (object names) in a user group, where the group is an *object* with a *set property* whose *property value* consists of the list (set) of member users.

Property name identifies the property and can be from 1 to 15 characters long. Programmers can define their own names; however, the following names are defined by Novell:

LOGIN_CONTROL
ACCOUNT_SERVERS
ACCOUNT_BALANCE
PASSWORD
SECURITY_EQUALS
GROUP_MEMBERS
GROUPS_I'M_IN
NET_ADDRESS
IDENTIFICATION
OPERATORS

Property security determines who can access the property for either viewing or updating. It is similar to object security and has the same encoding.

The *Property values flag* indicates whether a property has a value (0x00 = no value present, 0xFF = value present).

Values of a Property

The values of a property are maintained in 128-byte segment records. More than one segment can exist. Each segment is numbered, and each Read or Write operation that you specify deals with one entire segment.

Filling in the Structs

In many of the structs used by the Bindery Services functions, you will see a name field preceded by a name_length field. For example:

```
typedef unsigned int   word;
typedef unsigned char  byte;


struct {
       word buffer_len
       byte name_length;    /* Set to 48 */
       char name [48];
       byte object_flag;
       } request_buffer;
```

For each of these "name-length" fields, NetWare uses the length value to know the size of the next field (name). If you were to put a value of 6 in the name_length field, NetWare would expect the name field to be declared as follows:

```
char name [6];
```

So that you can use the same struct to refer to any possible name, you should always set the name_length field to a value that represents the maximum size of the name field:

```
request_buffer.name_length = 48;
strcpy(request_buffer.name, "BARRY");
```

Because the string you put in the name field is null-terminated (that is, it is a normal C string), NetWare properly uses only the portion of the name up to the terminating ("/O") byte. The length field tells NetWare where the next field begins (not necessarily the length of the name string itself). The alternative would be to not use a struct at all, but to build a memory area "on the fly." This alternative approach would be more difficult to code. The simpler approach is shown here.

Finally, to set the buffer_len field, you can code:

```
request_buffer.buffer_len = sizeof(request_buffer) - 2;
```

because the buffer_len field expresses the total length of the struct, but does not include itself.

Add Bindery Object to Set 0xE3, type 0x41

Description: This function adds an object to a set property. The member_object_type and member_object_name that you specify are used to check that object's object ID, and the result is added to the set of values for the specified property.

Request Buffer:

```
struct
    {
    word buffer_length;
    byte type;
    nw_int object_type;
    byte object_name_length;        /* Set to 48 */
    char object_name[48];
    byte property_name_length;      /* Set to 16 */
    char property_name[16];
    nw_int member_object_type;
    byte member_object_length;      /* Set to 48 */
    char member_object_name[48];
    } request_buffer;
```

Reply Buffer:

```
struct
    {
    word buffer_length;
    } reply_buffer;
```

Input Registers:	AH	0xE3
	DS:SI	Far pointer to request_buffer
	ES:DI	Far pointer to reply_buffer

Output Registers:	AL	Completion code
	0x00	Success
	0x96	Server out of memory
	0xE9	Member already exists
	0xEB	Not a set property
	0xF0	Wild card not allowed
	0xF8	No privilege to modify property
	0xFB	No such property
	0xFC	No such object
	0xFE	Server bindery locked
	0xFF	Bindery failure

Change Bindery Object Password 0xE3, type 0x40

Description: This function changes the password of an object. If the object does not already have a property named PASSWORD, one is added to the object with a property security of 0x44 (NetWare-only, Read-Write). Both the old and new passwords can be zero length; both must be uppercase.

Request Buffer:

```
struct
    {
    word buffer_length;
    byte type;
    nw_int object_type;
    byte object_name_length;        /* Set to 48  */
    char object_name[48];
    byte old_password_length;       /* Set to 127 */
    char old_password[127];
    byte new_password_length;       /* Set to 127 */
    char new_password[127];
    } request_buffer;
```

Reply Buffer:

```
struct
    {
    word buffer_length;
    } reply_buffer;
```

Input Registers:	AH	0xE3
	DS:SI	Far pointer to request_buffer
	ES:DI	Far pointer to reply_buffer

Output Registers:	AL	Completion code
	0x00	Success
	0x96	Server out of memory
	0xF0	Wild card not allowed
	0xF8	No privilege to modify property
	0xFC	No such object
	0xFE	Server bindery locked
	0xFF	Password error

Change Bindery Object Security   0xE3, type 0x38

Description: Object security can be modified with this function. It requires SUPERVISOR rights, and cannot be used to set or clear Net-Ware-only, Read-Write security.

Request Buffer:

```
struct
    {
    word buffer_length;
    byte type;
    byte new_object_security;
    nw_int object_type;
    byte object_name_length;        /* Set to 48 */
    char object_name[48];
    } request_buffer;
```

Reply Buffer:

```
struct
    {
    word buffer_length;
    } reply_buffer;
```

Input Registers:	AH	0xE3
	DS:SI	Far pointer to request_buffer
	ES:DI	Far pointer to reply_buffer

Output Registers:	AL	Completion code
	0x00	Success
	0x96	Server out of memory
	0xF0	Wild card not allowed
	0xF1	Invalid bindery security
	0xFC	No such object
	0xFE	Server bindery locked
	0xFF	Bindery failure

Change Property Security   0xE3, type 0x3B

Description: This function updates the property security of a particular object's property. You cannot set a property's security mask to a level greater than the workstation currently holds.

Request Buffer:

```
struct
    {
    word buffer_length;
    byte type;
    nw_int object_type;
    byte object_name_length;        /* Set to 48 */
    char object_name[48];
    byte new_property_security;
    byte property_name_length;      /* Set to 16 */
    char property_name[16];
    } request_buffer;
```

Reply Buffer:

```
struct
    {
    word buffer_length;
    } reply_buffer;
```

Input Registers:	AH	0xE3
	DS:SI	Far pointer to `request_buffer`
	ES:DI	Far pointer to `reply_buffer`

Output Registers:	AL	Completion code
	0x00	Success
	0x96	Server out of memory
	0xE9	Member already exists
	0xEB	Not a set property
	0xF0	Wild card not allowed
	0xF1	Invalid bindery security
	0xF8	No privilege to modify property
	0xFB	No such property
	0xFC	No such object
	0xFE	Server bindery locked
	0xFF	Bindery failure

Close Bindery 0xE3, type 0x44

Description: This function closes both bindery files (NET$BIND.SYS and NET$BVAL.SYS). These files are normally open and locked; however, you must close them before you perform a global operation such as backing up (archiving) the bindery. You do not have to close the bindery to do any of the update actions described in this section. Close Bindery requires SUPERVISOR privileges. *Caution:* While the bindery is closed, the network is effectively asleep, so do not keep the bindery closed any longer than necessary.

Request Buffer:

```
struct
    {
    word buffer_length;
    byte type;
    } request_buffer;
```

Reply Buffer:

```
struct
    {
    word buffer_length;
    } reply_buffer;
```

Input Registers:	AH	0xE3
	DS:SI	Far pointer to request_buffer
	ES:DI	Far pointer to reply_buffer

Output Registers:	AL	Completion code
		0x00 Success

Create Bindery Object   0xE3, type 0x32

Description: This service, which requires SUPERVISOR-level rights, creates an object and gives it its object-level characteristics.

Request Buffer:

```
struct
    {
    word buffer_length;
    byte type;
    byte object_flag;
    byte object_security;
    nw_int object_type;
    byte object_name_length;        /* Set to 48 */
    char object_name[48];
    } request_buffer;
```

Reply Buffer:

```
struct
    {
    word buffer_length;
    } reply_buffer;
```

Input Registers:	AH	0xE3
	DS:SI	Far pointer to request_buffer
	ES:DI	Far pointer to reply_buffer

Output Registers:	AL	Completion code
		0x00 Success
		0x96 Server out of memory

0xEE	Object already exists
0xEF	Invalid name
0xF0	Wild card not allowed
0xF1	Invalid bindery security
0xF5	No privilege to create object
0xFE	Server bindery locked
0xFF	Bindery failure

Create Property   0xE3, type 0x39

Description: This service adds a property to an object and gives the property its characteristics. To use this service, you must have Read-Write access to the object.

Request Buffer:

```
struct
    {
    word buffer_length;
    byte type;
    nw_int object_type;
    byte object_name_length;        /* Set to 48 */
    char object_name[48];
    byte new_property_flags;
    byte new_property_security;
    byte property_name_length;      /* Set to 16 */
    char property_name[16];
    } request_buffer;
```

Reply Buffer:

```
struct
    {
    word buffer_length;
    } reply_buffer;
```

Input Registers:	AH	0xE3
	DS:SI	Far pointer to request_buffer
	ES:DI	Far pointer to reply_buffer
Output Registers:	AL	Completion code
	0x00	Success
	0x96	Server out of memory
	0xED	Property already exists

0xEF	Invalid name
0xF0	Wild card not allowed
0xF1	Invalid bindery security
0xF7	No property-create privilege
0xFC	No such object
0xFE	Server bindery locked
0xFF	Bindery failure

Delete Bindery Object   0xE3, type 0x33

Description: This service, which requires SUPERVISOR-level rights, deletes an object.

Request Buffer:

```
struct
    {
    word buffer_length;
    byte type;
    nw_int object_type;
    byte object_name_length;        /* Set to 48 */
    char object_name[48];
    } request_buffer;
```

Reply Buffer:

```
struct
    {
    word buffer_length;
    } reply_buffer;
```

Input Registers:	AH	0xE3
	DS:SI	Far pointer to request_buffer
	ES:DI	Far pointer to reply_buffer

Output Registers:	AL	Completion code
	0x00	Success
	0x96	Server out of memory
	0xEF	Invalid name
	0xF0	Wild card not allowed
	0xF4	No object-delete privilege
	0xFC	No such object
	0xFE	Server bindery locked
	0xFF	Bindery failure

Delete Bindery Object   0xE3, type 0x42
from Set

Description: This service, which requires Write privileges at the property level, deletes an object ID (corresponding to the given object name and object type) from a set property.

Request Buffer:

```
struct
    {
    word buffer_length;
    byte type;
    nw_int object_type;
    byte object_name_length;         /* Set to 48 */
    char object_name[48];
    byte property_name_length;       /* Set to 16 */
    char property_name[16];
    nw_int member_object_type;
    byte member_object_name_length; /* Set to 48 */
    char member_object_name[48];
    } request_buffer;
```

Reply Buffer:

```
struct
    {
    word buffer_length;
    } reply_buffer;
```

Input Registers:	AH	0xE3
	DS:SI	Far pointer to `request_buffer`
	ES:DI	Far pointer to `reply_buffer`

Output Registers:	AL	Completion code
	0x00	Success
	0x96	Server out of memory
	0xEA	No such member
	0xEB	Not a set property
	0xF0	Wild card not allowed
	0xF8	No privilege to modify property
	0xFB	No such property
	0xFC	No such object
	0xFE	Server bindery locked
	0xFF	Bindery failure

Delete Property   0xE3, type 0x3A

Description: This service deletes one property or more from an object.
The property name can contain wild-card characters. The service
requires Write access to both the object and the property.

Request Buffer:

```
struct
    {
    word buffer_length;
    byte type;
    nw_int object_type;
    byte object_name_length;        /* Set to 48 */
    char object_name[48];
    byte property_name_length;      /* Set to 16 */
    char property_name[16];
    } request_buffer;
```

Reply Buffer:

```
struct
    {
    word buffer_length;
    } reply_buffer;
```

Input Registers:	AH	0xE3
	DS:SI	Far pointer to request_buffer
	ES:DI	Far pointer to reply_buffer

Output Registers:	AL	Completion code
	0x00	Success
	0x96	Server out of memory
	0xF1	Invalid bindery security
	0xF6	No property-delete privilege
	0xFB	No such property
	0xFC	No such object
	0xFE	Server bindery locked
	0xFF	Bindery failure

Get Bindery Access Level   0xE3, type 0x46

Description: This service returns the workstation's access level, as well as the workstation or user's object ID, to the bindery.

Request Buffer:

```
struct
    {
    word buffer_length;
    byte type;
    } request_buffer;
```

Reply Buffer:

```
struct
    {
    word buffer_length;
    byte access_level;
    nw_long object_id;
    } reply_buffer;
```

Input Registers:	AH	0xE3
	DS:SI	Far pointer to `request_buffer`
	ES:DI	Far pointer to `reply_buffer`
Output Registers:	AL	Completion code
		0x00 Success

Get Bindery Object ID   0xE3, type 0x35

Description: This service, which requires Read access to the object, returns an object's unique object ID number.

Request Buffer:

```
struct
    {
    word buffer_length;
    byte type;
    nw_int object_type;
    byte object_name_length;        /* Set to 48 */
    char object_name[48];
    } request_buffer;
```

Reply Buffer:

```
struct
    {
    word buffer_length;
    nw_long object_id;
    nw_int object_type;
    char object_name[48];
    } reply_buffer;
```

Input Registers:	AH	0xE3
	DS:SI	Far pointer to request_buffer
	ES:DI	Far pointer to reply_buffer

Output Registers:	AL	Completion code
	0x00	Success
	0x96	Server out of memory
	0xEF	Invalid name
	0xF0	Wild card not allowed
	0xFC	No such object
	0xFE	Server bindery locked
	0xFF	Bindery failure

Get Bindery Object Name   0xE3, type 0x36

Description: This service, which requires Read access to the object, returns the object name and object type that correspond to a particular object ID number.

Request Buffer:

```
struct
    {
    word buffer_length;
    byte type;
    nw_long object_id;
    } request_buffer;
```

Reply Buffer:

```
struct
    {
    word buffer_length;
    nw_long object_id;
```

```
nw_int object_type;
char object_name[48];
} reply_buffer;
```

Input Registers:	AH	0xE3
	DS:SI	Far pointer to request_buffer
	ES:DI	Far pointer to reply_buffer

Output Registers:	AL	Completion code
		0x00 Success
		0x96 Server out of memory
		0xFC No such object
		0xFE Server bindery locked
		0xFF Bindery failure

Is Bindery Object in Set? 0xE3, type 0x43

Description: This service returns an indication of whether one object (specified by its object name and object type) is in a particular set property for another given object. The candidate member object is first searched for in the bindery. If the object exists, its corresponding object ID number then is used as a search argument in a scan of the values of the given property of the given object. If the object is found, a Completion code of 0x00 is returned. If the candidate member object does not exist, a Completion code of 0xFC is returned. If the candidate member object exists but is not in the set of object ID numbers for the given object or property, a Completion code of 0xEA is returned. This service requires Read access to the object and property.

Request Buffer:

```
struct
    {
    word buffer_length;
    byte type;
    nw_int object_type;
    byte object_name_length;        /* Set to 48 */
    char object_name[48];
    byte property_name_length;      /* Set to 16 */
    char property_name[16];
```

```
        nw_int member_object_type;
        byte member_object_length;      /* Set to 48 */
        char member_object_name[48];
        } request_buffer;
```

Reply Buffer:

```
    struct
        {
        word buffer_length;
        } reply_buffer;
```

Input Registers:	AH	0xE3
	DS:SI	Far pointer to `request_buffer`
	ES:DI	Far pointer to `reply_buffer`

Output Registers:	AL	Completion code
	0x00	Success
	0x96	Server out of memory
	0xEA	No such member
	0xEB	Not a set property
	0xF0	Wild card not allowed
	0xF9	No privilege to read property
	0xFB	No such property
	0xFC	No such object
	0xFE	Server bindery locked
	0xFF	Bindery failure

Open Bindery   0xE3, type 0x45

Description: This service, which requires SUPERVISOR-level rights, reopens the bindery after a previous Close Bindery call.

Request Buffer:

```
    struct
        {
        word buffer_length;
        byte type;
        } request_buffer;
```

Reply Buffer:

```
struct
    {
    word buffer_length;
    } reply_buffer;
```

Input Registers:	AH	0xE3
	DS:SI	Far pointer to request_buffer
	ES:DI	Far pointer to reply_buffer

Output Registers:	AL	Completion code
		0x00 Success

Read Property Value   0xE3, type 0x3D

Description: This service returns, as a 128-byte segment, the value (or part of the value) of a given property for a given object. The field request_buffer.segment_number should be set to 1 for the first call and incremented for each subsequent call. Then the field reply_buffer.more_segments is set to 0 when the last (or only) segment is returned; the field is 0xFF for all intermediate segments. A request for a nonexistent segment returns a Completion code of 0xEC.

Request Buffer:

```
struct
    {
    word buffer_length;
    byte type;
    nw_int object_type;
    byte object_name_length;        /* Set to 48 */
    char object_name[48];
    byte segment_number;
    byte property_name_length;      /* Set to 16 */
    char property_name[16];
    } request_buffer;
```

Reply Buffer:

```
struct
    {
    word buffer_length;
    byte property_value[128];
```

```
    byte more_segments;
    byte property_flags;
    } reply_buffer;
```

Input Registers:	AH	0xE3
	DS:SI	Far pointer to request_buffer
	ES:DI	Far pointer to reply_buffer

Output Registers:	AL	Completion code
	0x00	Success
	0x96	Server out of memory
	0xEC	No such segment
	0xF0	Wild card not allowed
	0xF1	Invalid bindery security
	0xF9	No privilege to read property
	0xFB	No such property
	0xFC	No such object
	0xFE	Server bindery locked
	0xFF	Bindery failure

Rename Bindery Object   0xE3, type 0x34

Description: This service, which requires SUPERVISOR-level rights, renames an object. The object ID number is not changed.

Request Buffer:

```
struct
    {
    word buffer_length;
    byte type;
    nw_int object_type;
    byte old_object_name_length;    /* Set to 48 */
    char old_object_name[48];
    byte new_object_name_length;    /* Set to 48 */
    char new_object_name[48];
    } request_buffer;
```

Reply Buffer:

```
struct
    {
    word buffer_length;
    } reply_buffer;
```

Input Registers:	AH	0xE3
	DS:SI	Far pointer to request_buffer
	ES:DI	Far pointer to reply_buffer

Output Registers:	AL	Completion code
	0x00	Success
	0x96	Server out of memory
	0xEF	Invalid name
	0xF0	Wild card not allowed
	0xF3	No privilege to rename objects
	0xFC	No such object
	0xFE	Server bindery locked
	0xFF	Bindery failure

Scan Bindery for Object   0xE3, type 0x37

Description: This service searches the bindery for an object (by its type and name) and returns information about the object. Wild cards can be used in both the type and name fields, in which case this service can be called repeatedly to obtain all matching objects. For the first call, the field request_buffer.last_object_id should be set to 0xFFFFFFFF. For subsequent calls, this field should be set to the value of reply_buffer.object_id that the previous call returned. When there are no more matching entries, a Completion code of 0xFC (no such object) is returned.

Request Buffer:

```
struct
    {
    word buffer_length;
    byte type;
    nw_long last_object_id;
```

```
    nw_int object_type;
    byte object_name_length;        /* Set to 48 */
    char object_name[48];
    } request_buffer;
```

Reply Buffer:

```
    struct
        {
        word buffer_length;
        nw_long object_id;
        nw_int object_type;
        char object_name[48];
        byte object_flag;
        byte object_security;
        byte object_has_properties;
        } reply_buffer;
```

Input Registers:	AH	0xE3
	DS:SI	Far pointer to request_buffer
	ES:DI	Far pointer to reply_buffer

Output Registers:	AL	Completion code
	0x00	Success
	0x96	Server out of memory
	0xEF	Invalid name
	0xFC	No such object
	0xFE	Server bindery locked
	0xFF	Bindery failure

Scan for Property   0xE3, type 0x3C

Description: This service retrieves each property (one per call) for a given object. Wild cards are not allowed in the object name or the object type. For the first call, request_buffer.sequence_number field should be set to 0xFFFFFFFF. For subsequent calls, this field should be set to the value of reply_buffer.sequence_number that the previous call returned. The reply_buffer.more_properties field is set to 0x00 for the last entry, and to 0xFF for all intermediate entries. When there are no more matching entries, a Completion code of 0xFB (no such property) is returned.

Request Buffer:

```
struct
    {
    word buffer_length;
    byte type;
    nw_int object_type;
    byte object_name_length;        /* Set to 48 */
    char object_name[48];
    nw_long sequence_number;
    byte property_name_length;      /* Set to 16 */
    char property_name[16];
    } request_buffer;
```

Reply Buffer:

```
struct
    {
    word buffer_length;
    char property_name[16];
    byte property_flags;
    byte property_security;
    nw_long sequence_number;
    byte property_has_value;
    byte more_properties;
    } reply_buffer;
```

Input Registers:	AH	0xE3
	DS:SI	Far pointer to request_buffer
	ES:DI	Far pointer to reply_buffer

Output Registers:	AL	Completion code
	0x00	Success
	0x96	Server out of memory
	0xF1	Invalid bindery security
	0xFB	No such property
	0xFC	No such object
	0xFE	Server bindery locked
	0xFF	Bindery failure

Verify Bindery Object Password   0xE3, type 0x3F

Description: After comparing the password supplied in the request_buffer to the password stored in the bindery for an object, this service then returns a Completion code indicating whether the two passwords are equal. The password stored in the bindery is a value of the predefined PASSWORD property, which is a required property for any object intended to log into a file server. The property value can be null. The password supplied in the request_buffer can either be uppercase or null (an empty string). This call does not require that the requesting workstation be logged into the file server.

Request Buffer:

```
struct
    {
    word buffer_length;
    byte type;
    nw_int object_type;
    byte object_name_length;        /* Set to 48  */
    char object_name[48];
    byte password_length;           /* Set to 128 */
    char password[128];
    } request_buffer;
```

Reply Buffer:

```
struct
    {
    word buffer_length;
    } reply_buffer;
```

Input Registers:	AH	0xE3
	DS:SI	Far pointer to request_buffer
	ES:DI	Far pointer to reply_buffer

Output Registers:	AL	Completion code
	0x00	Success
	0x96	Server out of memory
	0xF0	Wild card not allowed
	0xFB	No such property
	0xFC	No such object
	0xFE	Server bindery locked
	0xFF	Bindery failure

Write Property Value   0xE3, type 0x3E

Description: This service writes, as a 128-byte segment, the value (or part of the value) of a given property for a given object. A value can span from 1 to 255 segments. Each segment is numbered and the segments must be created in sequence. This is done by setting the field request_buffer.segment_number to 1 for the first call and incrementing the field for each subsequent call. Therefore, a value longer than 128 bytes can be split into multiple segments. Of course, the values you store can fit inside one 128-byte segment. If the value is shorter than 128 bytes, you use only the first sequence of bytes (however many are required) of the segment; the remainder is unused.

This call is useful only for Item properties; the values of set properties should be managed only with the Add Bindery Object to Set function. If you are overwriting existing segments and want to truncate the overall length of the value at the current segment, you can set the field request_buffer.erase_remaining_segments to 0. If you set this field to 0xFF, subsequent segments can continue to exist. This service requires Write privileges at the property level.

Request Buffer:

```
struct
    {
    word buffer_length;
    byte type;
    nw_int object_type;
    byte object_name_length;        /* Set to 48 */
    char object_name[48];
    byte segment_number;
    byte erase_remaining_segments;
    byte property_name_length;      /* Set to 16 */
    char property_name[16];
    byte property_value_segment[128];
    } request_buffer;
```

Reply Buffer:

```
struct
    {
    word buffer_length;
    } reply_buffer;
```

Input Registers: AH   0xE3
                       DS:SI   Far pointer to `request_buffer`
                       ES:DI   Far pointer to `reply_buffer`

Output Registers: AL   Completion code

0x00	Success
0x96	Server out of memory
0xE8	Not item property
0xEC	No such segment
0xF0	Wild card not allowed
0xF1	Invalid bindery security
0xF8	No privilege to modify property
0xFB	No such property
0xFC	No such object
0xFE	Server bindery locked
0xFF	Bindery failure

Connection Services

The services in this category enable you to perform *login*, *attach*, and *logout* operations from within your application.

The NetWare shell program running on each workstation maintains two internal tables, the *Server Name Table* and the *Connection ID Table*. Both tables can hold as many as eight entries. The number of the table entry (1-8) identifies the file server. Each entry in the Server Name Table is simply a 48-byte string containing the name of a file server. Each corresponding entry in the Connection ID Table looks like this:

```
struct
    {
    byte in_use_flag;
    byte order_number;
    byte network_number[4];
    byte node_address[6];
    byte socket_number[2];
    byte receive_timeout[2];
    byte routing_node[6];
    byte packet_sequence_number;
    byte connection_number;
    byte connection_status;
    byte maximum_timeout[2];
    byte reserved[5];
    } connect_id_table[8];
```

Attach to File Server   0xF1, type 0x00

Description: This service attaches the workstation to the specified file server. The workstation must already be logged into at least one file server, and can be attached to as many as eight file servers.

Input Registers:	AH	0xF1
	AL	0
	DL	Server connection ID (1-8)
Output Registers:	AL	Completion code
		0x00 Success
		0xF8 Already attached
		0xF9 No free connection slots at the file server
		0xFA No more server slots
		0xFC Unknown file server
		0xFE Server bindery locked
		0xFF No response from the server (illegal server address)

Detach from File Server   0xF1, type 0x01

Description: This service detaches the workstation from the specified file server.

Input Registers:	AH	0xF1
	AL	1
	DL	Server connection ID (1-8)
Output Registers:	AL	Completion code
		0x00 Success
		0xFF Connection does not exist

Enter Login Area   0xE3, type 0x0A

Description: This service puts the workstation in the file server's SYS:LOGIN directory and tells NetWare the name of the subdirectory beneath SYS:LOGIN in which the LOGIN utility is located. Not particularly useful in application programs, this call is used mostly by the Boot ROM chips found in diskless workstations.

Request Buffer:

```
struct
    {
    word buffer_length;
    byte type;
    byte number_of_local_drives;
    byte subdirectory_name_length;
    char subdirectory_name[255];
    } request_buffer;
```

Reply Buffer:

```
struct
    {
    word buffer_length;
    } reply_buffer;
```

Input Registers:	AH	0xE3
	DS:SI	Far pointer to request_buffer
	ES:DI	Far pointer to reply_buffer

Output Registers:	AL	Completion code
		0x00 Success

Get Connection Information   0xE3, type 0x16

Description: This service returns information about the object that is logged in as the specified connection number. The connection number ranges from 1 to 100 and is obtainable with a call to either Get Connection Number or Get Object Connection Numbers. The login_time field returned in the reply_buffer is a 7-byte character array:

Byte	Meaning
login_time[0]	Year, in the range 0 to 99 (0 = 1980)
login_time[1]	Month, 1 to 12
login_time[2]	Day, 1 to 31
login_time[3]	Hour, 0 to 23

`login_time[4]`	Minute, 0 to 59
`login_time[5]`	Second, 0 to 59
`login_time[6]`	Day of week, 0 to 6 (0 = Sunday)

Request Buffer:

```
struct
    {
    word buffer_length;
    byte type;
    byte connection_number;
    } request_buffer;
```

Reply Buffer:

```
struct
    {
    word buffer_length;
    nw_long object_id;
    nw_int  object_type;
    char    object_name[48];
    char    login_time[7]
    } reply_buffer;
```

Input Registers:	AH	0xE3
	DS:SI	Far pointer to `request_buffer`
	ES:DI	Far pointer to `reply_buffer`

Output Registers:	AL	Completion code
		0x00 Success

Get Connection Number   0xDC

Description: This service returns the connection number that the workstation uses to communicate with the default file server.

Input Registers:	AH	0xDC

Output Registers:	AL	Connection number (1-100)
	CL	First digit of connection number
	CH	Second digit of connection number

Get Internet Address   0xE3, type 0x13

Description: This service obtains a connection's internetwork address, which consists of a network number, node address, and socket number (see Chapter 3, "PC-to-PC Communications Concepts"). The socket number returned by this function is the one the workstation uses to communicate with the file server; do not use it yourself.

Request Buffer:

```
struct
    {
    word buffer_length;
    byte type;
    byte connection_number;
    } request_buffer;
```

Reply Buffer:

```
struct
    {
    word buffer_length;
    byte network_number[4];
    byte node_address[6];
    byte socket_number[2];
    } reply_buffer;
```

Input Registers:	AH	0xE3
	DS:SI	Far pointer to `request_buffer`
	ES:DI	Far pointer to `reply_buffer`
Output Registers:	AL	Completion code
		0x00 Success

Get Object Connection   0xE3, type 0x15 Numbers

Description: This service returns an array of from 0 to 100 connection numbers under which the given object is logged on. Objects are defined in the Bindery Services reference section.

Request Buffer:

```
struct
    {
    word buffer_length;
    byte type;
    nw_int object_type;
    byte object_name_length;
    char object_name[48];
    } request_buffer;
```

Reply Buffer:

```
struct
    {
    word buffer_length;
    byte number_of_connections;
    byte connection_numbers[100];
    } reply_buffer;
```

Input Registers:	AH	0xE3
	DS:SI	Far pointer to `request_buffer`
	ES:DI	Far pointer to `reply_buffer`

Output Registers:	AL	Completion code
		0x00 Success

Login to File Server   0xE3, type 0x14

Description: This service logs an object (normally a user) into the default file server.

Request Buffer:

```
struct
    {
    word buffer_length;
    byte type;
    nw_int object_type;
    byte object_name_length;
    char object_name[48];
    byte password_length;
    char password[128];
    } request_buffer;
```

Reply Buffer:

```
struct
    {
    word buffer_length;
    } reply_buffer;
```

Input Registers:	AH	0xE3
	DS:SI	Far pointer to request_buffer
	ES:DI	Far pointer to reply_buffer

Output Registers:	AL	Completion code
		0x00 Success
		0xFF Bad password

Logout   0xD7

Description: The object at a workstation is logged off all file servers, detached from all file servers except for the default, and placed in the SYS:LOGIN directory.

Input Registers:	AH	0xD7

Output Registers: None

Logout from File Server   0xF1, type 0x02

Description: This service logs out a workstation (object) from the specified file server.

Input Registers:	AH	0xF1
	AL	2
	DL	Server connection ID (1-8)

Output Registers: None

Print Services

As was discussed in Chapter 4, "DOS-Level Programming," the functions offered by NetWare under the category of Print Services provide you with a variety of controls over how things are printed. Your application can switch between the local and network printer or printers and can specify the number of copies, the tab-expansion factor, the form type, the banner-page text, and other parameters. When NetWare intercepts print data (from Interrupt hex 17) and sends it instead to a network printer, the process is termed *capturing*.

Many of the functions defined under this category use the following data structure; if your software uses certain Print Services functions, the structure's first 42 bytes (up through form_name) can be modified, except for status:

```
struct    PRINT_CONTROL_DATA
    {
    unsigned char status;
    unsigned char print_flags;
    unsigned char tab_size;
    unsigned char server_printer;
    unsigned char number_copies;
    unsigned char form_type;
    unsigned char reserved1;
    unsigned char banner_text[13];
    unsigned char reserved2;
    unsigned char local_lpt_device;
    unsigned int  flush_timeout_count;
    unsigned char flush_on_close;
    unsigned int  maximum_lines;
    unsigned int  maximum_chars
    unsigned char form_name[13];
    unsigned char lpt_flag;
    unsigned char file_flag;
    unsigned char timeout_flag;
    char far      *setup_string_ptr;
    char far      *reset_string_ptr;
    unsigned char connect_id_queue_print_job;
    unsigned char in_progress;
    unsigned char print_queue_flag;
    unsigned char print_job_valid;
    unsigned long print_queue_id;
    unsigned int  print_job_number;
    };
```

Cancel LPT Capture   0xDF, type 0x02

Description: This service cancels the capturing of print stream data to the default printer. The print queue item is deleted and capturing is turned off (the local printer regains control).

Input Registers:	AH	0xDF
	DL	2

Output Registers:	AL	Completion code
		0x00 Success

Cancel Specific   0xDF, type 0x06
LPT Capture

Description: This service cancels the capturing of print stream data to a specific printer. The print queue item is deleted and capturing is turned off (the local printer regains control).

Input Registers:	AH	0xDF
	DL	6
	DH	LPT device (0 = LPT1, 1 = LPT2, 2 = LPT3)

Output Registers:	AL	Completion code
		0x00 Success

End Print Capture   0xDF, type 0x01

Description: This service releases the print queue item for printing and ends capturing for the default print device (the local printer regains control).

Input Registers:	AH	0xDF
	DL	1

Output Registers:	AL	Completion code
		0x00 Success

End Specific Print Capture   0xDF, type 0x05

Description: This service releases a specific printer's print queue item for printing and ends capturing (the local printer regains control).

Input Registers:	AH	0xDF
	DL	5
	DH	LPT device (0 = LPT1, 1 = LPT2, 2 = LPT3)
Output Registers:	AL	Completion code
		0x00 Success

Flush Capture   0xDF, type 0x03

Description: This service releases the default printer's print queue item for printing but continues the capturing of print data.

Input Registers:	AH	0xDF
	DL	5
Output Registers:	AL	Completion code
		0x00 Success

Flush Specific Capture   0xDF, type 0x07

Description: This service releases the specified printer's print queue item for printing but continues the capturing of print data.

Input Registers:	AH	0xDF
	DL	7
	DH	LPT device (0 = LPT1, 1 = LPT2, 2 = LPT3)
Output Registers:	AL	Completion code
		0x00 Success

Get Banner User Name   0xB8, type 0x08

Description: This service returns the user name that is printed on banner pages, if set; otherwise, the name of the user logged in at the workstation.

Reply Buffer:

```
char banner_user_name[12];
```

Input Registers:	AH	0xB8
	AL	8
	ES:BX	Far pointer to reply_buffer
Output Registers:	AL	Completion code
		0x00 Success

Get Default Printer Capture Data   0xB8, type 0x00

Description: This service returns a filled-in PRINT_CONTROL_DATA structure, as defined earlier.

Reply Buffer:

```
struct PRINT_CONTROL_DATA      reply_buffer;
```

Input Registers:	AH	0xB8
	AL	0
	CX	Length of reply_buffer
	ES:BX	Far pointer to reply_buffer
Output Registers:	AL	Completion code
		0x00 Success

Get Default Local Printer   0xB8, type 0x04

Description: This service returns a number corresponding to the default print device currently set up for capturing.

Input Registers:	AH	0xB8
	AL	4

Output Registers:	DH	Default LPT device (0 = LPT1, 1 = LPT2, 2 = LPT3)

Get Capture Status　　　0xF0, type 0x03

Description: This service indicates whether capturing is currently active for the default print device.

Input Registers:	AH	0xF0
	AL	3
Output Registers:	AH	Completion code
		0x00　Capturing not active
		0xFF　Capturing is active
	AL	Connection ID (1-8) (returned only if capturing is active)

Get Printer Status　　　0xE0, type 0x06

Description: This service returns the current status of a specified network printer. Because a file server can manage as many as five print devices (three parallel, two serial), the printer_number field can range from 0 to 4.

Request Buffer:

```
struct
    {
    word buffer_length;
    byte type;
    byte printer_number; /* 0-4 */
    } request_buffer;
```

Reply Buffer:

```
struct
    {
    word buffer_length;
    byte printer_halted;       /* O=active, 0xFF=stopped */
    byte printer_offline;      /* 1=offline */
    byte form_type;            /* 0-255 */
    byte target_printer_number; /* same as above, unless */
                               /* rerouted */
```

```
} reply_buffer;
```

Input Registers:	AH	0xE0
	DS:SI	Far pointer to `request_buffer`
	ES:DI	Far pointer to `reply_buffer`
Output Registers:	AL	Completion code
	0x00	Success
	0xFF	No such printer

Get Specified Printer Capture Data   0xB8, type 0x02

Description: This service returns a filled-in PRINT_CONTROL_DATA structure, as defined earlier, for a specific print device.

Reply Buffer:

```
struct PRINT_CONTROL_DATA    reply_buffer;
```

Input Registers:	AH	0xB8
	AL	2
	CX	Length of `reply_buffer`
	ES:BX	Far pointer to `reply_buffer`
	DH	Printer number (0 = LPT1, 1 = LPT2, 2 = LPT3)
Output Registers:	AL	Completion code
	0x00	Success

Set Banner User Name   0xB8, type 0x09

Description: This service sets the user name that is printed on banner pages.

Request Buffer:

```
char banner_user_name[12];
```

Input Registers:	AH	0xB8
	AL	9
	ES:BX	Far pointer to `request_buffer`
Output Registers:	AL	Completion code
	0x00	Success

Set Capture Print Queue   0xB8, type 0x06

Description: This service targets the next print capture to a specified print queue.

Input Registers:	AH	0xB8
	AL	6
	DH	Print device (0 = LPT1, 1 = LPT2, 2 = LPT3)
	BX:CX	Queue ID (bindery object ID number)
Output Registers:	AL	Completion code
	0x00	Success
	0xFF	Print job already queued

Set Default Printer Capture Data   0xB8, type 0x01

Description: With this service, you can change any of the first 42 bytes (up through `form_name`, except for the status field) of the `print_control` data structure for the default print device.

Reply Buffer:

```
struct PRINT_CONTROL_DATA        reply_buffer;
```

Input Registers:	AH	0xB8
	AL	1
	CX	`reply_buffer` length (1-42)
	ES:BX	Far pointer to `reply_buffer`
Output Registers:	AL	Completion code
	0x00	Success

Set Default   0xB8, type 0x05
Local Printer

Description: This function, which remains in effect until it is recalled or the workstation is rebooted, designates the default local print device (LPT1, LPT2, or LPT3). The designated device becomes the selected printer for the default print-capture functions in this category.

Input Registers:	AH	0xB8
	AL	5
	DH	Print device (0 = LPT1, 1 = LPT2, 2 = LPT3)
Output Registers:	AL	Completion code
		0x00 Success

Set Specified Printer   0xB8, type 0x03
Capture Data

Description: With this service, you can change any of the first 42 bytes (up through `form_name`, except for the *status* field) of the `print_control` data structure for the specified print device.

Request Buffer:

```
struct PRINT_CONTROL_DATA        request_buffer;
```

Input Registers:	AH	0xB8
	AL	3
	CX	`request_buffer` length (1-42)
	DH	Print device (0 = LPT1, 1 = LPT2, 2 = LPT3)
	ES:BX	Far pointer to `request_buffer`
Output Registers:	AL	Completion code
		0x00 Success

Specify Capture File   0xE0, type 0x09

Description: This service creates a disk file and directs that the next capture of print stream data go into the file. The previous contents of the file, if any, are lost. The service must be used for the default print device, not a specific print device. The file is closed when the application invokes a Cancel Capture, End Capture, or Flush Capture function call. This service requires Read, Write, and Create rights in the target directory.

Request Buffer:

```
struct
    {
    word buffer_length;
    byte type;
    byte directory_handle;    /* 0 */
    byte file_path_length;    /* 1-255 */
    char file_path[255];      /* full path and file name */
    } request_buffer;
```

Reply Buffer:

```
struct
    {
    word buffer_length;
    } reply_buffer;
```

Input Registers:	AH	0xE0
	AL	9
	DS:SI	Far pointer to `request_buffer`
	ES:DI	Far pointer to `reply_buffer`

Output Registers:	AL	Completion code
		0x00 Success
		0x9C Invalid path

Start LPT Capture 　　　　 0xDF, type 0x00

Description: This service starts a capture of print data to the default print device. Characters subsequently sent to the default printer are redirected to a network printer. The current settings in the default printer's PRINT_CONTROL_DATA structure are used to manage the printout.

Input Registers:	AH	0xDF
	AL	0

Output Registers:	AL	Completion code
		0x00 Success

Start Specific LPT Capture — 0xDF, type 0x04

Description: This service starts a capture of print data to the specified print device. Characters subsequently sent to that printer are redirected to a network printer. The current settings in the specified printer's PRINT_CONTROL_DATA structure are used to manage the printout. The print material is sent to its final destination when the application issues an End Specific Capture or a Flush Specific Capture call.

Input Registers:	AH	0xDF
	AL	4
	DH	Print device (0 = LPT1, 1 = LPT2, 2 = LPT3)
Output Registers:	AL	Completion code
		0x00 Success

Synchronization Services

You can consider the services in this category as extensions to the PC DOS file-sharing and record-locking services. However, these services really exist at a lower level than the DOS functions. The sharing and locking calls you issue to DOS are translated into equivalent Synchronization Services calls as part of the redirection of DOS functions that occurs in the NetWare shell/redirector software. Therefore, the file server does not need to know anything about PC DOS function calls (even redirected ones); it only has to be capable of handling the NetWare-specific functions it receives from the shell/redirector or directly from your application.

This section focuses on the Synchronization Services that deal with physical file or record locks. See Chapter 2, "Multiuser Concepts," and Chapter 4, "DOS-Level Programming," for further discussion of these services.

Clear File — 0xED

Description: This service unlocks the specified file and removes it from the log table for a workstation.

Request Buffer:

```
char file_path[255];      /* drive, path, and file name */
```

Input Registers:	AH	0xED
	DS:DX	Far pointer to request_buffer string

Output Registers:	AL	Completion code
		0x00 Success
		0xFF File not found

Clear File Set   0xCF

Description: This service unlocks all files in the log table for a workstation and removes them from the log table.

Input Registers:	AH	0xCF

Output Registers:	None

Clear Physical Record   0xBE

Description: This service unlocks the specified physical record and removes it from the log table.

Input Registers:	AH	0xBE
	BX	File handle (from DOS function 3C, 3D, or 5B)
	CX:DX	Record's location in the file
	SI:DI	Record's length (file region)

Output Registers:	AL	Completion code
		0x00 Success
		0xFF No locked record found

Clear Physical Record   0xC4
Set

Description: This service unlocks all physical records in the log table and removes them from the log table.

Input Registers:	AH	0xC4
Output Registers:	None	

Get Lock Mode   0xC6, type 0x02

Description: This service returns the current Lock mode flag. This flag indicates whether NetWare should recognize the time-out value specified for certain function calls. Set the flag to 0 for early versions of NetWare (earlier than NetWare 4.61). NetWare 4.61 and all versions of Advanced NetWare 286 and 386 require a lock flag value of 1. The default is 0.

Input Registers:	AH	0xC6
	AL	2
Output Registers:	AL	Current Lock mode

Lock File Set   0xCB

Description: This service attempts to lock all files in the log table. The time-out value indicates how long NetWare will wait for an already locked file to become unlocked (available). A value of 0 means no-wait.

Input Registers:	AH	0xCB
	BP	Time-out limit, in 1/18 second
Output Registers:	AL	Completion code
		0x00 Success
		0xFE Timed out (could not acquire all locks)
		0xFF Failure

Lock Physical   0xC2
Record Set

Description: This service attempts to lock all physical records in the log table. The time-out value indicates how long NetWare will wait for an already locked file to become unlocked (available). A value of 0 means no wait. The lock directive denotes the type of locking to be performed:

00   Lock records with exclusive locks
01   Lock with SHAREABLE, Read-Only locks

Input Registers:	AH	0xC2
	AL	Lock directive
	BP	Time-out limit, in 1/18 second

Output Registers:	AL	Completion code
	0x00	Success
	0xFE	Timed out (could not acquire all locks)
	0xFF	Failure

Log File   0xEB

Description: This service puts a file in the log table. Optionally, you can attempt to lock the file using this service.

Request Buffer:

```
char file_path[255];      /* drive, path, and file name */
```

Input Registers:	AH	0xEB
	AL	Lock directive:
	0	Log file
	1	Log and lock file
	BP	Time-out limit (needed only if lock directive = 1)
	DS:DX	Far pointer to request_buffer

Output Registers:	AL	Completion code
	0x00	Success
	0x96	Server out of memory
	0xFE	Timed out (lock not acquired)
	0xFF	Hardware failure

Log Physical Record   0xBC

Description: This service logs a physical record in the log table. Optionally, you can also attempt to lock the record using this service.

Input Registers:	AH	0xBC
	AL	Lock directive:
		0 Log the record
		1 Log and lock record with an exclusive lock
		3 Log and lock record with a SHAREABLE, Read-Only lock
	BX	File handle (from DOS function 3C, 3D, or 5B)
	BP	Time-out limit, in 1/18 second
	CX:DX	File position of record
	SI:DI	Record length
Output Registers:	AL	Completion code
		0x00 Success
		0x96 Server out of memory
		0xFE Timed out (lock not acquired)
		0xFF Failure

Release File   0xEC

Description: This service unlocks a file that was previously logged and locked. The entry in the log table is not removed.

Request Buffer:

```
char file_path[255]        /* drive, path, and file name */
```

Input Registers:	AH	0xEC
	DS:DX	Far pointer to request_buffer
Output Registers:	AL	Completion code
		0x00 Success
		0xFF File not found

Release File Set   0xCD

Description: This service unlocks all files logged in the log table; the entries are not removed from the table.

Input Registers: AH   0xCD

Output Registers: None

Release Physical   0xBD
Record

Description: This service unlocks a physical record in the log table, but does not remove the entry from the table.

Input Registers:	AH	0xBD
	BX	File handle (from DOS function 3C, 3D, or 5B)
	CX:DX	File position of record
	SI:DI	Record length
Output Registers:	AL	Completion code
		0x00 Success
		0xFF Locked record not found

Release Physical   0xC3
Record Set

Description: This service unlocks all physical records in the log table, but does not remove the entries from the table.

Input Registers: AH   0xC3

Output Registers: None

Set Lock Mode 0xC6

Description: This service sets the current Lock mode flag. This flag indicates whether NetWare should recognize the time-out value specified for certain function calls. Set the flag to 0 for early versions of NetWare (earlier than NetWare 4.61). NetWare 4.61 and all versions of Advanced NetWare 286 and 386 require a lock flag value of 1. The default is 0.

Input Registers: AH 0xC6

AL Lock mode (0 or 1)

Output Registers: None

Transaction Tracking Services

Chapter 4, "DOS-Level Programming," discussed related file updates and the need for a mechanism for maintaining consistency among the data in two or more related files. I mapped out in pseudocode such a mechanism you can develop yourself, involving journaling and rollback. However, if you don't mind writing your application in a Novell-specific fashion, a mechanism called *Transaction Tracking Services* (TTS) is provided for you. When TTS is enabled and properly used, it guarantees that either all related updates take place or none of them do.

TTS is available only on file servers using the SFT Advanced NetWare and NetWare 386 products. Also, the server must be configured to use TTS when it is "NETGEN'd." Finally, for TTS to be able to treat a file specially, the file must be marked *Transactional* with the Set Extended File Attributes service. (With all these prerequisites, you would think that TTS would seldom be used; this is not the case, however, primarily because applications that make TTS calls work okay even on non-TTS networks—except, of course, that transaction tracking is not performed on such networks.)

TTS does both implicit and explicit transaction tracking. *Implicit* means that activity to a Transactional file is tracked record-by-record without requiring TTS-aware programming. *Explicit* means that TTS (as Novell puts it) "allows applications to neatly bracket file update sequences with locking and TTS system calls." You incorporate TTS calls in your application to delimit updates to related files, and TTS makes sure that half-finished operations do not corrupt the relationships and consistencies in the data.

The server can simultaneously monitor 1 to 200 transactions; exactly how many transactions is specified when the server is "NETGEN'd." Because a "before" image of each update is kept on the server, TTS requires extra disk space. Also, because journaling takes extra I/O, TTS can slow things down just a little. The extra data protection that TTS provides, however, can well justify the extra disk space and I/O time.

Get Extended File Attributes   0xB6, type 0x00

Description: This service returns the NetWare-specific *Extended File Attributes* for a named file. (See the Set Extended File Attributes call.)

Request Buffer:

```
char file_path[255]      /* drive, path, and file name */
```

Input Registers:	AH	0xB6
	AL	0
	DS:DX	Far pointer to request_buffer
Output Registers:	AL	Completion code
		0x00 Success
		0xFE No privilege
		0xFF File not found

Set Extended File Attributes   0xB6, type 0x01

Description: This service sets the NetWare-specific Extended File Attributes for a named file. Bit 5 (bit mask 0x10) of the attribute byte defines whether the file is Transactional. Setting the attribute to 0x10 makes TTS aware of the file. While this bit is set, the file cannot be deleted or renamed. Bit 6 (bit mask 0x20) of the attribute byte defines whether NetWare indexed the file. Indexing makes accessing different records within the file take less time; usually you should index files accessed randomly at the record level that are larger than 2 megabytes.

Request Buffer:

```
char file_path[255]        /* drive, path, and file name */
```

Input Registers:	AH	0xB6
	AL	1
	CL	Extended file attributes

Bit position 76543210	*Meaning*
...0....	TTS off for this file
...1....	TTS enabled
..0.....	File is not indexed
..1.....	Indexing enabled

	DS:DX	Far pointer to request_buffer

Output Registers:	AL	Completion code
	0x00	Success
	0xFE	No privilege
	0xFF	File not found

TTS Abort Transaction   0xC7, type 0x03

Description: This service lets you "manually" abort a transaction, causing the files involved in the current transaction to be restored to their original state prior to the start of the transaction. If TTS acquired automatic physical record locks while the transaction was active, they are released.

Input Registers:	AH	0xC7
	AL	3

Output Registers:	Carry flag clear	
	AL	Completion code
		0x00 Success
	Carry flag set	
	AL	Completion code
		0xFD TTS is presently disabled

0xFE	Transaction ended; records locked
0xFF	No explicit transaction is active

TTS Begin Transaction   0xC7, type 0x00

Description: This service is used to start an explicit transaction. When this call is made, TTS begins tracking writes to Transactional files, automatically acquiring a physical record lock on all records being written, except for those records already locked. If TTS places a lock, the lock is left in place until a TTS End Transaction call or a TTS Abort Transaction call.

Input Registers: AH   0xC7

AL   0

Output Registers: Carry flag clear

AL   Completion code

0x00   Success

Carry flag set

AL   Completion code

0x96   Out of dynamic work space

0xFE   Implicit transaction is already active (it is now converted to an explicit transaction)

0xFF   Explicit transaction is already active (it continues normally)

TTS End Transaction   0xC7, type 0x01

Description: This service is used to end an explicit transaction. File server I/O continues even after this call returns; TTS supplies a Transaction Reference Number that you can use to determine when the transaction is actually finished. Call the TTS Transaction Status function for that Transaction Reference Number to see whether the transaction I/O finished. Any automatically acquired physical record locks are released.

Input Registers:	AH	0xC7
	AL	1

Output Registers: Carry flag clear

	AL	Completion code
		0x00 Success
		0xFD Transaction tracking disabled
		0xFE Transaction ended; records still locked (transaction is backed out)
	CX:DX	Transaction Reference Number

Carry flag set

	AL	Completion code
		0xFF No explicit transaction active

TTS Get Application Thresholds   0xC7, type 0x05

Description: This service returns threshold information about application-level logical or physical records. TTS uses this information for implicit transactions. (See the TTS Set Application Thresholds call.)

Input Registers:	AH	0xC7
	AL	5

Output Registers:	AL	Completion code
		0x00 Success
	CL	Logical record lock threshold (0 to 225)
	CH	Physical record lock threshold (0 to 225)

TTS Get Workstation Thresholds   0xC7, type 0x07

Description: This service returns threshold information about workstation-level logical or physical record locks. TTS uses this information for implicit transactions. (See the TTS Set Workstation Thresholds call.)

Input Registers:	AH	0xC7
	AL	7
Output Registers:	AL	Completion code
		0x00 Success
	CL	Logical record lock threshold (0 to 225)
	CH	Physical record lock threshold (0 to 225)

TTS Is Available   0xC7, type 0x02

Description: This service returns an indication of whether TTS is available and active on the default file server.

Input Registers:	AH	0xC7
	AL	2
Output Registers:	AL	Completion code
		0x00 TTS not available
		0x01 TTS available
		0xFD TTS currently disabled

TTS Set Application Thresholds   0xC7, type 0x06

Description: This service sets logical or physical record lock thresholds at the application level. If the number of logical or physical record locks exceeds these thresholds, TTS starts an implicit transaction. The default threshold for logical and physical locks is 0. A threshold of 0xFF turns off the generation of implicit transactions for that lock type. You should turn off implicit transaction tracking if your application is designed to use explicit transactions but sometimes generates unwanted implicit transactions just because of the way it locks records. The threshold values you specify with this function are temporarily in effect until your application terminates.

Input Registers:	AH	0xC7
	AL	6
	CL	Logical record lock threshold (0 to 225)
	CH	Physical record lock threshold (0 to 225)
Output Registers:	AL	Completion code
		0x00 Success

TTS Set Workstation Thresholds   0xC7, type 0x08

Description: This service sets workstation-level, logical or physical record lock thresholds. If the number of logical or physical record locks exceeds these thresholds, TTS starts an implicit transaction. The default threshold for logical and physical locks is 0. A threshold of 0xFF turns off the generation of implicit transactions for that lock type. You should turn off implicit transaction tracking if your application is designed to use explicit transactions but sometimes generates unwanted implicit transactions just because of the way it locks records. The threshold values you set with this function survive the termination of your application; only making another call to this function or rebooting the workstation will reset them.

Input Registers:	AH	0xC7
	AL	8
	CL	Logical record lock threshold (0 to 225)
	CH	Physical record lock threshold (0 to 225)
Output Registers:	AL	Completion code
		0x00 Success

TTS Transaction Status   0xC7, type 0x04

Description: This service returns an indication of whether a transaction has been completely written to disk. Because it uses a "lazy-write" caching algorithm in the file server, NetWare can take several seconds to actually record the transaction on the surface of the network disk.

Input Registers:	AH	0xC7
	AL	4
	CX:DX	Transaction Reference Number (returned by TTS End Transaction)
Output Registers:	AL	Completion code
		0x00 Success
		0xFF Not yet completely written to disk

Workstation Services

The services in this category provide information about the NetWare shell/redirector program running on the workstation, and let you control certain workstation environmental factors, such as the following:

❑ Whether NetWare performs cleanup actions when a program terminates

❑ Whether critical errors should be returned to your program or cause an `Abort, Retry, Fail?` message to appear

The NetWare shell program running on each workstation maintains two internal tables, the Server Name Table and the Connection ID Table. Both tables can hold as many as eight entries. The number of the table entry (1-8) identifies the file server. Each entry in the Server Name Table is simply a 48-byte string containing the name of a file server. Each corresponding entry in the Connection ID Table looks like this:

```
struct
    {
    byte in_use_flag;
    byte order_number;
    byte network_number[4];
```

```
    byte node_address[6];
    byte socket_number[2];
    byte receive_timeout[2];
    byte routing_node[6];
    byte packet_sequence_number;
    byte connection_number;
    byte connection_status;
    byte maximum_timeout[2];
    byte reserved[5];
    } connect_id_table[8];
```

The addresses (returned as far pointers) of these two tables are available through function calls in this category.

End of Job   0xD6

Description: This service prompts cleanup actions at both the workstation and the file server, releasing file and record locks, closing network and local files, and resetting Error mode and Lock mode. The Synchronization Services section discussed Lock mode. Error mode is discussed later in this section as part of the Set Error Mode call. Unless you call Set End of Job Status, the NetWare shell automatically calls this function when your application terminates and returns to DOS.

Input Registers:	AH	0xD6	
	BX	0x0000	for current process only
		0xFFFF	for all processes on workstation

Output Registers:	None

Get Connection ID   0xEF, type 0x03
Table Pointer

Description: This service returns a far pointer to the Connection ID Table within the NetWare shell program.

Input Registers:	AH	0xEF
	AL	3
Output Registers:	ES:SI	Far pointer to workstation's Connection ID Table

Get File Server Name Table Pointer   0xEF, type 0x04

Description: This service returns a far pointer to the File Server Name Table within the NetWare shell program.

Input Registers:	AH	0xEF
	AL	4
Output Registers:	ES:SI	Far pointer to workstation's Server Name Table

Get Shell Version Information   0xEA, type 0x01

Description: This service returns information about the workstation's environment.

Reply Buffer:

```
byte reply_buffer[40]
    /* (Filled with four concatenated, null-terminated
       strings. The first string contains the name of the
       workstation's operating system (for example, "MS DOS").
       The second string contains the version of the
       operating system.  The third string contains an
       identification of the type of computer (e.g, "IBM PC").
       And the fourth string contains a more generic
       identification of the type of computer (e.g, "IBM"). */
```

Input Registers:	AH	0xEA
	AL	1
	BX	0
	ES:DI	Far pointer to reply_buffer

Output Registers:	AH	Workstation operating system (0 = PC DOS)
	AL	Customization code
	BH	Major NetWare shell version
	BL	Minor NetWare shell version
	CL	Shell revision number
	ES:SI	Far pointer to `reply_buffer`

Set End of Job Status　　0xBB

Description: This service turns on or off the automatic cleanup actions performed by the NetWare shell program when an application terminates.

Input Registers:	AH	0xBB	
	AL	End of Job flag	
		0	Disabled
		1	Enabled

| Output Registers: | AL | Previous setting of the End of Job flag |

Set NetWare　　0xDD
Error Mode

Description: This service tells NetWare how you want it to handle critical errors (the kind that normally invoke Interrupt 24 [hex]). Error mode 0 is the default. The setting of Error mode affects only DOS function calls; direct calls to NetWare services return Completion codes as described in this section. You can also choose to install your own Interrupt 24 handler.

Input Registers:	AH	0xDD	
	DL	Error mode	
		0	Ask user `Abort, Retry, Fail?`

| | 1 | Do not do Int 24; return NetWare error to program |
| | 2 | Do not do Int 24; return DOS error to program |

Output Registers: AL Previous setting of Error mode

OS/2 Services

This section includes reference material on the `DosOpen()`, `DosClose()`, `DosFileLocks()`, and `DosBufReset()` functions, as well as material on the O/S kernel API calls that deal with named pipes.

In addition to the file-oriented programmer services described in this section, OS/2 also offers a protected-mode implementation of NETBIOS that applications can use for PC-to-PC communications. OS/2 NETBIOS is similar to the DOS-based NETBIOS, which is described separately in this reference section.

You will recall from Chapter 1, "The Basics of Networking," that an application wanting to create a named pipe is considered the *server* (not to be confused with file server) and the application at the other end of the pipe is considered the *client*. A named pipe is a file whose name has a particular format (the path and extension are optional):

`\PIPE\`*path*`\`*name.ext*

A named pipe typically is used as follows: the server application calls `DosMakeNmPipe()` to create a named pipe, and then it uses `DosConnectNmPipe()` to wait until the client has opened the pipe with a call to `DosOpen()`. The communication link is two-way; both the server and client can use `DosWrite()` and `DosRead()` calls to put data in the pipe or to remove data from it. `DosPeekNmPipe()` can be used to inspect data in the pipe without removing the data. At the end of the pipe's lifetime, the server can close the pipe with a DosClose() call and destroy the pipe with DosDisConnectNmPipe(). Named Pipes can be treated as simple data streams or, if you want, as message pipes. In the latter case, each call to DosRead() fetches one message at a time from the pipe.

In the function definitions that follow, the data types byte, word, and dword are used as though the following #define statements are in effect:

```
#define byte    unsigned char
#define word    unsigned int
#define dword   unsigned long
```

DosBufReset

Description: This function takes data that was written to a file but is still sitting in OS/2's internal buffers, and flushes the data to the output device (usually a disk). The directory entry for the file is updated. If the *handle* parameter is −1, all buffers for all open files associated with the current process are written to disk.

Prototype:
```
word DosBufReset(word handle);
```

Returns: 0 on success, nonzero on error

DosCallNmPipe

Description: Using this function, a client workstation can perform a series of actions in one fell swoop: the named pipe is opened; a message record is written to the pipe; a message is read from the pipe; and the pipe is closed. The server workstation must have opened the pipe in message mode. If you specify an input buffer too small to hold the entire incoming message, you can call this function again to receive the remainder of the message.

As was mentioned earlier, you must specify the *pipename* parameter in the form \PIPE*path**filename.ext*. The write_length parameter indicates how many bytes are written from write_buffer. The input_length parameter gives the length of the input_buffer area. The item that actual_length_ptr points to is set to the length of the incoming message. And the timeout_interval parameter specifies the number of milliseconds to wait for the incoming message before returning an error. You can also set timeout_interval to 0 to tell OS/2 to use its default time-out value, or you can set timeout_value to −1 to indicate that you want to wait indefinitely.

Prototype:
```
word DosCallNmPipe( char far *pipename,
                    char far *write_buffer,
                    word write_length,
                    char far *input_buffer,
                    word input_length,
                    word far *actual_length_ptr,
                    long timeout_interval);
```

Returns: 0 on success, nonzero on error

DosClose

Description: This function does the following:

❏ Closes the file associated with the file or pipe handle

❏ Flushes any buffered, written data to disk

❏ Updates the directory entry

If either the server or the client closes a named pipe handle that is in the "connected" state, the state of the pipe is changed to "closing." If the pipe is not in the "connected" state and is closed by the server (pipe creator), the pipe is destroyed.

Prototype:
```
word DosClose(word handle);
```

Returns: 0 on success, nonzero on error

DosConnectNmPipe

Description: This function is used by the server workstation, never by the client. If the pipe was opened in blocking mode, this function waits until the client workstation opens the pipe with a call to DosOpen(). If the server workstation opens the pipe in non-blocking mode and the client workstation has not yet opened the other end of the pipe, this function returns an error code; if the client workstation opens the pipe, the function returns a 0. In nonblocking mode, this function can be used inside a loop to poll for the client to open the pipe, but you should use DosSleep() in the polling loop to make sure that you do not drain CPU resources while you wait. The parameter handle was returned by DosMakeNmPipe().

Prototype:

    word DosConnectNmPipe(word handle);

Returns: 0 if the client workstation has opened the pipe, otherwise a nonzero error code

DosDisConnectNmPipe

Description: A server workstation uses this function to abruptly "break the pipe." When this call finishes, the client workstation can no longer read from or write to the named pipe. Any unread data remaining in the pipe is abandoned.

Prototype:

    word DosDisConnectNmPipe(word handle);

Returns: 0 on success, nonzero on error

DosFileLocks

Description: This function locks or unlocks a file region. If a null pointer is specified for either parameter, the corresponding action (lock or unlock) is not performed. However, if both parameters are present, the unlock action is performed before the lock action. Locking beyond end-of-file is not an error. Do not overlap regions. A child process does not inherit access to a locked region of a file.

Prototype:
```
struct LOCK_INFO
    {
    dword file_offset;
    dword region_length;
    };

word DosFileLocks(word handle,
                  struct LOCK_INFO far *unlock_info,
                  struct LOCK_INFO far *lock_info);
```

Returns: 0 on success, nonzero on error

DosMakeNmPipe

Description: This function creates a new named pipe. The workstation that calls this function is termed the *server*. If successful, this function returns a handle that you use in other functions to refer to the pipe.

The *pipename* parameter must be a string in the following format: \PIPE*path**filename.ext*. The open_mode parameter specifies the following:

open_mode, high byte

> *Bits*
> FEDCBA98   *Meaning*
> ..xxxxxx   Reserved
> .x......   write_through flag
> x.......   Reserved

open_mode, low byte

> *Bits*
> 76543210   *Meaning*
> xxx   access_mode
> .xxxx...   Reserved
> x.......   Inheritance

If the write_through flag is a 0, write operations are buffered. If the flag is a 1, write operations cause data to flow immediately into the pipe. The access_mode bits indicate whether the pipe is bidirectional (010), server-to-client (001), or client-to-server (000). The inheritance bit indicates whether a child process can inherit the pipe handle (0 = inheritable, 1 = not inheritable).

The `pipe_mode` parameter specifies the following:

Bits

FFEDCBA98 76543210	*Meaning*
.... xxxxxxxx	`max_instance_count`
.......x	`read_mode`
......x.	Reserved
.....x..	`write_mode`
.xxxx...	Reserved
x.......	`blocking_mode`

These parameters are defined as follows:

❏ `max_instance_count` denotes the maximum number of instances of the pipe that can exist (255 = no limit).

❏ `read_mode` specifies whether the pipe will be read as a simple stream of bytes (0) or as either a series of distinct messages or as a stream of bytes (1).

❏ `write_mode` identifies whether data is written to the pipe as a stream of bytes (0) or as a series of distinct messages (1).

❏ `blocking_mode` indicates that a read or write operation should wait (block) until the specified number of bytes are read or written (0), or that the Read or Write operation should return immediately to the application if it cannot be completely satisfied (1).

The `outbound_size` field tells how many bytes will be allocated for the pipe's output buffer. `inbound_size` does the same for the pipe's input buffer. If you specify 0 for either of these parameters, a default buffer size of 1,024 bytes is used.

Set the `timeout_interval` to the number of milliseconds that `DosWaitNmPipe()` and `DosConnectNmPipe()` will wait before returning to your application (specifying 0 tells OS/2 to use its default of 50 milliseconds).

Prototype:

```
word DosMakeNmPipe(char far *pipename,
                   word far *handle,
                   word open_mode,
                   word pipe_mode,
                   word outbound_size,
                   word inbound_size,
                   dword timeout_interval);
```

Returns: 0 on success, nonzero on error

DosOpen

Description: This function opens a file or an existing named pipe, or creates a new file, and returns a handle that you use in subsequent references to the file. If you are creating a new file, set the attribute and `initial_filesize` parameters to indicate the file's attribute and initial size allocation. The current file position is set to 0 (the first byte). A client workstation uses this function to open a named pipe; the pipe defaults to *blocking* and *byte stream* modes. Issue a call to `DosSetNmPHandState()` if you want to change these default characteristics. The `open_mode` parameter has a slightly different definition for named pipes; see the description of `open_mode` bit-fields that follows.

The *action* parameter returned indicates one of the following:

1. File existed and was opened

2. File did not exist and was created

3. File existed and was replaced

Code the *attribute* parameter for a new file with the following:

Bits FEDCBA98 76543210	*Meaning*
....x	Read-Only
....x.	Hidden
....x..	System
....xx...	Reserved
....x.....	Archive
xxxxxxxx xx......	Reserved

The bits of `open_flag` have the following meaning:

Bits FEDCBA98 76543210	*Meaning*
....0000	Fail if file exists
....0001	Open if file exists
....0010	Replace if file exists
.... 0000....	Fail if file does not exist
.... 0001....	Create if file does not exist
xxxxxxxx	Reserved

Except for named pipes, code `open_mode` according to the following bit-fields:

Bits

FEDCBA98 76543210	*Meaning*
....000	Access mode: Read-Only
....001	Access mode: Write-Only
....010	Access mode: Read-Write
....x...	Reserved
.... .001....	Sharing mode: Deny Read-Write (exclusive)
.... .010....	Sharing mode: Deny Write
.... .011....	Sharing mode: Deny Read
.... .100....	Sharing mode: Deny None (fully shared)
.... 0.......	Inheritable by child process
.... 1.......	Not inheritable by child process
...xxxxx	Reserved
..0.....	Let system handle critical errors
..1.....	Return error to program
.0......	OK if writes are buffered
.1......	Do not buffer writes
0.......	Normal file open
1.......	Open entire volume as a file (do not use on network disks!)

For a named pipe, bits 3 through D and bit F of `open_mode` must be 0. Also, bits 0 through 2 are defined as `pipe_mode` rather than `access_mode`:

Bits

76543210	*Meaning*
.....000	Inbound pipe (client to server)
.....001	Outbound pipe (server to client)
.....010	Bidirectional

Prototype:

```
word DosOpen(char far *file name,
             word far *handle,
             word far *action,
             dword initial_filesize,
             word attribute,
             word open_flag,
             word open_mode,
             dword reserved);
```

Returns: 0 on success, nonzero on error

DosPeekNmPipe

Description: As its name implies, this function lets you peek at the data in the named pipe without actually removing the data from the pipe. DosPeekNmPipe() attempts to transfer buffer_size bytes into buffer, but the function does not block (wait) if it cannot fill the buffer. The actual number of bytes is placed in actual_size, and the pipe_data_ptr structure receives the number of bytes remaining in the pipe and the number of bytes remaining in the current message. Finally, pipe_status returns one of the following four statuses of the named pipe:

1. Disconnected

2. Listening

3. Connected

4. Closing

Prototype:
```
struct PIPE_DATA
    {
    word bytes_left_in_pipe;
    word bytes_left_in_message;
    };

word DosPeekNmPipe(word handle,
                char far *buffer,
                word buffer_size,
                word far *actual_size,
                struct PIPE_DATA far *pipe_data_ptr,
                word *pipe_status);
```

Returns: 0 on success, nonzero on error

DosQNmPHandState

Description: This function returns information about a named pipe in the *state* variable:

```
Bits
FEDCBA98 76543210    Meaning
........ xxxxxxxx    max_instance_count
.......x ........    read_mode
......x. ........    Reserved
```

```
.....X.. ........          write_mode
..XXX... ........          Reserved
.X...... ........          server_client
X....... ........          blocking_mode
```

server_client is a 0 if the workstation making the call is the client, and 1 if the workstation is the server. The other bit-fields are described under DosMakeNmPipe().

Prototype:

```
word DosQNmPHandState(word handle, word far *state);
```

Returns: 0 on success, nonzero on error

DosQNmPipeInfo

Description: This function returns information about a named pipe. You should set the info_level parameter to 1 before calling this function. The returned information is placed in a structure (PIPE_INFO) whose size you specify in the last parameter, pipe_info_size.

Prototype:

```
struct PIPE_INFO
    {
    word output buffer size (outbound data);
    word input buffer size (inbound data);
    byte max_instances;
    byte actual_instance_count;
    byte pipe_name_length;
    char pipe_name[255];
    };

word DosQNmPipeInfo(word handle,
                    word info_level,
                    struct PIPE_INFO far *pipe_info_ptr,
                    word pipe_info_size);
```

Returns: 0 on success, nonzero on error

DosQNmPipeSemState

Description: This function provides information about a named pipe associated with a given system semaphore (see the section that describes `DosSetNmPipeSem()`). The information is returned as a series of 6-byte entries in the SEM_INFO structure:

```
struct SEM_INFO
    {
    byte pipe_status;
    byte wait_status;
    word semaphore_key;
    word bytes_available;
    } [xx];
```

The entries provide the following information:

❑ `pipe_status` is a 0 if the pipe is empty, 1 if data is available in the pipe, 2 if the pipe has some free space, or 3 if the pipe is closing.

❑ `wait_status` is a 0 if the other workstation is not waiting for pipe data, or a 1 if the other workstation is waiting for data.

❑ `semaphore_key` is the key associated with the semaphore handle.

❑ `bytes_available` represents the number of bytes available to be read (if `pipe_status` is a 1) or the free space inside the pipe (if `pipe_status` is a 2).

OS/2 returns information about all named pipes related to the given semaphore, unless of course `sem_info_size` specifies an array of SEM_INFO structures too small to receive the information.

Prototype:
```
word DosQNmPipeSemState(dword sem_handle,
                        struct SEM_INFO far *sem_info,
                        word sem_info_size);
```

Returns: 0 on success, nonzero on error

DosSetNmPHandState

Description: This function establishes a new `read_mode` and `blocking_mode` for an open named pipe. You should code state as follows:

Bits	
FEDCBA98 76543210	*Meaning*
.... xxxxxxx	Reserved
........0	`read_mode`: byte-stream only
........1	`read_mode`: byte-stream or message-stream
.xxxxxx.	Reserved
0.......	`blocking_mode`: wait for read or write to complete
1.......	`blocking_mode`: return from read or write (with error code) if read or write operation cannot be immediately satisfied

Prototype:

```
word DosSetNmPHandState(word handle, word state);
```

Returns: 0 on success, nonzero on error

DosSetNmPipeSem

Description: This function attaches a system semaphore to a named pipe, or replaces a semaphore already attached. The semaphore is cleared when either (1) the other workstation places data in the pipe to be read, or (2) the pipe becomes less than full (so that more data can be written). The semaphore key that you assign is returned when you later call `DosQNmPipeSemState()`; because several named pipes can be associated with a single semaphore, you can use the key to distinguish which pipe needs to be serviced.

Prototype:

```
word DosSetNmPipeSem(word handle,
                     dword semaphore_handle,
                     word  semaphore_key);
```

Returns: 0 on success, nonzero on error

DosTransactNmPipe

Description: This function sends a message to the other workstation and then receives a message from the other workstation. `DosTransactNmPipe()` waits for the incoming message regardless of how the pipe's blocking mode is set. The actual number of bytes received is placed in `actual_bytes`. If the read buffer is too small, an error is returned and the remainder of the message can be obtained with another call to this function. An error is also returned if the pipe is in byte-stream-only mode, or if the pipe is not empty when this function is called.

Prototype:
```
word DosTransactNmPipe(word handle,
                       char far *write_buffer,
                       word write_buffer_size,
                       char far *read_buffer,
                       word read_buffer_size,
                       word *actual_bytes);
```

Returns: 0 on success, nonzero on error

DosWaitNmPipe

Description: A client workstation uses this function to wait until an instance of a named pipe is available. If you call `DosOpen()` and receive an error telling you that the pipe is busy (that is, the maximum number of instances of the pipe are already in use), you can use this function to wait until you can open the named pipe. When an instance of the pipe becomes available, `DosWaitNmPipe()` returns 0. The timeout parameter specifies, in milliseconds, how long to wait for the pipe to become available. Code a *timeout* value of 0 to use the pipe default (50 milliseconds); code a value of -1 to wait indefinitely.

Prototype:
```
word DosWaitNmPipe(char far *pipename, dword timeout);
```

Returns: 0 on success, nonzero on error

NETBIOS Functions

This section contains reference information on the NETBIOS functions for PC-to-PC communications.

A NETBIOS function is invoked in three steps:

1. Filling in the proper fields of a Network Control Block (NCB)

2. Setting up the ES:BX register pair as a far pointer to the NCB

3. Performing an Interrupt 5C (hex)

Many commands have both wait and no-wait options. When you specify the wait option, or if the command does not have a no-wait option, the call to NETBIOS (Interrupt 5C) does not return to your program until the command is executed. On some commands the wait option can be risky, because an unforeseen error situation (such as a hardware error or power loss at the other workstation) can mean that your program waits forever for a response that never comes. NETBIOS does the following when you specify the no-wait option:

❏ Initiates the operation, sets the final return code to 0xff, and returns to your program with an immediate return code

❏ Continues the operation in the background

❏ Detects the completion of the event

❏ Sets the final return code to the proper value

❏ Calls the POST routine (if one is specified in the NCB)

359

A POST routine must function exactly like an interrupt service routine. NETBIOS invokes the routine when a no-wait command is executed and the POST_FUNC field in the NCB is not NULL. The following conditions are true at the outset of the POST routine:

- ❏ Interrupts are off.
- ❏ ES:BX forms a far pointer to the NCB associated with the completed event.
- ❏ AL contains a copy of the final return code (same as that within the NCB).
- ❏ The other registers (DS, and so on) have no particular value.
- ❏ DOS function calls may not be safe to perform from within the POST routine.

The POST routine should save the registers, set DS (and any other registers) as necessary, process as quickly as possible the NCB that ES:BX points to, restore the registers, and finish by executing an IRET instruction. (Accomplishing these steps in C is not that difficult; see Chapter 5, "PC-to-PC NETBIOS Programming.")

The following definition of an NCB is used throughout this reference section:

```
typedef unsigned char byte;
typedef unsigned int  word;

/* Network Control Block (NCB)  */

typedef struct
    {
    byte NCB_COMMAND;             /* command ID for this NCB    */
    byte NCB_RETCODE;             /* immediate return code      */
    byte NCB_LSN;                 /* local session number       */
    byte NCB_NUM;                 /* network name number        */
    void far *NCB_BUFFER_PTR;     /* pointer to message packet  */
    word NCB_LENGTH;              /* length of message packet   */
    byte NCB_CALLNAME[16];        /* name of the other computer */
    byte NCB_NAME[16];            /* our network name           */
    byte NCB_RTO;                 /* receive time-out, 1/2 secs. */
    byte NCB_STO;                 /* send time-out, in 1/2 secs. */
    void interrupt (*NCB_POST)(); /* POST function pointer      */
    byte NCB_LANA_NUM;            /* adapter number (0 or 1)    */
    byte NCB_CMD_CPLT;            /* final return code          */
    byte NCB_RESERVE[14];         /* reserved area              */
    }
    NCB;
```

Reset Adapter   0x32 (wait)

Description: This command resets NETBIOS, erasing and clearing all session information, deleting all names (except for the permanent node name) from the name table, and resetting the maximum number of sessions and the maximum number of outstanding NCBs. New values for these maximums can be supplied as part of the Reset command.

If you want to alter the default maximums for number of sessions and number of outstanding NCBs, code the new values in the NCB_LSN and NCB_NUM fields (respectively) before performing the Reset command. If these NCB fields are zero (0x00) when you issued the Reset command, the defaults of six sessions and 12 NCBs are used. For best performance, code these values to be as small as possible.

If a workstation has two adapters, this command resets NETBIOS only as it affects the adapter specified in the NCB_LANA_NUM field.

The Reset command does not affect the traffic and error statistics (see the Adapter Status command).

Caution: Do not use this command when running under the IBM PC LAN Program. It clears the PCLP sessions and deletes the PCLP names, resulting in network errors.

NCB Input Fields:

NCB_COMMAND	0x32
NCB_LSN	Maximum sessions, or 0x00 for default
NCB_NUM	Maximum NCBs, or 0x00 for default
NCB_LANA_NUM	0 = adapter 1, 1 = adapter 2

NCB Output Fields:

NCB_CMD_CPLT	Final return code

Immediate Return Code: None

Final Return Code:		
	0x00	Success
	0x03	Invalid command
	0x23	Invalid NCB_LANA_NUM
	0x40-0x4F	Unusual network condition
	0x50-0xFE	Adapter malfunction

Cancel 0x35 (wait)

Description: This command cancels an outstanding NETBIOS command. Place the address of the NCB whose pending command is to be canceled in the NCB_BUFFER_PTR field (it requires a far pointer). The return code from the Cancel command pertains only to the Cancel operation, indicating nothing about the command being canceled. The NCB_CMD_CPLT field in the NCB being canceled identifies the return code of the canceled command.

The following commands cannot be canceled:

Add Name	Send Datagram
Add Group Name	Session Status
Delete Name	Reset Adapter
Reset Adapter	Another Cancel command
Send Broadcast Datagram	Unlink

NCB Input Fields:

NCB_COMMAND	0x35
NCB_BUFFER_PTR	Far pointer to NCB to be canceled
NCB_LANA_NUM	0 = adapter 1, 1 = adapter 2

NCB Output Fields:

NCB_CMD_CPLT	Final return code

Immediate Return Code: None

Final Return Code:	0x00	Success
	0x03	Invalid command
	0x23	Invalid LAN adapter number
	0x24	Command executed during cancellation
	0x26	Command cannot be canceled
	0x40-0x4F	Unusual network condition
	0x50-0xFE	Adapter malfunction

Get Adapter Status 0x33 (wait), 0xB3 (no-wait)

Description: This command obtains status information about any workstation's network adapter, local or remote, currently active on the network. You specify the workstation by placing any one of the names by which it is known in the NCB_CALLNAME field. To obtain status information about the local workstation, you can put an asterisk (*) in the first byte of NCB_CALLNAME. Tell NETBIOS where to put the returned data by placing a far pointer to the following structure in the NCB_BUFFER_PTR field, and then placing the structure length in the NCB_LENGTH field. The returned area must be at least 60 bytes.

After the call, NCB_LENGTH contains the actual number of bytes returned. The returned data is in three distinct parts:

❑ 6 bytes of network adapter ID

❑ 52 bytes of error or traffic information

❑ 2 bytes containing a count of the names in the name table plus 18 bytes of information about each name table entry, repeated as many times as necessary for the number of names in the name table

```
/*    The following structures describe the layout      */
/*    of Adapter Status information returned by the      */
/*    DXMTOMOD.SYS implementation of NETBIOS. Other      */
/*    implementations may return slightly different      */
/*    data.                                              */

typedef struct {
        unsigned char    card_id[6];
        unsigned char    release_level;
        unsigned char    reserved1;
        unsigned char    type_of_adapter;
        unsigned char    old_or_new_parameters;
        unsigned int     reporting_period_minutes;

        unsigned int     frame_reject_recvd_count;
        unsigned int     frame_reject_sent_count;
        unsigned int     recvd_I_frame_errors;

        unsigned int     unsuccessful_transmissions;
        unsigned long    good_transmissions;
        unsigned long    good_receptions;
        unsigned int     retransmissions;
        unsigned int     exhausted_resource_count;
        unsigned int     t1_timer_expired_count;
```

```
unsigned int    t1_timer_expired_count;
char            reserved2[4];
unsigned int    available_ncbs;
unsigned int    max_ncbs_configured;
unsigned int    max_ncbs_possible;
unsigned int    buffer_or_station_busy_count;
unsigned int    max_datagram_size;
unsigned int    pending_sessions;
unsigned int    max_sessions_configured;
unsigned int    max_sessions_possible
unsigned int    max_frame_size;
int             name_count;
struct {
    char            tbl_name[16];
    unsigned char   tbl_name_number;
    unsigned char   tbl_name_status;
    } name_table[20];
}
ADAPTER_DATA;
```

You construct a permanent node name by prefixing the 6 bytes of `card_id` (returned in the preceding structure) with 10 bytes of binary 0s. The resulting 16-byte character array is *not* a normal C string, because it is not null-terminated. You can use `memcpy()`, but not `strcpy()`, on the array.

NCB Input Fields:

NCB_COMMAND	0x33 or 0xB3
NCB_BUFFER_PTR	Far pointer to ADAPTER_DATA area
NCB_LENGTH	Size of ADAPTER_DATA area
NCB_CALLNAME	Name of other workstation, or *
NCB_LANA_NUM	0 = adapter 1, 1 = adapter 2
NCB_POST	Far pointer to a POST routine, or NULL

NCB Output Fields:

NCB_LENGTH	Actual bytes returned
NCB_RETCODE	Immediate return code
NCB_CMD_CPLT	Final return code

Immediate Return Code:

0x00	No immediate error
0x03	Invalid command
0x21	Interface busy

	0x22	Too many commands outstanding
	0x23	Invalid NCB_LANA_NUM
	0x40-0x4F	Unusual network condition
	0x50-0xFE	Adapter malfunction
Final Return Code:	0x00	Success
	0x01	Invalid buffer length
	0x03	Invalid command
	0x05	Command timed out
	0x06	Buffer too small (remaining data is lost)
	0x0B	Command canceled
	0x15	Invalid name
	0x19	Name conflict detected
	0x21	Interface busy
	0x22	Too many commands outstanding
	0x23	Invalid NCB_LANA_NUM
	0x40-0x4F	Unusual network condition
	0x50-0xFE	Adapter malfunction

Unlink   0x70 (wait)

Description: A workstation booted from the network (rather than from its own disk or diskette drives) uses this command to effectively disconnect itself from the network. This command does not apply to normal workstations; it is intended to be used by diskless workstations.

If you install a special ROM chip on the network adapter card (the Remote Program Load feature), the workstation loads PC DOS from the file server when you turn on the power. The workstation establishes a special session with the file server. When this command is issued, the special session is dropped and redirection of disk I/O to and from the file server is terminated.

NCB Input Fields:

NCB_COMMAND	0x70
NCB_LANA_NUM	Adapter to unlink

NCB Output Fields:

NCB_CMD_CPLT   Final return code

Immediate Return Code: None

Final Return Code:

0x00	Success
0x03	Invalid command
0x21	Interface busy
0x23	Invalid NCB_LANA_NUM
0x40-0x4F	Unusual network condition
0x50-0xFE	Adapter malfunction

Add Name   0x30 (wait), 0xB0 (no-wait)

Description: This command adds the 16-byte name specified in NCB_NAME to the name table as a unique name. An error is returned if any other workstation is already using the name as either a name or a group name. You build the name string by padding spaces on the right and inserting a null character (\0) in the last character position, as shown in the following example:

```
char netbios_name[16];

strcpy(netbios_name, "BARRY");
while (strlen(netbios_name) < 15)
        strcat(netbios_name, " ");
```

NETBIOS assigns a number to the name you have added and returns this number in the NCB_NUM field. Use this number in datagram commands and in Receive Any commands.

NCB Input Fields:

NCB_COMMAND	0x30 or 0xB0
NCB_NAME	Name you want to add
NCB_POST	Far pointer to POST routine, or NULL
NCB_LANA_NUM	0 = adapter 1, 1 = adapter 2

NCB Output Fields:

NCB_NUM	Assigned name number
NCB_RETCODE	Immediate return code
NCB_CMD_CPLT	Final return code

Immediate Return Code:	0x00	No immediate error
	0x03	Invalid command
	0x21	Interface busy
	0x22	Too many commands outstanding
	0x23	Invalid NCB_LANA_NUM
	0x40-0x4F	Unusual network condition
	0x50-0xFE	Adapter malfunction
Final Return Code:	0x00	Success
	0x03	Invalid command
	0x09	No resource available
	0x0D	Name already in use by this workstation
	0x0E	Name table is full
	0x15	Invalid name
	0x16	Name already in use by another workstation
	0x19	Name conflict (NETBIOS internal error)
	0x21	Interface busy
	0x22	Too many commands outstanding
	0x23	Invalid NCB_LANA_NUM
	0x40-0x4F	Unusual network condition
	0x50-0xFE	Adapter malfunction

Add Group Name 0x36 (wait), 0xB6 (no-wait)

Description: This command adds the 16-byte name specified in NCB_NAME to the name table as a group name. An error is returned if any other workstation is already using the name as a unique name. Other workstations can simultaneously use the name as a group name. You build the name string by padding spaces on the right and inserting a null character (\0) in the last character position, as shown in the following example:

```
char netbios_name[16];

strcpy(netbios_name, "TEAM_ONE");
while (strlen(netbios_name) < 15)
    strcat(netbios_name, " ");
```

NETBIOS assigns a number to the name you have added and returns this number in the NCB_NUM field. Use this number in datagram commands and in Receive Any commands.

NCB Input Fields:

NCB_COMMAND	0x36 or 0xB6
NCB_NAME	Group name you want to add
NCB_POST	Far pointer to POST routine, or NULL
NCB_LANA_NUM	0 = adapter 1, 1 = adapter 2

NCB Output Fields:

NCB_NUM	Assigned name number
NCB_RETCODE	Immediate return code
NCB_CMD_CPLT	Final return code

Immediate Return Code:

0x00	No immediate error
0x03	Invalid command
0x21	Interface busy
0x22	Too many commands outstanding
0x23	Invalid NCB_LANA_NUM
0x40-0x4F	Unusual network condition
0x50-0xFE	Adapter malfunction

Final Return Code:

0x00	Success
0x03	Invalid command
0x09	No resource available
0x0D	Name already in use by this workstation
0x0E	Name table is full
0x15	Invalid name
0x16	Name already in use by another workstation
0x21	Interface busy
0x22	Too many commands outstanding
0x23	Invalid NCB_LANA_NUM
0x40-0x4F	Unusual network condition
0x50-0xFE	Adapter malfunction

Delete Name

0x31 (wait), 0xB1 (no-wait)

Description: This command deletes the 16-byte name specified in NCB_NAME from the name table. An error is returned if the name has an active session; the name is marked as `deregistered`, but the name is actually deleted after its sessions are closed. You should use the Hang Up command to terminate any active sessions before deleting the name. If the name has a Listen, Receive Any, Receive Datagram, or Receive Broadcast Datagram command pending when the Delete Name command is issued, the name is deleted but the pending command is terminated with a `Name was deleted` error code. It is preferable to use the Cancel command to explicitly terminate the outstanding Listen or other command before issuing the Delete Name.

NCB Input Fields:

NCB_COMMAND	0x31 or 0xB1
NCB_NAME	Name to be deleted
NCB_POST	Far pointer to a POST routine, or NULL
NCB_LANA_NUM	0 = adapter 1, 1 = adapter 2

NCB Output Fields:

NCB_RETCODE	Immediate return code
NCB_CMD_CPLT	Final return code

Immediate Return Code:

0x00	No immediate error
0x03	Invalid command
0x21	Interface busy
0x22	Too many commands outstanding
0x23	Invalid NCB_LANA_NUM
0x40-0x4F	Unusual network condition
0x50-0xFE	Adapter malfunction

Final Return Code:

0x00	Success
0x03	Invalid command
0x0F	Name marked `deregistered` (active sessions)
0x15	Invalid name
0x21	Interface busy
0x22	Too many commands outstanding

0x23	Invalid NCB_LANA_NUM
0x40-0x4F	Unusual network condition
0x50-0xFE	Adapter malfunction

Call   0x10 (wait), 0x90 (no-wait)

Description: This command establishes a session with the workstation named in NCB_CALLNAME. A session can be established between names on two different workstations or between two names on a single workstation.

If multiple workstations use the name as a group name and have issued Listen commands, the Call command establishes only one session. However, you can open multiple sessions between the same pair of names by issuing multiple Call sequences (multiple Listen commands must be outstanding, of course). The name specified in NCB_NAME—which must be one of the names in the local name table—identifies the local side of the session.

If the named workstation does not have an outstanding Listen command pending, the Call command is retried several times before returning an error to your program. If the Call command is successful, a local session number (LSN) is returned to your program. Subsequent session activities (Send, Receive, and Hang Up commands) use the assigned LSN to refer to this session.

Time-out intervals for subsequent Send and Receive commands are specified in the Call NCB, not in the individual Send and Receive commands. The NCB_STO (Send Time Out) and NCB_RTO (Receive Time Out) fields are given in 500-millisecond (half second) increments. Setting either field to a value of 0 means that no time-out will occur for the corresponding command.

NCB Input Fields:

NCB_COMMAND	0x10 or 0x90
NCB_CALLNAME	Name of the listening workstation
NCB_NAME	Local name performing the Call
NCB_RTO	Receive time-out, in 1/2 seconds
NCB_STO	Send time-out, in 1/2 seconds
NCB_POST	Far pointer to a POST routine, or NULL
NCB_LANA_NUM	0 = adapter 1, 1 = adapter 2

NCB Output Fields:

NCB_LSN	The assigned local session number
NCB_RETCODE	Immediate return code
NCB_CMD_CPLT	Final return code

Immediate Return Code:	0x00	No immediate error
	0x03	Invalid command
	0x09	No resource available
	0x15	Invalid name
	0x21	Interface busy
	0x22	Too many commands outstanding
	0x23	Invalid NCB_LANA_NUM
	0x40-0x4F	Unusual network condition
	0x50-0xFE	Adapter malfunction

Final Return Code:	0x00	Success
	0x03	Invalid command
	0x09	No resource available
	0x05	Timed out
	0x0B	Command canceled
	0x11	Local session table full
	0x12	Session open rejected
	0x14	No answer, or no such name
	0x15	Invalid name
	0x18	Session ended abnormally
	0x19	Name conflict
	0x21	Interface busy
	0x22	Too many commands outstanding
	0x23	Invalid NCB_LANA_NUM
	0x40-0x4F	Unusual network condition
	0x50-0xFE	Adapter malfunction

Listen   0x11 (wait), 0x91 (no-wait)

Description: This command answers a Call and opens a session with the workstation named in NCB_CALLNAME. If the first byte of NCB_CALLNAME is an asterisk (*), it means "Listen for a call to our name (NCB_NAME) from anyone." You can establish a session between names on two different workstations or between two names on a single workstation.

If you have multiple Listens outstanding, a Listen command for a specific name takes priority over a Listen command for any name. You can open multiple sessions between the same pair of names by issuing multiple Call/Listen sequences. The name specified in NCB_NAME—which must be one of the names in the local name table—identifies the local side of the session.

If the Listen command is successful, it returns a local session number (LSN) to your program. Subsequent session activities (Send, Receive, and Hang Up commands) use the assigned LSN to refer to this session. Also, if you are Listening for a Call from anyone, the NCB_CALLNAME field returns the name of the Calling workstation.

Time-out intervals for subsequent Send and Receive commands are specified in the Listen NCB, not in the individual Send and Receive commands. The NCB_STO (Send Time Out) and NCB_RTO (Receive Time Out) fields are given in 500-millisecond (half second) increments. Setting either field to a value of 0 means that no time-out will occur for the corresponding command. The Listen command itself does not time out. Use the wait option carefully.

NCB Input Fields:

NCB_COMMAND	0x11 or 0x91
NCB_CALLNAME	Name to Listen for (* = anyone)
NCB_NAME	Local (Listening) name
NCB_RTO	Receive time-out, in half seconds
NCB_STO	Send time-out, in half seconds
NCB_POST	Far pointer to a POST routine, or NULL
NCB_LANA_NUM	0 = adapter 1, 1 = adapter 2

NCB Output Fields:

NCB_LSN	The assigned local session number
NCB_CALLNAME	Caller's name if "Listening for anyone"
NCB_RETCODE	Immediate return code
NCB_CMD_CPLT	Final return code

Immediate Return Code:

0x00	No immediate error
0x03	Invalid command
0x09	No resource available
0x15	Invalid name
0x21	Interface busy

	0x22	Too many commands outstanding
	0x23	Invalid NCB_LANA_NUM
	0x40-0x4F	Unusual network condition
	0x50-0xFE	Adapter malfunction
Final Return Code:	0x00	Success
	0x03	Invalid command
	0x09	No resource available
	0x0B	Command canceled
	0x11	Local session table full
	0x15	Invalid name
	0x17	Name was deleted
	0x18	Session ended abnormally
	0x19	Name conflict
	0x21	Interface busy
	0x22	Too many commands outstanding
	0x23	Invalid NCB_LANA_NUM
	0x40-0x4F	Unusual network condition
	0x50-0xFE	Adapter malfunction

Hang Up 0x12 (wait), 0x92 (no-wait)

Description: This command closes the session identified by the local session number (NCB_LSN). Both partners in the session should issue this call at the end of the session.

Any pending Receive commands for this LSN are terminated and their NCB_CMD_CPLT fields are set to 0x0A (session closed). However, pending Send commands are given roughly 20 seconds to finish, after which they too are terminated with error code 0x0A (unless, of course, they are completed successfully). If a pending Send command is not executed within 20 seconds, the Hang Up command itself returns with an error code 0x05 (timed out), and the session ends. Finally, if one or more Receive Any commands are outstanding when the Hang Up command is issued, one of those Receive Any commands returns with error code 0x0A (session closed). Any other commands outstanding when the Hang Up command is issued return with error code 0x18 (session ended abnormally).

As the preceding discussion suggests, you should coordinate the commands issued by both partners so that none is outstanding when the Hang Up is issued.

NCB Input Fields:

NCB_COMMAND	0x12 or 0x92
NCB_LSN	Local session number
NCB_POST	Far pointer to a POST routine, or NULL
NCB_LANA_NUM	0 = adapter 1, 1 = adapter 2

NCB Output Fields:

NCB_RETCODE	Immediate return code
NCB_CMD_CPLT	Final return code

Immediate Return Code:

0x00	No immediate error
0x03	Invalid command
0x21	Interface busy
0x22	Too many commands outstanding
0x23	Invalid NCB_LANA_NUM
0x40-0x4F	Unusual network condition
0x50-0xFE	Adapter malfunction

Final Return Code:

0x00	Success
0x03	Invalid command
0x05	Timed out
0x08	Invalid local session number
0x0A	Session closed
0x0B	Command canceled
0x18	Session ended abnormally
0x21	Interface busy
0x22	Too many commands outstanding
0x23	Invalid NCB_LANA_NUM
0x40-0x4F	Unusual network condition
0x50-0xFE	Adapter malfunction

Send 0x14 (wait), 0x94 (no-wait)

Description: This command sends 1 to 65,535 bytes of data to the NETBIOS session partner associated with the local session number that NCB_LSN specifies. You place the address of the data in NCB_BUFFER_PTR as a far pointer, and you set the length in NCB_LENGTH.

A Hang Up command issued while Send commands are pending causes an error situation, which is discussed in the Hang Up command description. The period during which the Send must execute successfully (Send Time Out) is given in the corresponding Call or Listen command, not by the Send command itself. If this time period expires before the other workstation receives the data, the session terminates abnormally and a "timed out" error (0x05) is returned in the Send NCB. (This differs with a Receive command that times out, for which the session is not terminated.) Furthermore, if the Send command is not completed successfully for *any* reason, the session ends.

If multiple Send commands are outstanding, the other workstation receives them in the proper order (first-in, first-out).

Avoid issuing a Send command unless the other workstation has issued a corresponding Receive command.

NCB Input Fields:

NCB_COMMAND	0x14 or 0x94
NCB_LSN	Local session number
NCB_BUFFER_PTR	Far pointer to data to be sent
NCB_LENGTH	Number of bytes to send
NCB_POST	Far pointer to a POST routine, or NULL
NCB_LANA_NUM	0 = adapter 1, 1 = adapter 2

NCB Output Fields:

NCB_RETCODE	Immediate return code
NCB_CMD_CPLT	Final return code

Immediate Return Code:

0x00	No immediate error
0x03	Invalid command
0x21	Interface busy
0x22	Too many commands outstanding
0x23	Invalid NCB_LANA_NUM
0x40-0x4F	Unusual network condition
0x50-0xFE	Adapter malfunction

Final Return Code:

0x00	Success
0x03	Invalid command
0x05	Timed out

0x08	Invalid local session number
0x0A	Session closed
0x0B	Command canceled
0x18	Session ended abnormally
0x21	Interface busy
0x22	Too many commands outstanding
0x23	Invalid NCB_LANA_NUM
0x40-0x4F	Unusual network condition
0x50-0xFE	Adapter malfunction

Send No ACK   0x71 (wait), 0xF1 (no-wait)

Description: This command works exactly like the Send command, except that Send No ACK does not require an acknowledgment from the receiving workstation and therefore operates a little quicker.

NCB Input Fields:

NCB_COMMAND	0x71 or 0xf1
NCB_LSN	Local session number
NCB_BUFFER_PTR	Far pointer to data to be sent
NCB_LENGTH	Number of bytes to send
NCB_POST	Far pointer to a POST routine, or NULL
NCB_LANA_NUM	0 = adapter 1, 1 = adapter 2

NCB Output Fields:

NCB_RETCODE	Immediate return code
NCB_CMD_CPLT	Final return code

Immediate Return Code:

0x00	No immediate error
0x03	Invalid command
0x21	Interface busy
0x22	Too many commands outstanding
0x23	Invalid NCB_LANA_NUM
0x40-0x4F	Unusual network condition
0x50-0xFE	Adapter malfunction

Final Return Code:	0x00	Success
	0x03	Invalid command
	0x05	Timed out
	0x08	Invalid local session number
	0x0A	Session closed
	0x0B	Command canceled
	0x18	Session ended abnormally
	0x21	Interface busy
	0x22	Too many commands outstanding
	0x23	Invalid NCB_LANA_NUM
	0x40-0x4F	Unusual network condition
	0x50-0xFE	Adapter malfunction

Chain Send   0x17 (wait), 0x97 (no-wait)

Description: This command functions exactly like the Send command, except that Chain Send sends two data buffers rather than just one. The two data buffers are concatenated and sent as a single message. The first two bytes of NCB_CALLNAME are used to specify the length of the second buffer, and the next four bytes of NCB_CALLNAME are used as a far pointer to the second buffer. The total size of both buffers can be as much as 131,070 bytes.

NCB Input Fields:

NCB_COMMAND	0x17 or 0x97
NCB_LSN	Local session number
NCB_BUFFER_PTR	Far pointer to first data buffer
NCB_LENGTH	Length of first data buffer
NCB_CALLNAME	Length of second buffer in first two bytes; address (far pointer) of buffer in following four bytes
NCB_POST	Far pointer to a POST routine, or NULL
NCB_LANA_NUM	0 = adapter 1, 1 = adapter 2

NCB Output Fields:

| NCB_RETCODE | Immediate return code |
| NCB_CMD_CPLT | Final return code |

Immediate Return Code:

0x00	No immediate error
0x03	Invalid command
0x21	Interface busy
0x22	Too many commands outstanding
0x23	Invalid NCB_LANA_NUM
0x40-0x4F	Unusual network condition
0x50-0xFE	Adapter malfunction

Final Return Code:

0x00	Success
0x03	Invalid command
0x05	Timed out
0x08	Invalid local session number
0x0A	Session closed
0x0B	Command canceled
0x18	Session ended abnormally
0x21	Interface busy
0x22	Too many commands outstanding
0x23	Invalid NCB_LANA_NUM
0x40-0x4F	Unusual network condition
0x50-0xFE	Adapter malfunction

Chain Send No ACK 0x72 (wait), 0xf2 (no-wait)

Description: This command functions exactly like the Chain Send command, except that Chain Send No ACK does not require an acknowledgment from the receiving workstation, and therefore operates a little quicker than the more reliable Chain Send command.

NCB Input Fields:

NCB_COMMAND	0x72 or 0xf2
NCB_LSN	Local session number
NCB_BUFFER_PTR	Far pointer to first data buffer
NCB_LENGTH	Length of first data buffer
NCB_CALLNAME	Length of second buffer in first two bytes; address (far pointer) of buffer in following four bytes
NCB_POST	Far pointer to a POST routine, or NULL
NCB_LANA_NUM	0 = adapter 1, 1 = adapter 2

NCB Output Fields:

NCB_RETCODE	Immediate return code
NCB_CMD_CPLT	Final return code

Immediate Return Code:

0x00	No immediate error
0x03	Invalid command
0x21	Interface busy
0x22	Too many commands outstanding
0x23	Invalid NCB_LANA_NUM
0x40-0x4F	Unusual network condition
0x50-0xFE	Adapter malfunction

Final Return Code:

0x00	Success
0x03	Invalid command
0x05	Timed out
0x08	Invalid local session number
0x0A	Session closed
0x0B	Command canceled
0x18	Session ended abnormally
0x21	Interface busy
0x22	Too many commands outstanding
0x23	Invalid NCB_LANA_NUM
0x40-0x4F	Unusual network condition
0x50-0xFE	Adapter malfunction

Receive 0x15 (wait), 0x95 (no-wait)

Description: This command receives data Sent (or Chain Sent) by the other session-partner workstation. If different types of Receive commands are outstanding, they are processed in the following order: Receive, Receive Any for a specified name, and Receive Any for any name. The time-out interval for the Receive command is specified in the Call or Listen command and not here in the Receive. A time-out error (0x05) does not cause the session to be aborted. For an explanation of what happens when a Hang Up is issued when outstanding Receive commands are pending, see the description of the Hang Up command.

Error code 0x06 is returned if you give NETBIOS a receive buffer too small for the incoming message. However, you can issue another Receive command to read the remainder of the data (before the end of the time-out interval). The number of bytes actually received is returned in NCB_LENGTH.

NCB Input Fields:

NCB_COMMAND	0x15 or 0x95
NCB_LSN	Local session number
NCB_BUFFER_PTR	Far pointer to input buffer
NCB_LENGTH	Length of input buffer
NCB_POST	Far pointer to a POST routine, or NULL
NCB_LANA_NUM	0 = adapter 1, 1 = adapter 2

NCB Output Fields:

NCB_LENGTH	Actual number of bytes received
NCB_RETCODE	Immediate return code
NCB_CMD_CPLT	Final return code

Immediate Return Code:

0x00	No immediate error
0x03	Invalid command
0x21	Interface busy
0x22	Too many commands outstanding
0x23	Invalid NCB_LANA_NUM
0x40-0x4F	Unusual network condition
0x50-0xFE	Adapter malfunction

Final Return Code:

0x00	Success
0x03	Invalid command
0x05	Timed out
0x06	Receive buffer too small
0x08	Invalid local session number
0x0A	Session closed
0x0B	Command canceled
0x18	Session ended abnormally
0x21	Interface busy
0x22	Too many commands outstanding
0x23	Invalid NCB_LANA_NUM
0x40-0x4F	Unusual network condition
0x50-0xFE	Adapter malfunction

Receive Any   0x16 (wait), 0x96 (no-wait)

Description: This command receives data from any of your session partners. You specify your name number (assigned by NETBIOS when the Add Name or Add Group Name commands were performed) rather than the local session number in this call. If you set the NCB_NUM field to 0xFF, this command receives data from any session partner for any of your names.

For an explanation of what happens if a Hang Up command is issued when outstanding Receive Any commands are pending, see the description of Hang Up. The Receive Any command does not time-out; use the wait option carefully.

Error code 0x06 is returned if you give NETBIOS a receive buffer too small for the incoming message. However, you can issue another Receive Any command to read the remainder of the data (before the end of the time-out interval). The number of bytes actually received is returned in NCB_LENGTH.

Caution: Do not use the Receive Any command when running under the IBM PC LAN Program. This command blocks PCLP from properly receiving messages.

NCB Input Fields:

NCB_COMMAND	0x16 or 0x96
NCB_NUM	Name number (0xFF = receive from any partner)
NCB_BUFFER_PTR	Far pointer to input buffer
NCB_LENGTH	Length of input buffer
NCB_POST	Far pointer to a POST routine, or NULL
NCB_LANA_NUM	0 = adapter 1, 1 = adapter 2

NCB Output Fields:

NCB_LENGTH	Actual number of bytes received
NCB_NUM	Name number of name receiving the data
NCB_RETCODE	Immediate return code
NCB_CMD_CPLT	Final return code

Immediate Return Code:

0x00	No immediate error
0x03	Invalid command
0x21	Interface busy

	0x22	Too many commands outstanding
	0x23	Invalid NCB_LANA_NUM
	0x40-0x4F	Unusual network condition
	0x50-0xFE	Adapter malfunction
Final Return Code:	0x00	Success
	0x03	Invalid command
	0x06	Receive buffer too small
	0x0A	Session closed
	0x0B	Command canceled
	0x13	Invalid name number
	0x17	Name deleted
	0x18	Session ended abnormally
	0x19	Name conflict
	0x21	Interface busy
	0x22	Too many commands outstanding
	0x23	Invalid NCB_LANA_NUM
	0x40-0x4F	Unusual network condition
	0x50-0xFE	Adapter malfunction

Session Status   0x34 (wait), 0xB4 (no-wait)

Description: This command obtains status information about the sessions, if any, associated with a given NCB_NAME. If the first byte of NCB_NAME is an asterisk (*), information about all names in the local name table is returned.

A return code of 0x06 (buffer too small) causes any data that could not fit in the input buffer to be discarded.

The following structures show the layout of the information returned by this command:

```
/* information about each session:           */
/*    local session number                   */
/*    session state:                         */
/*        1 - Listen pending                 */
/*        2 - Call pending                   */
/*        3 - Session established            */
```

```
/*       4 - Hang Up pending                      */
/*       5 - Hang Up complete                     */
/*       6 - Session ended abnormally             */
/*    local workstation name                      */
/*    remote (partner) workstation name           */
/*    number of Receive commands outstanding      */
/*    number of Send commands outstanding         */

typedef struct {
      byte lsn;
      byte state;
      char local_name[16];
      char remote_name[16];
      byte recv_count;
      byte send_count;
      }
      A_SESSION;



/* information about the specified name:          */
/*    name number, number of sessions,            */
/*    number of outstanding Receive Datagrams,    */
/*    number of outstanding Receive Any commands, */
/*    and data about each session.                */

typedef struct {
      byte name_num;
      byte session_count;
      byte datagrams_outstanding;
      byte receive_any_outstanding;
      A_SESSION session_data[40];
      }
      STATUS_INFO;
```

NCB Input Fields:

NCB_COMMAND	0x34 or 0xB4
NCB_BUFFER_PTR	Address (far pointer) of status buffer
NCB_LENGTH	Size of status buffer
NCB_NAME	* = all local names
NCB_POST	Far pointer to a POST routine, or NULL
NCB_LANA_NUM	0 = adapter 1, 1 = adapter 2

NCB Output Fields:

NCB_LENGTH	Actual number of bytes returned
NCB_RETCODE	Immediate return code
NCB_CMD_CPLT	Final return code

Immediate Return Code:

0x00	No immediate error
0x03	Invalid command
0x15	Invalid name
0x21	Interface busy
0x22	Too many commands outstanding
0x23	Invalid NCB_LANA_NUM
0x40-0x4F	Unusual network condition
0x50-0xFE	Adapter malfunction

Final Return Code:

0x00	Success
0x01	Invalid buffer length
0x03	Invalid command
0x06	Receive buffer too small
0x19	Name conflict
0x21	Interface busy
0x22	Too many commands outstanding
0x23	Invalid NCB_LANA_NUM
0x40-0x4F	Unusual network condition
0x50-0xFE	Adapter malfunction

Send Datagram   0x20 (wait), 0xA0 (no-wait)

Description: This command sends a datagram to a unique name or to a group name. The datagram can be 1 to 512 bytes long. You do not need to have a session already established before using this command; however, the command does not guarantee that the datagram will be received.

NCB Input Fields:

NCB_COMMAND	0x20 or 0xA0
NCB_NUM	Name number assigned when name added

NCB_CALLNAME	Destination workstation name
NCB_BUFFER_PTR	Far pointer to output buffer
NCB_LENGTH	Size of output buffer (1-512 bytes)
NCB_POST	Far pointer to POST routine, or NULL
NCB_LANA_NUM	0 = adapter 1, 1 = adapter 2

NCB Output Fields:

NCB_RETCODE	Immediate return code
NCB_CMD_CPLT	Final return code

Immediate Return Code:	0x00	No immediate error
	0x03	Invalid command
	0x21	Interface busy
	0x22	Too many commands outstanding
	0x23	Invalid NCB_LANA_NUM
	0x40-0x4F	Unusual network condition
	0x50-0xFE	Adapter malfunction

Final Return Code:	0x00	Success
	0x01	Invalid buffer length
	0x03	Invalid command
	0x13	Invalid name number
	0x19	Name conflict
	0x21	Interface busy
	0x22	Too many commands outstanding
	0x23	Invalid NCB_LANA_NUM
	0x40-0x4F	Unusual network condition
	0x50-0xFE	Adapter malfunction

Send Broadcast Datagram   0x22 (wait), 0xA2 (no-wait)

Description: This command sends a datagram to all workstations that have issued an outstanding Receive Broadcast Datagram (other workstations do not receive the message). If a Receive Broadcast Datagram is outstanding at the local workstation, it too receives the message. If multiple Receive Broadcast Datagram commands are outstanding at a workstation, they all receive the one message.

NCB Input Fields:

NCB_COMMAND	0x22 or 0xA2
NCB_NUM	Name number assigned when name added
NCB_BUFFER_PTR	Far pointer to output buffer
NCB_LENGTH	Size of output buffer (1-512 bytes)
NCB_POST	Far pointer to a POST routine, or NULL
NCB_LANA_NUM	0 = adapter 1, 1 = adapter 2

NCB Output Fields:

NCB_RETCODE	Immediate return code
NCB_CMD_CPLT	Final return code

Immediate Return Code:		
	0x00	No immediate error
	0x03	Invalid command
	0x21	Interface busy
	0x22	Too many commands outstanding
	0x23	Invalid NCB_LANA_NUM
	0x40-0x4F	Unusual network condition
	0x50-0xFE	Adapter malfunction

Final Return Code:		
	0x00	Success
	0x01	Invalid buffer length
	0x03	Invalid command
	0x13	Invalid name number
	0x21	Interface busy
	0x22	Too many commands outstanding
	0x23	Invalid NCB_LANA_NUM
	0x40-0x4F	Unusual network condition
	0x50-0xFE	Adapter malfunction

Receive Datagram 0x21 (wait), 0xA1 (no-wait)

Description: This command receives a datagram (but not a Broadcast Datagram) sent by any user to a unique name or to a group name in the local name table. The datagram can be as much as 512 bytes long. You do not need to have a session already established before issuing this command. If set to 0xFF, the NCB_NUM field signifies that a datagram can be received from any user for any of the names in the local name table. If the datagram is longer than specified in NCB_LENGTH, the remainder of the message data is discarded.

This command does not time-out; use the wait option carefully.

NCB Input Fields:

NCB_COMMAND	0x21 or 0xA1
NCB_NUM	Name number, or 0xFF
NCB_BUFFER_PTR	Far pointer to input buffer
NCB_LENGTH	Size of input buffer (1-512 bytes)
NCB_POST	Far pointer to a POST routine, or NULL
NCB_LANA_NUM	0 = adapter 1, 1 = adapter 2

NCB Output Fields:

NCB_CALLNAME	Name of other workstation
NCB_LENGTH	Actual number of bytes received
NCB_RETCODE	Immediate return code
NCB_CMD_CPLT	Final return code

Immediate Return Code:	0x00	No immediate error
	0x03	Invalid command
	0x21	Interface busy
	0x22	Too many commands outstanding
	0x23	Invalid NCB_LANA_NUM
	0x40-0x4F	Unusual network condition
	0x50-0xFE	Adapter malfunction

Final Return Code:	0x00	Success
	0x01	Invalid buffer length
	0x03	Invalid command
	0x06	Buffer too small
	0x0B	Command canceled
	0x13	Invalid name number
	0x17	Name deleted
	0x19	Name conflict
	0x21	Interface busy
	0x22	Too many commands outstanding
	0x23	Invalid NCB_LANA_NUM
	0x40-0x4F	Unusual network condition
	0x50-0xFE	Adapter malfunction

Receive Broadcast Datagram   0x23 (wait), 0xA3 (no-wait)

Description: This command receives a Broadcast Datagram (but not regular datagrams) sent by any user. The datagram can be as much as 512 bytes long. You do not need to have a session already established before issuing this command. If the datagram is longer than specified in NCB_LENGTH, the remainder of the message data is discarded.

This command does not time-out; use the wait option carefully.

NCB Input Fields:

NCB_COMMAND	0x21 or 0xA1
NCB_NUM	Name number, or 0xFF
NCB_BUFFER_PTR	Far pointer to input buffer
NCB_LENGTH	Size of input buffer (1-512 bytes)
NCB_POST	Far pointer to a POST routine, or NULL
NCB_LANA_NUM	0 = adapter 1, 1 = adapter 2

NCB Output Fields:

NCB_CALLNAME	Name of other workstation
NCB_LENGTH	Actual number of bytes received
NCB_RETCODE	Immediate return code
NCB_CMD_CPLT	Final return code

Immediate Return Code:	0x00	No immediate error
	0x03	Invalid command
	0x21	Interface busy
	0x22	Too many commands outstanding
	0x23	Invalid NCB_LANA_NUM
	0x40-0x4F	Unusual network condition
	0x50-0xFE	Adapter malfunction

Final Return Code:	0x00	Success
	0x01	Invalid buffer length
	0x03	Invalid command
	0x06	Buffer too small
	0x0B	Command canceled
	0x13	Invalid name number
	0x17	Name deleted
	0x19	Name conflict

0x21	Interface busy
0x22	Too many commands outstanding
0x23	Invalid NCB_LANA_NUM
0x40-0x4F	Unusual network condition
0x50-0xFE	Adapter malfunction

IPX and SPX Functions

This section contains reference information regarding the IPX and SPX protocols available under Novell NetWare. Some important techniques are briefly reviewed in this section, but you should refer to Chapter 5, "PC-to-PC NETBIOS Programming," for details about accessing the functions and their data structures, especially when direct access to CPU registers is required.

There are two ways to call IPX/SPX. The first method entails setting up the CPU registers (as specified for the given function) and performing a far call to an address that you have previously obtained. The entry point for method 1 is returned in the ES:DI register pair after calling Interrupt 2F (hex) with a multiplex number of 7A (hex) and a function code of 0. The entry point itself is a far pointer to a function. The following code shows how to obtain the function pointer (the first method's entry point):

```
void far (*ipx_spx)(void);     /* far pointer to function */

int  get_ipx_spx_pointer(void)
     {
     union REGS regs;
     struct SREGS sregs;

     regs.x.ax = 0x7A00;
     int86x(0x2F, &regs, &regs, &sregs);
```

```
if (regs.h.al != 0xFF)
    return -1;             /* IPX/SPX not installed! */

ipx_spx = MK_FP(sregs.es, regs.x.di);

return 0;                  /* entry point established */
}
```

Once you know this function pointer, calling IPX or SPX is a matter of setting up certain CPU registers (as specified in this section) and calling the function. This is easy to do in Turbo C (because it lets you directly access the CPU registers) but requires some assembler coding if you are using Microsoft C or Lattice C. The following is an example of how to call IPX/SPX in Turbo C:

```
void close_socket(unsigned socket)
    {
    _BX = 0x0001;
    _DX = socket;
    ipx_spx();      /* compiler generates a "far call" */
    }
```

The second method of calling IPX/SPX uses the older (but still supported) Interrupt 7A (hex) entry point into IPX/SPX. This entry point is easier for Microsoft C and Lattice C users to invoke:

```
void close_socket(unsigned socket)
    {
    union REGS regs;

    regs.x.bx = 0x0001;
    regs.x.dx = socket;
    int86(0x7A, &regs, &regs);
    }
```

The one drawback to using Interrupt 7A is that the IBM 3270 Emulation product also uses this interrupt. If you are using the Microsoft C or Lattice C compilers and want to avoid potential interrupt vector conflicts, see the discussion in Chapter 5 about constructing a custom assembler interface to IPX/SPX.

An Event Control Block (ECB) is associated with almost every IPX or SPX function. SPX in particular must draw from a pool of available ECBs that you submit. IPX/SPX uses some of the items internally in an ECB. However, you specify some items, which are described for each function call in this section and are marked /* you set */ in the following code. An ECB looks like this:

```
struct ECB
    {
    void far        *link_address;
    void far        (*event_svc_routine)();   /* you set */
    unsigned char   in_use;
    unsigned char   completion_code;
    unsigned char   socket_number[2];          /* you set */
    unsigned int    connection_id;
    unsigned int    reserved1;
    unsigned char   reserved2 [12];
    unsigned char   immediate_address [6];     /* you set */
    unsigned int    fragment_count;            /* you set */
    struct {
        void far    *address;                  /* you set */
        unsigned int length;                   /* you set */
        } fragment [2];
    };
```

IPX/SPX uses the link_address field internally. When you submit the ECB, IPX/SPX sets the in_use item to a nonzero value, which remains nonzero while the ECB is being processed and then is set to 0 when the event finishes (you can use the setting of this item to poll for the completion of the event.) When the event is complete, you can inspect the completion_code field to determine success or failure. You set socket_number to identify the socket you have opened and through which you are sending and receiving packets. *Note:* The high-order byte of socket_number occurs first. SPX returns the connection_id field after a successful SPXListenForConnection() call.

Before each IPXSendPacket() call, use IPXGetLocalTarget() to set the immediate_address field, which represents the node address of a bridge that the packet must cross to reach its destination. You set fragment_count to tell IPX/SPX how many packet fragments it must "gather" to form a complete packet. fragment[].address and fragment[].length describe the packet fragments themselves: the first fragment is always an IPX Header (30 bytes) or an SPX Header (42 bytes); the second fragment is usually one entire data buffer (as much as 546 bytes for IPX, or as much as 534 bytes for SPX).

If you specify an Event Service Routine (ESR) by putting a non-NULL function pointer in the Event Control Block's event_svc_routine field, IPX/SPX calls that function when the event associated with the ECB is complete. When the ESR is called, the following conditions are true:

❑ Interrupts are disabled.

❑ A far call invokes the ESR; you must declare it as follows: void far event_handler(void).

❑ A far pointer to the associated ECB is in the ES:SI register pair.

❑ The CPU registers are saved.

❑ The DS register does not necessarily point to your program's data area.

❑ The ECB's in_use field has been reset to 0.

To show what these conditions mean to a C program, an example of an ESR in Turbo C follows. Notice that direct access to the CPU registers is needed to properly set up the ESR:

```
void far event_handler(void)
    {
    struct ECB far *ecb_ptr;

    _AX = _ES;
    _DS = _AX;      /* establish addressability */
    ecb_ptr = MK_FP(_ES, _SI);
    global_return_code = ecb_ptr->completion_code;
    ecb_attention_flag = 1;  /* signal the main pgm */
    }
```

The format of an IPX Header follows:

```
struct IPXHEADER
    {
    unsigned int     checksum;
    unsigned int     length;
    unsigned char    transport_control;
    unsigned char    packet_type;                /* you set */
    unsigned char    dest_network_number[4];   /* you set */
    unsigned char    dest_network_node[6];     /* you set */
    unsigned char    dest_network_socket[2];   /* you set */
    unsigned char    source_network_number[4];
    unsigned char    source_network_node[6];
    unsigned char    source_network_socket[2];
    };
```

IPX sets the `checksum`, `length`, and `transport_control` fields, as well as the `source_network` fields (`number`, `node`, and `socket`). You set `packet_type` to 4 to distinguish an IPX packet from an SPX packet, and set the `dest_network` fields (`number`, `node`, and `socket`) to identify a packet's destination (refer to Chapter 6, "IPX and SPX Programming"). The destination can be a single workstation or (if *node* = 0xFF 0xFF 0xFF 0xFF 0xFF 0xFF) all workstations on the network. If you mix IPX and SPX calls in your program, do not use the same socket for both.

The following is an SPX Header:

```
struct SPXHEADER
    {
    unsigned int      checksum;
    unsigned int      length;
    unsigned char     transport_control;
    unsigned char     packet_type;
    unsigned char     dest_network_number[4];   /* you set */
    unsigned char     dest_network_node[6];     /* you set */
    unsigned char     dest_network_socket[2];   /* you set */
    unsigned char     source_network_number[4];
    unsigned char     source_network_node[6];
    unsigned char     source_network_socket[2];
    unsigned char     connection_control;
    unsigned char     datastream_type;          /* you set */
    unsigned int      source_connection_id;
    unsigned int      dest_connection_id;
    unsigned int      sequence_number;
    unsigned int      acknowledge_number;
    unsigned int      allocation_number;
    };
```

The first 30 bytes of the 42-byte SPX Header have the same layout as an IPX Header. You do not have to set `packet_type`; SPX does that for you automatically. The `dest_network` fields (`number`, `node`, and `socket`) identify a packet's destination, just as with IPX, except that *node* cannot contain a broadcast address. *Note:* A socket number is represented with its high-order byte first. `datastream_type` is a dual-purpose field that both you and SPX can use (see Chapter 6, "IPX and SPX Programming"). SPX sets and manages the other fields in the SPX Header. As was previously mentioned, do not use the same socket for IPX calls and SPX calls if you use both protocols in your program.

IPX Functions

IPXCancelEvent   0x06

Description: This function cancels a pending IPX or SPX event associated with a particular ECB. IPX returns a Completion code in the canceled ECB but does not invoke the ESR if one is specified in the ECB. If the cancellation is successful, the Completion code in the canceled ECB is set to 0xFC (event canceled). This Completion code is distinct from the Completion code returned in the AL register (see the output registers for this function).

The event to be canceled must not have been started yet (it must still be pending). ECBs related to the following two SPX functions must not be canceled by IPXCancelEvent (use SPXAbortConnection instead):

❑ SPXEstablishConnection

❑ SPXSendSequencedPacket

Input Register:	BX	0x06
	ES:SI	Far pointer to an ECB
Output Registers:	AL	Completion code
		0x00 Success
		0xF9 ECB cannot be canceled
		0xFF ECB is not in use

IPXCloseSocket   0x01

Description: Closes a socket. Any events associated with the socket are canceled. It is harmless to close a socket that is already closed. If you terminate your program without closing the socket or sockets, and if a pending ECB tries to call an Event Service Routine after your program is no longer in memory, you likely will crash the workstation.

Input Registers:	BX	0x01
	DX	Socket number
Output Registers:	none	

IPXDisconnectFromTarget   0x0B

Description: Network communications software drivers use this function to notify a listening node that communications to a specified socket are being terminated. The driver on the destination node reacts by de-allocating any virtual connection it has with the originating node. Do not call this function from within an ESR.

Request Buffer:

```
struct
    {
    byte dest_network_number[4];
    byte dest_node_address[6];
    byte dest_socket[2];
    } request_buffer;
```

Input Registers:	BX	0x0B
	ES:SI	Far pointer to request_buffer

Output Registers:	None

IPXGetInternetworkAddress   0x09

Description: This function returns the network number and node address of the workstation that calls it.

Reply Buffer:

```
struct
    {
    byte network_number[4];
    byte node_address[6];
    } reply_buffer;
```

Input Registers:	BX	0x09
	ES:SI	Far pointer to reply_buffer

Output Registers:	ES:SI	Far pointer to reply_buffer

IPXGetIntervalMarker   0x08

Description: This function returns a time marker measured in timer ticks. Each second, 18.2 timer ticks occur. A subsequent call to this function returns a time marker with a greater value; you can subtract the first marker value from the later one to get an idea of how much time has passed. The size of the returned field (16 bits) means that this command cannot be used to measure time periods longer than one hour.

Input Registers: BX   0x08

Output Registers: AX   Interval marker

Special Note: A better way to mark time in your program is to create a far pointer to the double-word timer tick that the computer automatically maintains:

```
unsigned long far *tick_ptr;
unsigned long then, now, interval;


tick_ptr = MK_FP(0x0040, 0x006C);   /* valid for IBM and */
                                    /* compatibles       */
then = *tick_ptr;

/* do something here that takes up some time */

now = *tick_ptr;
interval = now - then;
```

IPXGetLocalTarget   0x02

Description: For a given destination workstation, this function provides routing information you need when you construct an IPXSendPacket() ECB. Copy the node_address returned by this function into the immediate_address field of the ECB before calling IPXSendPacket(). Use the memcpy() library function (or an equivalent function) to copy the six bytes.

The returned node_address value is either the identification of the nearest bridge if the packet must cross a bridge on its way to the destination, or the node address of the destination workstation itself if there is no intervening bridge. In either case, copy the returned value to the `immediate_address` field.

If performance is a concern, you can use the necessary routing information contained in the ECB of a received packet to expedite the process. After an `IPXListenForPacket()` call finishes, save the `immediate_address` field from its ECB. Use this value to construct the ECB for your next `IPXSendPacket()` call to that same destination.

This function also returns an estimate of how much time a packet takes to reach the destination workstation. This value is represented in timer ticks (18.2 ticks per second).

You can call this function from within an ESR.

Request Buffer:

```
struct
    {
    byte dest_network_number[4];
    byte dest_node_address[6];
    byte dest_socket[2];
    } request_buffer;
```

Reply Buffer:

```
struct
    {
    byte node_address[6];
    } reply_buffer;
```

Input Registers:	BX	0x02
	ES:SI	Far pointer to `request_buffer`
	ES:DI	Far pointer to `reply_buffer`
Output Registers:	AL	Completion code
		0x00 Success
		0xFA No path to destination
	CX	Estimated transport time
	ES:DI	Far pointer to `reply_buffer`

IPXListenForPacket 0x04

Description: You issue one or more calls to this function to give IPX the address of a buffer in which IPX should place the next incoming message packet for a particular open socket. Each call gives IPX an ECB that it places in a pool of listening ECBs. IPX returns immediately to your program after each call, but waits in the background for incoming packets.

On receiving a packet, IPX selects one of the listening ECBs with a socket number that matches that of the incoming packet. Any one of the listening ECBs could be chosen. Still processing in background mode, IPX does the following:

❑ Sets the Completion code in the ECB

❑ Places the node address of the sender, or the local bridge that routed this packet, in the immediate_address field of the ECB

❑ Sets the in_use flag to 0

❑ Invokes the ESR associated with the ECB, if one is specified

You must previously have opened the socket with a call to IPXOpenSocket(). You should set the following fields in each ECB before calling IPXListenForPacket:

socket_number	The socket number you opened
event_svc_routine	A function pointer, or NULL
fragment_count	Typically a value of 2, to express both the incoming IPX Header and the incoming data message
fragment[0].address	A far pointer to an IPX Header buffer
fragment[0].length	The length of the IPX Header buffer (30 bytes)
fragment[1].address	A far pointer to a data area receiving the incoming message (can be as much as 546 bytes long)
fragment[1].length	The length of the data area

Input Registers:	BX	0x04	
	ES:SI	Far pointer to an ECB	
Output Registers:	AL	Immediate Completion code	
		0x00	Success (ECB added to pool)
		0xFF	Listening socket does not exist
ECB Completion Codes:		0x00	Packet successfully received
		0xFC	This event has been canceled
		0xFD	Buffer too small
		0xFF	Socket not open

IPXOpenSocket   0x00

Description: This function opens a socket for use by either IPX or SPX. If you specify a 0 value, IPX assigns a socket number in the range of 0x4000 to 0x8000. You use the open socket when you send or receive message packets. Also, to send message packets, you must know the socket number at the destination workstation.

If you specify the socket number, do not use values in the range 0x0000 to 0x0BB9 or higher than 0x8000; Novell has reserved or already assigned these values. You can contact Novell to obtain registered socket number assignments for your applications.

Note: The high-order byte of a socket number occurs first. This differs from the CPU's native, internal representation of numbers, so you must swap the bytes.

A socket can be short-lived or long-lived. If the socket is short-lived, it is closed when a program terminates or when an explicit call to IPXCloseSocket() is made. If long-lived, a socket is closed only by an explicit call to IPXCloseSocket(), which is particularly useful in Terminate and Stay Resident programs.

You can configure the maximum number of open sockets (as many as 150) at each workstation when you load the IPX software. The default is 20.

Input Registers:	BX	0x00
	AL	Socket longevity flag
		0x00 Short-lived
		0xFF Long-lived
	DX	Requested socket number (high byte first)
Output Registers:	AL	Completion code
		0x00 Success
		0xFE Socket table is full
		0xFF Socket already open
	DX	Assigned socket number

IPXRelinquishControl   0x0A

Description: You call this function inside your polling loops (while wait-ing for an IPX or SPX event to finish) to give IPX the CPU time it needs to process the event.

Input Registers:	BX	0x0A
Output Registers:	None	

IPXScheduleIPXEvent   0x05

Description: This function tells IPX to schedule the processing of the specified ECB for a later time. The delay period is specified in timer ticks (18.2 timer ticks per second). Setting the delay period to the maximum of 0xFFFF (65,535) causes a delay of about one hour. IPX returns to your application immediately after this call and then waits in the background until the delay period expires. When time is up, IPX initiates the event, sets the ECB's in_use field to 0, and invokes the ESR associated with the ECB (if non-NULL).

You use this function for events that involve sending or receiving packets. It is not used to defer SPXEstablishConnection() from establishing a connection, for example. The function is particularly useful inside an ESR when you want to process the completed ECB at a later time.

The associated ECB must contain a function pointer to an ESR (or a NULL pointer) and an open socket number.

Input Registers:	BX	0x05
	AX	Delay ticks
	ES:SI	Far pointer to an ECB
Output Registers:	None	

IPXSendPacket   0x03

Description: This function instructs IPX to gather the data fragments described in the ECB into a message packet and send the packet to the destination expressed in the ECB. IPX returns immediately to your program and performs the actual sending operation in the background. The delivery of the message packet is not guaranteed (because IPX is a datagram-based protocol). When the send attempt is completed, IPX does the following:

❑ Sets the Completion code in the ECB

❑ Sets the in_use flag to 0

❑ Invokes the ESR associated with the ECB, if one is specified (non-NULL function pointer)

If you know the user ID that is logged on at the destination workstation, but not the destination network or node address information, you can call GetObjectConnectionNumbers() and GetInternetAddress(), both of which are described under Connection Services in the section on Novell's Extended DOS Services.

You must previously have opened the source socket (through which the message packet will be sent) with a call to IPXOpenSocket(). Similarly, the application running on the destination workstation must have opened a socket (which you specify as dest_network_socket in the IPX Header) and must have issued one or more IPXListenForPacket() calls.

Before calling this function, you should set the following fields in the ECB:

socket_number	The (source) socket you opened
event_svc_routine	A function pointer, or NULL
immediate_address	See IPXGetLocalTarget

`fragment_count`	Typically a value of 2, to express both the outgoing IPX Header and the outgoing data message
`fragment[0].address`	A far pointer to an IPX Header buffer
`fragment[0].length`	The length of the IPX Header buffer (30 bytes)
`fragment[1].address`	A far pointer to a data area to be sent to the destination (can be as much as 546 bytes long)
`fragment[1].length`	The length of the data area

In addition, you must set the following fields in the IPX Header (described by the ECB's first fragment address):

`packet_type`	A value of 4
`dest_network_number` and `dest network node`	The workstation to which the message packet will be sent
`dest_network_socket`	A socket that the application running on the destination workstation opened

Input Registers:	BX	0x03
	ES:SI	Far pointer to an ECB
Output Registers:	None	
ECB (Final) Completion Codes:	0x00	Message sent (delivery not guaranteed)
	0xFC	This event has been canceled
	0xFD	Bad packet (packet is less than 30 or greater than 576 bytes; first fragment less than 30 bytes; or fragment count is 0)

0xFE	Undeliverable (destination workstation does not exist; no bridge or path to destination; destination socket not open; or destination is not listening)
0xFF	Hardware or network failure

SPX Functions

SPXAbortConnection   0x14

Description: This function aborts an SPX connection by abnormally terminating any outstanding SPX events. No notification of the abnormal termination is sent to the other workstation; it learns of the broken connection when error codes are returned to the application running on the other workstation.

The abnormal termination occurs in the background. SPX invokes the ESR of each terminated ECB (unless the ESR function pointer is NULL) after setting the ECB Completion code to 0xED (abnormal termination).

To perform an orderly and graceful termination of an SPX connection, use the SPXTerminateConnection() function rather than this function.

Input Registers:	BX	0x14
	DX	Connection ID
Output Registers:	None	

SPXInitialize   0x10

Description: This function determines whether SPX is running on this workstation; if so, the function also returns version and configuration information. SPX is not available in earlier versions of NetWare; therefore, detecting the presence of IPX does not automatically imply that SPX is loaded.

Input Registers:	BX	0x10
	AL	0x00
Output Registers:	AL	SPX installation flag
		0x00 Not installed
		0xFF Installed
	BH	SPX major version
	BL	SPX minor version
	CX	Maximum number of connections supported
	DX	Available number of connections

SPXEstablishConnection   0x11

Description: This function creates a connection between the originating workstation and the specified destination workstation. The destination workstation must be ready and waiting for the connection to be made, by having already called SPXListenForConnection(). To create the connection, follow these steps at the originating workstation:

1. Open a socket by calling IPXOpenSocket().

2. Do five SPXListenForSequencedPacket() calls to give SPX a pool of ECBs and packet buffers. SPX uses some of these ECBs and buffers internally; this usage is transparent to your program. Some ECBs and buffers are used to receive incoming message packets after the connection is created; the best way to process these ECBs and buffers is through an ESR. Fill in the following ECB fields for each call:

   ESR function pointer

   Socket Number—from step 1

   Fragment Count—a value of 2

First Fragment Pointer—address of an SPX Header

First Fragment Length—length of the SPX Header

Second Fragment Pointer—address of a packet buffer

Second Fragment Length—size of buffer (1-534 bytes)

3. Issue the SPXEstablishConnection() call. Fill in the following ECB fields for this call:

ESR function pointer

Socket Number—from step 1

Fragment Count—a value of 1

First Fragment Pointer—address of an SPX Header

First Fragment Length—length of the SPX Header

The SPX Header referenced by the First Fragment Pointer and Length should be initialized with the network number, node, and socket that identify the destination workstation.

You specify a retry count and a watchdog flag when you call SPXEstablishConnection(). A retry count tells SPX how many times to attempt sending a packet to the other workstation before giving up and returning an error to your program. Setting Retry Count to 0 lets SPX use its default retry count. The watchdog flag tells SPX whether to monitor the connection by sending periodic "Are you there?" packets to the other workstation. A value of 0 disables monitoring; a value of 1 enables it. If enabled, and if SPX detects that the connection was broken, SPX uses one of the ECBs associated with an outstanding SPXListenForSequencedPacket() call to signal the error. The chosen ECB's in_use flag is set to 0; its completion_code is set to 0xED (failed connection), and its ESR is invoked.

SPX returns to your program immediately after each of the calls to SPXListenForSequencedPacket() and after the call to SPXEstablishConnection(). SPX returning a Completion code of 0 in the AL register signifies that SPX is processing the connection request in the background. Any other immediate Completion code value indicates that SPX found something wrong and could not process the connection request.

The connection ID returned in the DX register after the call to SPXEstablishConnection() was assigned by SPX but cannot be used until the connection is actually created. SPX signals the establishment of the connection by setting the in_use flag of the SPXEstablishConnection() ECB to 0 and invoking the ESR associated with that ECB. SPX also returns the assigned connection ID in the source_connection_id field of the SPX Header pointed to by the SPXEstablishConnection() ECB's first fragment address. If SPX could not create the connection, an error code is returned in the completion_code field of the SPXEstablishConnection() ECB.

To cancel a pending SPXEstablishConnection() call, use SPXAbortConnection(), not IPXCancelEvent().

Input Registers:

BX	0x11	
AL	Retry Count	
	0	Use SPX default
	1-255	User-specified retry count
AH	Watchdog Flag	
	0	Disable
	1	Enable
ES:SI	Far pointer to an ECB	

Output Registers:

AL	Completion code	
	0x00	Success (SPX is attempting to make the connection)
	0xEF	Local connection table is full
	0xFD	Error in ECB; fragment count is not 1 or fragment length is not 42
	0xFF	Sending socket is not open
DX	Connection ID	

ECB Completion Codes:

0x00	Success (connection established)
0xED	No answer from destination
0xEF	Connection table became full
0xFC	Sending socket closed during background processing

0xFD   Error in ECB;
fragment count is not
1 or fragment length
is not 42

0xFF   Sending socket is not
open

SPXGetConnectionStatus   0x15

Description: This function returns status information about an existing SPX connection, as defined by the following `reply_buffer` structure declaration

Reply Buffer:

```
struct
{
byte connect_status;
        /* 1=waiting;      2=starting;    */
        /* 3=established;   4=terminating  */
byte watchdog;
        /* if the second bit is 1, monitoring is active */
word local_connect_id;
        /* this workstation's connection id */
word remote_connect_id;
        /* the other computer's connection id */
word sequence_num;
        /* the number of the next packet to be sent */
word local_acknowledge_num;
        /* the number of the next packet to receive */
word local_allocation_num;
        /* number of listen ECBs in SPX's pool */
word remote_acknowledge_num;
        /* other computer's next packet number */
word remote_allocation_num;
        /* other computer's number of listen ECBs */
byte local_socket[2];
        /* local socket number for this connection */
byte immediate_address[6];
        /* address of bridge or of destination node */
byte remote_network[4];
        /* other computer's network number */
```

```
byte remote_node[6];
        /* other computer's node address */
byte remote_socket[2];
        /* socket being used by the other computer */
word retransmit_count;
        /* the retry count that SPX is using */
word est_roundtrip_time;
        /* packet-send timeout value, in timer ticks */
word retransmitted_packets;
        /* number of re-sent packets */
word suppressed_packets;
        /* number of duplicate packets received */
} reply_buffer;
```

Input Registers:	BX	0x15
	DX	Connection ID
	ES:SI	Far pointer to `reply_buffer`

Output Registers:	AL	Completion code
		0x00 Success
		0xEE No such connection

SPXListenForConnection   0x12

Description: This function tells SPX to expect a request from another
workstation to establish a connection. SPX returns immediately
to your program and waits in the background for the request packet.
If the packet is received, SPX assigns a connection ID and signals
the creation of the connection by setting the in_use flag of the
`SPXListenForConnection()` ECB to 0, which sets the ECB's
`completion_code`, and invokes its ESR.

To enable SPX to successfully create the connection, follow these
steps:

1. Open a socket by calling `IPXOpenSocket()`.

2. Do five `SPXListenForSequencedPacket()` calls to give SPX
    a pool of ECBs and packet buffers. SPX uses some of these
    ECBs and buffers internally; this usage is transparent to your
    program. Some ECBs and buffers are used to receive
    incoming message packets after the connection is created;
    the best way to process these ECBs and buffers is through
    an ESR. Fill in these ECB fields for each of the five calls:

ESR function pointer

Socket Number—from step 1

Fragment Count—set to a value of 2

First Fragment Pointer—address of an SPX Header

First Fragment Length—length of the SPX Header

Second Fragment Pointer—address of a packet buffer

Second Fragment Length—size of buffer (1-534)

3. Issue the SPXListenForConnection() call. The ECB fields to fill in for this call are the following:

ESR function pointer

Socket Number—from step 1

Fragment Count—set to a value of 1

First Fragment Pointer—address of an SPX Header

First Fragment Length—length of the SPX Header

You specify a retry count and a watchdog flag when you call SPXListenForConnection(). Retry Count tells SPX how many times to attempt sending a packet to the other workstation before giving up and returning an error to your program. Setting Retry Count to 0 lets SPX use its default retry count. The watchdog flag tells SPX whether to monitor the connection by sending periodic "Are you there?" packets to the other workstation. A value of 0 disables monitoring; a value of 1 enables it. If SPX is enabled and detects that the connection has been broken, it uses one of the ECBs associated with an outstanding SPXListenForSequencedPacket() call to signal the error. The chosen ECB's in_use flag is set to 0; its completion_code is set to 0xED (failed connection), and its ESR is invoked.

When the connection is created, SPX returns a connection ID to your program in the connection_id field of the ECB associated with the SPXListenForConnection() call. The in_use flag in the ECB is set to 0, its completion_code is set, and the ESR specified in that ECB is invoked. If SPX could not create the connection, an error code is returned in the completion_code field of the SPXEstablishConnection() ECB.

If you need to cancel a pending SPXListenForConnection() call, use IPXCancelEvent().

Input Registers:	BX	0x12	
	AL	Retry Count	
		0	Use SPX default
		1-255	User-specified retry count
	AH	Watchdog Flag	
		0	Disable
		1	Enable
	ES:SI	Far pointer to an ECB	
Output Registers:	None		
ECB Completion Codes:		0x00	Success
		0xEF	Local connection table is full
		0xFC	Canceled by IPXCancelEvent
		0xFF	Socket not open

SPXListenForSequencedPacket   0x17

Description: This function gives SPX an ECB and a packet buffer it can use when it receives an incoming message packet. SPX places each ECB and buffer in a pool of listening ECBs and returns immediately to your program. On receiving a message packet, SPX selects one of the available listening ECBs for the specified socket number. The in_use flag of that ECB is set to 0, the completion_code is set, and the ESR is invoked.

Before calling this function, the ECB should be initialized as follows:

ESR function pointer

Socket Number

Fragment Count—set to 2

First Fragment Address—must point to an SPX Header

First Fragment Length—must be 42

Second Fragment Address—pointer to a data buffer

Second Fragment Length—size of the data buffer (up to 534 bytes)

When an application receives a packet with a `datastream_type` field of 0xFE, the application should recognize that the connection has been terminated and finish up its processing accordingly (see `SPXTerminateConnection`.)

Input Registers:	BX	0x17
	ES:SI	Far pointer to an ECB

Output Registers:	None	

ECB Completion Codes:	0x00	Success
	0xED	Connection failed
	0xFC	Canceled by `IPXCancelEvent`
	0xFD	Buffer too small
	0xFF	Socket not open, fragment count is 0, or the first fragment is not at least 42 bytes

SPXSendSequencedPacket   0x16

Description: This function tells SPX to send a message packet to the other workstation involved in a connection. SPX returns immediately to your program and performs the actual send operation in the background. When the operation is finished, the `in_use` flag of the associated ECB is set to 0, the `completion_code` is set, and the ESR is invoked.

Before calling this function, the ECB should be initialized as follows:

ESR function pointer

Fragment Count—set to 2

First Fragment Address—must point to an SPX Header

First Fragment Length—must be 42

Second Fragment Address—pointer to a data buffer

Second Fragment Length—size of the data buffer (up to 534 bytes)

The `connection_control` field and the `datastream_type` field of the SPX Header should both be set to 0 before calling this function.

Input Registers:	BX	0x16
	DX	Connection ID
	ES:SI	Far pointer to an ECB
Output Registers:	None	

ECB Completion Codes:		
	0x00	Success
	0xEC	The other workstation ended the connection (packet might not have been received)
	0xED	Connection aborted or failed
	0xEE	No such connection
	0xFC	Socket not open
	0xFD	Fragment count is 0, packet is too large, or the first fragment is not at least 42 bytes (connection is aborted)

SPXTerminateConnection   0x13

Description: This function terminates a connection. SPX returns immediately to your program; the termination operation occurs in the background.

Before calling this function, the ECB should be initialized as follows:

ESR function pointer

Fragment Count—must be 1

First Fragment Address—must point to an SPX Header

First Fragment Length—must be 42

SPX sets the datastream_type field in the SPX Header to 0xFE and sends the SPX Header as a packet to the other workstation. When the send operation is over, the in_use flag of the associated ECB is set to 0, the completion_code is set, and the ESR is invoked.

On receiving a packet with a datastream_type field of 0xFE, the application running at the other workstation should recognize that the connection has been terminated and finish up its processing accordingly.

Input Registers:	BX	0x13
	DX	Connection ID
	ES:SI	Far pointer to an ECB

| **Output Registers:** | None |

ECB Completion Codes:		0x00	Success
		0xEC	The other workstation ended the connection (packet might not have been received)
		0xED	Connection aborted or failed
		0xEE	No such connection
		0xFC	Socket not open
		0xFD	Fragment count is 0, packet is too large, or the first fragment is not at least 42 bytes (connection is aborted)

Part IV

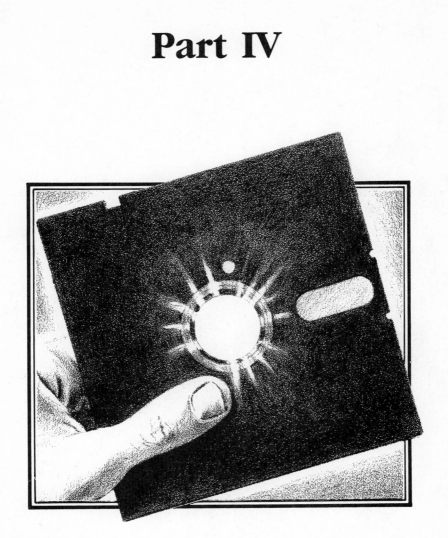

Appendixes

A

Source Listing for File/ Record Collision Tester

See Chapter 8, "Network Applications," for a discussion about what the following program does, how it works, and how to use it.

```c
/*  NETWORK.C  */

/*  a Local Area Network emulator  */
/*  written in Turbo C 2.0          */

#pragma  inline

#include <stdio.h>
#include <dos.h>
#include <fcntl.h>
#include <conio.h>
#include <io.h>
#include <bios.h>
#include <stdlib.h>
#include <string.h>
#include <stddef.h>
#include <stdarg.h>
#include <dir.h>
#include <mem.h>
#include <process.h>
```

```
void    main(int argc, char *argv[]);
void    init_program(void);
void    do_popup(void);
void    actual_popup(void);

void    open_file(void);
void    close_file(void);
void    lock_record(void);
void    unlock_record(void);
void    show_file(void);
void    show_status(void);

void    getkey(void);
int     kbdstring(char buff[], int max_chars);
int     get_vid_mode(void);
void    save_cursor(struct csavetype *csave);
void    restore_cursor(struct csavetype *csave);

void interrupt    int08 (void);
void interrupt    int09 (void);
void interrupt    int10 (unsigned bp,
                         unsigned di,
                         unsigned si,
                         unsigned ds,
                         unsigned es,
                         unsigned dx,
                         unsigned cx,
                         unsigned bx,
                         unsigned ax,
                         unsigned ip,
                         unsigned cs,
                         unsigned flags);
void interrupt   int13 (unsigned bp,
                         unsigned di,
                         unsigned si,
                         unsigned ds,
                         unsigned es,
                         unsigned dx,
                         unsigned cx,
                         unsigned bx,
                         unsigned ax,
                         unsigned ip,
                         unsigned cs,
                         unsigned flags);
```

```
              void interrupt   int16  (unsigned bp,
                                       unsigned di,
                                       unsigned si,
                                       unsigned ds,
                                       unsigned es,
                                       unsigned dx,
                                       unsigned cx,
                                       unsigned bx,
                                       unsigned ax,
                                       unsigned ip,
                                       unsigned cs,
                                       unsigned flags);
       void interrupt   int1b  (void);
       void interrupt   int1c  (void);
       void      interrupt int21(unsigned bp,
                                       unsigned di,
                                       unsigned si,
                                       unsigned ds,
                                       unsigned es,
                                       unsigned dx,
                                       unsigned cx,
                                       unsigned bx,
                                       unsigned ax,
                                       unsigned ip,
                                       unsigned cs,
                                       unsigned flags);
       void interrupt   int23  (void);
       void interrupt   int24  (unsigned bp,
                                       unsigned di,
                                       unsigned si,
                                       unsigned ds,
                                       unsigned es,
                                       unsigned dx,
                                       unsigned cx,
                                       unsigned bx,
                                       unsigned ax,
                                       unsigned ip,
                                       unsigned cs,
                                       unsigned flags);
       void interrupt   int28  (void);

       #define    TRUE          1
       #define    FALSE         0
       #define    LT            <0
```

```
#define    EQ            ==0
#define    GT            >0
#define    NE            !=0
#define    MY_STK_SIZE   1500
#define    LINE_LENGTH   81
#define    MAX_LINES     100
#define    FOUR_SECS     73

#define    BELL          7
#define    BS            8
#define    LINEFEED      10
#define    FORMFEED      12
#define    CR            13
#define    BACKTAB       15
#define    CTRLQ         17
#define    CTRLS         19
#define    CTRLX         24
#define    CTRLZ         26
#define    ESC           27

#define    ALTX          45
#define    ALTC          46
#define    ALTD          32
#define    ALTE          18
#define    ALTF          33
#define    ALTT          20
#define    ALTM          50
#define    ALTH          35
#define    HOMEKEY       71
#define    ENDKEY        79
#define    UPKEY         72
#define    DOWNKEY       80
#define    PGUPKEY       73
#define    PGDNKEY       81
#define    LEFTKEY       75
#define    INSKEY        82
#define    RIGHTKEY      77
#define    DELKEY        83
#define    CTRLLEFTKEY   115
#define    CTRLRIGHTKEY  116

#define    ALT           56
#define    RIGHT_SHIFT   54
```

```
#define     F1           59
#define     F2           60
#define     F3           61
#define     F4           62
#define     F5           63
#define     F6           64
#define     F7           65
#define     F8           66
#define     F9           67
#define     F10          68

struct      csavetype
            {
            unsigned int curloc;
            unsigned int curmode;
            };

struct      FILE_DATA
            {
            char name[81];
            int  handle;
            int  rec_length;
            int  lock_count;
            unsigned char inherit_flag;
            unsigned char sharing_flag;
            unsigned char access_flag;
            };

struct  FILE_DATA file_data[5];

char            filename[81];
unsigned char   file_inherit;
unsigned char   file_sharing;
unsigned char   file_access;
int             file_rec_len;
int             open_count;

unsigned int    paragraphs;
unsigned int    temp1, temp2;
unsigned int    current_ss;
unsigned int    current_sp;
unsigned int    save_ss;
unsigned int    save_sp;
```

```
unsigned int    far *our_mcb_size;
unsigned int    far *next_mcb_owner;
unsigned char   far *ourdta_ptr;
unsigned char   far *olddta_ptr;
unsigned char   far *our_mcb;
unsigned char   far *next_mcb;
unsigned char   far *prtsc_flag_ptr;
unsigned char   far *indos_ptr;
unsigned char   far *indos2_ptr;
unsigned char   far *kbd_flag_ptr;

unsigned int    ourpsp;
unsigned int    oldpsp;
unsigned int    break_state;

union    REGS   regs;
struct   SREGS  sregs;

void    interrupt (*oldint08)(void);
void    interrupt (*oldint09)(void);
void    interrupt (*oldint10)(void);
void    interrupt (*oldint13)(void);
void    interrupt (*oldint16)(void);
void    interrupt (*oldint1b)(void);
void    interrupt (*oldint1c)(void);
void    interrupt (*oldint21)(void);
void    interrupt (*oldint23)(void);
void    interrupt (*oldint24)(void);
void    interrupt (*oldint28)(void);
void    interrupt (*vectsave)(void);
void    interrupt (*vecthold)(void);

unsigned int    in_int08     = FALSE;
unsigned int    in_int09     = FALSE;
unsigned int    in_int10     = FALSE;
unsigned int    in_int13     = FALSE;
unsigned int    in_int16     = FALSE;
unsigned int    in_int21     = FALSE;
unsigned int    in_int28     = FALSE;
unsigned int    in_popup     = FALSE;
unsigned int    hot_flag     = FALSE;
unsigned int    de_install   = FALSE;
unsigned int    break_flag   = FALSE;
```

```
unsigned int      crit_err_flag   = FALSE;
unsigned int      we_are_last     = FALSE;
unsigned int      first_time      = TRUE;

unsigned int      tick_counter    = 0;
char              machine_name [16] = "01TEST          ";
unsigned char     network_drive;
char              string1 [LINE_LENGTH];

unsigned char     key_char;
unsigned char     extended_char;
unsigned int      i, j;
unsigned int      temp_ax;
unsigned int      temp_bx;
unsigned char     temp_ah;
unsigned char     temp_bl;

unsigned int      low_inten;
unsigned int      hi_inten;

unsigned char     *box_lines1[] =
                    {
                  "- [ LAN EMULATOR ]----------------------",
                  "                                        ",
                  "   E)xit to application                 ",
                  "   R)emove Emulator from RAM            ",
                  "   O)pen a file                         ",
                  "   C)lose a file                        ",
                  "   L)ock a record                       ",
                  "   U)nlock a record                     ",
                  "   S)how current files/locks            ",
                  "                                        ",
                  "                                        ",
                  "- (Select option by first letter)-------"
                    };
```

```c
unsigned char     *box_lines2[] =
                  {
            "_____",
            "                                       ",
            "                                       ",
            "                                       ",
            "                                       ",
            "                                       ",
            "                                       ",
            "                                       ",
            "                                       ",
            "                                       ",
            "                                       ",
            "                                       ",
            "       .                               ",
            "_____",
                  };

unsigned char     app_window_save [42*12*2];
struct csavetype app_cursor;
unsigned int      *our_stack;


/************************************/

void     interrupt int08(void)
    {
    in_int08 = TRUE;
    oldint08();
    enable();
    tick_counter++;

int08_p1:
    if (!hot_flag && !de_install)
        goto exit08;

int08_p2:
    if (in_int09 || in_int10 || in_int13
        || in_int16 || in_int21 || in_int28 || in_popup)
        goto exit08;

    if (*indos_ptr != 0)
        goto exit08;

    if (*indos2_ptr != 0)
        goto exit08;
```

```
        if (*prtsc_flag_ptr == 1)
            goto exit08;

    outportb(0x20, 0x0b);
    if (inportb(0x20)) goto exit08;

    in_popup = TRUE;
    do_popup();
    in_popup = FALSE;

exit08:
    in_int08 = FALSE;
    }


/**********************************/

void interrupt   int09 (void)
    {
    in_int09 = TRUE;
    oldint09();
    enable();

    if ( (*kbd_flag_ptr & 0x09) == 0x09 )
        {
        de_install = FALSE;
        hot_flag   = TRUE;
        }

    in_int09 = FALSE;
    }


/***********************************/

void     interrupt int10(unsigned bp,
                         unsigned di,
                         unsigned si,
                         unsigned ds,
                         unsigned es,
                         unsigned dx,
                         unsigned cx,
                         unsigned bx,
                         unsigned ax,
                         unsigned ip,
```

```
                        unsigned cs,
                        unsigned flags)
    {
    in_int10 = TRUE;
    enable();

    asm     push bp
     asm      pushf
    asm     CLI
     asm      call dword ptr _oldint10
    asm     pop  bp

    asm     pushf
    asm     pop flags
    ax    = _AX;
    bx    = _BX;
    cx    = _CX;
    dx    = _DX;
    in_int10 = FALSE;
    }


/**********************************/

void    interrupt int13(unsigned bp,
                        unsigned di,
                        unsigned si,
                        unsigned ds,
                        unsigned es,
                        unsigned dx,
                        unsigned cx,
                        unsigned bx,
                        unsigned ax,
                        unsigned ip,
                        unsigned cs,
                        unsigned flags)
    {
    in_int13 = TRUE;

    oldint13();
    enable();
    asm     pushf
    asm     pop flags
    ax    = _AX;
```

```c
     in_int13 = FALSE;
     }


/**********************************/

void     interrupt int16(unsigned bp,
                         unsigned di,
                         unsigned si,
                         unsigned ds,
                         unsigned es,
                         unsigned dx,
                         unsigned cx,
                         unsigned bx,
                         unsigned ax,
                         unsigned ip,
                         unsigned cs,
                         unsigned flags)
     {
     temp_ax  = _AX;
     temp_bx  = _BX;
     temp_ah  = _AH;
     in_int16 = TRUE;
     enable();

     if (temp_ax == 'BN')
         {
         temp_ax = 'bn';
         goto int16_exit;
         }

     if (in_popup)
         goto do_old16;

     if (temp_ah != 0)
         goto do_old16;

wait_for_key:
     _AH = 1;
     oldint16();
     asm     jz     popup_16

     goto do_old16;
```

```
popup_16:
    if (!hot_flag && !de_install)
        goto wait_for_key;

    if (in_int08 || in_int09 || in_int10 || in_int13
        || in_int21 || in_int28 || in_popup)
        goto wait_for_key;

    if (*indos_ptr != 0)
        goto wait_for_key;

    if (*indos2_ptr != 0)
        goto wait_for_key;

    if (*prtsc_flag_ptr == 1)
        goto wait_for_key;

    outportb(0x20, 0x0b);
    if (inportb(0x20))
        goto wait_for_key;

    in_popup = TRUE;
    do_popup();
    in_popup = FALSE;

    goto wait_for_key;

do_old16:
    _AX = temp_ax;
    oldint16();
    asm     pushf
    asm     pop flags
    temp_ax = _AX;
    temp_bx = _BX;

int16_exit:
    ax = temp_ax;
    bx = temp_bx;
    in_int16 = FALSE;
    }
```

```
/**********************************/

void interrupt  int1b (void)
    {
    enable();
    break_flag = TRUE;
    }

/**********************************/

void interrupt  int1c (void)
    {
    enable();
    }

/**********************************/

void    interrupt int21(unsigned bp,
                        unsigned di,
                        unsigned si,
                        unsigned ds,
                        unsigned es,
                        unsigned dx,
                        unsigned cx,
                        unsigned bx,
                        unsigned ax,
                        unsigned ip,
                        unsigned cs,
                        unsigned flags)
    {
    if (ax == 0x4409 || ax == 0x5e00)
        goto carry_on;

    asm     mov     sp, bp
    asm     pop     bp
    asm     pop     di
    asm     pop     si
    asm     pop     ds
    asm     pop     es
    asm     pop     dx
    asm     pop     cx
    asm     pop     bx
    asm     pop     ax
```

```c
/*  jmp dword ptr cs:[0]  */
    asm     db      02eh,0ffh,02eh,0000h,000h

carry_on:
    in_int21        = TRUE;

    if (ax == 0x4409)       /* network drives */
        {
        if (temp_bl == network_drive)
            dx = 0x1000;
        else
            dx = 0x0000;
        ax = 0;
        goto int21exit;
        }
    else                    /* machine name */
        {
        movedata(_DS, (unsigned) machine_name, ds, dx, 16);
        cx = 0x0101;
        ax = 0;
        }

int21exit:
    flags &= 0xfffe;        /* clear the carry flag */
    in_int21 = FALSE;
    }

/**********************************/
void interrupt  int23 (void)
    {
    enable();
    }

/**********************************/
void interrupt  int28 (void)
    {
    in_int28 = TRUE;
    enable();
    oldint28();

    if (!hot_flag && !de_install)
        goto exit28;
```

```
          if (in_int08 || in_int09 || in_int10 || in_int13
              || in_int16 || in_popup)
              goto exit28;

          if (*indos_ptr > 1)
              goto exit28;

          if (*indos2_ptr != 0)
              goto exit28;

          if (*prtsc_flag_ptr == 1)
              goto exit28;

          outportb(0x20, 0x0b);
          if (inportb(0x20)) goto exit28;

          in_popup = TRUE;
          do_popup();
          in_popup = FALSE;

exit28:
      in_int28 = FALSE;
      }


/**********************************/

void    interrupt int24(unsigned bp,
                        unsigned di,
                        unsigned si,
                        unsigned ds,
                        unsigned es,
                        unsigned dx,
                        unsigned cx,
                        unsigned bx,
                        unsigned ax,
                        unsigned ip,
                        unsigned cs,
                        unsigned flags)
      {
      temp1 = _AX;
      crit_err_flag = TRUE;

      if (_osmajor < 3)
          ax = (temp1 & 0xFF00);
```

```
    else
        ax = (temp1 & 0xFF00) | 0x03;
    }


/**********************************/

void    do_popup (void)
        {
        disable();
        current_ss = _SS;
        current_sp = _SP;
        _SS = save_ss;
        _SP = save_sp;
        enable();

        next_mcb       = MK_FP( (ourpsp) + *our_mcb_size, 0);
        next_mcb_owner = MK_FP(  ourpsp  + *our_mcb_size, 1);

        if (   *next_mcb_owner == 0x0000
           || *next_mcb_owner == 0xffff
           || *next_mcb_owner <  ourpsp  )
                we_are_last = TRUE;
        else
                we_are_last = FALSE;

        if (!de_install)
            goto process_popup;

        if (!we_are_last)
            goto do_popup_exit;

        regs.x.ax = 0x5000;
        regs.x.bx = ourpsp;
        intdos(&regs, &regs);
        setvect(0x08, oldint08);
        setvect(0x09, oldint09);
        setvect(0x10, oldint10);
        setvect(0x13, oldint13);
        setvect(0x16, oldint16);
        setvect(0x21, oldint21);
        setvect(0x28, oldint28);
        _AX = _CS;
        _ES = _AX;
```

```
        _AH = 0x49;
        geninterrupt(0x21);
        _ES = ourpsp;
        _BX = 0x2c;
        asm   mov es, es:[bx]
        _AH = 0x49;
        geninterrupt(0x21);
        _AX = 0x4c00;
        geninterrupt(0x21);

process_popup:
        break_state = getcbrk();
        oldint1b = getvect(0x1b);
        setvect(0x1b, int1b);
        oldint1c = getvect(0x1c);
        setvect(0x1c, int1c);
        oldint23 = getvect(0x23);
        setvect(0x23, int23);
        oldint24 = getvect(0x24);
        setvect(0x24, int24);
        olddta_ptr = getdta();
        setdta(ourdta_ptr);
        regs.x.ax = 0x5100;
        intdos(&regs, &regs);
        oldpsp = regs.x.bx;
        regs.x.ax = 0x5000;
        regs.x.bx = ourpsp;
        intdos(&regs, &regs);

        if (hot_flag)
            {
            save_cursor(&app_cursor);
            gettext(19, 7, 59, 18, app_window_save);
            actual_popup();
            puttext(19, 7, 59, 18, app_window_save);
            restore_cursor(&app_cursor);
            }

        regs.x.ax = 0x5000;
        regs.x.bx = oldpsp;
        intdos(&regs, &regs);
        setdta(olddta_ptr);
        setvect(0x24, oldint24);
```

```
            setvect(0x23, oldint23);
            setvect(0x1c, oldint1c);
            setvect(0x1b, oldint1b);
            setcbrk(break_state);

do_popup_exit:
            disable();
            _SS = current_ss;
            _SP = current_sp;
            enable();
            }


/**********************************/

void    actual_popup(void)
            {
            de_install      = FALSE;
            hot_flag        = FALSE;

show_menu1:
            window(1, 1, 80, 25);
            textattr(low_inten);
            for (i=0; i<12; i++)
                {
                gotoxy(19, i+7);
                cprintf("%s", box_lines1[i]);
                }
            window(20, 8, 58, 17);

win_key:
            gotoxy(1, 1);
            getkey();

            if (key_char == ESC)
                {
                goto exit_popup;
                }

            if (key_char == 'e' || key_char == 'E')
                goto exit_popup;

            if (key_char == 'r' || key_char == 'R')
                {
                de_install = TRUE;
```

```c
                goto exit_popup;
                }

        if (key_char == 'o' || key_char == 'O')
                {
                open_file();
                goto show_menu1;
                }

        if (key_char == 'c' || key_char == 'C')
                {
                close_file();
                goto show_menu1;
                }

        if (key_char == 'l' || key_char == 'L')
                {
                lock_record();
                goto show_menu1;
                }

        if (key_char == 'u' || key_char == 'U')
                {
                unlock_record();
                goto show_menu1;
                }

        if (key_char == 's' || key_char == 'S')
                {
                show_status();
                goto show_menu1;
                }

        goto win_key;

exit_popup:
        window(1, 1, 80, 25);
        }


/**********************************/
void    open_file(void)
        {
        window(1, 1, 80, 25);
```

```
textattr(low_inten);
for (i=0; i<12; i++)
    {
    gotoxy(19, i+7);
    cprintf("%s", box_lines2[i]);
    }

gotoxy(21, 7);
cprintf("[ OPEN A FILE ]");
window(20, 8, 58, 18);

if (open_count == 5)
    {
    gotoxy(1, 8);
    textattr(hi_inten);
    cprintf("Whoops. 5 files already open.");
    gotoxy(1, 9);
    cprintf("   (Press a key)");
    textattr(low_inten);
    gotoxy(1, 1);
    getkey();
    goto open_exit;
    }

gotoxy(1, 2);
cprintf("   Filename: ");
gotoxy(1, 3);
cprintf("Inheritance: ");
gotoxy(1, 4);
cprintf("    Sharing: ");
gotoxy(1, 5);
cprintf("     Access: ");
gotoxy(1, 6);
cprintf(" Record Len: ");

gotoxy(1, 8);
textattr(hi_inten);
cprintf("Enter filename and press  <enter>");
gotoxy(1, 9);
cprintf("(ESC if none)");
textattr(low_inten);
gotoxy(14, 2);
strcpy(filename, "");
```

```
            kbdstring(filename, 20);
            if (filename[0] == '\0')
                goto open_exit;

get_inherit:
            gotoxy(1, 8);
            textattr(hi_inten);
            cprintf("File is inheritable? (Y or N)     ");
            gotoxy(1, 9);
            cprintf("                                  ");
            textattr(low_inten);
            gotoxy(14, 3);
            getkey();

            if (key_char == 'y' || key_char == 'Y')
                file_inherit = 0x00;
            else
            if (key_char == 'n' || key_char == 'N')
                file_inherit = 0x80;
            else
                goto get_inherit;
            cprintf("%c", key_char);

get_sharing:
            gotoxy(1, 8);
            textattr(hi_inten);
            cprintf("1=Compatibility Mode; 2=Deny R/W;");
            gotoxy(1, 9);
            cprintf("3=Deny Write; 4=Deny Read; 5=None");
            textattr(low_inten);
            gotoxy(14, 4);
            getkey();

            if (key_char == '1')
                {
                file_sharing = 0x00;
                cprintf("Compatibility Mode");
                }
            else
            if (key_char == '2')
                {
                file_sharing = 0x10;
                cprintf("Deny Read/Write");
                }
```

```
        else
        if (key_char == '3')
            {
            file_sharing = 0x20;
            cprintf("Deny Write");
            }
        else
        if (key_char == '4')
            {
            file_sharing = 0x30;
            cprintf("Deny Read");
            }
        else
        if (key_char == '5')
            {
            file_sharing = 0x40;
            cprintf("Deny None");
            }
        else
            goto get_sharing;

        gotoxy(1, 8);
        cprintf("                              ");
        gotoxy(1, 9);
        cprintf("                              ");

get_access:
        gotoxy(1, 8);
        textattr(hi_inten);
        cprintf("1=Read access;  2=Write access    ");
        gotoxy(1, 9);
        cprintf("3=Read/Write access               ");
        textattr(low_inten);
        gotoxy(14, 5);
        getkey();

        if (key_char == '1')
            {
            file_access = 0x00;
            cprintf("Read access");
            }
```

```
            else
            if (key_char == '2')
                {
                file_access = 0x01;
                cprintf("Write access");
                }
            else
            if (key_char == '3')
                {
                file_access = 0x02;
                cprintf("Read/Write access");
                }
            else
                goto get_access;

            gotoxy(1, 8);
            cprintf("                          ");
            gotoxy(1, 9);
            cprintf("                          ");

    get_rec_len:
            gotoxy(1, 8);
            textattr(hi_inten);
            cprintf("Enter record length (1-32767)");
            gotoxy(1, 9);
            cprintf("and press  <enter>");
            textattr(low_inten);
            gotoxy(14, 6);
            file_rec_len = 0;
            strcpy(string1, "        ");
            kbdstring(string1, 7);
            if (string1[0] == '\0')
                goto get_rec_len;
            file_rec_len = atoi(string1);
            if (file_rec_len < 1)
                goto get_rec_len;

            gotoxy(1, 8);
            cprintf("                          ");
            gotoxy(1, 9);
            cprintf("                          ");
```

```
        regs.h.ah = 0x3d;
        regs.h.al = file_inherit | file_sharing | file_access;
        regs.x.dx = (unsigned) filename;
        intdos(&regs, &regs);

        if (regs.x.cflag)
            {
            gotoxy(1, 8);
            textattr(hi_inten);
            cprintf("Failed.  DOS error %d", regs.x.ax);
            gotoxy(1, 9);
            cprintf("  (Press a key)");
            textattr(low_inten);
            }
        else
            {
            open_count++;
            i = 0;
            while (file_data[i].handle != 0)
                i++;
            strcpy(file_data[i].name, filename);
            file_data[i].handle       = regs.x.ax;
            file_data[i].lock_count   = 0;
            file_data[i].rec_length   = file_rec_len;
            file_data[i].inherit_flag = file_inherit;
            file_data[i].sharing_flag = file_sharing;
            file_data[i].access_flag  = file_access;
            gotoxy(1, 8);
            textattr(hi_inten);
            cprintf("File successfully opened");
            gotoxy(1, 9);
            cprintf("  (Press a key)");
            textattr(low_inten);
            }

        gotoxy(1, 1);
        getkey();

open_exit:
        window(1, 1, 80, 25);
        }
```

```
void    close_file(void)
        {
        window(1, 1, 80, 25);
        textattr(low_inten);
        for (i=0; i<12; i++)
            {
            gotoxy(19, i+7);
            cprintf("%s", box_lines2[i]);
            }

        gotoxy(21, 7);
        cprintf("[ CLOSE A FILE ]");
        window(20, 8, 58, 18);

        if (open_count == 0)
            {
            gotoxy(1, 8);
            textattr(hi_inten);
            cprintf("Whoops. No files are open.");
            gotoxy(1, 9);
            cprintf("    (Press a key)");
            textattr(low_inten);
            gotoxy(1, 1);
            getkey();
            goto close_exit;
            }

        for (i=0; i<5; i++)
            {
            gotoxy(1, i+2);
            cprintf(" %d. ", i+1);
            if (file_data[i].handle)
                cprintf("%s", file_data[i].name);
            }

get_close:
        gotoxy(1, 8);
        textattr(hi_inten);
        cprintf("Which file? (1-5) ");
        gotoxy(1, 9);
        cprintf("(ESC if none)");
        textattr(low_inten);
        gotoxy(19, 8);
        getkey();
```

```
if (key_char == ESC)
    goto close_exit;

i = (int) key_char - '1';
if (i < 0 || i > 5)
    goto get_close;

if (file_data[i].handle == 0)
    goto get_close;

if (file_data[i].lock_count != 0)
    {
    gotoxy(1, 8);
    textattr(hi_inten);
    cprintf("%d records are still locked!", file_data[i].lock_count);
    gotoxy(1, 9);
    cprintf("File not closed.  (Press a key)");
    textattr(low_inten);
    gotoxy(1, 1);
    getkey();
    goto close_exit;
    }

regs.h.ah = 0x3e;
regs.x.bx = file_data[i].handle;
intdos(&regs, &regs);

if (regs.x.cflag)
    {
    gotoxy(1, 8);
    textattr(hi_inten);
    cprintf("Failed.  DOS error %d", regs.x.ax);
    gotoxy(1, 9);
    cprintf("   (Press a key)");
    textattr(low_inten);
    }
else
    {
    open_count-;
    file_data[i].handle = 0;
    gotoxy(1, 8);
    textattr(hi_inten);
    cprintf("%s closed", file_data[i].name);
```

```
                    gotoxy(1, 9);
                    cprintf("   (Press a key)");
                    textattr(low_inten);
                    }

            gotoxy(1, 1);
            getkey();

close_exit:
            window(1, 1, 80, 25);
            }

void    lock_record(void)
            {
            window(1, 1, 80, 25);
            textattr(low_inten);
            for (i=0; i<12; i++)
                {
                gotoxy(19, i+7);
                cprintf("%s", box_lines2[i]);
                }

            gotoxy(21, 7);
            cprintf("[ LOCK A RECORD ]");
            window(20, 8, 58, 18);

            if (open_count == 0)
                {
                gotoxy(1, 8);
                textattr(hi_inten);
                cprintf("Whoops. No files are open.");
                gotoxy(1, 9);
                cprintf("   (Press a key)");
                textattr(low_inten);
                gotoxy(1, 1);
                getkey();
                goto lock_exit;
                }

            for (i=0; i<5; i++)
                {
                gotoxy(1, i+2);
                cprintf(" %d. ", i+1);
```

```
            if (file_data[i].handle)
                cprintf("%s", file_data[i].name);
        }

get_lock_file:
        gotoxy(1, 8);
        textattr(hi_inten);
        cprintf("Which file? (1-5) ");
        gotoxy(1, 9);
        cprintf("(ESC if none)");
        textattr(low_inten);
        gotoxy(19, 8);
        getkey();

        if (key_char == ESC)
            goto lock_exit;

        i = (int) key_char - '1';
        if (i < 0 || i > 5)
            goto get_lock_file;

        if (file_data[i].handle == 0)
            goto get_lock_file;

get_lock_rec:
        gotoxy(1, 8);
        textattr(hi_inten);
        cprintf("Which record number? ");
        gotoxy(1, 9);
        cprintf("(numbers start at 1) ");
        textattr(low_inten);

        j = 0;
        strcpy(string1, "      ");
        gotoxy(22, 8);
        kbdstring(string1, 5);
        j = atoi(string1);
        if (j < 1)
            goto get_lock_rec;

        regs.h.ah = 0x5c;
        regs.h.al = 0x00;
        regs.x.bx = file_data[i].handle;
```

```
            regs.x.di = file_data[i].rec_length;
            regs.x.si = 0;
            regs.x.cx = 0;
            regs.x.dx = (j - 1) * file_data[i].rec_length;
            intdos(&regs, &regs);

            if (regs.x.cflag)
                {
                gotoxy(1, 8);
                textattr(hi_inten);
                cprintf("Failed.  DOS error %d    ", regs.x.ax);
                gotoxy(1, 9);
                cprintf("   (Press a key)            ");
                textattr(low_inten);
                }
            else
                {
                file_data[i].lock_count++;
                gotoxy(1, 8);
                textattr(hi_inten);
                cprintf("record %d locked          ", j);
                gotoxy(1, 9);
                cprintf("   (Press a key)            ");
                textattr(low_inten);
                }

            gotoxy(1, 1);
            getkey();

lock_exit:
        window(1, 1, 80, 25);
        }

void    unlock_record(void)
        {
        window(1, 1, 80, 25);
        textattr(low_inten);
        for (i=0; i<12; i++)
            {
            gotoxy(19, i+7);
            cprintf("%s", box_lines2[i]);
            }
```

```
        gotoxy(21, 7);
        cprintf("[ UNLOCK A RECORD ]");
        window(20, 8, 58, 18);

        if (open_count == 0)
            {
            gotoxy(1, 8);
            textattr(hi_inten);
            cprintf("Whoops. No files are open.");
            gotoxy(1, 9);
            cprintf("   (Press a key)");
            textattr(low_inten);
            gotoxy(1, 1);
            getkey();
            goto unlock_exit;
            }

        for (i=0; i<5; i++)
            {
            gotoxy(1, i+2);
            cprintf(" %d. ", i+1);
            if (file_data[i].handle)
                cprintf("%s", file_data[i].name);
            }

get_unlock_file:
        gotoxy(1, 8);
        textattr(hi_inten);
        cprintf("Which file? (1-5) ");
        gotoxy(1, 9);
        cprintf("(ESC if none)");
        textattr(low_inten);
        gotoxy(19, 8);
        getkey();

        if (key_char == ESC)
            goto unlock_exit;

        i = (int) key_char - '1';
        if (i < 0 || i > 5)
            goto get_unlock_file;

        if (file_data[i].handle == 0)
            goto get_unlock_file;
```

```
        if (file_data[i].lock_count == 0)
            {
            gotoxy(1, 8);
            textattr(hi_inten);
            cprintf("No records are locked!");
            gotoxy(1, 9);
            cprintf("  (Press a key)");
            textattr(low_inten);
            gotoxy(1, 1);
            getkey();
            goto unlock_exit;
            }

get_unlock_rec:
        gotoxy(1, 8);
        textattr(hi_inten);
        cprintf("Which record number? ");
        gotoxy(1, 9);
        cprintf("(numbers start at 1) ");
        textattr(low_inten);

        j = 0;
        strcpy(string1, "     ");
        gotoxy(22, 8);
        kbdstring(string1, 5);
        j = atoi(string1);
        if (j < 1)
            goto get_unlock_rec;

        regs.h.ah = 0x5c;
        regs.h.al = 0x01;
        regs.x.bx = file_data[i].handle;
        regs.x.di = file_data[i].rec_length;
        regs.x.si = 0;
        regs.x.cx = 0;
        regs.x.dx = (j - 1) * file_data[i].rec_length;
        intdos(&regs, &regs);

        if (regs.x.cflag)
            {
            gotoxy(1, 8);
            textattr(hi_inten);
            cprintf("Failed.  DOS error %d     ", regs.x.ax);
```

```
        gotoxy(1, 9);
        cprintf("   (Press a key)              ");
        textattr(low_inten);
        }
    else
        {
        file_data[i].lock_count--;
        gotoxy(1, 8);
        textattr(hi_inten);
        cprintf("record %d unlocked        ", j);
        gotoxy(1, 9);
        cprintf("   (Press a key)              ");
        textattr(low_inten);
        }

    gotoxy(1, 1);
    getkey();

unlock_exit:
    window(1, 1, 80, 25);
    }

void    show_file(void)
        {
        j = i;

        window(1, 1, 80, 25);
        textattr(low_inten);
        for (i=0; i<12; i++)
            {
            gotoxy(19, i+7);
            cprintf("%s", box_lines2[i]);
            }

        gotoxy(21, 7);
        cprintf("[ FILE/LOCK STATUS ]");
        window(20, 8, 58, 18);

        i = j;
        gotoxy(1, 2);
        cprintf("      Name: %s", file_data[i].name);
        gotoxy(1, 3);
        cprintf("    Handle: %5d", file_data[i].handle);
        gotoxy(1, 4);
```

```
            cprintf("Rec Length: %5d", file_data[i].rec_length);
            gotoxy(1, 5);
            cprintf("Lock Count: %5d", file_data[i].lock_count);
            gotoxy(1, 6);
            j =   file_data[i].inherit_flag
                | file_data[i].sharing_flag
                | file_data[i].access_flag;
            cprintf(" Open Mode:    %2.2x (hex)", j);

            gotoxy(1, 8);
            textattr(hi_inten);
            cprintf("(Press a key) ");
            textattr(low_inten);
            gotoxy(1, 1);
            getkey();
            }

void    show_status(void)
        {
        window(1, 1, 80, 25);
        textattr(low_inten);
        for (i=0; i<12; i++)
            {
            gotoxy(19, i+7);
            cprintf("%s", box_lines2[i]);
            }

        gotoxy(21, 7);
        cprintf("[ FILE/LOCK STATUS ]");
        window(20, 8, 58, 18);

        if (open_count == 0)
            {
            gotoxy(1, 8);
            textattr(hi_inten);
            cprintf("Whoops. No files are open.");
            gotoxy(1, 9);
            cprintf("   (Press a key)");
            textattr(low_inten);
            gotoxy(1, 1);
            getkey();
            goto status_exit;
            }
```

```
        for (i=0; i<5; i++)
            {
            gotoxy(1, i+2);
            cprintf(" %d. ", i+1);
            if (file_data[i].handle)
                cprintf("%s", file_data[i].name);
            }

get_status_file:
        gotoxy(1, 8);
        textattr(hi_inten);
        cprintf("Which file? (1-5) ");
        gotoxy(1, 9);
        cprintf("(ESC if none)");
        textattr(low_inten);
        gotoxy(19, 8);
        getkey();

        if (key_char == ESC)
            goto status_exit;

        i = (int) key_char - '1';
        if (i < 0 || i > 5)
            goto get_status_file;

        if (file_data[i].handle == 0)
            goto get_status_file;

        show_file();

status_exit:
        window(1, 1, 80, 25);
        }
/************************************/

int     kbdstring(char buff[], int max_chars)
        {
        unsigned int    i, j, insert_mode, ctype, res;
        unsigned char   row, col, trow, tcol;
        unsigned int    cblock;

        i = j = insert_mode = 0;
        if (get_vid_mode() == 7)
            cblock = 0x000D;
```

```
                   else
                       cblock = 0x0007;

                   _AH = 3;
                   _BH = 0;
                   geninterrupt(0x10);
                   ctype = _CX;
                   col = wherex();
                   row = wherey();
                   cprintf("%-*s", max_chars-1, buff);
                   gotoxy(col, row);

         ks1:      getkey();
                   tcol = wherex();
                   trow = wherey();
                   if (key_char == ESC)
                       {
                       buff[0] = '\0';
                       res = 0;
                       goto kbdstring_exit;
                       }

                   if (key_char == 0)
                       {
                       if (extended_char == INSKEY)
                           {
                           if (insert_mode)
                               {
                               insert_mode = FALSE;
                               _CX = ctype;
                               _AH = 1;
                               geninterrupt(0x10);
                               }
                           else
                               {
                               insert_mode = TRUE;
                               _CX = cblock;
                               _AH = 1;
                               geninterrupt(0x10);
                               }
                           }
```

```
        else
        if (extended_char == HOMEKEY)
            {
            i = 0;
            gotoxy(col, row);
            }
        else
        if (extended_char == ENDKEY)
            {
            i = strlen(buff);
            gotoxy(col+strlen(buff), row);
            }
        else
        if (extended_char == DELKEY)
            {
            for (j = i; j < strlen(buff); j++)
                buff[j] = buff[j+1];
            gotoxy(col, row);
            cprintf("%-*s", max_chars-1, buff);
            gotoxy(tcol, trow);
            }
        else
        if (extended_char == RIGHTKEY)
            {
            if (i < strlen(buff))
                {
                i++;
                gotoxy(tcol+1, trow);
                }
            }
        else
        if (extended_char == LEFTKEY)
            {
            if (i > 0)
                {
                i--;
                gotoxy(tcol-1, trow);
                }
            }
        }
    if (key_char == 0)
        goto ks1;
```

```
          if (key_char == BS)
             {
             if (i > 0)
                {
                i--;
                gotoxy(tcol-1, trow);
                }
             }

          if (key_char == CR)
             {
             res = 0;
             goto kbdstring_exit;
             }
          if (key_char < 32)
             goto ks1;
          if (i == max_chars-1)
             goto ks1;

     if (insert_mode)
             {
             for (j = strlen(buff)-1; j >= i; j--)
                 if (j < max_chars-2)
                     buff[j+1] = buff[j];
             buff[i++] = key_char;
             _CX = ctype;
             _AH = 1;
             geninterrupt(0x10);
             gotoxy(col, row);
             cprintf("%-*s", max_chars-1, buff);
             gotoxy(++tcol, trow);
             _CX = cblock;
             _AH = 1;
             geninterrupt(0x10);
             }
         else
             {
             buff[i++] = key_char;
             cprintf("%c", key_char);
             }

         goto ks1;
```

```
kbdstring_exit:
        _CX = ctype;
        _AH = 1;
        geninterrupt(0x10);
        return(res);
        }


/*********************************/


void    getkey(void)
        {
        unsigned int    k;

        k             = bioskey(0);
        key_char      = k & 0x00FF;
        extended_char = (k & 0xFF00) >> 8;
        }


/*********************************/


int     get_vid_mode(void)
        {
        regs.h.ah = 15;
        int86(0x10, &regs, &regs);
        regs.h.ah = 0;
        return(regs.x.ax);
        }


/*********************************/


void    save_cursor(struct csavetype *csave)
        {
        _AH = 3;
        _BH = 0;
        geninterrupt(0x10);
        csave->curloc  = _DX;
        csave->curmode = _CX;
        }


/*********************************/
```

```c
void    restore_cursor(struct csavetype *csave)
        {
        _DX = csave->curloc;
        _AH = 2;
        _BH = 0;
        geninterrupt(0x10);

        _CX = csave->curmode;
        _AH = 1;
        geninterrupt(0x10);
        }

/***********************************/
void    init_program(void)
        {
        if (get_vid_mode() == 7)
            {
            low_inten = 0x07;
            hi_inten  = 0x0f;
            }
        else
            {
            low_inten = 0x17;
            hi_inten  = 0x1f;
            }

        file_data[0].handle = 0;
        file_data[1].handle = 0;
        file_data[2].handle = 0;
        file_data[3].handle = 0;
        file_data[4].handle = 0;
        file_data[0].lock_count = 0;
        file_data[1].lock_count = 0;
        file_data[2].lock_count = 0;
        file_data[3].lock_count = 0;
        file_data[4].lock_count = 0;
        open_count = 0;

        clrscr();

        _AX = 'BN';
        geninterrupt(0x16);
```

```
if (_AX == 'bn')
    {
    gotoxy(1, 2);
    cprintf("The Local Area Network Emulator is already loaded.");
    gotoxy(1, 3);
    cprintf("Use ALT/RIGHT-SHIFT to activate it.");
    gotoxy(1, 5);
    exit(1);
    }

if (_osmajor < 3)
    {
    gotoxy(1, 2);
    cprintf("Early versions of DOS not supported...");
    gotoxy(1, 4);
    exit(1);
    }

regs.x.ax = 0x1000;
int86(0x2f, &regs, &regs);
if (regs.h.al != 0xff)
    {
    gotoxy(1, 2);
    cprintf("You must run SHARE.EXE before using the LAN Emulator.");
    gotoxy(1, 4);
    exit(1);
    }

sregs.ds = _DS;
regs.x.ax = 0x3400;
intdosx(&regs, &regs, &sregs);
indos_ptr = MK_FP(sregs.es, regs.x.bx);
if (_osmajor == 2)
    indos2_ptr = MK_FP(sregs.es, regs.x.bx + 1);
else
    indos2_ptr = MK_FP(sregs.es, regs.x.bx - 1);

prtsc_flag_ptr = MK_FP(0x0050, 0x0000);
kbd_flag_ptr   = MK_FP(0x0040, 0x0017);

if ( (our_stack = malloc(MY_STK_SIZE)) == NULL)
    {
    gotoxy(1, 2);
```

```
                cprintf("Insufficient memory.");
                gotoxy(1, 5);
                exit(1);
                }

        get_net_drive:
                gotoxy(1, 24);
                cprintf("Drive letter that will be your network drive: ");
                strcpy(string1, "      ");
                network_drive = 0;
                gotoxy(1, 25);
                kbdstring(string1, 5);
                strupr(string1);
                network_drive = string1[0] - '@';
                if (network_drive < 1 || network_drive > 20)
                    goto get_net_drive;


                }
        /**********************************/

        void    main(int argc, char *argv[])
                {
                init_program();

                clrscr();
                gotoxy(1, 3);
cprintf("NETWORK--a LAN Emulator.  Copyright (c) 1988 Barry R. Nance");
                gotoxy(1, 4);
                cprintf("Press ALT/RIGHT-SHIFT to activate this program.");
                gotoxy(1, 6);
                cprintf("As you test, the following conditions will exist:");
                gotoxy(1, 7);
                cprintf("     machine name: %s", machine_name);
                gotoxy(1, 8);
                cprintf("    Network Drive: %c:", network_drive + '@');
                gotoxy(1, 12);

                save_ss = _SS;
                save_sp = ( (unsigned) our_stack + MY_STK_SIZE ) - 2;

                ourdta_ptr = getdta();
                regs.x.ax = 0x5100;
                intdos(&regs, &regs);
                ourpsp = regs.x.bx;
```

```
our_mcb       = MK_FP(ourpsp-1, 0);
our_mcb_size  = MK_FP(ourpsp-1, 3);

oldint08 = getvect(0x08);
oldint09 = getvect(0x09);
oldint10 = getvect(0x10);
oldint13 = getvect(0x13);
oldint16 = getvect(0x16);
oldint28 = getvect(0x28);
oldint21 = getvect(0x21);
asm     mov ax, word ptr oldint21
asm     mov word ptr cs:[0000], ax
asm     mov ax, word ptr oldint21+2
asm     mov word ptr cs:[0002], ax

setvect(0x10, int10);
setvect(0x13, int13);
setvect(0x16, int16);
setvect(0x21, int21);
setvect(0x28, int28);
setvect(0x09, int09);
setvect(0x08, int08);

paragraphs = (save_ss + (save_sp >> 4) + 0x10) - ourpsp;
keep(0, paragraphs);
}


/***********************************/
```

Source Listing for
NETBIOS Microscope

See Chapter 8, "Network Applications," for a discussion of the following program:

```c
#include <stdio.h>
#include <stdlib.h>
#include <dos.h>
#include <mem.h>
#include <bios.h>
#include <conio.h>
#include <string.h>
#include <process.h>
#include <netbios.h>

#define MSG_SIZE 1001

/* - - - - - - - - - - - - - - - - - - - - - - */

char          message_out[MSG_SIZE];
char          message_in [MSG_SIZE];
char          string     [MSG_SIZE];
char          string2    [MSG_SIZE];
char          localname  [17];
```

```
char            remotename [17];
unsigned char   lsn;
unsigned char   name_number;
int             choice;
int             x;
int             cursor_x;
int             cursor_y;

/* - - - - - - - - - - - - - - - - - - - - - - - */

unsigned            ncb_segments[10];
unsigned            ncb_offsets [10];
unsigned volatile   ncb_head  = 0;
unsigned            ncb_tail  = 0;

/* - - - - - - - - - - - - - - - - - - - - - - - */

NCB     reset_ncb;
NCB     adapter_status_ncb;
NCB     session_status_ncb;
NCB     call_ncb;
NCB     listen_ncb;
NCB     add_name_ncb;
NCB     add_group_name_ncb;
NCB     delete_name_ncb;
NCB     send_ncb;
NCB     receive_ncb;
NCB     receive_any_ncb;
NCB     hangup_ncb;
NCB     temp_ncb;

/* - - - - - - - - - - - - - - - - - - - - - - - */

typedef struct {
        char            tbl_name[16];
        unsigned char   tbl_name_number;
        unsigned char   tbl_name_status;
        }
        NAME_TABLE;

typedef struct {
        unsigned char   card_id[6];
        unsigned char   unknown[52];
```

```
            int             name_count;
            NAME_TABLE      name_table[20];
            }
            ADAPTER_DATA;

    typedef struct {
            unsigned char   lsn;
            unsigned char   state;
            char            local_name[16];
            char            remote_name[16];
            unsigned char   recv_count;
            unsigned char   send_count;
            }
            A_SESSION;

    typedef struct {
            unsigned char   name_num;
            unsigned char   session_count;
            unsigned char   junk1;
            unsigned char   junk2;
            A_SESSION       session_data[40];
            }
            STATUS_INFO;

    ADAPTER_DATA    adapter_data;
    STATUS_INFO     session_info;


    /* - - - - - - - - - - - - - - - - - - - - - - - - */

    unsigned        es_reg, bx_reg;
    void interrupt  (*int_5C_vector)(void);
    char            screen_save[4000];

    char    *state_msg [7] = {
            "                ",
            "LISTEN pending",
            "CALL pending",
            "Active session",
            "HANG UP pending",
            "HANG UP complete",
            "Session abort"
            };
```

```
int     name_type;
char    *name_type_msg [2] = {
        "Unique name",
        "Group name "
        };


int     name_status;
char    *name_status_msg [8] = {
        "Reg. in progress   ",
        "                   ",
        "                   ",
        "                   ",
        "Registered         ",
        "De-registered      ",
        "Dupl detected      ",
        "Dupl; dereg pend.  "
        };
  unsigned char    *box[18] = {

    " [NetTest POST results]----------------------",
    "                                             ",
    "                                             ",
    "                                             ",
    "                                             ",
    "                                             ",
    "                                             ",
    "                                             ",
    "                                             ",
    "                                             ",
    "                                             ",
    "                                             ",
    "                                             ",
    "                                             ",
    "                                             ",
    "                                             ",
    "                                             ",
    "---------------------------------"
        };


char    *error_message[] = {
        "success",                  /*  00  */
        "invalid buffer length",    /*  01  */
        "ret code 02",              /*  02  */
        "invalid command",          /*  03  */
```

```
    "ret code 04",              /*  04  */
    "timed out",               /*  05  */
    "buffer too small",        /*  06  */
    "ret code 07",             /*  07  */
    "invalid session num",     /*  08  */
    "no resource",             /*  09  */
    "session closed",          /*  0A  */
    "command cancelled",       /*  0B  */
    "ret code 0C",             /*  0C  */
    "dupl. local name",        /*  0D  */
    "name table full",         /*  0E  */
    "active session",          /*  0F  */
    "ret code 10",             /*  10  */
    "session table full",      /*  11  */
    "no one listening",        /*  12  */
    "invalid name num",        /*  13  */
    "no answer",               /*  14  */
    "no local name",           /*  15  */
    "name in use",             /*  16  */
    "name is deleted",         /*  17  */
    "abnormal end",            /*  18  */
    "name conflict",           /*  19  */
    "ret code 1A",             /*  1A  */
    "ret code 1B",             /*  1B  */
    "ret code 1C",             /*  1C  */
    "ret code 1D",             /*  1D  */
    "ret code 1E",             /*  1E  */
    "ret code 1F",             /*  1F  */
    "ret code 20",             /*  20  */
    "card busy",               /*  21  */
    "too many cmds",           /*  22  */
    "invalid card num",        /*  23  */
    "cancel done",             /*  24  */
    "ret code 25",             /*  25  */
    "cannot cancel"            /*  26  */
};

/* - - - - - - - - - - - - - - - - - - - - - - - - */
```

```c
void    NetBios(NCB far *ncb_ptr)
        {
        _ES     = FP_SEG(ncb_ptr);
        _BX     = FP_OFF(ncb_ptr);
        _AX     = 0x0100;
        geninterrupt(0x5c);
        }

/* - - - - - - - - - - - - - - - - - - - - - - - - */

void    expand_to_16_chars(char *name)
        {
        char *p;
        char tmp[17];
        int  i;

memset(tmp, ' ', 15);
        p = name;
        i = 0;
        while (i < 15 && *p)
            {
            tmp[i] = *p;
            i++;
            p++;
            }
        tmp[15] = '\0';
        strcpy(name, tmp);
        }

/* - - - - - - - - - - - - - - - - - - - - - - - - */

void    report_result(void)
        {
        int i, j;

        gettext(1, 1, 80, 25, screen_save);
        cursor_x = wherex();
        cursor_y = wherey();
        for (i=0; i<18; i++)
            {
            gotoxy(5, i+1);
            cprintf("%s", box[i]);
            }
        window(6, 2, 70, 17);
```

```c
    movedata(ncb_segments[ncb_tail], ncb_offsets[ncb_tail],
        FP_SEG(&temp_ncb), FP_OFF(&temp_ncb),
        sizeof(NCB));
    ncb_tail++;
    if (ncb_tail == 10)
        ncb_tail = 0;

    if (temp_ncb.NCB_LENGTH == MSG_SIZE - 1)
        temp_ncb.NCB_LENGTH = 0;

    if (temp_ncb.NCB_LENGTH > 320)
        temp_ncb.NCB_LENGTH = 320;

    switch (temp_ncb.NCB_COMMAND)
        {
        case RESET         : {strcpy(string, "RESET ADAPTER"); break;}
        case STATUS        : {strcpy(string, "ADAPTER STATUS");break;}
        case ADD_NAME      : {strcpy(string, "ADD NAME");     break;}
        case ADD_GROUP_NAME: {strcpy(string, "ADD GRP NAME"); break;}
        case DELETE_NAME   : {strcpy(string, "DELETE NAME");  break;}
        case LISTEN        : {strcpy(string, "LISTEN");       break;}
        case CALL          : {strcpy(string, "CALL");         break;}
        case HANG_UP       : {strcpy(string, "HANG UP");      break;}
        case SEND          : {strcpy(string, "SEND");         break;}
        case RECEIVE       : {strcpy(string, "RECEIVE");      break;}
        case RECEIVE_ANY   : {strcpy(string, "RECEIVE ANY");  break;}
        case SESSION_STATUS: {strcpy(string, "SESSION STATUS");break;}
        default            : {strcpy(string, "<unknown>");    break;}
        }

    gotoxy(1, 1);
    cprintf("Command: %s", string);

    if (temp_ncb.NCB_RETCODE <= 0x26)
        strcpy(string, error_message[temp_ncb.NCB_RETCODE]);
    else
    if (temp_ncb.NCB_RETCODE == 0xff)
        strcpy(string, "command pending");
    else
        strcpy(string, "adapter malfunction");

    if (temp_ncb.NCB_CMD_CPLT <= 0x26)
        strcpy(string2, error_message[temp_ncb.NCB_CMD_CPLT]);
```

```
            else
            if (temp_ncb.NCB_CMD_CPLT == 0xff)
                strcpy(string2, "command pending");
            else
                strcpy(string2, "adapter malfunction");

        gotoxy(1, 2);
        cprintf("Immed: %s.  Final: %s.", string, string2);

        if (temp_ncb.NCB_RETCODE > 0 || temp_ncb.NCB_CMD_CPLT > 0)
            goto report_exit;

        if (temp_ncb.NCB_COMMAND == STATUS)
            {
            gotoxy(1, 4);
            cprintf("Card ID (hex): ");
            for (i=0; i<6; i++)
                cprintf("%2.2X ", (int) adapter_data.card_id[i]);
            gotoxy(1, 6);
            cprintf("NetBIOS data block (hex): ");
            for (i=0, j=7; i<52; i++)
                {
                if (i % 16 == 0)
                    gotoxy(1, j++);
                cprintf("%2.2X  ", (int) adapter_data.unknown[i]);
                }
            gotoxy(1, 14);
            cprintf("Local name table items: %d", adapter_data.name_count);
            gotoxy(15, 16);
            cprintf("(Press a key)");
            bioskey(0);
            if (adapter_data.name_count == 0) goto report_exit;
            clrscr();
            for (i=0, j=2; i<adapter_data.name_count; i++)
                {
                adapter_data.name_table[i].tbl_name[15] = '\0';
                name_status = (int) adapter_data.name_table[i].tbl_name_status;
                name_status &= 0x0007;
                name_type = (int) adapter_data.name_table[i].tbl_name_status;
                name_type &= 0x0080;
                name_type = (name_type == 0x0080)? 1 : 0;
                if (i > 9)
```

```c
                {
                gotoxy(15, 16);
                cprintf("(Press a key)");
                bioskey(0);
                clrscr();
                j = 2;
                }
            gotoxy(1, j++);
            cprintf("%s  (#%d)  %s  %s",
                adapter_data.name_table[i].tbl_name,
                (int) adapter_data.name_table[i].tbl_name_number,
                name_status_msg [name_status],
                name_type_msg   [name_type]);
            }
        }
    else
    if (temp_ncb.NCB_COMMAND == ADD_NAME
      || temp_ncb.NCB_COMMAND == ADD_GROUP_NAME)
        {
        gotoxy(1, 5);
        cprintf("Name number = %d.", (int) temp_ncb.NCB_NUM);
        }
    else
    if (temp_ncb.NCB_COMMAND == CALL)
        {
        gotoxy(1, 5);
        cprintf("Session established.  LSN = %d.", (int) temp_ncb.NCB_LSN);
        }
    else
    if (temp_ncb.NCB_COMMAND == LISTEN)
        {
        gotoxy(1, 5);
        strncpy(string, temp_ncb.NCB_CALLNAME, 16);
        string[16] = '\0';
        cprintf("Session established with '%s'.  LSN = %d.",
                string, (int) temp_ncb.NCB_LSN);
        }
    else
    if (temp_ncb.NCB_COMMAND == RECEIVE
      || temp_ncb.NCB_COMMAND == RECEIVE_ANY)
        {
        gotoxy(1, 5);
        cprintf("Message says: ");
        for (i=0, j=6; i<temp_ncb.NCB_LENGTH; i++)
```

```
            {
            if (i % 60 == 0)
                gotoxy(1, j++);
            cprintf("%c", message_in[i]);
            }
        }
    else
    if (temp_ncb.NCB_COMMAND == SESSION_STATUS)
        {
        gotoxy(1, 4);
        cprintf("Names: %d   sessions: %d",
            (int) session_info.name_num, (int) session_info.session_count);
        if (session_info.session_count == 0) goto report_exit;
        j = 5;
        for (i=0; i<session_info.session_count; i++)
            {
            if (i > 5)
                {
                gotoxy(15, 16);
                cprintf("(Press a key)");
                bioskey(0);
                clrscr();
                j = 5;
                }
            gotoxy(1, j++);
            cprintf("lsn = %d  (%s)  recvcount = %d  sendcount = %d",
                    (int) session_info.session_data[i].lsn,
                    state_msg[(int) session_info.session_data[i].state],
                    (int) session_info.session_data[i].recv_count,
                    (int) session_info.session_data[i].send_count );
            gotoxy(1, j++);
            session_info.session_data[i].local_name[15] = '\0';
            session_info.session_data[i].remote_name[15] = '\0';
            cprintf("localname = '%s'   remotename = '%s'",
                    session_info.session_data[i].local_name,
                    session_info.session_data[i].remote_name);
            }
        }
    else
    if (temp_ncb.NCB_COMMAND == HANG_UP)
        {
        gotoxy(1, 5);
        cprintf("Session closed.");
        }
```

```
report_exit:
        gotoxy(15, 16);
        cprintf("(Press a key)");
        bioskey(0);
        window(1, 1, 80, 25);
        gotoxy(cursor_x, cursor_y);
        puttext(1, 1, 80, 25, screen_save);
        }

/* - - - - - - - - - - - - - - - - - - - - - - - */

void interrupt      post(void)
        {
        es_reg  = _ES;
        bx_reg  = _BX;
        ncb_segments[ncb_head] = es_reg;
        ncb_offsets [ncb_head] = bx_reg;
        ncb_head++;

        if (ncb_head == 10)
            ncb_head = 0;
        }

/* - - - - - - - - - - - - - - - - - - - - - - - */

void    main(int argc, char *argv[])
        {
        int_5C_vector = getvect(0x5C);
        if (int_5C_vector == (void far *) NULL)
            {
            printf("NetBios not loaded (Int5C not present).\n");
            exit(0);
            }

        memset(&temp_ncb, 0, sizeof(NCB));
        temp_ncb.NCB_COMMAND = 0x7F;
        NetBios(&temp_ncb);
        if (temp_ncb.NCB_RETCODE != 03)
            {
            printf("NetBios not loaded (No response from Int5C).\n");
            exit(0);
            }
```

```
show_menu:
        clrscr();
        choice = 0;

        printf("NET-TEST Menu:\n\n");
        printf(" 0...exit\n");
        printf(" 1...reset adapter\n");
        printf(" 2...adapter status\n");
        printf(" 3...add name\n");
        printf(" 4...add group name\n");
        printf(" 5...delete name\n");
        printf(" 6...call\n");
        printf(" 7...listen\n");
        printf(" 8...send\n");
        printf(" 9...receive\n");
        printf("10...receive any\n");
        printf("11...hang up\n");
        printf("12...session status\n\n");
        printf("    Choice? ");

get_choice:
        if (ncb_head != ncb_tail)
            report_result();

        if (!bioskey(1))
            goto get_choice;

        gets(string);
        printf("\n");
        if (strlen(string) == 0) goto show_menu;

        choice = atoi(string);
        if (choice < 0 || choice > 12) goto show_menu;

        switch (choice)
            {
            case 0 :{printf("Exiting.\n"); exit(0);}
            case 1 :{
                    printf("Are you sure (Y/N)? ");
                    gets(string);
                    strlwr(string);
                    if (string[0] != 'y') break;
                    printf("Resetting adapter...\n");
```

```
        memset(&reset_ncb, 0, sizeof(NCB));
        reset_ncb.NCB_COMMAND = RESET;
        NetBios(&reset_ncb);
        printf("Return Code = %d.   (press a key)",
            (int) reset_ncb.NCB_RETCODE);
        bioskey(0);
        break;
        }
case 2 :{
        printf("GET STATUS -- Enter name of adapter: ");
        gets(remotename);
        if (strlen(remotename) == 0) break;
        expand_to_16_chars(remotename);
        memset(&adapter_status_ncb, 0, sizeof(NCB));
        adapter_status_ncb.NCB_COMMAND = STATUS;
        adapter_status_ncb.POST_FUNC = post;
        strcpy(adapter_status_ncb.NCB_CALLNAME, remotename);
        adapter_status_ncb.NCB_BUFFER_OFFSET  =FP_OFF(&adapter_data);
        adapter_status_ncb.NCB_BUFFER_SEGMENT =FP_SEG(&adapter_data);
        adapter_status_ncb.NCB_LENGTH  = sizeof(ADAPTER_DATA);
        memset(&adapter_data, 0, sizeof(ADAPTER_DATA));
        NetBios(&adapter_status_ncb);
        break;
        }
case 3 :{
        printf("ADD NAME -- Enter name: ");
        gets(localname);
        if (strlen(localname) == 0) break;
        expand_to_16_chars(localname);
        memset(&add_name_ncb, 0, sizeof(NCB));
        add_name_ncb.NCB_COMMAND = ADD_NAME;
        strcpy(add_name_ncb.NCB_NAME, localname);
        add_name_ncb.POST_FUNC = post;
        NetBios(&add_name_ncb);
        break;
        }
case 4 :{
        printf("ADD GROUP NAME -- Enter name: ");
        gets(localname);
        if (strlen(localname) == 0) break;
        expand_to_16_chars(localname);
        memset(&add_group_name_ncb, 0, sizeof(NCB));
        add_group_name_ncb.NCB_COMMAND = ADD_GROUP_NAME;
        strcpy(add_group_name_ncb.NCB_NAME, localname);
```

```
            add_group_name_ncb.POST_FUNC = post;
            NetBios(&add_group_name_ncb);
            break;
            }
    case 5 :{
            printf("DELETE NAME -- Enter name: ");
            gets(localname);
            if (strlen(localname) == 0) break;
            expand_to_16_chars(localname);
            memset(&delete_name_ncb, 0, sizeof(NCB));
            delete_name_ncb.NCB_COMMAND = DELETE_NAME;
            strcpy(delete_name_ncb.NCB_NAME, localname);
            delete_name_ncb.POST_FUNC = post;
            NetBios(&delete_name_ncb);
            break;
            }
    case 6 :{
            printf("CALL -- Enter remote name to call: ");
            gets(remotename);
            if (strlen(remotename) == 0) break;
            printf("        Enter local (calling) name: ");
            gets(localname);
            if (strlen(localname) == 0) break;
            expand_to_16_chars(remotename);
            expand_to_16_chars(localname);
            memset(&call_ncb, 0, sizeof(NCB));
            call_ncb.NCB_COMMAND = CALL;
            strcpy(call_ncb.NCB_NAME,     localname);
            strcpy(call_ncb.NCB_CALLNAME, remotename);
            call_ncb.NCB_RTO = 0;
            call_ncb.NCB_STO = 0;
            call_ncb.POST_FUNC = post;
            NetBios(&call_ncb);
            break;
            }
    case 7 :{
            printf("LISTEN -- Enter remote name to listen for: ");
            gets(remotename);
            if (strlen(remotename) == 0) break;
            printf("              Enter local (listening) name: ");
            gets(localname);
            if (strlen(localname) == 0) break;
            expand_to_16_chars(remotename);
```

```
                        expand_to_16_chars(localname);
                        memset(&listen_ncb, 0, sizeof(NCB));
                        listen_ncb.NCB_COMMAND = LISTEN;
                        strcpy(listen_ncb.NCB_NAME,      localname);
                        strcpy(listen_ncb.NCB_CALLNAME, remotename);
                        listen_ncb.NCB_RTO = 60;
                        listen_ncb.NCB_STO = 0;
                        listen_ncb.POST_FUNC = post;
                        NetBios(&listen_ncb);
                        break;
                        }
                case 8 :{
                        printf("SEND -- Enter message to be sent: ");
                        gets(message_out);
                        if (strlen(message_out) == 0) break;
                        printf("           Enter session number: ");
                        gets(string);
                        if (strlen(string) == 0) break;
                        x = atoi(string);
                        if (x < 1 || x > 254) break;
                        lsn = (unsigned char) x;
                        memset(&send_ncb, 0, sizeof(NCB));
                        send_ncb.NCB_COMMAND = SEND;
                        send_ncb.NCB_LSN     = lsn;
                        send_ncb.NCB_LENGTH  = strlen(message_out) + 1;
                        send_ncb.NCB_BUFFER_OFFSET  = FP_OFF(message_out);
                        send_ncb.NCB_BUFFER_SEGMENT = FP_SEG(message_out);
                        send_ncb.POST_FUNC = post;
                        NetBios(&send_ncb);
                        break;
                        }
                case 9 :{
                        printf("RECEIVE -- Enter session number: ");
                        gets(string);
                        if (strlen(string) == 0) break;
                        x = atoi(string);
                        if (x < 1 || x > 254) break;
                        lsn = (unsigned char) x;
                        memset(&receive_ncb, 0, sizeof(NCB));
                        receive_ncb.NCB_COMMAND = RECEIVE;
                        receive_ncb.NCB_LSN     = lsn;
                        receive_ncb.NCB_LENGTH  = MSG_SIZE - 1;
                        receive_ncb.NCB_BUFFER_OFFSET  = FP_OFF(message_in);
```

```
                receive_ncb.NCB_BUFFER_SEGMENT = FP_SEG(message_in);
                receive_ncb.POST_FUNC = post;
                NetBios(&receive_ncb);
                break;
                }
        case 10:{
                printf("RECEIVE ANY -- Enter name number: ");
                gets(string);
                if (strlen(string) == 0) break;
                x = atoi(string);
                if (x < 1 || x > 255) break;
                name_number = (unsigned char) x;
                memset(&receive_any_ncb, 0, sizeof(NCB));
                receive_any_ncb.NCB_COMMAND = RECEIVE_ANY;
                receive_any_ncb.NCB_NUM      = name_number;
                receive_any_ncb.NCB_LENGTH   = MSG_SIZE - 1;
                receive_any_ncb.NCB_BUFFER_OFFSET  = FP_OFF(message_in);
                receive_any_ncb.NCB_BUFFER_SEGMENT = FP_SEG(message_in);
                receive_any_ncb.POST_FUNC = post;
                NetBios(&receive_any_ncb);
                break;
                }
        case 11:{
                printf("HANG UP -- Enter session number: ");
                gets(string);
                if (strlen(string) == 0) break;
                x = atoi(string);
                if (x < 1 || x > 254) break;
                lsn = (unsigned char) x;
                memset(&hangup_ncb, 0, sizeof(NCB));
                hangup_ncb.NCB_COMMAND = HANG_UP;
                hangup_ncb.NCB_LSN     = lsn;
                hangup_ncb.POST_FUNC   = post;
                NetBios(&hangup_ncb);
                break;
                }
        case 12:{
                printf("GET SESSION STATUS -- Enter name:");
                gets(localname);
                if (strlen(localname) == 0) break;
                expand_to_16_chars(localname);
                memset(&session_status_ncb, 0, sizeof(NCB));
                session_status_ncb.NCB_COMMAND = SESSION_STATUS;
```

```
                strcpy(session_status_ncb.NCB_NAME, localname);
                session_status_ncb.NCB_LENGTH  = sizeof(STATUS_INFO);
                session_status_ncb.NCB_BUFFER_OFFSET  = FP_OFF(&session_info);
                session_status_ncb.NCB_BUFFER_SEGMENT = FP_SEG(&session_info);
                session_status_ncb.POST_FUNC = post;
                NetBios(&session_status_ncb);
                break;
                }
        default : break;
        }

    goto show_menu;
    }

/* - - - - - - - - - - - - - - - - - - - - - - - */
```

Source Listing for RPE.C

A discussion about how this program works is in Chapter 8, "Network Applications." Its companion, REMOTE.C, is listed in Appendix D.

```
/*
 *            Remote Program Executioner   (RPE)
 *
 * The "Executioner" takes calls from other workstations consisting
 * of messages that tell it to execute programs or DOS commands.
 * It returns a "job ticket" to each caller.  A queue of up to 50
 * pending jobs is maintained.
 *
 * Copyright (c) 1989 Barry Nance
 * All Rights Reserved
 *
 *
 * Written for Turbo C version 2.0.
 * Use the HUGE memory model to compile this program.
 *
 */

/* - - - - - - - - - - - - - - - - - - - - - - - - - */
#include <stdio.h>
#include <stdlib.h>
#include <dos.h>
```

```c
#include <bios.h>
#include <mem.h>
#include <fcntl.h>
#include <io.h>
#include <conio.h>
#include <string.h>
#include <time.h>
#include <process.h>
#include <alloc.h>

#include <netbios.h>
void    interrupt background_listen(void);

#define TRUE   1
#define FALSE  0


/* - - - - - - - - - - - - - - - - - - - - - - - */

unsigned extern _stklen = 2000;

NCB     cancel_ncb;
NCB     listen_ncb;
NCB     add_group_name_ncb;
NCB     delete_name_ncb;
NCB     send_ncb;
NCB     receive_ncb;
NCB     hangup_ncb;


NCB     temp_ncb;

void interrupt  (*int_5C_vector)(void);

char    ch;
char    string[201];
char    *exec_prog;
char    *exec_parms;
char    path[81];
char    logname[81];
char    outname[81];
char    machine_name[16];
int     log_handle;
int     job_number;
int     background_activity;
```

```
int     executing;
int     i;
unsigned u;
unsigned char general_error;

struct  RUN_PACKET
        {
        char    packet_flag;
        char    program_and_commandline[133];
        };

struct  RUN_PACKET run_packet;

struct  QUEUE_INFO
        {
        int     queue_count;
        int     queue_head;
        int     queue_tail;
        struct  RUN_PACKET run_queue[50];
        int     next_jobnum[50];
        };

struct  QUEUE_INFO queue_info;

struct  JOB_PACKET
        {
        char    status_flag;
        char    our_name[16];
        char    job[9];
        };

struct  JOB_PACKET job_packet;

long    start_time;
long    stop_time;

unsigned paragraphs;
char    *transient;

/* - - - - - - - - - - - - - - - - - - - - - - - - */
/*
 *  A function to call NetBIOS (via Int 5C).
 *
 *
 */
```

```
void    NetBios(NCB *ncb_ptr)
        {
        ncb_ptr->NCB_CMD_CPLT = OxFF;

        _ES     = FP_SEG(ncb_ptr);
        _BX     = FP_OFF(ncb_ptr);
        _AX     = 0x0100;

        geninterrupt(Ox5c);
        }


/* - - - - - - - - - - - - - - - - - - - - - - */
/*
 * Expand 'name' to be a 16 byte string, padded
 * on the right with spaces, and null-terminated.
 * (Doesn't work with 'permanent node names'.)
 */
void    expand_to_16_chars(char *name)
        {
        char *p;
        char tmp[17];
        int  i;

        memset(tmp, ' ', 15);
        p = name;
        i = 0;
        while (i < 15 && *p)
            {
            tmp[i] = *p;
            i++;
            p++;
            }
        tmp[15] = '\0';
        strcpy(name, tmp);
        }


/* - - - - - - - - - - - - - - - - - - - - - - */
/*
 * Format a log file entry, lock the file, write
 * the entry, and unlock the file.  Abort if a serious
 * error occurs.
 */
```

```
void    log(char *log_message)
        {
        char    line[201];
        char    *str_time;
        long    now;
        int     retry_count;

        time(&now);
        str_time = ctime(&now);
        str_time[strlen(str_time) - 1] = '\0';
        sprintf(line, "%s <%s> ==> %s\n",
                str_time,
                machine_name,
                log_message);

        printf("%s", line);

        retry_count = 0;
        while ( lock(log_handle, 0x00000000l, 0x0FFFFFFFl) )
            if (++retry_count > 100)
                {
                printf("SYSTEM ERROR.  Could not lock the log file.\n");
                close(log_handle);
                exit(1);
                }

        write(log_handle, line, strlen(line));

        retry_count = 0;
        while ( unlock(log_handle, 0x00000000l, 0x0FFFFFFFl) )
            if (++retry_count > 100)
                {
                printf("SYSTEM ERROR.  Could not unlock the log file.\n");
                close(log_handle);
                exit(1);
                }

        close(dup(log_handle));
        }
```

```
/* - - - - - - - - - - - - - - - - - - - - - - - */
/*
 *  Build the 'add_group_name' NCB and send it out
 *  across the network.
 *
 */
void     net_add_group_name(char *name)
         {
         memset(&add_group_name_ncb, 0, sizeof(NCB));
         add_group_name_ncb.NCB_COMMAND = ADD_GROUP_NAME;
         strcpy(add_group_name_ncb.NCB_NAME, name);
         expand_to_16_chars(add_group_name_ncb.NCB_NAME);
         NetBios(&add_group_name_ncb);
         }


/* - - - - - - - - - - - - - - - - - - - - - - - */
/*
 *     Build the 'delete_name' NCB and send it out
 *     across the network.
 *
 */
void     net_delete_name(char *name)
         {
         memset(&delete_name_ncb, 0, sizeof(NCB));
         delete_name_ncb.NCB_COMMAND = DELETE_NAME;
         strcpy(delete_name_ncb.NCB_NAME, name);
         expand_to_16_chars(delete_name_ncb.NCB_NAME);
         NetBios(&delete_name_ncb);
         }


/* - - - - - - - - - - - - - - - - - - - - - - - */
/*
 *     Build the 'listen' NCB and send it out
 *     across the network.  Set the POST address to
 *     point to a 'background' routine to handle a caller.
 */
void     net_listen_post(char *caller, char *us,
                       void interrupt (*post_function)(),
                       unsigned char rto, unsigned char sto)

         {
         memset(&listen_ncb, 0, sizeof(NCB));
         listen_ncb.NCB_COMMAND = LISTEN;
         strcpy(listen_ncb.NCB_NAME,     us);
```

```
        strcpy(listen_ncb.NCB_CALLNAME, caller);
        expand_to_16_chars(listen_ncb.NCB_NAME);
        expand_to_16_chars(listen_ncb.NCB_CALLNAME);
        listen_ncb.POST_FUNC = post_function;
        listen_ncb.NCB_RTO = rto;
        listen_ncb.NCB_STO = sto;
        NetBios(&listen_ncb);
        }

/* - - - - - - - - - - - - - - - - - - - - - - - */
/*
 *    Build the 'cancel' NCB and send it out
 *    across the network.
 *
*/
void    net_cancel(NCB *np)
        {
        memset(&cancel_ncb, 0, sizeof(NCB));
        cancel_ncb.NCB_COMMAND = CANCEL;
        cancel_ncb.NCB_BUFFER_OFFSET  = FP_OFF(np);
        cancel_ncb.NCB_BUFFER_SEGMENT = FP_SEG(np);
        NetBios(&cancel_ncb);
        }

/* - - - - - - - - - - - - - - - - - - - - - - - */
/*
 *    Build the 'receive' NCB and send it out
 *    across the network.  When the operation completes,
 *    let NetBIOS call the POST routine to handle it.
*/
void    net_receive_post(unsigned char lsn,
                         void interrupt (*post_function)(),
                         void *packet_ptr, int packet_len)
        {
        memset(&receive_ncb, 0, sizeof(NCB));
        receive_ncb.NCB_COMMAND = RECEIVE;
        receive_ncb.NCB_LSN = lsn;
        receive_ncb.NCB_LENGTH = packet_len;
        receive_ncb.NCB_BUFFER_OFFSET  = FP_OFF(packet_ptr);
        receive_ncb.NCB_BUFFER_SEGMENT = FP_SEG(packet_ptr);
        receive_ncb.POST_FUNC = post_function;
        NetBios(&receive_ncb);
        }
```

```
/* - - - - - - - - - - - - - - - - - - - - - - - */
/*
 *    Build the 'send' NCB and send it out
 *    across the network.
 *
 */
void    net_send(unsigned char lsn,void *packet_ptr, int packet_len)
        {
        memset(&send_ncb, 0, sizeof(NCB));
        send_ncb.NCB_COMMAND = SEND;
        send_ncb.NCB_LSN = lsn;
        send_ncb.NCB_LENGTH = packet_len;
        send_ncb.NCB_BUFFER_OFFSET  = FP_OFF(packet_ptr);
        send_ncb.NCB_BUFFER_SEGMENT = FP_SEG(packet_ptr);
        NetBios(&send_ncb);
        }

/* - - - - - - - - - - - - - - - - - - - - - - - */
/*
 *    Build the 'hang up' NCB and send it out
 *    across the network.  Wait for completion.
 *
 */
void    net_hangup(unsigned char lsn)
        {
        memset(&hangup_ncb, 0, sizeof(NCB));
        hangup_ncb.NCB_COMMAND = HANG_UP;
        hangup_ncb.NCB_LSN = lsn;
        NetBios(&hangup_ncb);
        }

/* - - - - - - - - - - - - - - - - - - - - - - - */
/*
 *  Find job in the pending queue and remove it
 *  by marking it with a packet flag of 'C'
 *  (or return a 'job not found' indication).
 */

void    cancel_job (int job)
        {
        int  x;

        sprintf(job_packet.job, "J%4.4d", job);
        x = queue_info.queue_tail;
```

```
        while (x != queue_info.queue_head)
            {
            if (queue_info.next_jobnum[x] == job)
                {
                queue_info.run_queue[x].packet_flag = 'C';
                job_packet.status_flag = 'C';
                return;
                }
            if (++x == 50) x = 0;
            }
        job_packet.status_flag = 'E';
        }

/* - - - - - - - - - - - - - - - - - - - - - - - - - */
/*
 * This function is called by NetBIOS when a POSTed
 * receive completes (meaning that someone sent us a
 * status packet, a cancel packet, or a run packet
 * that goes into the queue).
 *
 */
void    interrupt background_receive(void)
        {
        char *job_token;

        general_error = receive_ncb.NCB_CMD_CPLT;
        if (general_error != 0)
            goto bg_receive_exit;

forget_it:
        if (run_packet.packet_flag == 'X')
            goto bg_close_session;

        if (queue_info.queue_count > 45)
            {
            job_packet.status_flag = 'Z';
        net_send(listen_ncb.NCB_LSN, &job_packet, sizeof(job_packet));
            goto bg_close_session;
            }

status_response:
  if (strnicmp(run_packet.program_and_commandline, "status", 6) == 0)
      {
      net_send(listen_ncb.NCB_LSN, &queue_info, sizeof(queue_info));
```

```
                goto bg_close_session;
                }

cancel_a_job:
        if (strnicmp(run_packet.program_and_commandline, "cancel", 6) == 0)
                {
                job_token = strtok(run_packet.program_and_commandline, "Jj");
                if (job_token != NULL)
                    i = atoi( strtok(NULL, " \n") );
                cancel_job(i);
                net_send(listen_ncb.NCB_LSN, &job_packet, sizeof(job_packet));
                goto bg_close_session;
                }

queue_the_job:
        strcpy(queue_info.run_queue
                    [queue_info.queue_head].program_and_commandline,
                run_packet.program_and_commandline);
        queue_info.run_queue[queue_info.queue_head].packet_flag = 'Q';
        sprintf(job_packet.job, "J%4.4d", ++job_number);
        job_packet.status_flag = 'J';
        queue_info.next_jobnum[queue_info.queue_head] = job_number;

        if (++queue_info.queue_head == 50) queue_info.queue_head = 0;
        queue_info.queue_count++;

        net_send(listen_ncb.NCB_LSN, &job_packet, sizeof(job_packet));

bg_close_session:
        net_hangup(listen_ncb.NCB_LSN);
        if (strnicmp(run_packet.program_and_commandline, "quit", 4) == 0)
            goto bg_receive_exit;

reissue_listen:
        net_listen_post("*", "RPE", background_listen, 20, 20);

bg_receive_exit:
        background_activity = FALSE;
        }

/* - - - - - - - - - - - - - - - - - - - - - - - */
/*
```

```
        *  This function is activated when a 'call RPE' command
        *  is issued by another workstation.
        *
        */
        void     interrupt background_listen(void)
                 {
                 general_error = listen_ncb.NCB_CMD_CPLT;
                 if (general_error != 0)
                     goto bg_listen_exit;

                 background_activity = TRUE;

                 strcpy(job_packet.our_name, machine_name);
                 strcpy(job_packet.job, "          ");

                 if (executing)
                     job_packet.status_flag = 'Q';
                 else
                     job_packet.status_flag = 'J';

                 net_send(listen_ncb.NCB_LSN, &job_packet, sizeof(job_packet));

                 net_receive_post(listen_ncb.NCB_LSN,
                               background_receive,
                               &run_packet, sizeof(run_packet));

        bg_listen_exit:
                 ;
                 }

        /* - - - - - - - - - - - - - - - - - - - - - - - */
        /*
         *  Execute the next item in the queue.
         */

        void     execute_program(int job)
                 {
        /*
         *
         *  if a call is still underway, let it finish.
         *
         */
                 while (background_activity)
                     ;
```

```
/*
 * As mentioned below, we want to force Command.Com to reload
 * its transient (high-memory) portion.  This avoids an obscure
 * DOS bug and makes RPE a little more bullet-proof.
 */
        for (i=0; i<8000; i++)
            transient[i] = 0;


/*
 *
 * Mention how many jobs are awaiting execution.  Log this job.
 *
 */

        if (queue_info.queue_count != 0)
            {
            sprintf(string, "%d job(s) awaiting execution",
                    queue_info.queue_count);
            log(string);
            }

         sprintf(job_packet.job, "J%4.4d", job);
         log(job_packet.job);


/*
 * If the caller is instructing us to quit (remotely), we do so.
 *
 *
 */


        if (strnicmp(run_packet.program_and_commandline, "quit", 4) == 0)
            {
            log("RPE ended remotely.");
            close(log_handle);
            net_hangup(listen_ncb.NCB_LSN);
            while (hangup_ncb.NCB_CMD_CPLT == 0xFF)
                ;
            net_delete_name("RPE");
            while (delete_name_ncb.NCB_CMD_CPLT == 0xFF)
                ;
            exit(0);
            }
```

```
/*
 * Now construct the DOS command line that we'll pass to the
 * system() function, just as if it were to be executed at a
 * DOS prompt.  Redirect 'stdout' output to a job-specific file.
 */

        sprintf(string, "%s >%sJ%4.4d.OUT",
            run_packet.program_and_commandline,
            path,
            job);
        log(string);

/*
 * Execute the program (or DOS command).  For statistical purposes,
 * keep track of elapsed time.
 *
 */

        executing = TRUE;
        time(&start_time);
        system(string);
        time(&stop_time);
        executing = FALSE;

/*
 * Log the completion of the program/command.
 *
 */

        sprintf(string, "Job %4.4d completed.  %ld elapsed second(s).",
                job, (long) stop_time - start_time );
        log(string);
        }

/* - - - - - - - - - - - - - - - - - - - - - - - - - */
/*
 * The program starts here.
 *
 * Initialize job_number, then figure out where the transient
 * portion of Command.Com is located.  We'll use this later to
 * zero that area, because we want to force Command.Com to
 * reload it.  This avoids an obscure bug in PC/DOS.
 *
 */
```

```c
void    main (int argc, char *argv[])
        {
        general_error = 0;

        job_number = 0;
        paragraphs = (biosmemory() - 8) * 64;
        transient  = MK_FP(paragraphs, 0);

        background_activity = FALSE;
        queue_info.queue_head = 0;
        queue_info.queue_tail = 0;

/*
 * Abort if we're running on top of a DOS version earlier than 3.0.
 * Also, check to see if SHARE.EXE has been run (to support file-
 * sharing).  Finally, make sure NetBIOS is present.
 */
Step_1:
        if (_osmajor < 3)
            {
            printf("ERROR. Early versions of DOS not supported.\n");
            exit(1);
            }

        _AX = 0x1000;
        geninterrupt(0x2F);
        if (_AL != 0xFF)
            {
            printf("ERROR. 'Share.Exe' (file sharing support) not loaded.\n");
            exit(1);
            }

        _DX = (unsigned) &machine_name[0];
        _AX = 0x5E00;
        geninterrupt(0x21);
        if (_CH == 0)
            {
            printf("ERROR.  Machine name not set.\n");
            exit(1);
            }
```

```
            i = strlen(machine_name) - 1;
            while (i > 0 && machine_name[i] == ' ')
                {
                machine_name[i] = '\0';
                i-;
                }

            int_5C_vector = getvect(0x5C);
            if (int_5C_vector == (void far *) NULL)
                {
                printf("ERROR. NetBios not loaded (Int5C not present).\n");
                exit(1);
                }

            memset(&temp_ncb, 0, sizeof(NCB));
            temp_ncb.NCB_COMMAND = 0x7F;
            NetBios(&temp_ncb);
            if (temp_ncb.NCB_RETCODE != 03)
                {
        printf("ERROR. NetBios not loaded (No response from Int5C).\n");
                exit(1);
                }

/*
 *   Do an 'add group name' call, to make us available on
 *   the network.
 *
 */
Step_2:
            printf("Adding name 'RPE' to the network...");

            net_add_group_name("RPE");
            while (add_group_name_ncb.NCB_CMD_CPLT == 0xFF)
                ;

            printf("\n");
            if (add_group_name_ncb.NCB_CMD_CPLT != 0)
                {
                printf("ERROR.  NetBios said: %s.\n",
                  net_error_message[(int)add_group_name_ncb.NCB_CMD_CPLT]);
                exit(1);
                }
```

```
/*
 *  Now find out the drive and directory in which the log file
 *  should be written.  Open it for shared access (if it's
 *  necessary to create it, we'll have to close it and re-open
 *  it because file-creation confers exclusive access, which we
 *  don't want).
*/
Step_3:
        printf("Specify network Drive:\\Path for log file: ");
        gets(path);
        if (strlen(path) == 0)
            goto Step_3;

        if (path[strlen(path)-1] != '\\')
            strcat(path, "\\");
        strcpy(logname, path);
        strcat(logname, "RPE.LOG");
        strupr(logname);

        printf("Log file is %s (append/shared)\n", logname);

        if ( (log_handle = creatnew(logname, 0)) != -1)
            close(log_handle);
        log_handle = open(logname, O_RDWR | O_APPEND | O_TEXT | O_DENYNONE);

        if (log_handle == -1)
            {
            net_delete_name("RPE");
            while (delete_name_ncb.NCB_CMD_CPLT == 0xFF)
                ;
            printf("ERROR. Could not open log file.\n");
            exit(1);
            }

        log("RPE started.");

/*
 *  Issue a Listen-to-anyone command.  Set the receive-timeout
 *  and send-timeout fields to 20 500-ms periods (10 seconds)
 *  each.  If someone calls, invoke the 'background_listen()'
 *  routine.
*/
```

```
Step_4:
        net_listen_post("*", "RPE", background_listen, 20, 20);

/*
 *  Let people know we're waiting for something to do,
 *  and tell how to stop the program.
 */

Step_5:
        log("Waiting for work.  Press 'ESC' to stop RPE. ");

/*
 *  While we're waiting for a call, look for a press of the
 *  ESCape key, to see if someone wants to stop the program.
 *  Confirm the response.  To stop RPE, we need to leave
 *  things the way we found them, so we cancel the
 *  outstanding 'listen' command, delete our name from the
 *  name table, and then go back to DOS.
 *
 */
Step_6:
        while (!general_error)
            {
            if (bioskey(1))
                if ( (ch = (char) getch()) == 27 )
                    {
                    log("Terminate RPE (Yes/No)? ");
                    gets(string);
                    if (string[0] == 'Y' || string[0] == 'y')
                        {
                        log("RPE ended.");
                        close(log_handle);
                        net_cancel(&listen_ncb);
                        while (cancel_ncb.NCB_CMD_CPLT == 0xFF)
                            ;
                        net_delete_name("RPE");
                        while (delete_name_ncb.NCB_CMD_CPLT == 0xFF)
                            ;
                        exit(0);
                        }
```

```
                        goto Step_5;
                        }
               if (queue_info.queue_head != queue_info.queue_tail)
                  {
                  strcpy(run_packet.program_and_commandline,
                           queue_info.run_queue
                              [queue_info.queue_tail].program_and_commandline);
                  job_number = queue_info.next_jobnum[queue_info.queue_tail];
                  if (queue_info.run_queue
                           [queue_info.queue_tail].packet_flag != 'C')
                     {
                     queue_info.run_queue
                              [queue_info.queue_tail].packet_flag = 'E';
                     execute_program(job_number);
                     }
                  queue_info.queue_count--;
                  if (++queue_info.queue_tail == 50) queue_info.queue_tail = 0;
                  }
            }


/*
 * If an error occurs, we want to stop the program as
 * gracefully as possible.  So, we make sure we cancel
 * any outstanding 'listen' and delete the name 'RPE'
 * before going back to DOS.
 */

      sprintf(string, "RPE aborted--%s",
               net_error_message[general_error]);
      log(string);
      close(log_handle);
      net_cancel(&listen_ncb);
      while (cancel_ncb.NCB_CMD_CPLT == 0xFF)
         ;
      net_delete_name("RPE");
      while (delete_name_ncb.NCB_CMD_CPLT == 0xFF)
         ;
      exit(1);
      }
```

APPENDIX D

Source Listing for REMOTE.C

For a discussion on how this program works, please see Chapter 8, "Network Applications." Its companion, RPE.C, is in Appendix C.

```
/*
 *          Remote -- A "Job" Dispatcher
 *
 * "Remote" sends messages to "RPE" (which you run on a separate
 * workstation), telling it to execute programs or DOS commands.
 * A "job ticket" is issued back to REMOTE by RPE for each job.
 *
 * Because the program or DOS command runs remotely, your
 * computer is freed up immediately to do other work.
 *
 * Copyright (c) 1989 Barry Nance
 * All Rights Reserved
 *
 *
 * Written for Turbo C version 2.0.
 * Use the SMALL memory model to compile this program.
 *
 */
```

```c
/* - - - - - - - - - - - - - - - - - - - - - - - - - - */
#include <stdio.h>
#include <conio.h>
#include <stdlib.h>
#include <string.h>
#include <process.h>
#include <dos.h>

#include <netbios.h>

NCB     status_ncb;
NCB     call_ncb;
NCB     send_ncb;
NCB     receive_ncb;
NCB     hangup_ncb;
NCB     temp_ncb;

void interrupt  (*int_5C_vector)(void);

char    string[201];
char    our_name[16];
char    other_name[16];
char    i;
int     j;

char far *command_line;
char far *byte_count;

struct  RUN_PACKET
        {
        char    packet_flag;
        char    program_and_commandline[133];
        };

struct  RUN_PACKET run_packet;

struct  QUEUE_INFO
        {
        int     queue_count;
        int     queue_head;
        int     queue_tail;
        struct  RUN_PACKET run_queue[50];
        int     next_jobnum[50];
        };
```

```
struct   QUEUE_INFO queue_info;

struct   JOB_PACKET
         {
         char    status_flag;
         char    machine_name[16];
         char    job[9];
         };

struct   JOB_PACKET job_packet;

/* - - - - - - - - - - - - - - - - - - - - - - - */
/*
 *  Call NetBIOS, via Interrupt 5C.
 */
void     NetBios(NCB far *ncb_ptr)
         {
         ncb_ptr->NCB_CMD_CPLT = 0xFF;

         _ES     = FP_SEG(ncb_ptr);
         _BX     = FP_OFF(ncb_ptr);
         _AX     = 0x0100;

         geninterrupt(0x5c);
         }


/* - - - - - - - - - - - - - - - - - - - - - - - */
/*
 *  Expand a NetBIOS name by padding on the right
 *  with spaces.
 */
void     expand_to_16_chars(char *name)
         {
         char *p;
         char tmp[17];
         int  i;

         memset(tmp, ' ', 15);
         p = name;
         i = 0;
         while (i < 15 && *p)
             {
             tmp[i] = *p;
```

```
            i++;
            p++;
            }
        tmp[15] = '\0';
        strcpy(name, tmp);
        }


/* - - - - - - - - - - - - - - - - - - - - - - - */
/*
 *  Build and send an 'adapter status' command
 */
void    net_status(char far *buffer, int len)
        {
        memset(&status_ncb, 0, sizeof(NCB));
        status_ncb.NCB_COMMAND = STATUS;
        strcpy(status_ncb.NCB_CALLNAME, "*");
        expand_to_16_chars(status_ncb.NCB_CALLNAME);
        status_ncb.NCB_LENGTH = len;
        status_ncb.NCB_BUFFER_OFFSET  = FP_OFF(buffer);
        status_ncb.NCB_BUFFER_SEGMENT = FP_SEG(buffer);
        NetBios(&status_ncb);
        }


/* - - - - - - - - - - - - - - - - - - - - - - - */
/*
 *  "Call" another workstation.
 */
void    net_call(char *who, char *us, unsigned char rto, unsigned char sto)
        {
        memset(&call_ncb, 0, sizeof(NCB));
        call_ncb.NCB_COMMAND = CALL;
        memcpy(call_ncb.NCB_NAME,     us, 16);
        strcpy(call_ncb.NCB_CALLNAME, who);
        expand_to_16_chars(call_ncb.NCB_CALLNAME);
        call_ncb.NCB_RTO = rto;
        call_ncb.NCB_STO = sto;
        NetBios(&call_ncb);
        }


/* - - - - - - - - - - - - - - - - - - - - - - - */
/*
 *  Issue a "receive" command to NetBIOS.
 */
```

```
void    net_receive(unsigned char lsn, void far *packet_ptr, int packet_len)
        {
        memset(&receive_ncb, 0, sizeof(NCB));
        receive_ncb.NCB_COMMAND = RECEIVE;
        receive_ncb.NCB_LSN = lsn;
        receive_ncb.NCB_LENGTH = packet_len;
        receive_ncb.NCB_BUFFER_OFFSET  = FP_OFF(packet_ptr);
        receive_ncb.NCB_BUFFER_SEGMENT = FP_SEG(packet_ptr);
        NetBios(&receive_ncb);
        }

/* - - - - - - - - - - - - - - - - - - - - - - */
/*
 *  Build and send a message packet via NetBIOS.
 */
void    net_send(unsigned char lsn, void far *packet_ptr, int packet_len)
        {
        memset(&send_ncb, 0, sizeof(NCB));
        send_ncb.NCB_COMMAND = SEND;
        send_ncb.NCB_LSN = lsn;
        send_ncb.NCB_LENGTH = packet_len;
        send_ncb.NCB_BUFFER_OFFSET  = FP_OFF(packet_ptr);
        send_ncb.NCB_BUFFER_SEGMENT = FP_SEG(packet_ptr);
        NetBios(&send_ncb);
        }

/* - - - - - - - - - - - - - - - - - - - - - - */
/*
 *  Close a session with a "hang up" command.
 */
void    net_hangup(unsigned char lsn)
        {
        memset(&hangup_ncb, 0, sizeof(NCB));
        hangup_ncb.NCB_COMMAND = HANG_UP;
        hangup_ncb.NCB_LSN = lsn;
        NetBios(&hangup_ncb);
        }

/* - - - - - - - - - - - - - - - - - - - - - - */
/*
 *  The program starts here.
 *
```

```
 *   Basically, all we do is send our command line to "RPE"
 *   so that it can treat it as a program (or DOS command)
 *   to be executed remotely.
 *
 */
void    main(int argc, char *argv[])
        {
/*
 *   First, make sure that we're running under DOS 3.0 or later.
 *   Then check to make sure that SHARE.EXE has been run and that
 *   NetBIOS is active.
 */
Step_1:
        if (_osmajor < 3)
            {
            printf("ERROR. Early versions of DOS not supported.\n");
            exit(1);
            }

        _AX = 0x1000;
        geninterrupt(0x2F);
        if (_AL != 0xFF)
            {
            printf("ERROR. 'Share.Exe' (file sharing support) not loaded.\n");
            exit(1);
            }

        int_5C_vector = getvect(0x5C);
        if (int_5C_vector == (void far *) NULL)
            {
            printf("ERROR. NetBios not loaded (Int5C not present).\n");
            exit(1);
            }

        memset(&temp_ncb, 0, sizeof(NCB));
        temp_ncb.NCB_COMMAND = 0x7F;
        NetBios(&temp_ncb);
        if (temp_ncb.NCB_RETCODE != 03)
            {
            printf("ERROR. NetBios not loaded (No response from Int5C).\n");
            exit(1);
            }
```

```
/*
 *  We need a name to identify ourselves when we later issue the
 *  "call" command.  Let's use the "Permanent Node Name"...we build
 *  it by getting the first six bytes of the data area returned by
 *  the "adapter status" command, and prefixing them with ten bytes
 *  of binary zeroes.
 *
 *  Note that we only give the 'adapter status' command a buffer of
 *  60 bytes to fill.  We then deliberately ignore the almost certain
 *  NCB_CMD_CPLT return code of 6 ("data area too small").
 */
Step_2:
        net_status(string, 60);
        while (status_ncb.NCB_CMD_CPLT == 0xFF)
            ;
        if (status_ncb.NCB_CMD_CPLT != 0x00 && status_ncb.NCB_CMD_CPLT != 0x06)
            {
            printf("ERROR.  NetBios said: %s.\n",
                net_error_message[(int)status_ncb.NCB_CMD_CPLT]);
            exit(1);
            }

        memset(our_name, 0, 16);
        for (i=0; i<6; i++)
            our_name[i+10] = string[i];


/*
 *  REMOTE expects to be invoked like this:
 *
 *      C:> remote <progname> <command line parameters>
 *
 *  or this:
 *
 *      C:> remote <dos command> <command parameters>
 *
 *  So we go down inside the Program Segment Prefix to pick up
 *  REMOTE's command line, which will be sent to RPE.  If REMOTE
 *  is run without a command line, it simply exits after reminding
 *  the user that a command line is required.
 *
 *  The length of the command line is found in byte 0x80 (byte 128)
 *  of the PSP.  The bytes following the length are the command
 *  line, terminated by a carriage return.  For example:
 *
```

```
* (11)       C   O   P   Y       A   :   *   .   *   (13)
* ---  ---  ---  ---  ---  ---  ---  ---  ---  ---  ---  ---  ---
* 0x80  81  82  83  84  85  86  87  88  89  8A  8B  8C
*
* Note that the first byte following the length byte is normally
* a space character.  We bypass it.
*
*/
Step_3:
        byte_count   = MK_FP(_psp, 0x0080);
        command_line = MK_FP(_psp, 0x0081);

        if (*byte_count == 0)
            {
            printf("Usage: REMOTE <progname> <command line>\n");
            printf("    or REMOTE <dos command> <parms>\n");
            exit(1);
            }

        memset(run_packet.program_and_commandline, 0, 133);
        while (*command_line == ' ')
            ++command_line;

        i = 0;
        while (*command_line != 13 && *command_line != 0)
            {
            run_packet.program_and_commandline[i] = *command_line;
            ++command_line;
            ++i;
            }

/*
 * Issue a NetBIOS 'call' to establish a session with "RPE".
 *
 *
 */
Step_5:
        net_call("RPE", our_name, 20, 20);
        while (call_ncb.NCB_CMD_CPLT == 0xFF)
            ;

        if (call_ncb.NCB_CMD_CPLT != 0)
            {
```

```
            printf("Couldn't connect: %s\n",
                    net_error_message[call_ncb.NCB_CMD_CPLT]);
            printf("'Remote' ended (unsuccessfully).\n");
            exit(1);
            }

/*
 *  "RPE" always starts the conversation by sending us the machine-
 *  name of the computer it's running on (as part of 'job_packet').
 *  So the first thing we do is issue a 'receive' command in order
 *  to get that first message.
 */
Step_6:
        net_receive(call_ncb.NCB_LSN, &job_packet, sizeof(job_packet));
        while (receive_ncb.NCB_CMD_CPLT == 0xFF)
            ;

        if (receive_ncb.NCB_CMD_CPLT != 0)
            {
            printf("RPE aborted--%s\n",
                    net_error_message[receive_ncb.NCB_CMD_CPLT]);
            net_hangup(call_ncb.NCB_LSN);
            while (hangup_ncb.NCB_CMD_CPLT == 0xFF)
                ;
            printf("Remote ended due to error.\n");
            exit(1);
            }

        strcpy(other_name, job_packet.machine_name);
        j = strlen(other_name) - 1;
        while (j > 0 && other_name[j] == ' ')
            {
            other_name[j] = '\0';
            j--;
            }


/*
 *  If the job packet returned by "RPE" contains a 'packet_flag'
 *  of 'Q', it means that our job request will go into the queue.
 *  Let's ask if this is okay.
 *
 *  If 'packet_flag' is a 'Z', the queue is full.
 *
```

```
 *   If the user doesn't want the job placed in the awaiting-
 *   execution queue, we'll tell "RPE" to forget it.
 *
 *   If the command line contains 'quit', 'status', or 'cancel',
 *   pass it immediately to "RPE".
 *
 */
Step_7:
        if (strnicmp(run_packet.program_and_commandline, "quit", 4) == 0)
            goto Step_8;
        if (strnicmp(run_packet.program_and_commandline, "status", 6) == 0)
            goto Step_8;
        if (strnicmp(run_packet.program_and_commandline, "cancel", 6) == 0)
            goto Step_8;

        if (job_packet.status_flag == 'Z')
            {
            printf("The queue is full at this time.  Try later.\n");
            net_hangup(call_ncb.NCB_LSN);
            while (hangup_ncb.NCB_CMD_CPLT == 0xFF)
                ;
            printf("'Remote' ended due to error.\n");
            exit(1);
            }

        if (job_packet.status_flag == 'Q')
            {
            printf("\n");
            printf("RPE (%s) is busy...your request will go into the queue.\n",
                    other_name);
            printf("Is this okay (Yes/No)? ");
            do
                i = (char) getch();
                while (i != 'N' && i != 'n' && i != 'Y' && i != 'y');
            if (i == 'y' || i == 'Y')
                {
                printf("Yes...\n");
                goto Step_8;
                }
            printf("No...\n");
            printf("Job request cancelled.\n");
            run_packet.packet_flag = 'X';
```

```
        net_send(call_ncb.NCB_LSN, &run_packet, size of(run_packet));
        while (send_ncb.NCB_CMD_CPLT == OxFF)
            ;
        if (send_ncb.NCB_CMD_CPLT != O)
            {
            printf("NetBios error msg: %s\n",
                    net_error_message[send_ncb.NCB_CMD_CPLT]);
            net_hangup(call_ncb.NCB_LSN);
            while (hangup_ncb.NCB_CMD_CPLT == OxFF)
                ;
            printf("'Remote' ended due to error.\n");
            exit(1);
            }
        net_hangup(call_ncb.NCB_LSN);
        while (hangup_ncb.NCB_CMD_CPLT == OxFF)
            ;
        exit(O);
        }


/*
 *   Send "RPE" a message containing REMOTE's command line.
 *
 */
Step_8:
        run_packet.packet_flag = 'P';

        net_send(call_ncb.NCB_LSN, &run_packet, size of(run_packet));
        while (send_ncb.NCB_CMD_CPLT == OxFF)
            ;

        if (send_ncb.NCB_CMD_CPLT != O)
            {
            printf("NetBios error msg: %s\n",
                    net_error_message[send_ncb.NCB_CMD_CPLT]);
            net_hangup(call_ncb.NCB_LSN);
            while (hangup_ncb.NCB_CMD_CPLT == OxFF)
                ;
            printf("'Remote' ended due to error.\n");
            exit(1);
            }
```

```
/*
 *  If we sent a 'quit' command, we're stopping "RPE".  So we can
 *  quit, too.
 *
 */
Step_9:
        if (strnicmp(run_packet.program_and_commandline, "quit", 4) == 0)
            {
            printf("RPE (%s) will stop when the queue is empty.\n",
                    other_name);
            net_hangup(call_ncb.NCB_LSN);
            while (hangup_ncb.NCB_CMD_CPLT == 0xFF)
                ;
            exit(0);
            }


/*
 *  Receive a response from "RPE".
 *
 */
Step_10:
        if (strnicmp(run_packet.program_and_commandline, "status", 6) == 0)
            net_receive(call_ncb.NCB_LSN, &queue_info, size of(queue_info));
        else
        if (strnicmp(run_packet.program_and_commandline, "cancel", 6) == 0)
            net_receive(call_ncb.NCB_LSN, &job_packet, size of(job_packet));
        else
            net_receive(call_ncb.NCB_LSN, &job_packet, size of(job_packet));

        while (receive_ncb.NCB_CMD_CPLT == 0xFF)
            ;
        if (receive_ncb.NCB_CMD_CPLT != 0)
            {
            printf("RPE aborted--%s\n",
                    net_error_message[receive_ncb.NCB_CMD_CPLT]);
            net_hangup(call_ncb.NCB_LSN);
            while (hangup_ncb.NCB_CMD_CPLT == 0xFF)
                ;
            printf("Remote ended due to error.\n");
            exit(1);
            }
```

```
/*
 *  The dialog is finished; hang up on "RPE".
 *
 */

        net_hangup(call_ncb.NCB_LSN);
        while (hangup_ncb.NCB_CMD_CPLT == 0xFF)
            ;


/*
 *  Display the awaiting-execution queue.
 *
 */
Step_11:
        if (strnicmp(run_packet.program_and_commandline, "status", 6) == 0)
            {
            printf("\n");
            printf("There are %d job(s) in %s's queue.\n\n",
                    queue_info.queue_count,
                    other_name);
            if (queue_info.queue_count > 0)
                {
                printf("  JOB    COMMAND\n");
                printf("  -----  ------------------------------------\n");
                for (j=0; j<queue_info.queue_count; j++)
                    {
                    if (queue_info.run_queue
                            [queue_info.queue_tail].packet_flag == 'C')
                        strcpy(string, "CANCELLED");
                    else
                    if (queue_info.run_queue
                            [queue_info.queue_tail].packet_flag == 'E')
                        strcpy(string, "EXECUTING");
                    else
                        strcpy(string, "PENDING");
                    printf("  J%4.4d  %-40.40s  %s\n",
                        queue_info.next_jobnum[queue_info.queue_tail],
                        queue_info.run_queue
                            [queue_info.queue_tail].program_and_commandline,
                        string);
                    if (++queue_info.queue_tail == 50)
                        queue_info.queue_tail = 0;
                    }
                printf("\n");
                }
```

```
                    printf("Remote ended successfully.\n");
                    exit(0);
                    }


/*
 *   Display whether the job was canceled or not found in the queue.
 *
*/
Step_12:
            if (strnicmp(run_packet.program_and_commandline, "cancel", 6) == 0)
                    {
                    if (job_packet.status_flag == 'E')
                        printf("Job %s not found in %s's queue.\n",
                                job_packet.job,
                                other_name);
                    else
                        printf("Job %s cancelled in %s's queue.\n",
                                job_packet.job,
                                other_name);
                    printf("Remote ended successfully.\n");
                    exit(0);
                    }


/*
 *   Display the assigned job number.
 *
*/
Step_13:
            printf("\n");
            printf("Job # %s in queue on machine %s.\n",
                    job_packet.job,
                    other_name);
            printf("Remote ended successfully.\n");
            exit(0);
            }
```

E

Source Listing for the Postman Program

See Chapter 8, "Network Applications," for a discussion on what this program does, how it works, and how to use it.

```
/*      E-Mail  V1.00   (Postman)     */
/*      Written by Barry R. Nance     */

#pragma   inline

#include <stdio.h>
#include <dos.h>
#include <dir.h>
#include <mem.h>
#include <io.h>
#include <fcntl.h>
#include <errno.h>
#include <conio.h>
#include <bios.h>
#include <stdlib.h>
#include <string.h>
#include <stddef.h>
#include <stdarg.h>
#include <time.h>
#include <netbios.h>
```

```
void     send_mail(int first_item);
void     interrupt POST_routine(void);
void     process_mail(void);
int      fgetbuf(int fh);
int      fgetstring(int fh, char buff[], int max_chars);
void     beep(void);

#define TRUE        1
#define FALSE       0
#define LINEFEED    10
#define CR          13

#define ACK         1
#define HEADER      10
#define MAIL_DATA   20
#define MAIL_EOF    30
#define FILE_HDR    50
#define FILE_DATA   60
#define FILE_EOF    70
#define TRAILER     99

NCB      cancel_ncb;
NCB      add_name_ncb;
NCB      delete_name_ncb;
NCB      send_dg_ncb;
NCB      receive_dg_ncb;
NCB      temp_ncb;

void interrupt  (*int_5C_vector)(void);

char     machine_name[16];
char     mail_name[16];
char     caller[16];
char     addressee[16];
char     subject[31];
unsigned char name_number;

typedef struct
        {
        char    type;
        int     sequence;
        int     data_length;
        char    data[500];
        } MAIL_PACKET;
```

```
MAIL_PACKET packet_in;
MAIL_PACKET packet_out;

typedef struct
        {
        char    addressee[16];
        char    to_name[16];
        char    sender[16];
        char    maildate[17];
        char    subject[31];
        char    copy_flag;
        char    attachment_flag;
        char    attachment_name[66];
        char    cc_list[66];
        char    read_flag;
        char    crlf[2];
        } ENVELOPE;

ENVELOPE    envelope_in;
ENVELOPE    envelope_out;

int     errors_this_packet = 0;
int     send_handle = -1;
int     mail_handle = -1;
int     file_handle = -1;
int     expected_sequence = 1;
char    state = 0;

unsigned     paragraphs;
char         critical_error = FALSE;
int          i, j, k;
unsigned     temp1, temp2;
unsigned     temp_ax;
unsigned char temp_ah;
unsigned     old_ss, old_sp, our_ss, our_sp;
char         far *ourdta_ptr;
char         far *olddta_ptr;
char         far *our_mcb;
unsigned     far *our_mcb_size;
char         far *next_mcb;
unsigned     far *next_mcb_owner;
unsigned     ourpsp;
unsigned     oldpsp;
int          break_state;
```

```
void       interrupt (*oldint08)(void);
void       interrupt (*oldint09)(void);
void       interrupt (*oldint10)(void);
void       interrupt (*oldint13)(void);
void       interrupt (*oldint16)(void);
void       interrupt (*oldint1b)(void);
void       interrupt (*oldint1c)(void);
void       interrupt (*oldint23)(void);
void       interrupt (*oldint24)(void);
void       interrupt (*oldint28)(void);
char far            *kbd_flag_ptr;
unsigned char far   *indos_ptr;
unsigned char far   *indos2_ptr;
unsigned char     in_int08 = FALSE;
unsigned char     in_int09 = FALSE;
unsigned char     in_int10 = FALSE;
unsigned char     in_int13 = FALSE;
unsigned char     in_int16 = FALSE;
unsigned char     in_int28 = FALSE;
unsigned char     in_popup = FALSE;
unsigned char     de_install = FALSE;
unsigned char     mail_flag = FALSE;
unsigned char     new_mail  = FALSE;
unsigned char     incoming_msg = FALSE;
unsigned char     break_flag = FALSE;

unsigned char     trigger_outbasket= FALSE;
unsigned char     incoming_timeout = FALSE;
unsigned char     no_answer        = FALSE;

unsigned char     first_packet = FALSE;
long              tick_counter = 0l;

long              outbasket_alarm = 10920l;
long              incoming_alarm  = 0x0FFFFFFFl;
long              no_answer_alarm = 0x0FFFFFFFl;

char              mail_path[65];
char              io_buffer[512];
char              outname[81];
char              mailname[81];
char              filename[81];
char              string[101];
```

```
struct ffblk      find_block;
int               io_len    = 0;
unsigned int      fbufndx   = 2000;
unsigned int      fbufbytes = 0;
unsigned          *our_stack;


/* - - - - - - - - - - - - - - - - - - - - - - - - */


void    interrupt int08(void)
    {
    in_int08 = TRUE;
    oldint08();
    tick_counter++;
    enable();

    if (tick_counter > outbasket_alarm)
        {
        mail_flag = TRUE;
        trigger_outbasket = TRUE;
        }

    if (tick_counter > incoming_alarm)
        {
        mail_flag = TRUE;
        incoming_timeout = TRUE;
        }

    if (tick_counter > no_answer_alarm)
        {
        mail_flag = TRUE;
        no_answer = TRUE;
        }

    if (!de_install && !mail_flag)
        goto exit08;

    if (in_popup)
        goto exit08;

    if (in_int09 || in_int10 || in_int13 || in_int16 || in_int28)
        goto exit08;

    if (*indos_ptr != 0)
        goto exit08;
```

```
        if (*indos2_ptr != 0)
            goto exit08;

        outportb(0x20, 0x0b);
        if (inportb(0x20)) goto exit08;

        in_popup = TRUE;
        process_mail();
        in_popup = FALSE;

exit08:
    in_int08 = FALSE;
    }

void interrupt  int09 (void)
    {
    in_int09 = TRUE;
    oldint09();
    enable();
    in_int09 = FALSE;
    }

void    far int10(unsigned flags)
    {
    asm     pop  bp

    asm     push ax
    asm     push ds
    asm     mov  ax, DGROUP
    asm     mov  ds, ax
    asm     mov  _in_int10, 1
    asm     pop  ds
    asm     pop  ax

    asm     pushf
    asm     call    dword ptr cs:[0000h]
    asm     sti

    asm     push bp
    asm     mov  bp, sp
    asm     pushf
    asm     pop  flags
    asm     pop  bp
```

```
        asm     push ax
        asm     push ds
        asm     mov  ax, DGROUP
        asm     mov  ds, ax
        asm     mov  _in_int10, 0
        asm     pop  ds
        asm     pop  ax

        asm     iret
        }

void    far int13(unsigned flags)
        {
        asm     pop  bp

        asm     push ax
        asm     push ds
        asm     mov  ax, DGROUP
        asm     mov  ds, ax
        asm     mov  _in_int13, 1
        asm     pop  ds
        asm     pop  ax

        asm     pushf
        asm     call    dword ptr cs:[0004h]
        asm     sti

        asm     push bp
        asm     mov  bp, sp
        asm     pushf
        asm     pop  flags
        asm     pop  bp

        asm     push ax
        asm     push ds
        asm     mov  ax, DGROUP
        asm     mov  ds, ax
        asm     mov  _in_int13, 0
        asm     pop  ds
        asm     pop  ax

        asm     iret
        }
```

```
void     interrupt int16(unsigned bp,
                         unsigned di,
                         unsigned si,
                         unsigned ds,
                         unsigned es,
                         unsigned dx,
                         unsigned cx,
                         unsigned bx,
                         unsigned ax,
                         unsigned ip,
                         unsigned cs,
                         unsigned flags)
    {
    in_int16 = TRUE;
    enable();
    temp_ax = _AX;
    temp_ah = _AH;

    if (temp_ax == 'PO')
        {
        ax = 'po';
        es = FP_SEG( (void far *) mail_path);
        bx = FP_OFF( (void far *) mail_path);
        si = FP_OFF( (void far *) &outbasket_alarm);
        di = FP_OFF( (void far *) &new_mail);
        dx = FP_OFF( (void far *) &de_install);
        goto int16_exit;
        }

    if (temp_ah != 0)
        goto do_old16;

wait_for_key:
    _AH = 1;
    oldint16();
    asm     jz    check_flags

    goto do_old16;

check_flags:
    if (in_popup)
        oldint28();
```

```c
        if (!mail_flag && !de_install)
            goto wait_for_key;

        if (*indos_ptr != 0)
            goto wait_for_key;

        if (*indos2_ptr != 0)
            goto wait_for_key;

        outportb(0x20, 0x0b);
        if (inportb(0x20)) goto wait_for_key;

        in_popup = TRUE;
        process_mail();
        in_popup = FALSE;

        goto wait_for_key;

do_old16:
        _AX = temp_ax;
        oldint16();
        asm     pushf
        asm     pop flags
        ax      = _AX;
        bx      = _BX;
        cx      = _CX;
        dx      = _DX;

int16_exit:
        in_int16 = FALSE;
        }

void interrupt  int1b (void)
        {
        enable();
        break_flag = TRUE;
        }

void interrupt  int1c (void)
        {
        enable();
        }
```

```
void interrupt  int23 (void)
    {
    enable();
    }

void     interrupt int24(unsigned bp,
                         unsigned di,
                         unsigned si,
                         unsigned ds,
                         unsigned es,
                         unsigned dx,
                         unsigned cx,
                         unsigned bx,
                         unsigned ax,
                         unsigned ip,
                         unsigned cs,
                         unsigned flags)
    {
    temp1 = _AX;
    critical_error = TRUE;

    if (_osmajor < 3)
        ax = (temp1 & 0xFF00);
    else
        ax = (temp1 & 0xFF00) | 0x03;
    }

void     interrupt int28(void)
    {
    in_int28 = TRUE;
    oldint28();
    enable();

    if (!mail_flag && !de_install)
        goto exit28;

    if (in_popup)
        goto exit28;

    if (*indos_ptr > 1)
        goto exit28;

    if (*indos2_ptr != 0)
        goto exit28;
```

```
        outportb(0x20, 0x0b);
        if (inportb(0x20))
            goto exit28;

        in_popup = TRUE;
        process_mail();
        in_popup = FALSE;

exit28:
        in_int28 = FALSE;
        }

/* --------------------- */

/* - - - - - - - - - - - - - - - - - - - - - - - */
/*
 *  A function to call NetBIOS (via Int 5C).
 *
 *
*/
void    NetBios(NCB *ncb_ptr)
        {
        ncb_ptr->NCB_CMD_CPLT = 0xFF;

        _ES    = FP_SEG(ncb_ptr);
        _BX    = FP_OFF(ncb_ptr);
        _AX    = 0x0100;

        geninterrupt(0x5c);
        }

/* - - - - - - - - - - - - - - - - - - - - - - - */
/*
 *  Expand 'name' to be a 16 byte string, padded
 *  on the right with spaces, and null-terminated.
 *  (Doesn't work with 'permanent node names'.)
*/
void    expand_to_16_chars(char *name)
        {
        char *p;
        char tmp[17];
        int  i;
```

```
        memset(tmp, ' ', 15);
        p = name;
        i = 0;
        while (i < 15 && *p)
            {
            tmp[i] = *p;
            i++;
            p++;
            }
        tmp[15] = '\0';
        strcpy(name, tmp);
        }


/* - - - - - - - - - - - - - - - - - - - - - - */
/*
 *  Build the 'add_name' NCB and send it out
 *  across the network.
 *
 */
void    net_add_name(char *name)
        {
        memset(&add_name_ncb, 0, sizeof(NCB));
        add_name_ncb.NCB_COMMAND = ADD_NAME;
        strcpy(add_name_ncb.NCB_NAME, name);
        expand_to_16_chars(add_name_ncb.NCB_NAME);
        NetBios(&add_name_ncb);
        }


/* - - - - - - - - - - - - - - - - - - - - - - */
/*
 *    Build the 'delete_name' NCB
 *
 */
void    net_delete_name(char *name)
        {
        memset(&delete_name_ncb, 0, sizeof(NCB));
        delete_name_ncb.NCB_COMMAND = DELETE_NAME;
        strcpy(delete_name_ncb.NCB_NAME, name);
        expand_to_16_chars(delete_name_ncb.NCB_NAME);
        NetBios(&delete_name_ncb);
        }
```

```
/* - - - - - - - - - - - - - - - - - - - - - */
/*
 *      Build the 'cancel' NCB and send it out
 *      across the network.
 *
 */
void    net_cancel(NCB *np)
        {
        memset(&cancel_ncb, 0, sizeof(NCB));
        cancel_ncb.NCB_COMMAND = CANCEL;
        cancel_ncb.NCB_BUFFER_PTR = np;
        NetBios(&cancel_ncb);
        }

/* - - - - - - - - - - - - - - - - - - - - - - */
/*
 *      Build the 'receive datagram' NCB and send it out
 *      across the network.  When the operation completes,
 *      let NetBIOS call the POST routine to handle it.
 */
void    net_receive_dg_post(unsigned char name_num,
                          void interrupt (*post_function)(),
                          void *packet_ptr, int packet_len)
        {
        memset(&receive_dg_ncb, 0, sizeof(NCB));
        receive_dg_ncb.NCB_COMMAND = RECEIVE_DATAGRAM;
        receive_dg_ncb.NCB_NUM = name_num;
        receive_dg_ncb.NCB_LENGTH = packet_len;
        receive_dg_ncb.NCB_BUFFER_PTR = packet_ptr;
        receive_dg_ncb.POST_FUNC = post_function;
        NetBios(&receive_dg_ncb);
        }

/* - - - - - - - - - - - - - - - - - - - - - - */
/*
 *      Build the 'send datagram' NCB and send it out
 *      across the network.
 *
 */
void    net_send_dg(char *destination,
                  unsigned char name_num,
                  void *packet_ptr,
                  int packet_len)
```

```
        {
        memset(&send_dg_ncb, 0, sizeof(NCB));
        send_dg_ncb.NCB_COMMAND = SEND_DATAGRAM;
        send_dg_ncb.NCB_NUM = name_num;
        strcpy(send_dg_ncb.NCB_CALLNAME, destination);
        expand_to_16_chars(send_dg_ncb.NCB_CALLNAME);
        send_dg_ncb.NCB_LENGTH = packet_len;
        send_dg_ncb.NCB_BUFFER_PTR = packet_ptr;
        NetBios(&send_dg_ncb);
        }

/* - - - - - - - - - - - - - - - - - - - - - - - */


int     okay_to_unload(void)
        {
        next_mcb       = MK_FP( (ourpsp) + *our_mcb_size, 0);
        next_mcb_owner = MK_FP(  ourpsp  + *our_mcb_size, 1);

        if (   *next_mcb_owner == 0x0000
           || *next_mcb_owner == 0xffff
           || *next_mcb_owner <  ourpsp  )
                return TRUE;

        return FALSE;
        }

void    beep(void)
        {
        sound(880);
        delay(100);
        nosound();
        }

/* ----------------------- */


void    announce_mail(void)
        {
        char    linsav[160];
        int     n, cpos, ctype, vid_mode;

        _AH = 15;
        geninterrupt(0x10);
        _AH = 0;
        vid_mode = _AX;
        if (vid_mode != 2
```

```
            && vid_mode != 3
            && vid_mode != 7)
                {
                beep();
                delay(100);
                beep();
                delay(10);
                beep();
                return;
                }

    gettext(1, 25, 80, 25, linsav);
    _AH = 3;
    _BH = 0;
    geninterrupt(0x10);
    cpos  = _DX;
    ctype = _CX;

    gotoxy(1, 25);
    textcolor(BLACK);
    textbackground(LIGHTGRAY);
    cprintf("%-79.79s", "                          You have mail.");
    beep();

    for (n=0; n<20; n++)
        {
        delay(100);
        if (bioskey(1))
            {
            bioskey(0);
            break;
            }
        }

    puttext(1, 25, 80, 25, linsav);
    _DX = cpos;
    _AH = 2;
    _BH = 0;
    geninterrupt(0x10);
    _CX = ctype;
    _AH = 1;
    geninterrupt(0x10);
}
```

```
void     send_ack(void)
         {
         packet_in.type = ACK;
         packet_in.data_length = 0;
         net_send_dg(caller, name_number, &packet_in, 5);
         }

void     receive_incoming_mail(void)
         {
         long t;
         char filepart[10];
         char extpart[6];

         incoming_alarm = tick_counter + 1092l;

         switch (packet_in.type)
             {
             case HEADER :
                 {
                 strcpy(caller, receive_dg_ncb.NCB_CALLNAME);
                 state = 1;
                 first_packet = TRUE;
                 time(&t);
                 sprintf(string, "%ld", t);
                 strcpy(mailname, mail_path);
                 strcat(mailname, &string[3]);
                 strcat(mailname, ".IN");
                 mail_handle = _creat(mailname, 0);
                 if (mail_handle == -1)
                     return;
                 send_ack();
                 break;
                 }
             case MAIL_DATA :
                 {
                 write(mail_handle, packet_in.data,
                         packet_in.data_length);
                 if (first_packet)
                     {
                     memcpy(&envelope_in,
                             &packet_in.data, sizeof(ENVELOPE));
                     first_packet = FALSE;
                     }
```

```c
            send_ack();
            break;
            }
        case MAIL_EOF :
            {
            close(mail_handle);
            mail_handle = -1;
            send_ack();
            break;
            }
        case FILE_HDR :
            {
            fnsplit(envelope_in.attachment_name,
                    NULL, NULL, filepart, extpart);
            strcpy(filename, mail_path);
            strcat(filename, filepart);
            strcat(filename, extpart);
            file_handle = _creat(filename, 0);
            if (file_handle != -1)
                send_ack();
            break;
            }
        case FILE_DATA :
            {
            write(file_handle, packet_in.data,
                    packet_in.data_length);
            send_ack();
            break;
            }
        case FILE_EOF :
            {
            close(file_handle);
            file_handle = -1;
            send_ack();
            break;
            }
        case TRAILER :
            {
            new_mail = TRUE;
            incoming_alarm = 0x0FFFFFFFl;
            state = 0;
            expected_sequence = 0;
            send_ack();
            announce_mail();
```

```
                break;
                }
        default :
                {
                return;
                }
        };

        expected_sequence++;
        }

void    cancel_incoming_mail(void)
        {
        if (mail_handle != -1)
                {
                close(mail_handle);
                unlink(mailname);
                mail_handle = -1;
                }
        if (file_handle != -1)
                {
                close(file_handle);
                unlink(filename);
                file_handle = -1;
                }
        state = 0;
        expected_sequence = 1;
        }

void    send_next_packet(void)
        {
        int rc, retry_count;

        no_answer_alarm = tick_counter + 91l;
        errors_this_packet = 0;
        packet_out.sequence++;

        if (packet_out.type == TRAILER)
                {
                packet_out.type = HEADER;
                send_mail(0);
                return;
                }
```

```
if (packet_out.type == FILE_EOF)
    {
    retry_count = 0;
    do  rc = unlink(outname);
        while (rc != 0 && ++retry_count < 10);
    packet_out.type = TRAILER;
    net_send_dg(addressee, name_number, &packet_out, 5);
    return;
    }

if (packet_out.type == MAIL_EOF)
    {
    if (envelope_out.attachment_flag == 'N'
        || strcmp(envelope_out.addressee,
                envelope_out.sender) == 0)
        {
        retry_count = 0;
        do  rc = unlink(outname);
            while (rc != 0 && ++retry_count < 10);
        packet_out.type = TRAILER;
        net_send_dg(addressee, name_number, &packet_out, 5);
        return;
        }
    send_handle =
            open(envelope_out.attachment_name,
            O_RDWR | O_DENYALL);
    if (send_handle == -1)
        {
        retry_count = 0;
        do  rc = unlink(outname);
            while (rc != 0 && ++retry_count < 10);
        packet_out.type = TRAILER;
        net_send_dg(addressee, name_number, &packet_out, 5);
        return;
        }
    packet_out.type = FILE_HDR;
    packet_out.data_length = 0;
    net_send_dg(addressee, name_number, &packet_out, 5);
    return;
    }

if (packet_out.type == FILE_DATA
    || packet_out.type == FILE_HDR)
    {
```

```
            packet_out.type = FILE_DATA;
            packet_out.data_length
                = read(send_handle, packet_out.data, 500);
            if (packet_out.data_length == 0)
                {
                close(send_handle);
                send_handle = -1;
                packet_out.type = FILE_EOF;
                }
            net_send_dg(addressee, name_number,
                        &packet_out, packet_out.data_length+5);
            return;
            }

        if (packet_out.type == HEADER)
            {
            send_handle = open(outname, O_RDWR | O_DENYALL);
            if (send_handle == -1)
                return;
            }

        packet_out.type = MAIL_DATA;
        packet_out.data_length
            = read(send_handle, packet_out.data, 500);
        if (packet_out.data_length == 0)
            {
            close(send_handle);
            send_handle = -1;
            packet_out.type = MAIL_EOF;
            }

        net_send_dg(addressee, name_number,
                    &packet_out, packet_out.data_length+5);
        }

void    send_mail(int first_item)
        {
        int i, flag;

        if (!first_item && packet_out.type != HEADER)
            {
            if (++errors_this_packet < 10)
                {
                outbasket_alarm = tick_counter + 10920l;
```

```c
            no_answer_alarm = tick_counter + 91l;
            net_send_dg(addressee, name_number,
                        &packet_out, packet_out.data_length+5);
            return;
            }
        if (send_handle != -1)
            close(send_handle);
        }

    if (first_item)
        {
        strcpy(outname, mail_path);
        strcat(outname, "*.out");
        flag = findfirst(outname, &find_block, 0);
        }
    else
        flag = findnext(&find_block);

    if (flag != 0)
        {
        no_answer_alarm = 0x0FFFFFFFl;
        return;
        }

    outbasket_alarm = tick_counter + 10920l;
    no_answer_alarm = tick_counter + 91l;
    errors_this_packet = 0;

    packet_out.type = HEADER;
    packet_out.sequence = 1;
    packet_out.data_length = 0;

    strcpy(outname, mail_path);
    strcat(outname, find_block.ff_name);
    send_handle = open(outname, O_RDWR | O_DENYALL);
    if (send_handle == -1)
        return;
    i = read(send_handle, &envelope_out, sizeof(ENVELOPE));
    close(send_handle);
    send_handle = -1;
    if (i != sizeof(ENVELOPE))
        return;
    strcpy(addressee, envelope_out.addressee);
    strupr(addressee);
```

```
        net_send_dg(addressee, name_number, &packet_out, 5);
        }

void    post_office(void)
        {
        mail_flag = FALSE;

        if (incoming_msg)
            {
            incoming_msg = FALSE;
            if (receive_dg_ncb.NCB_CMD_CPLT != 0)
                {
                gotoxy(50, 1);
                cprintf("Mail error!  code = %d.",
                    (int) receive_dg_ncb.NCB_CMD_CPLT);
                gotoxy(1,1);
                cancel_incoming_mail();
                net_receive_dg_post(name_number,
                                    POST_routine,
                                    &packet_in,
                                    sizeof(MAIL_PACKET));
                }
            else
            if (packet_in.type == ACK)
                {
                send_next_packet();
                net_receive_dg_post(name_number,
                                    POST_routine,
                                    &packet_in,
                                    sizeof(MAIL_PACKET));
                }
            else
            if (packet_in.type == HEADER && state != 0)
                {
                net_receive_dg_post(name_number,
                                    POST_routine,
                                    &packet_in,
                                    sizeof(MAIL_PACKET));
                }
            else
            if (packet_in.sequence == expected_sequence)
                {
                receive_incoming_mail();
                net_receive_dg_post(name_number,
```

```
                                    POST_routine,
                                    &packet_in,
                                    sizeof(MAIL_PACKET));
            }
        else
        if (packet_in.sequence == expected_sequence - 1)
            {
            send_ack();
            net_receive_dg_post(name_number,
                                POST_routine,
                                &packet_in,
                                sizeof(MAIL_PACKET));
            }
        else
            {
            cancel_incoming_mail();
            net_receive_dg_post(name_number,
                                POST_routine,
                                &packet_in,
                                sizeof(MAIL_PACKET));
            }
        goto post_office_exit;
        }

    if (incoming_timeout)
        {
        incoming_timeout = FALSE;
        incoming_alarm   = 0xOFFFFFFFl;
        cancel_incoming_mail();
        goto post_office_exit;
        }

    if (no_answer)
        {
        no_answer = FALSE;
        send_mail(0);
        }

    if (trigger_outbasket)
        {
        trigger_outbasket = FALSE;
        outbasket_alarm   = tick_counter + 10920l;
        send_mail(1);
        }
```

```
post_office_exit:
        ;
        }

void    process_mail(void)
        {
        disable();
        old_ss = _SS;
        old_sp = _SP;
        _SS = our_ss;
        _SP = our_sp;
        enable();

        if (de_install)
            {
            if (!okay_to_unload())
                goto process_mail_exit;
            _AX = 0x5000;
            _BX = ourpsp;
            geninterrupt(0x21);
            setvect(0x08, oldint08);
            setvect(0x28, oldint28);
            setvect(0x09, oldint09);
            setvect(0x10, oldint10);
            setvect(0x13, oldint13);
            setvect(0x16, oldint16);
            net_cancel(&receive_dg_ncb);
            net_delete_name(mail_name);
            _ES = ourpsp;
            _BX = 0x2c;
            asm    mov es, es:[bx]
            _AH = 0x49;
            geninterrupt(0x21);
            _ES = ourpsp;
            _AH = 0x49;
            geninterrupt(0x21);
            asm    mov ax, word ptr next_mcb+2
            asm    inc ax
            asm    mov es, ax
            _AH = 0x49;
            geninterrupt(0x21);
            _AX = 0x4c00;
            geninterrupt(0x21);
            }
```

```
        break_state = getcbrk();
        oldint1b = getvect(0x1b);
        setvect(0x1b, int1b);
        oldint1c = getvect(0x1c);
        setvect(0x1c, int1c);
        oldint23 = getvect(0x23);
        setvect(0x23, int23);
        oldint24 = getvect(0x24);
        setvect(0x24, int24);
        olddta_ptr = getdta();
        setdta(ourdta_ptr);
        _AX = 0x5100;
        geninterrupt(0x21);
        oldpsp = _BX;
        _AX = 0x5000;
        _BX = ourpsp;
        geninterrupt(0x21);

        post_office();

        _AX = 0x5000;
        _BX = oldpsp;
        geninterrupt(0x21);
        setdta(olddta_ptr);
        setvect(0x24, oldint24);
        setvect(0x23, oldint23);
        setvect(0x1c, oldint1c);
        setvect(0x1b, oldint1b);
        setcbrk(break_state);

process_mail_exit:
        disable();
        _SS = old_ss;
        _SP = old_sp;
        enable();
        }

void    interrupt POST_routine(void)
        {
        incoming_msg = TRUE;
        mail_flag   = TRUE;
        }


/* ---------------------- */
```

```
void    main(int argc, char *argv[])
        {
        _fmode = O_BINARY;

        if (_osmajor < 2)
            {
            cprintf("\r\n");
            cprintf("Early versions of DOS not supported...\r\n");
            exit(1);
            }
        _AX = 'PO';
        geninterrupt(0x16);
        if (_AX == 'po')
            {
            cprintf("\r\n");
            cprintf("The PostMan program was already loaded.\r\n");
            exit(1);
            }

        if ( (our_stack = malloc(1000)) == NULL)
            {
            cprintf("\r\n");
            cprintf("Insufficient memory...\r\n");
            exit(1);
            }

        getcwd(mail_path, 64);
        if (mail_path[strlen(mail_path) - 1] != '\\')
            strcat(mail_path, "\\");

        our_ss    = _DS;
        our_sp    = FP_OFF( (void far *) our_stack) + 998;

        _AX = 0x3400;
        geninterrupt(0x21);
        temp2 = _BX;
        temp1 = _ES;
        indos_ptr = MK_FP(temp1, temp2);
        if (_osmajor == 2)
            indos2_ptr = MK_FP(temp1, temp2 + 1);
        else
            indos2_ptr = MK_FP(temp1, temp2 - 1);
```

```c
delay(10);
kbd_flag_ptr    = MK_FP(0x0040, 0x0017);

_DX = FP_OFF( (void far *) machine_name);
_AX = 0x5E00;
geninterrupt(0x21);
if (_CH == 0)
    {
    printf("ERROR.  Machine name not set.\n");
    exit(1);
    }
machine_name[14] = '\0';
strupr(machine_name);
strcpy(mail_name, "!");
strcat(mail_name, machine_name);

i = strlen(machine_name) - 1;
while (i > 0 && machine_name[i] == ' ')
    {
    machine_name[i] = '\0';
    i-;
    }

int_5C_vector = getvect(0x5C);
if (int_5C_vector == NULL)
    {
    printf("ERROR. NetBios not loaded (Int5C not present).\n");
    exit(1);
    }

memset(&temp_ncb, 0, sizeof(NCB));
temp_ncb.NCB_COMMAND = 0x7F;
NetBios(&temp_ncb);
if (temp_ncb.NCB_RETCODE != 03)
    {
    printf("ERROR. NetBios not loaded (No response from Int5C).\n");
    exit(1);
    }

printf("Adding mailing address (%s) to the network...", machine_name);
net_add_name(mail_name);
while (add_name_ncb.NCB_CMD_CPLT == 0xFF)
    ;
```

```
printf("\n");
if (add_name_ncb.NCB_CMD_CPLT != 0)
    {
    printf("ERROR.  NetBios said: %s.\n",
        net_error_message[(int)add_name_ncb.NCB_CMD_CPLT]);
    exit(1);
    }

name_number = add_name_ncb.NCB_NUM;
cprintf("\r\n\r\n");
cprintf("PostMan is loaded.\r\n");
cprintf("Run the 'MAIL' program to see your IN/OUT baskets.\r\n");

ourdta_ptr = getdta();
_AX = 0x5100;
geninterrupt(0x21);
ourpsp = _BX;
our_mcb         = MK_FP(ourpsp-1, 0);
our_mcb_size    = MK_FP(ourpsp-1, 3);
oldint08 = getvect(0x08);
oldint09 = getvect(0x09);
oldint10 = getvect(0x10);
oldint13 = getvect(0x13);
oldint16 = getvect(0x16);
oldint28 = getvect(0x28);

asm       mov ax, word ptr oldint10
asm       mov word ptr cs:[0000h], ax
asm       mov ax, word ptr oldint10+2
asm       mov word ptr cs:[0002h], ax
asm       mov ax, word ptr oldint13
asm       mov word ptr cs:[0004h], ax
asm       mov ax, word ptr oldint13+2
asm       mov word ptr cs:[0006h], ax

setvect(0x10, (void interrupt (*)()) int10);
setvect(0x13, (void interrupt (*)()) int13);
setvect(0x16, int16);
setvect(0x09, int09);
setvect(0x28, int28);
setvect(0x08, int08);
```

```
net_receive_dg_post(name_number,
                    POST_routine,
                    &packet_in,
                    sizeof(MAIL_PACKET));

paragraphs = (our_ss + (our_sp >> 4) + 1) - ourpsp;
keep(0, paragraphs);
}
```

Source Listing for the Electronic Mail Program

```
/*      E-Mail  V1.00  (Mail)       */
/*      Written by Barry R. Nance    */

#pragma   inline

#include <stdio.h>
#include <dos.h>
#include <dir.h>
#include <mem.h>
#include <io.h>
#include <fcntl.h>
#include <errno.h>
#include <conio.h>
#include <bios.h>
#include <stdlib.h>
#include <string.h>
#include <stddef.h>
#include <stdarg.h>
#include <time.h>

void    do_popup(void);
void    actual_popup(void);
int     get_vid_mode(void);
void    getkey(void);
```

```
void      vidtype(void);
int       kbdstring(char buff[], int max_chars);
int       fgetbuf(int fh);
int       fgetstring(int fh, char buff[], int max_chars);
void      message(char *s);
void      ask_yn(char *s);
void      beep(void);

#define    TRUE          1
#define    FALSE         0
#define    LT            <0
#define    EQ            ==0
#define    GT            >0
#define    NE            !=0
#define    ALT           56
#define    RIGHT_SHIFT   54
#define    BELL          7
#define    BS            8
#define    LINEFEED      10
#define    FORMFEED      12
#define    CR            13
#define    TAB           9
#define    BACKTAB       15
#define    CTRLQ         17
#define    CTRLS         19
#define    CTRLX         24
#define    CTRLZ         26
#define    ESC           27
#define    ALTX          45
#define    ALTC          46
#define    ALTS          31
#define    ALTD          32
#define    ALTE          18
#define    ALTF          33
#define    ALTT          20
#define    ALTM          50
#define    ALTH          35
#define    ALT1          120
#define    ALT2          121
#define    ALT3          122
#define    ALT4          123
#define    ALT5          124
#define    ALT6          125
#define    ALT7          126
```

```
#define    ALT8         127
#define    ALT9         128
#define    HOMEKEY      71
#define    ENDKEY       79
#define    UPKEY        72
#define    DOWNKEY      80
#define    PGUPKEY      73
#define    PGDNKEY      81
#define    LEFTKEY      75
#define    INSKEY       82
#define    RIGHTKEY     77
#define    DELKEY       83
#define    CTRLLEFTKEY  115
#define    CTRLRIGHTKEY 116
#define    F1           59
#define    F2           60
#define    F3           61
#define    F4           62
#define    F5           63
#define    F6           64
#define    F7           65
#define    F8           66
#define    F9           67
#define    F10          68
#define    ALT_F10      113

/* ------------------------------------------ */
char    machine_name[16];
char    mail_name[16];
char    addressee[16];
char    subject[31];

typedef struct
        {
        char    mailfile[13];
        char    mailname[16];
        char    maildate[17];
        char    subject[31];
        char    read_flag;
        } BASKET;

BASKET outbasket[50];
BASKET inbasket[50];
```

```
typedef struct
        {
        char    addressee[16];
        char    to_name[16];
        char    sender[16];
        char    maildate[17];
        char    subject[31];
        char    copy_flag;
        char    attachment_flag;
        char    attachment_name[66];
        char    cc_list[66];
        char    read_flag;
        char    crlf[2];
        } ENVELOPE;


ENVELOPE     envelope;

char     edit_area[1920];
char     *edit_line[24];


unsigned     paragraphs;
char         critical_error = FALSE;
int          i, j, k;
unsigned     temp1, temp2, temp3, temp4, temp5;
unsigned     temp_ax;
unsigned char temp_ah;
unsigned     old_ss, old_sp, our_ss, our_sp;
char         far *ourdta_ptr;
char         far *olddta_ptr;
char         far *our_mcb;
unsigned     far *our_mcb_size;
char         far *next_mcb;
unsigned     far *next_mcb_owner;
unsigned     ourpsp;
unsigned     oldpsp;
int          break_state;
void     interrupt (*oldint08)(void);
void     interrupt (*oldint09)(void);
void     interrupt (*oldint10)(void);
void     interrupt (*oldint13)(void);
void     interrupt (*oldint16)(void);
void     interrupt (*oldint1b)(void);
void     interrupt (*oldint1c)(void);
void     interrupt (*oldint23)(void);
```

```
void      interrupt (*oldint24)(void);
void      interrupt (*oldint28)(void);
char far           *kbd_flag_ptr;
unsigned char far  *indos_ptr;
unsigned char far  *indos2_ptr;
unsigned char     in_int08 = FALSE;
unsigned char     in_int09 = FALSE;
unsigned char     in_int10 = FALSE;
unsigned char     in_int13 = FALSE;
unsigned char     in_int16 = FALSE;
unsigned char     in_int28 = FALSE;
unsigned char     in_popup = FALSE;
unsigned char     hotkey_flag = FALSE;
unsigned char     de_install = FALSE;
unsigned char     break_flag = FALSE;

long far          *outbasket_alarm_ptr;
unsigned char far *postman_deinstall_ptr;
unsigned char far *new_mail_ptr;

char              mail_path[65];
int               in_count, out_count;
int               top_inbasket, top_outbasket;
int               inbasket_choice;
int               outbasket_choice;
int               which_basket;
int               redraw_list;
char              io_buffer[512];
char              filename[81];
char              string[101];
int               handle    = 0;
int               io_len    = 0;
unsigned int      fbufndx   = 2000;
unsigned int      fbufbytes = 0;

int               curr_item, old_item;
unsigned char     reg_fg = LIGHTGRAY;
unsigned char     reg_bg = BLUE;
unsigned char     msg_fg = BLACK;
unsigned char     msg_bg = CYAN;
int               cursor_save;
int               cursor_type;
unsigned          vidmode;
unsigned char     curr_vid_mode;
```

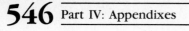

```
unsigned char    key_char;
unsigned char    extended_char;
char             app_screen [4000];
unsigned long    file_bytes;

char    *empty_basket[7] =
    {
    "                    ",
    "                    ",
    "                    ",
    "                    ",
    "       empty        ",
    "                    ",
    "                    "
    };

char    *one_letter[7] =
    {
    "                    ",
    "                    ",
    "                    ",
    "                    ",
    "                    ",
    "                    ",
    "                    "
    };

char    *multiple_letters[7] =
    {
    "                    ",
    "                    ",
    "                    ",
    "                    ",
    "                    ",
    "                    ",
    "                    "
    };
```

```
char      *send_icon[7] =
    {
"                                      ",
"      ===                             ",
"      =========                       ",
"      =========                       ",
"      =========                       ",
"      =========                       ",
"                                      "
    };

char      *list_icon[11] =
    {
"                                                      ",
"                                                      ",
"                                                      ",
"                                                      ",
"                                                      ",
"                                                      ",
"                                                      ",
"                                                      ",
"                                                      ",
"                                                      ",
"                                                      "
    };

unsigned               *our_stack;

/* - - - - - - - - - - - - - - - - - - - - - - - - - */

void    interrupt int08(void)
    {
    in_int08 = TRUE;
    oldint08();
    enable();

    if (!hotkey_flag && !de_install)
        goto exit08;

    if (in_popup)
        goto exit08;

    if (in_int09 || in_int10 || in_int13 || in_int16 || in_int28)
        goto exit08;
```

```c
        if (*indos_ptr != 0)
            goto exit08;

        if (*indos2_ptr != 0)
            goto exit08;

        outportb(0x20, 0x0b);
        if (inportb(0x20)) goto exit08;

        in_popup = TRUE;
        do_popup();
        in_popup = FALSE;

exit08:
        in_int08 = FALSE;
        }

void interrupt  int09 (void)
        {
        in_int09 = TRUE;
        oldint09();
        enable();
        if ( (*kbd_flag_ptr & 0x09) == 0x09 )
            {
            de_install = FALSE;
            hotkey_flag= TRUE;
            }
        in_int09 = FALSE;
        }

void    far int10(unsigned flags)
        {
        asm     pop  bp

        asm     push ax
        asm     push ds
        asm     mov  ax, DGROUP
        asm     mov  ds, ax
        asm     mov  _in_int10, 1
        asm     pop  ds
        asm     pop  ax

        asm     pushf
        asm     call    dword ptr cs:[0000h]
        asm     sti
```

```
        asm     push bp
        asm     mov  bp, sp
        asm     pushf
        asm     pop  flags
        asm     pop  bp

        asm     push ax
        asm     push ds
        asm     mov  ax, DGROUP
        asm     mov  ds, ax
        asm     mov  _in_int10, 0
        asm     pop  ds
        asm     pop  ax

        asm     iret
        }

void    far int13(unsigned flags)
        {
        asm     pop  bp

        asm     push ax
        asm     push ds
        asm     mov  ax, DGROUP
        asm     mov  ds, ax
        asm     mov  _in_int13, 1
        asm     pop  ds
        asm     pop  ax

        asm     pushf
        asm     call    dword ptr cs:[0004h]
        asm     sti

        asm     push bp
        asm     mov  bp, sp
        asm     pushf
        asm     pop  flags
        asm     pop  bp

        asm     push ax
        asm     push ds
        asm     mov  ax, DGROUP
        asm     mov  ds, ax
        asm     mov  _in_int13, 0
        asm     pop  ds
        asm     pop  ax
```

```
    asm     iret
    }

void    interrupt int16(unsigned bp,
                        unsigned di,
                        unsigned si,
                        unsigned ds,
                        unsigned es,
                        unsigned dx,
                        unsigned cx,
                        unsigned bx,
                        unsigned ax,
                        unsigned ip,
                        unsigned cs,
                        unsigned flags)
    {
    in_int16 = TRUE;
    enable();
    temp_ax = _AX;
    temp_ah = _AH;

    if (temp_ax == 'MA')
        {
        ax = 'ma';
        goto int16_exit;
        }

    if (temp_ah != 0)
        goto do_old16;

wait_for_key:
    _AH = 1;
    oldint16();
    asm     jz    popup_16
    goto do_old16;

popup_16:
    if (in_popup)
        {
        if (*new_mail_ptr)
            {
            ax = 0x0000;
            goto int16_exit;
            }
        oldint28();
        }
```

```
        if (!hotkey_flag && !de_install)
            goto wait_for_key;

        if (*indos_ptr != 0)
            goto wait_for_key;

        if (*indos2_ptr != 0)
            goto wait_for_key;

        outportb(0x20, 0x0b);
        if (inportb(0x20)) goto wait_for_key;

        in_popup = TRUE;
        do_popup();
        in_popup = FALSE;

        goto wait_for_key;

do_old16:
        _AX = temp_ax;
        oldint16();
        asm     pushf
        asm     pop flags
        ax      = _AX;
        bx      = _BX;
        cx      = _CX;
        dx      = _DX;

int16_exit:
        in_int16 = FALSE;
        }

void interrupt  int1b (void)
        {
        enable();
        break_flag = TRUE;
        }

void interrupt  int1c (void)
        {
        enable();
        }
```

552 Part IV: Appendixes

```c
void interrupt  int23 (void)
    {
    enable();
    }

void     interrupt int24(unsigned bp,
                         unsigned di,
                         unsigned si,
                         unsigned ds,
                         unsigned es,
                         unsigned dx,
                         unsigned cx,
                         unsigned bx,
                         unsigned ax,
                         unsigned ip,
                         unsigned cs,
                         unsigned flags)
    {
    temp1 = _AX;
    critical_error = TRUE;

    if (_osmajor < 3)
        ax = (temp1 & 0xFF00);
    else
        ax = (temp1 & 0xFF00) | 0x03;
    }

void     interrupt int28(void)
    {
    in_int28 = TRUE;
    oldint28();
    enable();

    if (!hotkey_flag && !de_install)
        goto exit28;

    if (in_popup)
        goto exit28;

    if (*indos_ptr > 1)
        goto exit28;

    if (*indos2_ptr != 0)
        goto exit28;
```

```
        outportb(0x20, 0x0b);
        if (inportb(0x20)) goto exit28;

        in_popup = TRUE;
        do_popup();
        in_popup = FALSE;

exit28:
        in_int28 = FALSE;
        }

    /* ------------------------------------------ */

void    beep(void)
        {
        sound(880);
        delay(100);
        nosound();
        }

void    save_screen(unsigned left, unsigned top,
                        unsigned right, unsigned bottom, char *buf,
                        int *curpos, int *curtype)
        {
        gettext(left, top, right, bottom, buf);

        _AH = 3;
        _BH = 0;
        geninterrupt(0x10);
        *curpos  = _DX;
        *curtype = _CX;
        }

void    restore_screen(unsigned left, unsigned top,
                        unsigned right, unsigned bottom, char *buf,
                        int *curpos, int *curtype)
        {
        puttext(left, top, right, bottom, buf);

        _DX = *curpos;
        _AH = 2;
        _BH = 0;
        geninterrupt(0x10);
        _CX = *curtype;
```

```
            _AH = 1;
            geninterrupt(0x10);
            }

void    getkey(void)
            {
            int     k;

            k               = bioskey(0);
            key_char        = k & 0x00FF;
            extended_char   = (k & 0xFF00) >> 8;
            }

int     kbdstring(char buff[], int max_chars)
            {
            int             i, j, insert_mode, ctype, res;
            unsigned char   row, col, trow, tcol;
            unsigned int    cblock;

            i = j = insert_mode = 0;
            if (get_vid_mode() == 7)
                cblock = 0x000D;
            else
                cblock = 0x0007;

            _AH = 3;
            _BH = 0;
            geninterrupt(0x10);
            ctype = _CX;
            col = wherex();
            row = wherey();

            textcolor(msg_fg);
            textbackground(msg_bg);
            cprintf("%-*s", max_chars-1, buff);
            gotoxy(col, row);

ks1:        getkey();
            tcol = wherex();
            trow = wherey();

            if (key_char == ESC)
                {
                memset(buff, 0, max_chars);
```

```
        res = 0;
        goto kbdstring_exit;
        }

if (key_char == 0)
    {
    if (extended_char == INSKEY)
        {
        if (insert_mode)
            {
            insert_mode = FALSE;
            _CX = ctype;
            _AH = 1;
            geninterrupt(0x10);
            }
        else
            {
            insert_mode = TRUE;
            _CX = cblock;
            _AH = 1;
            geninterrupt(0x10);
            }
        }
    else
    if (extended_char == HOMEKEY)
        {
        i = 0;
        gotoxy(col, row);
        }
    else
    if (extended_char == ENDKEY)
        {
        i = strlen(buff);
        gotoxy(col+strlen(buff), row);
        }
    else
    if (extended_char == DELKEY)
        {
        for (j = i; j < strlen(buff); j++)
            buff[j] = buff[j+1];
        buff[max_chars] = '\0';
        gotoxy(col, row);
        textcolor(msg_fg);
        textbackground(msg_bg);
```

```
            cprintf("%-*s", max_chars-1, buff);
            gotoxy(tcol, trow);
            }
        else
        if (extended_char == RIGHTKEY)
            {
            if (i < strlen(buff))
                {
                i++;
                gotoxy(tcol+1, trow);
                }
            }
        else
        if (extended_char == LEFTKEY)
            {
            if (i > 0)
                {
                i--;
                gotoxy(tcol-1, trow);
                }
            }
        }

    if (key_char == 0)
        goto ks1;

    if (key_char == BS)
        {
        if (i > 0)
            {
            i--;
            gotoxy(tcol-1, trow);
            }
        }

    if (key_char == CR)
        {
        res = 0;
        goto kbdstring_exit;
        }

    if (key_char < 32)
        goto ks1;
```

```
            if (i == max_chars-1)
                goto ks1;

            if (insert_mode)
                {
                for (j = strlen(buff)-1; j >= i; j--)
                    if (j < max_chars-2)
                        buff[j+1] = buff[j];
                buff[i++] = key_char;
                buff[max_chars] = '\0';
                _CX = ctype;
                _AH = 1;
                geninterrupt(0x10);
                gotoxy(col, row);
                textcolor(msg_fg);
                textbackground(msg_bg);
                cprintf("%-*s", max_chars-1, buff);
                gotoxy(++tcol, trow);
                _CX = cblock;
                _AH = 1;
                geninterrupt(0x10);
                }
            else
                {
                buff[i++] = key_char;
                textcolor(msg_fg);
                textbackground(msg_bg);
                cprintf("%c", key_char);
                }

            goto ks1;

    kbdstring_exit:
            _CX = ctype;
            _AH = 1;
            geninterrupt(0x10);

            return(res);
            }


    /***********************************/

    int     fgetbuf(int fh)
            {
```

```
fgetbuf01:
        if (fbufndx < fbufbytes)
            return( (int) io_buffer[fbufndx++]);

        io_len = read(fh, io_buffer, 512);
        if (io_len == -1)
            {
            fbufndx = 2000;
            return(-1);
            }

        fbufbytes = io_len;
        if (fbufbytes == 0)
            {
            fbufndx = 2000;
            return(-1);
            }

        fbufndx = 0;
        goto fgetbuf01;
        }


/**********************************/

int     fgetstring(int fh, char buff[], int max_chars)
        {
        int i, c;
        char ch;

        setmem(buff, max_chars, 0);
        i = 0;

fgs1:   if (i == max_chars - 1)
            {
            buff[i] = '\0';
            return(0);
            }
        if ( (c = fgetbuf(fh)) == -1 )
            {
            buff[i] = '\0';
            return(-1);
            }
        ch = (char) c;
        if (ch == CR)
            goto fgs1;
```

```
            if (ch == LINEFEED)
                {
                buff[i] = '\0';
                return(0);
                }

            buff[i++] = ch;
            goto fgs1;
            }

void    ask_yn(char *s)
        {
        char    linsav[160];
        int     cpos, ctype;

        save_screen(1,25,80,25, linsav, &cpos, &ctype);
        gotoxy(1, 25);
        cprintf("%-79.79s", " ");
        gotoxy(1, 25);
        cprintf("%s (y/n) ", s);

ask10:

        getkey();
        if ( key_char != 'y' && key_char != 'Y'
          && key_char != 'n' && key_char != 'N' )
            goto ask10;

        key_char |= 0x20;
        restore_screen(1,25,80,25, linsav, &cpos, &ctype);
        }

void    message(char *s)
        {
        char    linsav[160];
        int     cpos, ctype;

        save_screen(1,25,80,25, linsav, &cpos, &ctype);
        gotoxy(1, 25);
        cprintf("%-64.64s<Press a key.> ", s);
        getkey();
        restore_screen(1,25,80,25, linsav, &cpos, &ctype);
        }
```

```
int     okay_to_unload(void)
        {
        next_mcb       = MK_FP( (ourpsp) + *our_mcb_size, 0);
        next_mcb_owner = MK_FP(  ourpsp  + *our_mcb_size, 1);

        if (  *next_mcb_owner == 0x0000
           || *next_mcb_owner == 0xffff
           || *next_mcb_owner <  ourpsp  )
                return TRUE;

        return FALSE;
        }

void    show_help(int context)
        {
        int     help_handle, row, j;
        char    *p;
        char    str80[81];
        char    itemid[4];
        char    pageid[4];

        if ( (p = searchpath("mail.hlp")) == NULL || critical_error )
            {
            critical_error = FALSE;
            beep();
            message("ERROR.   'MAIL.HLP' not found.");
            return;
            }

        strcpy(str80, p);
        help_handle = open(str80, O_RDONLY | O_DENYNONE);
        if (help_handle < 1)
            {
            beep();
            message("ERROR.   'MAIL.HLP' not found.");
            return;
            }

        sprintf(itemid, "%1d", context);
        strcpy(pageid, "pg");
        strcat(pageid, itemid);
        i = fgetstring(help_handle, str80, 80);
        while (strcmp(str80, pageid) NE && i != -1)
            i = fgetstring(help_handle, str80, 80);
```

```
another_one:
        i = fgetstring(help_handle, str80, 80);
        row = 0;
        textcolor(msg_fg);
        textbackground(msg_bg);
        clrscr();

        while (strchr(str80, FORMFEED) == NULL && i != -1 && row < 24)
            {
            gotoxy(1, ++row);
            for (j=0; j<strlen(str80); j++)
                {
                if (str80[j] == 01)
                    {
                    textcolor(msg_bg);
                    textbackground(msg_fg);
                    }
                else
                if (str80[j] == 02)
                    {
                    textcolor(msg_fg);
                    textbackground(msg_bg);
                    }
                else
                    cprintf("%c", str80[j]);
                }
            i = fgetstring(help_handle, str80, 80);
            }

        if (i != -1)
            {
            message(" ESC to leave Help; any other key to see more Help. ");
            if (key_char != ESC)
                {
                i = fgetstring(help_handle, str80, 80);
                goto another_one;
                }
            }
        else
            message(" ");

        close(help_handle);
        }
```

```
int     get_vid_mode(void)
        {
        _AH = 15;
        geninterrupt(0x10);
        _AH = 0;
        return _AX;
        }

void    sort_basket(BASKET basket[], int count)
        {
        int     i, n1, n2;
        BASKET  temp;

        i = 0;
        while (i < count - 1)
            {
            n1 = atoi(basket[i].mailfile);
            n2 = atoi(basket[i+1].mailfile);
            if (n2 < n1)
                {
                temp = basket[i];
                basket[i] = basket[i+1];
                basket[i+1] = temp;
                i = 0;
                }
            else
                {
                i++;
                }
            }
        }

void    check_inbasket(void)
        {
        int  i, flag;
        struct ffblk findblock;

        for (i=0; i<50; i++)
            memset(&inbasket[i], 0, sizeof(BASKET));

        in_count = 0;
        strcpy(filename, mail_path);
        strcat(filename, "*.in");
        flag = findfirst(filename, &findblock, 0);
        while (flag == 0 && in_count < 50)
```

```
              {
              strcpy(inbasket[in_count].mailfile, findblock.ff_name);
              strcpy(filename, mail_path);
              strcat(filename, findblock.ff_name);
              handle = open(filename, O_RDWR | O_DENYALL);
              if (handle == -1)
                  return;
              i = read(handle, &envelope, sizeof(ENVELOPE));
              if (i == sizeof(ENVELOPE))
                  {
                  strcpy(inbasket[in_count].mailname,
                          &envelope.sender[1]);
                  strcpy(inbasket[in_count].maildate,
                          envelope.maildate);
                  strcpy(inbasket[in_count].subject,
                          envelope.subject);
                  inbasket[in_count].read_flag = envelope.read_flag;
                  }
              close(handle);
              in_count++;
              flag = findnext(&findblock);
              }
          sort_basket(inbasket, in_count);
          }

void      check_outbasket(void)
          {
          int  i, flag;
          struct ffblk findblock;

          for (i=0; i<50; i++)
              memset(&outbasket[i], 0, sizeof(BASKET));

          out_count = 0;
          strcpy(filename, mail_path);
          strcat(filename, "*.out");
          flag = findfirst(filename, &findblock, 0);
          while (flag == 0 && out_count < 50)
              {
              strcpy(outbasket[out_count].mailfile, findblock.ff_name);
              strcpy(filename, mail_path);
              strcat(filename, findblock.ff_name);
              handle = open(filename, O_RDWR | O_DENYALL);
              if (handle == -1)
                  return;
```

```
        i = read(handle, &envelope, sizeof(ENVELOPE));
        if (i == sizeof(ENVELOPE))
            {
            strcpy(outbasket[out_count].mailname,
                    &envelope.addressee[1]);
            strcpy(outbasket[out_count].maildate,
                    envelope.maildate);
            strcpy(outbasket[out_count].subject,
                    envelope.subject);
            outbasket[out_count].read_flag = envelope.read_flag;
            }
        close(handle);
        out_count++;
        flag = findnext(&findblock);
        }
    sort_basket(outbasket, out_count);
    }

void    get_attached_filename(void)
        {
        int h;

get_name:
        textcolor(reg_fg);
        textbackground(reg_bg);
        clrscr();

        textcolor(msg_fg);
        textbackground(msg_bg);
        gotoxy(1, 25);
        cprintf(
" Enter filename to attach (if any), including drive:\path. Then press enter. ");

        gotoxy(1, 1);
        envelope.attachment_flag = 'N';
        cprintf("Attach file: ");
        kbdstring(envelope.attachment_name, 65);

        textcolor(reg_fg);
        textbackground(reg_bg);
        gotoxy(1, 25);
        clreol();
```

```
            if (strlen(envelope.attachment_name) > 0)
                {
                h = open(envelope.attachment_name, O_RDONLY);
                if (h == -1)
                    {
                    textcolor(msg_fg);
                    textbackground(msg_bg);
                    gotoxy(2, 25);
                    if (errno == ENOENT)
                        cprintf("ERROR. No file by that name (press a key)");
                    else
                        cprintf("ERROR. Cannot access file.  (press a key)");
                    getkey();
                    goto get_name;
                    }
                close(h);
                envelope.attachment_flag = 'Y';
                }
        }


void     editor(char *filename)
         {
         int     i, column, row, ed_handle, count, insert_mode;
         char    CRLF[3] = {13, 10, 0};
         char    cc_sequence[2] = {'A', 0};
         char    cc_string[66];
         char    current_date[30];
         char    cc_filename[81];
         long    t;
         char    *p;

         textcolor(reg_fg);
         textbackground(reg_bg);
         clrscr();

         for (row=0; row<24; row++)
             memset(edit_line[row], 0, 80);
         ed_handle = open(filename, O_RDWR | O_DENYALL);
         fbufndx = 2000;
         if (ed_handle == -1)
             {
             if (errno != ENOENT)
                 {
                 clrscr();
                 gotoxy(1, 1);
```

```
                cprintf("I/O Error; can't open file.  (Press a key)");
                getkey();
                return;
                }
        memset(&envelope, 0, sizeof(ENVELOPE));
        gotoxy(1, 1);
        cprintf("TO: ");
        memset(addressee, 0, 16);
        kbdstring(addressee, 15);
        if (strlen(addressee) == 0)
                {
                textcolor(reg_fg);
                textbackground(reg_bg);
                clrscr();
                return;
                }
        textcolor(reg_fg);
        textbackground(reg_bg);
        gotoxy(1, 3);
        cprintf("SUBJECT: ");
        memset(subject, 0, 31);
        kbdstring(subject, 30);
        strcpy(edit_line[0], "TO: ");
        strcat(edit_line[0], addressee);
        strcpy(edit_line[1], "SUBJECT: ");
        strcat(edit_line[1], subject);
        textcolor(reg_fg);
        textbackground(reg_bg);
        clrscr();
        gotoxy(1, 1);
        cprintf("%s", edit_line[0]);
        gotoxy(1, 2);
        cprintf("%s", edit_line[1]);
        }
   else
        {
        i = read(ed_handle, &envelope, sizeof(ENVELOPE));
        if (i != sizeof(ENVELOPE))
                {
                close(ed_handle);
                clrscr();
                gotoxy(1, 1);
                cprintf("Error...can't read envelope. (Press a key)");
                getkey();
```

```
                        return;
                        }
                if (envelope.copy_flag == 'Y')
                        {
                        textcolor(reg_fg);
                        textbackground(reg_bg);
                        clrscr();
                        textcolor(msg_fg);
                        textbackground(msg_bg);
                        gotoxy(1, 25);
                        cprintf(
    " This is a CC: copy.  Respecify the destination name, then press enter. ");
                        gotoxy(1, 3);
                        cprintf("Destination: ");
                        memset(addressee, 0, 16);
                        strcpy(addressee, &envelope.addressee[1]);
                        kbdstring(addressee, 15);
                        textcolor(reg_fg);
                        textbackground(reg_bg);
                        gotoxy(1, 25);
                        clreol();
                        if (strlen(addressee) == 0)
                                {
                                close(ed_handle);
                                return;
                                }
                        memset(envelope.addressee, 0, 16);
                        strcpy(envelope.addressee, "!");
                        strcat(envelope.addressee, addressee);
                        while (strlen(envelope.addressee) < 15)
                                strcat(envelope.addressee, " ");
                        strupr(envelope.addressee);
                        lseek(ed_handle, 0L, SEEK_SET);
                        write(ed_handle, &envelope, sizeof(ENVELOPE));
                        close(ed_handle);
                        return;
                        }
                strcpy(edit_line[0], "TO: ");
                strcat(edit_line[0], &envelope.addressee[1]);
                strcpy(edit_line[1], "SUBJECT: ");
                strcat(edit_line[1], envelope.subject);
                textcolor(reg_fg);
                textbackground(reg_bg);
                clrscr();
```

```
        gotoxy(1, 1);
        cprintf("%s", edit_line[0]);
        gotoxy(1, 2);
        cprintf("%s", edit_line[1]);
        fbufndx = 2000;
        for (row=2; row<24; row++)
            {
            i = fgetstring(ed_handle, edit_line[row], 80);
            if (i == -1) break;
            gotoxy(1, row + 1);
            cprintf("%s", edit_line[row]);
            }
        close(ed_handle);
        }
    row = 4; column = 1; insert_mode = 0;

    textcolor(msg_fg);
    textbackground(msg_bg);
    gotoxy(2, 25);
    cprintf(
"ESC-Quit F2-Save   F4-Erase EOL   F5-Insert Line   F10-
Delete Line            ");
    textcolor(reg_fg);
    textbackground(reg_bg);

    window(1, 1, 80, 24);

editor_keypress:
    gotoxy(column, row);
    getkey();

    if (key_char == ESC)
        {
        window(1, 1, 80, 25);
        gotoxy(1, 25);
        clreol();
        gotoxy(2, 25);
        textcolor(msg_fg);
        textbackground(msg_bg);
        cprintf("Are you sure? (y/n) ");
        getkey();
        if (key_char == 'Y' || key_char == 'y')
            {
            textcolor(reg_fg);
```

```
                        textbackground(reg_bg);
                        clrscr();
                        return;
                        }
                textcolor(msg_fg);
                textbackground(msg_bg);
                gotoxy(2, 25);
                cprintf(
"ESC-Quit  F2-Save   F4-Erase EOL    F5-Insert Line    F10-
Delete Line             ");
                insert_mode = 0;
                textcolor(reg_fg);
                textbackground(reg_bg);
                window(1, 1, 80, 24);
                }
          else
          if (key_char >= 32 && key_char <= 127)
              {
              if (row == 1 && column < 5)
                  goto editor_keypress;
              if (row == 2 && column < 10)
                  goto editor_keypress;
              if (row == 24 && column == 80)
                  goto editor_keypress;
              while (strlen(edit_line[row-1]) < column - 1)
                  strcat(edit_line[row-1], " ");
              if (insert_mode)
                  {
                  if (edit_line[row-1][78] != ' '
                     && edit_line[row-1][78] != '\0')
                      goto editor_keypress;
                  for (i=78; i>=column-1; i--)
                      edit_line[row-1][i+1] = edit_line[row-1][i];
                  edit_line[row-1][column-1] = key_char;
                  edit_line[row-1][79] = '\0';
                  gotoxy(1, row);
                  cprintf("%s", edit_line[row-1]);
                  }
              else
                  {
                  edit_line[row-1][column-1] = key_char;
                  cprintf("%c", key_char);
                  }
```

```
        if (column < 80)
            {
            column++;
            }
        else
        if (row < 24)
            {
            column = 1;
            row++;
            }
    }
else
if (key_char == CR)
    {
    if (insert_mode && row < 24)
        {
        if (row == 1 && column < 5)
            goto editor_keypress;
        if (row == 2 && column < 10)
            goto editor_keypress;
        for (i=23; i>row; i--)
            strcpy(edit_line[i], edit_line[i-1]);
        memset(edit_line[row], 0, 80);
        if (edit_line[row-1][column-1] != '\0')
            strcpy(edit_line[row], &edit_line[row-1][column-1]);
        for (i=column-1; i<80; i++)
            edit_line[row-1][i] = '\0';
        clreol();
        row++;
        column = 1;
        gotoxy(1, row);
        insline();
        gotoxy(1, row);
        cprintf("%s", edit_line[row-1]);
        }
    else
        {
        if (row < 24)
            {
            column = 1;
            row++;
            }
        }
    }
```

```
              else
              if (key_char == BS)
                  {
                  key_char = 0;
                  extended_char = LEFTKEY;
                  }
              else
              if (key_char == TAB && column < 72)
                  {
                  column += 4;
                  }

      if (key_char == 0)
          {
          if (extended_char == F2)
              {
              window(1, 1, 80, 25);
              ed_handle = _creat(filename, 0);
              if (ed_handle == -1)
                  {
                  clrscr();
                  gotoxy(1, 1);
                  cprintf("I/O Error; can't open file.  (Press a key)");
                  getkey();
                  return;
                  }
              count = 24;
              for (row=23; row >1; row--)
                  {
                  if (strlen(edit_line[row]) > 0)
                      break;
                  count--;
                  }
              edit_line[0][19] = '\0';
              strupr(edit_line[0]);
              time(&t);
              strcpy(current_date, ctime(&t));
              current_date[16] = '\0';
              edit_line[1][39] = '\0';
              get_attached_filename();
              textcolor(msg_fg);
              textbackground(msg_bg);
              gotoxy(1, 25);
              cprintf(
```

```
" Enter CC: names (if any) separated by commas or spaces.  Then press enter. ");
                gotoxy(1, 3);
                cprintf("CC: ");
                kbdstring(envelope.cc_list, 65);
                textcolor(reg_fg);
                textbackground(reg_bg);
                gotoxy(1, 25);
                clreol();
                strcpy(envelope.addressee, "!");
                strcat(envelope.addressee, &edit_line[0][4]);
                while (strlen(envelope.addressee) < 15)
                    strcat(envelope.addressee, " ");
                strcpy(envelope.to_name, &envelope.addressee[1]);
                strcpy(envelope.sender, mail_name);
                strcpy(envelope.maildate, current_date);
                strcpy(envelope.subject, &edit_line[1][9]);
                envelope.read_flag = 'N';
                envelope.copy_flag = 'N';
                envelope.crlf[0] = 13;
                envelope.crlf[1] = 10;
                i = write(ed_handle, &envelope, sizeof(ENVELOPE));
                for (row=2; row<count; row++)
                    {
                    i = strlen(edit_line[row]);
                    if (i > 0)
                        write(ed_handle, edit_line[row], i);
                    write(ed_handle, CRLF, 2);
                    }
                write(ed_handle, CRLF, 2);
                close(ed_handle);
                strcpy(cc_string, envelope.cc_list);
                cc_sequence[0] = 'A';
                time(&t);
                p = strtok(cc_string, " ,");
                while (p != NULL && strlen(p) < 16)
                    {
                    strcpy(envelope.addressee, "!");
                    strcat(envelope.addressee, p);
                    while (strlen(envelope.addressee) < 15)
                        strcat(envelope.addressee, " ");
                    strupr(envelope.addressee);
                    envelope.copy_flag = 'Y';
                    sprintf(current_date, "%ld", t);
                    strcpy(cc_filename, mail_path);
```

```
                    strcat(cc_filename, &current_date[3]);
                    strcat(cc_filename, cc_sequence);
                    cc_sequence[0]++;
                    strcat(cc_filename, ".OUT");
                    ed_handle = _creat(cc_filename, 0);
                    write(ed_handle, &envelope, sizeof(ENVELOPE));
                    for (row=2; row<count; row++)
                        {
                        i = strlen(edit_line[row]);
                        if (i > 0)
                            write(ed_handle, edit_line[row], i);
                        write(ed_handle, CRLF, 2);
                        }
                    write(ed_handle, CRLF, 2);
                    close(ed_handle);
                    p = strtok(NULL, " ,");
                    }
                which_basket = 0;
                redraw_list = TRUE;
                *outbasket_alarm_ptr = 0l;
                clrscr();
                return;
                }
        else
        if (extended_char == F4)
            {
            if (row == 1 && column < 5)
                goto editor_keypress;
            if (row == 2 && column < 10)
                goto editor_keypress;
            for (i=column-1; i<80; i++)
                edit_line[row-1][i] = '\0';
            clreol();
            }
        else
        if (extended_char == F5)
            {
            if (row < 3)
                goto editor_keypress;
            for (i=23; i>row-1; i--)
                strcpy(edit_line[i], edit_line[i-1]);
            memset(edit_line[row-1], 0, 80);
            insline();
            }
```

```
        else
        if (extended_char == F10)
            {
            if (row < 3)
                goto editor_keypress;
            for (i=row-1; i<24; i++)
                strcpy(edit_line[i], edit_line[i+1]);
            memset(edit_line[23], 0, 80);
            delline();
            }
        else
        if (extended_char == INSKEY)
            {
            insert_mode = ~insert_mode;
            window(1, 1, 80, 25);
            gotoxy(72, 25);
            textcolor(msg_fg);
            textbackground(msg_bg);
            if (insert_mode)
                cprintf("INSERT");
            else
                cprintf("      ");
            textcolor(reg_fg);
            textbackground(reg_bg);
            window(1, 1, 80, 24);
            }
        else
        if (extended_char == HOMEKEY)
            {
            if (row == 1)
                column = 5;
            else
            if (row == 2)
                column = 10;
            else
            column = 1;
            }
        else
        if (extended_char == ENDKEY)
            {
            column = strlen(edit_line[row-1]) + 1;
            }
        else
        if (extended_char == DELKEY)
            {
```

```
                if (row == 1 && column < 5)
                    goto editor_keypress;
                if (row == 2 && column < 10)
                    goto editor_keypress;
                for (i=column-1; i<79; i++)
                    edit_line[row-1][i] = edit_line[row-1][i+1];
                edit_line[row-1][79] = '\0';
                gotoxy(1, row);
                clreol();
                cprintf("%s", edit_line[row-1]);
                }
        else
        if (extended_char == RIGHTKEY)
            {
            if (column < 80)
                {
                column++;
                }
            else
                {
                if (row < 24)
                    {
                    column = 1;
                    row++;
                    }
                }
            }
        else
        if (extended_char == LEFTKEY)
            {
            if (column > 1)
                {
                column--;
                }
            else
                {
                if (row > 1)
                    {
                    row--;
                    column = strlen(edit_line[row-1]) + 1;
                    }
                }
            }
```

```
            else
            if (extended_char == UPKEY)
                {
                if (row > 1)
                    row--;
                }
            else
            if (extended_char == DOWNKEY)
                {
                if (row < 24)
                    row++;
                }
            }

        goto editor_keypress;
        }

void    browse(char *filename)
        {
        int     i, j, count, row, browse_handle;
        char    formfeed = 12;
        char    CRLF[3] = {13, 10, 0};
        long    t;

open_browse:
        textcolor(reg_fg);
        textbackground(reg_bg);
        clrscr();

    for (row=0; row<24; row++)
        memset(edit_line[row], 0, 80);
    browse_handle = open(filename, O_RDWR | O_DENYALL);
    if (browse_handle == -1)
        {
        clrscr();
        gotoxy(1, 1);
        cprintf("I/O Error; can't open file.  (Press a key)");
        getkey();
        return;
        }
    i = read(browse_handle, &envelope, sizeof(ENVELOPE));
    if (i != sizeof(ENVELOPE))
        {
        clrscr();
        gotoxy(1, 1);
```

```
            cprintf("Error...can't read envelope. (Press a key)");
            getkey();
            return;
            }
        sprintf(edit_line[0],
            "TO: %-16.16s   FROM: %-16.16s   DATE: %-16.16s",
                    envelope.to_name,
                    &envelope.sender[1],
                    envelope.maildate);
        sprintf(edit_line[1], "SUBJECT: %s", envelope.subject);
        textcolor(reg_fg);
        textbackground(reg_bg);
        clrscr();
        gotoxy(1, 1);
        cprintf("%s", edit_line[0]);
        gotoxy(1, 2);
        cprintf("%s", edit_line[1]);
        fbufndx = 2000;
        for (row=2; row<24; row++)
            {
            i = fgetstring(browse_handle, edit_line[row], 80);
            if (i == -1) break;
            gotoxy(1, row + 1);
            cprintf("%s", edit_line[row]);
            }
        if (envelope.read_flag == 'N')
            {
            envelope.read_flag = 'Y';
            lseek(browse_handle, 0l, SEEK_SET);
            write(browse_handle, &envelope, sizeof(ENVELOPE));
            }
        close(browse_handle);

        gotoxy(1, 24);
        if (strlen(envelope.cc_list) > 0)
            cprintf("CC: %s", envelope.cc_list);

        gotoxy(70, 24);
        if (envelope.attachment_flag == 'Y')
            cprintf("ATTACHMENT");

browse_prompt:
        textcolor(msg_fg);
        textbackground(msg_bg);
        gotoxy(2, 25);
```

```
        if (which_basket == 0)
            {
            cprintf(
" ESC - Exit    D - Delete Mail    S - Save as file    P - Print   R - Reply ");
            }
        else
            {
            cprintf(
"     ESC - Exit         C - Change Contents       D - Delete This Mail      ");
            }

        textcolor(reg_fg);
        textbackground(reg_bg);

browse_key:
        gotoxy(80, 25);
        getkey();

        if (key_char == ESC)
            {
            clrscr();
            return;
            }

        if (key_char == 'd' || key_char == 'D')
            {
            unlink(filename);
            clrscr();
            return;
            }

        if (which_basket == 1)
            if (key_char == 'c' || key_char == 'C')
                {
                editor(filename);
                clrscr();
                return;
                }

        if (which_basket == 0)
            {
            if (key_char == 'r' || key_char == 'R')
                {
                strcpy(string, envelope.addressee);
```

```
        strcpy(envelope.addressee, envelope.sender);
        strcpy(envelope.sender, string);
        envelope.attachment_flag = 'N';
        memset(envelope.attachment_name, 0, 66);
        time(&t);
        sprintf(string, "%ld", t);
        strcpy(io_buffer, mail_path);
        strcat(io_buffer, &string[3]);
        strcat(io_buffer, ".OUT");
        strcpy(string, io_buffer);
        handle = _creat(string, 0);
        if (handle == -1)
            {
            textcolor(msg_fg);
            textbackground(msg_bg);
            gotoxy(2, 25);
            clreol();
            cprintf(" Error.  Could not create file. ");
            textcolor(reg_fg);
            textbackground(reg_bg);
            getkey();
            goto open_browse;
            }
        write(handle, &envelope, sizeof(ENVELOPE));
        close(handle);
        editor(string);
        goto open_browse;
        }
    if (key_char == 's' || key_char == 'S')
        {
        textcolor(reg_fg);
        textbackground(reg_bg);
        memset(filename, 0, 81);
        gotoxy(2, 25);
        clreol();
        cprintf("Save as: ");
        kbdstring(filename, 65);
        textcolor(reg_fg);
        textbackground(reg_bg);
        if (strlen(filename) == 0)
            goto browse_prompt;
        handle = _creat(filename, 0);
        if (handle == -1)
            {
            textcolor(msg_fg);
```

```
                textbackground(msg_bg);
                gotoxy(2, 25);
                clreol();
                cprintf(" Error.  Could not create file. ");
                textcolor(reg_fg);
                textbackground(reg_bg);
                getkey();
                goto browse_prompt;
                }
            count = 24;
            for (i=23; i>1; i--)
                {
                if (strlen(edit_line[i]) > 0)
                    break;
                count--;
                }
            for (i=0; i<count; i++)
                {
                j = strlen(edit_line[i]);
                if (j > 0)
                    write(handle, edit_line[i], j);
                write(handle, CRLF, 2);
                }
            write(handle, CRLF, 2);
            close(handle);
            goto browse_prompt;
            }
    if (key_char == 'p' || key_char == 'P')
        {
        handle = open("LPT1", O_WRONLY);
        if (handle == -1)
            {
            textcolor(msg_fg);
            textbackground(msg_bg);
            gotoxy(2, 25);
            clreol();
            cprintf(" Error.  Could not open printer. ");
            textcolor(reg_fg);
            textbackground(reg_bg);
            getkey();
            goto browse_prompt;
            }
        count = 24;
        for (i=23; i>1; i--)
```

```
                {
                if (strlen(edit_line[i]) > 0)
                    break;
                count--;
                }
            for (i=0; i<count; i++)
                {
                j = strlen(edit_line[i]);
                if (j > 0)
                    write(handle, edit_line[i], j);
                write(handle, CRLF, 2);
                }
            write(handle, CRLF, 2);
            write(handle, &formfeed, 1);
            close(handle);
            goto browse_prompt;
            }
        }

    goto browse_key;
    }

void    show_icon(int x, int y, char *icon[])
        {
        int i;

        for (i=0; i<7; i++)
            {
            gotoxy(x, y++);
            cprintf("%s", icon[i]);
            }
        }

void    actual_popup(void)
        {
        long t;

        de_install = FALSE;
        hotkey_flag= FALSE;

reset_trays:
        redraw_list= TRUE;
        inbasket_choice = 0;
        outbasket_choice = 0;
```

```
        top_inbasket = 0;
        top_outbasket = 0;

show_menu:
        textcolor(reg_fg);
        textbackground(reg_bg);
        clrscr();
        gotoxy(2, 1);
        cprintf(
"          ,  (cursor keys) move light bar.   selects item.          ");

        gotoxy(2, 2);
        cprintf(
"_____");

show_prompts:
        textcolor(reg_fg);
        textbackground(reg_bg);
        gotoxy(2, 24);
        cprintf(
"_____");
        gotoxy(2, 25);
        cprintf(
" F1-Help    S-Send Mail    I-Inbasket    O-Outbasket    X-Exit    F10-Unload ");

show_send_item:
        show_icon(2, 3, send_icon);
        gotoxy(9, 10);
        cprintf("S)end");

show_list:
        for (i=0, j=12; i<11; i++)
            {
            gotoxy(4, j++);
            cprintf("%s", list_icon[i]);
            }

show_baskets:
        *new_mail_ptr = FALSE;
        check_inbasket();
        check_outbasket();
        textcolor(reg_fg);
        textbackground(reg_bg);
```

```
if (in_count == 0)
    show_icon(25, 3, empty_basket);
else
if (in_count == 1)
    show_icon(25, 3, one_letter);
else
    show_icon(25, 3, multiple_letters);
gotoxy(28, 10);
cprintf("I)n (%2d items)", in_count);

if (out_count == 0)
    show_icon(52, 3, empty_basket);
else
if (out_count == 1)
    show_icon(52, 3, one_letter);
else
    show_icon(52, 3, multiple_letters);
gotoxy(54, 10);
cprintf("O)ut (%2d undeliv.)", out_count);

textcolor(reg_bg);
textbackground(reg_fg);
gotoxy(30, 3);
cprintf("E-Mail for %s", machine_name);

if (which_basket == 0)
    {
    textcolor(reg_fg);
    textbackground(reg_bg);
    gotoxy(2, 23);
    cprintf("%-79.79s", " ");
    gotoxy(6, 13);
    textcolor(reg_bg);
    textbackground(reg_fg);
    cprintf(" %-16.16s   %-30.30s   %-17.17s",
        "FROM", "SUBJECT", "DATE");
    gotoxy(6, 21);
    cprintf("%-25.25s %-44.44s",
        " ", "INBASKET STATUS");
    window(6, 14, 75, 20);
    textcolor(msg_fg);
    textbackground(msg_bg);
    if (redraw_list) clrscr();
    if (in_count == 0)
```

```
                    {
                    gotoxy(28, 1);
                    cprintf("<empty>");
                    }
            else
                    {
                    for (i=0, j=1; i<7; i++)
                        {
                        k = i + top_inbasket;
                        if (k == in_count) break;
                        gotoxy(1, j++);
                        if (k == inbasket_choice)
                            {
                            textcolor(msg_bg);
                            textbackground(msg_fg);
                            }
                        else
                            {
                            textcolor(msg_fg);
                            textbackground(msg_bg);
                            }
                        if (inbasket[k].read_flag == 'Y')
                            cprintf("*");
                        else
                            cprintf(" ");
                        cprintf("%-16.16s   %-30.30s   %-16.16s",
                            inbasket[k].mailname,
                            inbasket[k].subject,
                            inbasket[k].maildate);
                        }
                    }
                }
        else
                {
                textcolor(reg_bg);
                textbackground(reg_fg);
                gotoxy(2, 23);
                cprintf(
"   Delivery of outbasket items is deferred while you browse the outbasket.    ");
                gotoxy(6, 13);
                cprintf(" %-16.16s   %-30.30s   %-17.17s",
                    "TO", "SUBJECT", "DATE");
                gotoxy(6, 21);
                cprintf("%-25.25s %-44.44s",
```

```
                         " ", "OUTBASKET STATUS");
                 window(6, 14, 75, 20);
                 textcolor(msg_fg);
                 textbackground(msg_bg);
                 if (redraw_list) clrscr();
                 if (out_count == 0)
                     {
                     gotoxy(28, 1);
                     cprintf("<empty>");
                     }
                 else
                     {
                     for (i=0, j=1; i<7; i++)
                         {
                         k = i + top_outbasket;
                         if (k == out_count) break;
                         gotoxy(1, j++);
                         if (k == outbasket_choice)
                             {
                             textcolor(msg_bg);
                             textbackground(msg_fg);
                             }
                         else
                             {
                             textcolor(msg_fg);
                             textbackground(msg_bg);
                             }
                         cprintf(" %-16.16s   %-30.30s   %-16.16s",
                             outbasket[k].mailname,
                             outbasket[k].subject,
                             outbasket[k].maildate);
                         }
                     }
                 }

         textcolor(reg_fg);
         textbackground(reg_bg);
         window(1, 1, 80, 25);
         redraw_list = FALSE;
         gotoxy(80, 25);

get_menu_key:
         getkey();
         if (*new_mail_ptr)
```

```
            {
            *new_mail_ptr = FALSE;
            redraw_list   = TRUE;
            goto show_baskets;
            }

    if (key_char == CR)
        {
        if (which_basket == 0 && in_count > 0)
            {
            strcpy(filename, mail_path);
            strcat(filename,
                inbasket[inbasket_choice].mailfile);
            browse(filename);
            goto reset_trays;
            }
        else
        if (which_basket == 1 && out_count > 0)
            {
            strcpy(filename, mail_path);
            strcat(filename,
                outbasket[outbasket_choice].mailfile);
            browse(filename);
            goto reset_trays;
            }
        }

    if (key_char == 0 && extended_char == DOWNKEY)
        {
        if (which_basket == 0)
            {
            if (inbasket_choice < in_count - 1)
                inbasket_choice++;
            if (inbasket_choice > top_inbasket + 6)
                top_inbasket++;
            }
        else
            {
            if (outbasket_choice < out_count - 1)
                outbasket_choice++;
            if (outbasket_choice > top_outbasket + 6)
                top_outbasket++;
            }
        goto show_baskets;
        }
```

```
if (key_char == 0 && extended_char == UPKEY)
    {
    if (which_basket == 0)
        {
        if (inbasket_choice > 0)
            inbasket_choice--;
        if (inbasket_choice < top_inbasket)
            top_inbasket--;
        }
    else
        {
        if (outbasket_choice > 0)
            outbasket_choice--;
        if (outbasket_choice < top_outbasket)
            top_outbasket--;
        }
    goto show_baskets;
    }

if (key_char == 's' || key_char == 'S')
    {
    time(&t);
    sprintf(string, "%ld", t);
    strcpy(filename, mail_path);
    strcat(filename, &string[3]);
    strcat(filename, ".OUT");
    editor(filename);
    goto reset_trays;
    }

if (key_char == 'i' || key_char == 'I')
    {
    if (*outbasket_alarm_ptr == 0xOFFFFFFFL)
        *outbasket_alarm_ptr = 0l;
    which_basket = 0;
    redraw_list  = TRUE;
    goto show_baskets;
    }

if (key_char == 'o' || key_char == 'O')
    {
    *outbasket_alarm_ptr = 0xOFFFFFFFL;
    which_basket = 1;
    redraw_list  = TRUE;
```

```
            goto show_baskets;
            }

        if (key_char == 'x' || key_char == 'X')
            goto exit_popup;

        if (key_char == 0 && extended_char == F1)
            {
            show_help(1);
            redraw_list  = TRUE;
            goto show_menu;
            }

        if (key_char == 0 && extended_char == F10)
            {
            de_install = TRUE;
            goto exit_popup;
            }

        if (key_char == 0 && extended_char == ALT_F10)
            {
            *postman_deinstall_ptr = TRUE;
            de_install = TRUE;
            goto exit_popup;
            }

        goto get_menu_key;

exit_popup:
        hotkey_flag   = FALSE;
        if (*outbasket_alarm_ptr == 0x0FFFFFFFL)
            *outbasket_alarm_ptr = 0l;
        }

void    do_popup(void)
        {
        disable();
        old_ss = _SS;
        old_sp = _SP;
        _SS = our_ss;
        _SP = our_sp;
        enable();
```

```
        if (de_install)
            {
            if (!okay_to_unload()) goto do_popup_exit;
            _AX = 0x5000;
            _BX = ourpsp;
            geninterrupt(0x21);
            setvect(0x08, oldint08);
            setvect(0x28, oldint28);
            setvect(0x09, oldint09);
            setvect(0x10, oldint10);
            setvect(0x13, oldint13);
            setvect(0x16, oldint16);
            _ES = ourpsp;
            _BX = 0x2c;
            asm    mov es, es:[bx]
            _AH = 0x49;
            geninterrupt(0x21);
            _ES = ourpsp;
            _AH = 0x49;
            geninterrupt(0x21);
            asm    mov ax, word ptr next_mcb+2
            asm    inc ax
            asm    mov es, ax
            _AH = 0x49;
            geninterrupt(0x21);
            _AX = 0x4c00;
            geninterrupt(0x21);
            }

process_popup:
        curr_vid_mode = get_vid_mode();
        if (curr_vid_mode != 2
            && curr_vid_mode != 3
            && curr_vid_mode != 7)
                {
                beep();
                delay(100);
                beep();
                hotkey_flag = FALSE;
                goto do_popup_exit;
                }

        break_state = getcbrk();
        oldint1b = getvect(0x1b);
```

```
            setvect(0x1b, int1b);
            oldint1c = getvect(0x1c);
            setvect(0x1c, int1c);
            oldint23 = getvect(0x23);
            setvect(0x23, int23);
            oldint24 = getvect(0x24);
            setvect(0x24, int24);
            olddta_ptr = getdta();
            setdta(ourdta_ptr);
            _AX = 0x5100;
            geninterrupt(0x21);
            oldpsp = _BX;
            _AX = 0x5000;
            _BX = ourpsp;
            geninterrupt(0x21);

            save_screen(1,1,80,25, app_screen,
                                &cursor_save, &cursor_type);
            actual_popup();
            restore_screen(1,1,80,25, app_screen,
                                &cursor_save, &cursor_type);

            _AX = 0x5000;
            _BX = oldpsp;
            geninterrupt(0x21);
            setdta(olddta_ptr);
            setvect(0x24, oldint24);
            setvect(0x23, oldint23);
            setvect(0x1c, oldint1c);
            setvect(0x1b, oldint1b);
            setcbrk(break_state);

do_popup_exit:
            disable();
            _SS = old_ss;
            _SP = old_sp;
            enable();
            }

/* ------------------------------------------ */

void    main(int argc, char *argv[])
        {
        char far *path_ptr;
```

```
_fmode = O_BINARY;
if (_osmajor < 2)
    {
    cprintf("\r\n");
    cprintf("Early versions of DOS not supported...\r\n");
    exit(1);
    }

_AX = 'PO';
geninterrupt(Ox16);
temp_ax = _AX;
temp2   = _BX;
temp1   = _ES;
temp3   = _SI;
temp4   = _DX;
temp5   = _DI;
if (temp_ax == 'po')
    {
    path_ptr = MK_FP(temp1, temp2);
    for (i=O; i<65; i++)
        {
        mail_path[i] = *path_ptr;
        path_ptr++;
        }
    outbasket_alarm_ptr = MK_FP(temp1, temp3);
    postman_deinstall_ptr = MK_FP(temp1, temp4);
    new_mail_ptr = MK_FP(temp1, temp5);
    }
else
    {
    cprintf("\r\n");
    cprintf("You must run the PostMan program\r\n");
    cprintf("before you can send/receive mail.\r\n");
    exit(1);
    }

_AX = 'MA';
geninterrupt(Ox16);
if (_AX == 'ma')
    {
    cprintf("\r\n");
    cprintf("The E-Mail program was already loaded.\r\n");
    cprintf("Use ALT/RIGHT-SHIFT to activate it.\r\n");
    exit(1);
    }
```

```
if ( (our_stack = malloc(1000)) == NULL)
    {
    cprintf("\r\n");
    cprintf("Insufficient memory...\r\n");
    exit(1);
    }

curr_vid_mode = get_vid_mode();
if (curr_vid_mode == 7)
    {
    reg_fg = LIGHTGRAY;
    reg_bg = BLACK;
    msg_fg = WHITE;
    msg_bg = BLACK;
    }

for (i=0; i<24; i++)
    edit_line[i] = &edit_area[i*80];

our_ss    = _DS;
our_sp    = FP_OFF( (void far *) our_stack) + 998;

_AX = 0x3400;
geninterrupt(0x21);
temp2 = _BX;
temp1 = _ES;
indos_ptr = MK_FP(temp1, temp2);
if (_osmajor == 2)
    indos2_ptr = MK_FP(temp1, temp2 + 1);
else
    indos2_ptr = MK_FP(temp1, temp2 - 1);

delay(10);
kbd_flag_ptr   = MK_FP(0x0040, 0x0017);
cprintf("\r\n\r\n");
cprintf("E-Mail Program is loaded.\r\n");
cprintf("Press ALT/RIGHT-SHIFT to activate the program.\r\n\r\n");

_DX = FP_OFF( (void far *) machine_name);
_AX = 0x5E00;
geninterrupt(0x21);
if (_CH == 0)
    {
    printf("ERROR.  Machine name not set.\n");
```

```
        exit(1);
        }
machine_name[14] = '\0';
strupr(machine_name);
strcpy(mail_name, "!");
strcat(mail_name, machine_name);

i = strlen(machine_name) - 1;
while (i > 0 && machine_name[i] == ' ')
    {
    machine_name[i] = '\0';
    i--;
    }

ourdta_ptr = getdta();
_AX = 0x5100;
geninterrupt(0x21);
ourpsp = _BX;
our_mcb       = MK_FP(ourpsp-1, 0);
our_mcb_size  = MK_FP(ourpsp-1, 3);
oldint08 = getvect(0x08);
oldint09 = getvect(0x09);
oldint10 = getvect(0x10);
oldint13 = getvect(0x13);
oldint16 = getvect(0x16);
oldint28 = getvect(0x28);

asm     mov ax, word ptr oldint10
asm     mov word ptr cs:[0000h], ax
asm     mov ax, word ptr oldint10+2
asm     mov word ptr cs:[0002h], ax
asm     mov ax, word ptr oldint13
asm     mov word ptr cs:[0004h], ax
asm     mov ax, word ptr oldint13+2
asm     mov word ptr cs:[0006h], ax

setvect(0x10, (void interrupt (*)()) int10);
setvect(0x13, (void interrupt (*)()) int13);
setvect(0x16, int16);
setvect(0x09, int09);
setvect(0x28, int28);
setvect(0x08, int08);
```

```
        de_install = FALSE;
        hotkey_flag= TRUE;

        paragraphs = (our_ss + (our_sp >> 4) + 1) - ourpsp;
        keep(0, paragraphs);
        }
```

Source Listing for NETBIOS.H

The following header file is used by the C programs whose source code listings appear in these appendixes.

```
    /* NETBIOS.H */

typedef unsigned char byte;
typedef unsigned int  word;

/* Network Control Block (NCB)  */

typedef struct
    {
byte NCB_COMMAND;              /* command id                       */
byte NCB_RETCODE;             /* immediate return code            */
byte NCB_LSN;                 /* local session number             */
byte NCB_NUM;                 /* network name number              */
void far *NCB_BUFFER_PTR;     /* address of message packet        */
word NCB_LENGTH;             /* length of message packet         */
byte NCB_CALLNAME[16];       /* name of the other computer       */
byte NCB_NAME[16];           /* our network name                 */
byte NCB_RTO;                /* receive time-out in 500 ms. incrs. */
```

```
    byte NCB_STO;                        /* send time-out - 500 ms. increments */
    void interrupt (*POST_FUNC)(void);   /* address of POST routine            */
    byte NCB_LANA_NUM;                   /* adapter number (0 or 1)            */
    byte NCB_CMD_CPLT;                   /* final return code                  */
    byte NCB_RESERVE[14];                /* Reserved area                      */
    }
    NCB;


/* NetBIOS error return messages  */

char    *net_error_message[] = {
        "success",                  /*  00  */
        "invalid buffer length",    /*  01  */
        "ret code 02",              /*  02  */
        "invalid command",          /*  03  */
        "ret code 04",              /*  04  */
        "timed out",                /*  05  */
        "buffer too small",         /*  06  */
        "ret code 07",              /*  07  */
        "invalid session num",      /*  08  */
        "no resource",              /*  09  */
        "session closed",           /*  0A  */
        "command cancelled",        /*  0B  */
        "ret code 0C",              /*  0C  */
        "dupl. local name",         /*  0D  */
        "name table full",          /*  0E  */
        "active session",           /*  0F  */
        "ret code 10",              /*  10  */
        "session table full",       /*  11  */
        "no one listening",         /*  12  */
        "invalid name num",         /*  13  */
        "no answer",                /*  14  */
        "no local name",            /*  15  */
        "name in use",              /*  16  */
        "name is deleted",          /*  17  */
        "abnormal end",             /*  18  */
        "name conflict",            /*  19  */
        "ret code 1A",              /*  1A  */
        "ret code 1B",              /*  1B  */
        "ret code 1C",              /*  1C  */
        "ret code 1D",              /*  1D  */
        "ret code 1E",              /*  1E  */
        "ret code 1F",              /*  1F  */
```

```
        "ret code 20",              /*  20  */
        "card busy",                /*  21  */
        "too many cmds",            /*  22  */
        "invalid card num",         /*  23  */
        "cancel done",              /*  24  */
        "ret code 25",              /*  25  */
        "cannot cancel"             /*  26  */
    };

/* Symbolic names for NetBIOS commands  */

#define RESET                       0x32
#define CANCEL                      0x35
#define STATUS                      0xb3
#define STATUS_WAIT                 0x33
#define TRACE                       0xf9
#define TRACE_WAIT                  0x79
#define UNLINK                      0x70
#define ADD_NAME                    0xb0
#define ADD_NAME_WAIT               0x30
#define ADD_GROUP_NAME              0xb6
#define ADD_GROUP_NAME_WAIT         0x36
#define DELETE_NAME                 0xb1
#define DELETE_NAME_WAIT            0x31
#define CALL                        0x90
#define CALL_WAIT                   0x10
#define LISTEN                      0x91
#define LISTEN_WAIT                 0x11
#define HANG_UP                     0x92
#define HANG_UP_WAIT                0x12
#define SEND                        0x94
#define SEND_WAIT                   0x14
#define SEND_NO_ACK                 0xf1
#define SEND_NO_ACK_WAIT            0x71
#define CHAIN_SEND                  0x97
#define CHAIN_SEND_WAIT             0x17
#define CHAIN_SEND_NO_ACK           0xf2
#define CHAIN_SEND_NO_ACK_WAIT      0x72
#define RECEIVE                     0x95
#define RECEIVE_WAIT                0x15
#define RECEIVE_ANY                 0x96
#define RECEIVE_ANY_WAIT            0x16
#define SESSION_STATUS              0xb4
```

```
#define SESSION_STATUS_WAIT          0x34
#define SEND_DATAGRAM                0xa0
#define SEND_DATAGRAM_WAIT           0x20
#define SEND_BCST_DATAGRAM           0xa2
#define SEND_BCST_DATAGRAM_WAIT      0x22
#define RECEIVE_DATAGRAM             0xa1
#define RECEIVE_DATAGRAM_WAIT        0x21
#define RECEIVE_BCST_DATAGRAM        0xa3
#define RECEIVE_BCST_DATAGRAM_WAIT   0x23
```

H

Library Source Listing
for IPX.C

The following Turbo C code calls IPX functions. The code is explained in Chapter 6, "IPX and SPX Programming."

```c
/*
 *  IPX.C -- helper routines for accessing IPX services
 *  from Turbo C.
 */

#include <stdlib.h>
#include <dos.h>
#include <mem.h>
#include <string.h>
#include <ipx.h>

void far        (*ipx_spx)(void);

int     ipx_spx_installed(void)
        {
        union REGS      regs;
        struct SREGS    sregs;

        regs.x.ax = 0x7a00;
        int86x(0x2f, &regs, &regs, &sregs);
        if (regs.h.al != 0xff) return -1;
```

```
          ipx_spx = MK_FP(sregs.es, regs.x.di);
          _BX = 0x0010;
          _AL = 0x00;
          ipx_spx();
          if (_AL == 0x00) return 0;

          return 1;
          }

int       ipx_cancel_event(struct ECB *ecb_ptr)
          {
          _ES = FP_SEG( (void far *) ecb_ptr);
          _SI = FP_OFF( (void far *) ecb_ptr);
          _BX = 0x0006;
          ipx_spx();
          _AH = 0;
          return _AX;
          }

void      close_socket(unsigned int socket)
          {
          if (ipx_spx_installed() < 1) return;
          _BX = 0x0001;
          _DX = socket;
          ipx_spx();
          }

int       open_socket(unsigned int socket)
          {
          if (ipx_spx_installed() < 1) return -1;
          _DX = socket;
          _BX = 0x0000;
          _AL = 0xFF;
          ipx_spx();
          _AH = 0;
          return _AX;
          }

int       get_local_target(unsigned char *dest_network,
                           unsigned char *dest_node,
                           unsigned int  dest_socket,
                           unsigned char *bridge_address)
          {
          unsigned int    temp_ax;
```

```
              struct {
                      unsigned char    network_number [4];
                      unsigned char    physical_node  [6];
                      unsigned int     socket;
                      } request_buffer;

              struct {
                      unsigned char    local_target [6];
                      } reply_buffer;

      memcpy(request_buffer.network_number, dest_network, 4);
      memcpy(request_buffer.physical_node, dest_node, 6);
      request_buffer.socket = dest_socket;

      _ES = FP_SEG( (void far *) &request_buffer);
      _SI = FP_OFF( (void far *) &request_buffer);
      _DI = FP_OFF( (void far *) &reply_buffer);
      _BX = 0x0002;
      ipx_spx();
      _AH = 0;
      temp_ax = _AX;
      memcpy(bridge_address, reply_buffer.local_target, 6);
      return temp_ax;
      }

void  let_ipx_breath(void)
      {
      _BX = 0x000A;
      ipx_spx();
      }

void  ipx_listen_for_packet(struct ECB *ecb_ptr)
      {
      _ES = FP_SEG( (void far *) ecb_ptr);
      _SI = FP_OFF( (void far *) ecb_ptr);
      _BX = 0x0004;
      ipx_spx();
      }

void  ipx_send_packet(struct ECB *ecb_ptr)
      {
      _ES = FP_SEG( (void far *) ecb_ptr);
      _SI = FP_OFF( (void far *) ecb_ptr);
      _BX = 0x0003;
```

```
        ipx_spx();
        }

int     get_internet_address(unsigned char connection_number,
                        unsigned char *network_number,
                        unsigned char *physical_node)
        {
        union REGS      regs;
        struct SREGS    sregs;

        struct {
                unsigned int    len;
                unsigned char   buffer_type;
                unsigned char   connection_number;
                } request_buffer;

        struct {
                unsigned int    len;
                unsigned char   network_number [4];
                unsigned char   physical_node  [6];
                unsigned int    server_socket;
                } reply_buffer;

        regs.h.ah = 0xe3;
        request_buffer.len = 2;
        request_buffer.buffer_type = 0x13;
        request_buffer.connection_number = connection_number;

        reply_buffer.len = 12;

        regs.x.si = FP_OFF( (void far *) &request_buffer);
        sregs.ds  = FP_SEG( (void far *) &request_buffer);
        regs.x.di = FP_OFF( (void far *) &reply_buffer);
        sregs.es  = FP_SEG( (void far *) &reply_buffer);
        int86x(0x21, &regs, &regs, &sregs);

        memcpy(network_number, reply_buffer.network_number, 4);
        memcpy(physical_node,  reply_buffer.physical_node,  6);
        regs.h.ah = 0;
        return regs.x.ax;
        }

unsigned int    get_1st_connection_num (char *who)
        {
```

```c
        union REGS      regs;
        struct SREGS    sregs;

        struct {
                unsigned int    len;
                unsigned char   buffer_type;
                unsigned int    object_type;
                unsigned char   name_len;
                unsigned char   name [47];
                } request_buffer;

        struct {
                unsigned int    len;
                unsigned char   number_connections;
                unsigned char   connection_num [100];
                } reply_buffer;

        regs.h.ah = 0xe3;

        request_buffer.len = 51;
        request_buffer.buffer_type = 0x15;
        request_buffer.object_type = 0x0100;
        request_buffer.name_len   = (unsigned char) strlen(who);
        strcpy(request_buffer.name, who);

        reply_buffer.len = 101;

        regs.x.si = FP_OFF( (void far *) &request_buffer);
        sregs.ds  = FP_SEG( (void far *) &request_buffer);
        regs.x.di = FP_OFF( (void far *) &reply_buffer);
        sregs.es  = FP_SEG( (void far *) &reply_buffer);

        int86x(0x21, &regs, &regs, &sregs);

        if (regs.h.al != 0) return 0;
        if (reply_buffer.number_connections == 0) return 0;

        regs.h.ah = 0;
        regs.h.al = reply_buffer.connection_num[0];
        return regs.x.ax;
        }

unsigned char get_connection_number(void)
        {
```

```
          _AH = 0xDC;
          geninterrupt(0x21);
          return _AL;
          }


void      get_user_id(unsigned char connection_number,
                  unsigned char *user_id)
          {
          union REGS      regs;
          struct SREGS    sregs;

          struct {
                  unsigned int     len;
                  unsigned char    buffer_type;
                  unsigned char    connection_number;
                  } request_buffer;

          struct {
                  unsigned int     len;
                  unsigned char    object_id[4];
                  unsigned char    object_type[2];
                  char             object_name[48];
                  char             login_time[7];
                  } reply_buffer;

          regs.h.ah = 0xe3;
          request_buffer.len = 2;
          request_buffer.buffer_type = 0x16;
          request_buffer.connection_number = connection_number;


          reply_buffer.len = 61;


          regs.x.si = FP_OFF( (void far *) &request_buffer);
          sregs.ds  = FP_SEG( (void far *) &request_buffer);
          regs.x.di = FP_OFF( (void far *) &reply_buffer);
          sregs.es  = FP_SEG( (void far *) &reply_buffer);
          int86x(0x21, &regs, &regs, &sregs);

          strncpy(user_id, reply_buffer.object_name, 48);
          }
```

Header Source Listing for Use with IPX.C

This header file is used by the Turbo C code in Appendix H, "Library Source Listing for IPX.C."

```
/*
 *  IPX.H -- see 'ipx.c'.
 *
 */

struct IPXHEADER
    {
    unsigned int     checksum;
    unsigned int     length;
    unsigned char    transport_control;
    unsigned char    packet_type;
    unsigned char    dest_network_number [4];
    unsigned char    dest_network_node   [6];
    unsigned int     dest_network_socket;
    unsigned char    source_network_number [4];
    unsigned char    source_network_node   [6];
    unsigned int     source_network_socket;
    };
```

```
struct ECB
    {
    void far        *link_address;
    void far        (*event_service_routine)(void);
    unsigned char   in_use;
    unsigned char   completion_code;
    unsigned int    socket_number;
    unsigned int    connection_id;      /* from SPX Listen */
    unsigned int    rest_of_workspace;
    unsigned char   driver_workspace [12];
    unsigned char   immediate_address [ 6];
    unsigned int    packet_count;
    struct {
        void far    *address;
        unsigned int length;
        } packet [2];
    };


int     ipx_spx_installed(void);
int     ipx_cancel_event(struct ECB *ecb_ptr);
void    close_socket(unsigned int socket);
int     open_socket(unsigned int socket);
int     get_local_target(unsigned char *dest_network,
                         unsigned char *dest_node,
                         unsigned int   dest_socket,
                         unsigned char *bridge_address);
void    let_ipx_breath(void);
void    ipx_listen_for_packet(struct ECB *ecb_ptr);
void    ipx_send_packet(struct ECB *ecb_ptr);
int     get_internet_address(unsigned char connection_number,
                             unsigned char *network_number,
                             unsigned char *physical_node);
unsigned int    get_1st_connection_num (char *who);
unsigned char get_connection_number(void);
void    get_user_id(unsigned char connection_number,
                    unsigned char *user_id);
```

DOS Error Codes

The following error codes are given in hexadecimal:

01	Invalid function
02	File not found
03	Path not found
04	No more file handles (too many open files)
05	Access denied
06	Invalid handle
07	Memory control blocks damaged
08	Insufficient memory
09	Invalid memory block address
0A	Invalid environment
0B	Invalid format
0C	Invalid access code
0D	Invalid data
0E	Reserved
0F	Invalid drive specified
10	Attempt to remove current directory
11	Not same device
12	No more files
13	Attempt to write on write-protected diskette
14	Unknown unit
15	Drive not ready

16	Unknown command
17	Data (CRC) error
18	Bad request structure length
19	Seek error
1A	Unknown media error
1B	Sector not found
1C	Printer out of paper
1D	Write fault
1E	Read fault
1F	General failure
20	Sharing violation
21	Lock violation
22	Invalid disk change
23	FCB unavailable
24	Sharing buffer overflow
25-31	Reserved
32	Network request not supported
33	Remote computer not listening
34	Duplicate name on network
35	Network name not found
36	Network busy
37	Network device no longer exists
38	NETBIOS command limit exceeded
39	Network adapter hardware error
3A	Incorrect response from network
3B	Unexpected network error
3C	Incompatible remote adapter
3D	Print queue full
3E	Not enough disk space for print file
3F	Print file was deleted
40	Network name was deleted
41	Access denied
42	Network device type incorrect
43	Network name not found
44	Network name limit exceeded
45	NETBIOS session limit exceeded
46	Temporarily paused
47	Network request not accepted
48	Print or disk redirection is paused
49-4F	Reserved
50	File exists
51	Reserved
52	Cannot make directory entry

53	Fail on Interrupt 24
54	Too many redirections
55	Duplicate redirection
56	Invalid password
57	Invalid parameter
58	Network data fault

K

OS/2 Error Codes

The following error codes are given in decimal:

01	Invalid function
02	File not found
03	Path not found
04	Too many open files
05	Access denied
06	Invalid handle
07	Arena trashed
08	Not enough memory
09	Invalid block
10	Bad environment
11	Bad format
12	Invalid access
13	Invalid data
15	Invalid drive
16	Current directory
17	Not same device
18	No more files
19	Write protect
20	Bad unit
21	Not ready
22	Bad command
23	CRC

24	Bad length
25	Seek
26	Not DOS disk
27	Sector not found
28	Out of paper
29	Write fault
30	Read fault
31	General failure
32	Sharing violation
33	Lock violation
34	Wrong disk
35	FCB unavailable
36	Sharing buffer exceeded
50	Not supported
80	File exists
81	Dup FCB
82	Cannot make
83	Fail—Int 24
84	Out of structures
85	Already assigned
86	Invalid password
87	Invalid parameter
88	Net write fault
89	No proc slots
90	Not frozen
91	Tovfl
92	Tdup
93	No items
95	Interrupt
100	Too many semaphores
101	Excl sem already owned
102	Sem is set
103	Too many sem requests
104	Invalid at interrupt time
105	Sem owner died
106	Sem user limit
107	Disk change
108	Drive locked
109	Broken pipe
110	Open failed
111	Buffer overflow
112	Disk full
113	No more search handles
114	Invalid target handle

115	Protection violation
116	VIO KBD request
117	Invalid category
118	Invalid verify switch
119	Bad driver level
120	Call not implemented
121	Sem timeout
122	Insufficient buffer
123	Invalid name
124	Invalid level
125	No volume label
126	Mod not found
127	Proc not found
128	Wait no children
129	Child not complete
130	Direct access handle
131	Negative seek
132	Seek on device
133	Is join target
134	Is joined
135	Is substed
136	Not joined
137	Not substed
138	Join to join
139	Subst to subst
140	Join to subst
141	Subst to join
142	Busy drive
143	Same drive
144	Dir not root
145	Dir not empty
146	Is subst path
147	Is join path
148	Path busy
149	Is subst target
150	System trace
151	Invalid event count
152	Too many muxwaiters
153	Invalid list format
154	Label too long
155	Too many TCBs
156	Signal refused
157	Discarded
158	Not locked

159	Bad threadID addr
160	Bad arguments
161	Bad pathname
162	Signal pending
163	Uncertain media
164	Max thrds reached
165	Monitors not supported
166	Unc driver not installed
167	Lock failed
168	SwapIO failed
169	Swapin failed
170	Busy
180	Invalid segment number
181	Invalid callgate
182	Invalid ordinal
183	Already exists
184	No child process
185	Child alive nowait
186	Invalid flag number
187	Sem not found
188	Invalid starting codeseg
189	Invalid stackseg
190	Invalid moduletype
191	Invalid EXE signature
192	EXE marked invalid
193	Bad EXE format
194	Iterated data exceeds 64k
195	Invalid minallocsize
196	Dynlink from invalid ring
197	IOPL not enabled
198	Invalid segdpl
199	Autodataseg exceeds 64k
200	Ring2seg must be movable
201	Reloc chain xeeds seglim
202	Inf loop in reloc chain
203	Env var not found
204	Not current ctry
205	No signal sent
206	Filename exced range
207	Ring2 stack in use
208	Meta expansion too long
209	Invalid signal number
210	Thread 1 inactive
211	Info not avail

212	Locked
213	Bad dynalink
214	Too many modules
215	Nesting not allowed
230	Bad pipe
231	Pipe busy
232	No data
233	Pipe not connected
234	More data
240	VC disconnected
303	Invalid procID
304	Invalid pdelta
305	Not descendant
306	Not session manager
307	Invalid pclass
308	Invalid scope
309	Invalid threadid
310	DOSsub shrink
311	DOSsub nomem
312	DOSsub overlap
313	DOSsub badsize
314	DOSsub badflag
315	DOSsub badselector
316	MR msg too long
317	MR mid not found
318	MR un acc msgf
319	MR inv msgf format
320	MR inv ivcount
321	MR un perform
322	TS wakeup
323	TS semhandle
324	TS notimer
326	TS handle
327	TS datetime
328	Sys internal
329	Queue current name
330	Queue proc not owned
331	Queue proc owned
332	Queue duplicate
333	Queue element not exist
334	Queue no memory
335	Queue invalid name
336	Queue invalid priority
337	Queue invalid handle

338	Queue link not found
339	Queue memory error
340	Queue prev at end
341	Queue proc no access
342	Queue empty
343	Queue name not exist
344	Queue not initialized
345	Queue unable to access
346	Queue unable to add
347	Queue unable to init
349	VIO invalid mask
350	VIO ptr
351	VIO aptr
352	VIO rptr
353	VIO cptr
354	VIO lptr
355	VIO mode
356	VIO width
357	VIO attr
358	VIO row
359	VIO col
360	VIO toprow
361	VIO botrow
362	VIO rightcol
363	VIO leftcol
364	SCS call
365	SCS value
366	VIO wait flag
367	VIO unlock
368	SGS not session mgr
369	SMG invalid SG ID
369	SMG invalid session ID
370	SMG no SG
370	SMG no sessions
371	SMG grp not found
371	SMG session not found
372	SMG set title
373	KBD parameter
374	KBD no device
375	KBD invalid iowait
376	KBD invalid length
377	KBD invalid echo mask
378	KBD invalid input mask
379	Mon invalid parms

380	Mon invalid devname
381	Mon invalid handle
382	Mon buffer too small
383	Mon buffer empty
384	Mon data too large
385	Mouse no device
386	Mouse inv handle
387	Mouse inv parms
388	Mouse can't reset
389	Mouse display parms
390	Mouse inv module
391	Mouse inv entry pt
392	Mouse inv mask
393	Mouse no data
394	Mouse ptr drawn
395	Invalid frequency
396	NLS no country file
397	NLS open failed
398	NLS no ctry code
398	No country or codepage
399	NLS table truncated
400	NLS bad type
401	NLS type not found
402	VIO SMG only
403	VIO invalid asciiz
404	VIO deregister
405	VIO no popup
406	VIO existing popup
407	KBD SMG only
408	KBD invalid asciiz
409	KBD invalid mask
410	KBD register
411	KBD deregister
412	Mouse SMG only
413	Mouse invalid asciiz
414	Mouse invalid mask
415	Mouse register
416	Mouse deregister
417	SMG bad action
418	SMG invalid call
419	SCS sg not found
420	SCS not shell
421	VIO invalid parms
422	VIO function owned

423	VIO return
424	SCS invalid function
425	SCS not session mgr
426	VIO register
427	VIO no mode thread
428	VIO no save restore thrd
429	VIO in bg
430	VIO illegal during popup
431	SMG not baseshell
432	SMG bad statusreq
433	Queue invalid wait
434	VIO lock
435	Mouse invalid iowait
436	VIO invalid handle
437	VIO illegal during lock
438	VIO invalid length
439	KBD invalid handle
440	KBD no more handle
441	KBD cannot create KCB
442	KBD codepage load incomplete
443	KBD invalid codepage ID
444	KBD no codepage support
445	KBD focus required
446	KBD focus already active
447	KBD keyboard busy
448	KBD invalid codepage
449	KBD unable to focus
450	SMG session non select
451	SMG session not foregrnd
452	SMG session not parent
453	SMG invalid start mode
454	SMG invalid related opt
455	SMG invalid bond option
456	SMG invalid select opt
457	SMG start in background
458	SMG invalid stop option
459	SMG bad reserve
460	SMG process not parent
461	SMG invalid data length
462	SMG not bound
463	SMG retry sub alloc
464	KBD detached
465	VIO detached
466	Mouse detached

467	VIO font
468	VIO user font
469	VIO bad CP
470	VIO no CP
472	Invalid code page
473	CP list too small
474	CP not moved
475	Mode switch init
476	Code page not found
477	Unexpected slot returned
478	SMG invalid trace option
479	VIO internal resource
480	VIO shell init
481	SMG no hard errors
482	CP switch incomplete
483	VIO transparent popup
484	Critsec overflow
485	Critsec underflow
486	VIO bad reserve
487	Invalid address
488	Zero selectors requested
489	Not enough selectors avail
490	Invalid selector
491	SMG invalid program type
492	SMG invalid pgm control
493	SMG invalid inherit opt
494	VIO extended SG
495	VIO not pres mgr SG
496	VIO shield owned
497	VIO no more handles
498	VIO see error log
499	VIO associated DC
500	KBD no console
501	Mouse no console
502	Mouse invalid handle
503	SMG invalid debug parms
504	KBD extended SG
505	Mouse extended SG
506	SMG invalid icon file

NETBIOS Error Codes

The following error codes are given in hexadecimal:

01	Illegal buffer length
03	Invalid command
05	Timed out
06	Message incomplete
07	Send No ACK data was not received
08	Invalid local session number
09	No resource available (temporary condition)
0A	Session closed
0B	Command cancelled
0D	Duplicate name in local name table
0E	Local name table full
0F	Name has active sessions; is de-registered
11	Local session table full
12	Session open rejected
13	Invalid name number
14	Can't find name called
15	Name not found, or illegal name
16	Name in use on remote adapter
17	Name deleted
18	Session abnormal termination
19	Name conflict detected
21	Interface busy

22	Too many outstanding commands
23	Invalid adapter number
24	Command completed while cancel occurred
26	Command not valid to cancel
30	Name defined by another environment
34	Environment not defined — must issue Reset
35	Resources exhausted — try later
36	Maximum applications exceeded
37	No Service Access Points available
38	Requested resource not available
39	Invalid NCB address
3A	Reset may not be issued inside POST routine
3B	Invalid NCB_DD_ID value
3C	NetBIOS attempt to lock user storage failed
3F	NetBIOS device driver open error
40	OS/2 error detected
4E-4F	Network status error
F6-FA	Adapter error
FB	NetBIOS program not loaded
FC	Adapter open failed
FD	Unexpected adapter close
FE	NetBIOS not active

IPX and SPX Error Codes

The following error codes are given in hexadecimal:

EC Connection severed by remote workstation
ED No answer from destination, or connection failed
EE No such connection
EF Local connection table is full
F9 ECB cannot be canceled
FA No path to destination
FC ECB not active, or has been canceled
FD Invalid packet length
FE Socket table is full, or packet is undeliverable
FF Dest socket not open, local socket already open, or network failure

Disk Contents

This appendix contains a list of the files contained on the two companion disks.

Disk 1

SOURCE Directory

GETNAME.ASM
NAME.ASM
SETNAME.ASM
MAIL.C
NETTEST.C
NETWORK.C
POSTMAN.C
REMOTE.C
RPE.C
NETBIOS.H

NetWare Directory

BINDLIST.C
IPX.C
MAIL.C
POSTMAN.C
IPX.H

Disk 2:

EXES Directory

GETNAME.EXE
MAIL.EXE
NAME.EXE
NETTEST.EXE
NETWORK.EXE
POSTMAN.EXE
REMOTE.EXE
RPE.EXE
SETNAME.EXE
MAIL.HLP

NetWare Directory

POSTMAN.EXE
BINDLIST.EXE
MAIL.EXE
MAIL.HLP

Index

C

G

H

I

J–L

O

P

W

More Computer Knowledge from Que